Lecture Notes in Artificial Intelligence 642

Subseries of Lecture Notes in Computer Science
Edited by J. Siekmann

Lecture Notes in Computer Science
Edited by G. Goos and J. Hartmanis

K. P. Jantke (Ed.)

Analogical and Inductive Inference

International Workshop AII '92
Dagstuhl Castle, Germany, October 5-9, 1992
Proceedings

Springer-Verlag
Berlin Heidelberg New York
London Paris Tokyo
Hong Kong Barcelona
Budapest

Series Editor

Jörg Siekmann
University of Saarland
German Research Center for Artificial Intelligence (DFKI)
Stuhlsatzenhausweg 3, W-6600 Saarbrücken 11, FRG

Volume Editor

Klaus P. Jantke
TH Leipzig, FB Mathematik and Informatik
Postfach 66, O-7030 Leipzig, FRG

CR Subject Classification (1991): I.2.2, I.2.6, D.1.2

ISBN 3-540-56004-1 Springer-Verlag Berlin Heidelberg New York
ISBN 0-387-56004-1 Springer-Verlag New York Berlin Heidelberg

Typesetting: Camera ready by author/editor
Printing and binding: Druckhaus Beltz, Hemsbach/Bergstr.
45/3140-543210 - Printed on acid-free paper

Preface

AII'92 is the third workshop in the AII series started in 1986. The proceedings of the first and second conferences have been published as Lecture Notes in Computer Science 265 and Lecture Notes in Artificial Intelligence 397.

Learning is obviously an important phenomenon of natural intelligence. Therefore, despite restricted specifications of the area of artificial intelligence, learning is a central issue of artificial intelligence research. There is abundant evidence of the human ability to learn from possibly incomplete information. In human communication one usually provides only incomplete information with respect to some target phenomenon to be described or specified. Inductive inference originating from Gold's seminal paper (E.M. Gold, Language Identification in the Limit, Information and Control 10 (1967), 447-474) offers a firm mathematical basis for investigating the crucial problems of learning from possibly incomplete information. Similarly to learning from possibly incomplete information, human communication exhibits an amazing ability to draw analogical conclusions or to perform analogical constructions. This works although there is not much agreement about the gist of analogy. B. Indurkhya's paper in the present volume points to crucial problems.

The AII workshops are focused on all formal approaches to algorithmic learning particularly emphasising analogical reasoning and inductive inference. Both areas are currently attracting a considerable interest in particular settings. Analogical reasoning plays a crucial role in the currently booming field of case-based reasoning. In the field of inductive logic programming, a couple of new techniques have been developed for inductive inference.

The AII events are always intended to bridge the gap between several research communities. The basic areas of concern are theoretical computer science, artificial intelligence, and cognitive sciences.

The program committee of AII'92 consisted of S. Arikawa, J.M. Barzdins, B. Buchanan, R.P. Daley, L. De Raedt, U. Furbach, D.R. Hofstadter, B. Indurkhya, K.P. Jantke, C.H. Smith, M. Warmuth, and S. Wrobel. The program committee invited a number of distinguished scientists to deliver invited talks at AII'92. The second part contains 16 selected papers from a larger number of submissions. I am grateful to all members of the program committee and to all referees for their work. I particularly acknowledge the assistance provided by my research group, the Algorithmic Learning Group at Leipzig University of Technology. Steffen Lange did an especially important job behind the scene as the organising secretary of AII'92. Last but not least, the excellent conditions of the International Conference and Research Center for Computer Science at Dagstuhl Castle provided a firm basis for preparing AII'92.

Leipzig, July 1992   Klaus P. Jantke

List of Referees for AII′92

H. Adé
A. Albrecht
S. Arikawa
J.M. Barzdins
H.-R. Beick
G. Brewka
M. Bruynooghe
R.P. Daley
L. De Raedt
B. Fronhöfer
U. Furbach

W. Gasarch
C.M. Hamann
E. Hirowatari
D.R. Hofstadter
W. Hower
B. Indurkhya
K.P. Jantke
Y. Kodratoff
S. Lange
S. O'Hara
E. Pippig

M.M. Richter
G. Sablon
P. Scholz
S. Schönherr
J. Siekmann
C.H. Smith
M. Velauthapillai
M. Warmuth
R. Wiehagen
S. Wrobel
T. Zeugmann

Table of Contents

Representing the Spatial/Kinematic Domain and Lattice Computers[*]

John Case[1], Dayanand S. Rajan[2], and Anil M. Shende[3]

[1] Department of Computer and Information Sciences
University of Delaware
Newark, DE 19716, USA

[2] Department of Mathematics
Indian Institute of Technology
New Delhi 110016
India

[3] Department of Computer Science
Bucknell University
Lewisburg
PA 17837
USA

Abstract. An approach to analogical representation for objects and their motions in space is proposed.

This approach involves lattice computer architectures and associated algorithms and is shown to be abstracted from the behavior of human beings mentally solving spatial/kinematic puzzles. There is also discussion of where in this approach the modeling of human cognition leaves off and the engineering begins.

The possible relevance of the approach to a number of issues in Artificial Intelligence is discussed. These issues include efficiency of sentential versus analogical representations, common sense reasoning, update propagation, learning performance tasks, diagrammatic representations, spatial reasoning, metaphor, human categorization, and pattern recognition.

Lastly there is a discussion of the somewhat related approach involving cellular automata applied to computational physics.

[*] The research was supported in part by NSF Grant CCR 8713846. We would like to thank Dan Chester for helpful comments on the exposition in an earlier draft. The email address for communication regarding this paper is 'case@cis.udel.edu'.

1   Introduction

An important aspect of approaches to solving problems is the *representation scheme* employed for knowledge about the problem. In this paper, we propose a particular *vivid, analogical* [Sel88] representation for solving problems in the *spatial/kinematic* domain: lattice computer architectures and associated algorithms.

We argue, partly with evidence from the Clinical and Experimental Psychology and Artificial Intelligence literatures, that our approach is superior to approaches using sentential representations (see Sections 2, 5.1, and 5.3 below).

The physical sciences provide problems in the spatial/kinematic domain as do many puzzles and situations ostensibly requiring common sense. Solutions to such problems, at least from the physical sciences, are usually predictions of events in the course of the *unfolding* of a phenomenon under consideration, e.g., predictions of the motions of the participating objects. For spatial puzzle solving, the finding of solutions might involve some trial and error motion of objects in space rather than the tracking of deterministic simulations of physical phenomena. In any case, the knowledge-base for solving spatial problems is the representation of the objects participating, their motions, and the, usually finite, region of space in which the "action" takes place or is to take place.

Most physical phenomena involve the spatial/kinematic domain. Hence, our approach may be well-suited for scientific computing (See Sections 3, 4, and 5.4 below). Scientific computing provides but a subset of the problems we have in mind for our approach (see Section 5.3 below). To what extent our project is cognitive science or engineering is discussed in Sections 5.1 and 5.2 below. We'll give a brief progress report below on how far we've gotten with our lattice computer project in Section 4, but first we motivate it in the next two sections, Sections 2 and 3.

2   Motivations for our Approach

Our lattice computer project [CRS90b, CRS90a, She91, CRS91a, CRS91c, CRS91b, RS91] (see Section 4 below) was motivated by trying to find a computer architecture naturally fitted to solving problems in the spatial/kinematic domain. For example, we were and are interested in it as an eventual computer vehicle for the learning of non-verbal performance tasks (see Section 5.3 below). Our approach to representing the spatial/kinematic domain originally came out of thinking about

- the work of Nobelist Roger Sperry and others [Spe74, Orn72, Kin82, SD85] on lateralization of cognitive functions in the human brain and
- the ingenious reaction-time experiments of Shepard (with students) [SM71, SF72, SC82] and Kosslyn (also with students) [Kos80, Kos83] on human subjects *mentally* solving *spatial/kinematic* puzzles

(see also Section 5.1 below).

The work on lateralization of cognitive functions in the human brain shows us that the half of the brain (right half) that is good at spatial puzzles is not good at verbal puzzles and vice-versa. It occurred to us, then, to look to *non-verbal* representation schemes for the computer solution of spatial/kinematic problems. Kinsbourne

[Kin82] posits, among other things, that the right brain hemisphere provides a *spatial framework*.

[SM71] showed that the time it takes people to *mentally* match pictures of two congruent, complex 3-dimensional objects, one rotated with respect to the other, is *linear* in the angle between them. In general, the reaction-time experiments on "mental-imagery" are consistent with human beings employing an *analogical* (see also [Fun80, RN74, Slo71, Slo85, Sel88, For81, For83, Hin79, Bro81, MD84, LS87]) representation scheme for spatial/kinematic problems. It is as if we project a mental analog of space and mentally move analogs of objects around in it, at least in simple cases, with timing approximately linear in the real time it would take to move the corresponding real objects similarly in real space. At least that is a more parsimonious model (consistent with the data) of human representation for spatial/kinematic domains than assuming that people subconsciously directly solve systems of equations, multiply matrices, or run automatic theorem provers and then subconsciously make the reaction-time experiments come out suggesting a more analogical approach.

As will be seen in Section 4, our lattice computer architectures *are* spatial frameworks discretely representing space, and, as will be noted, our associated algorithms (so far developed) carry out *discrete but analogical* simulations of motion in space *approximately in real-time*: 'approximately in real-time' means, here, as close as possible to linear in real-time.

3 Inherent Parallelism and Ergonomics

It occurred to us that in the physical movement of a solid object, each particle of the object moves *in parallel* with each other particle; the particles do not move first one, then another, then another, ... It appears, then, that most sentential and mathematical representations do not, and perhaps cannot, directly make use of *this* inherent parallelism in spatial phenomena. To be sure, many *parallel* numerical algorithms which can simulate the motion of objects in space too (e.g., Kung and Leiserson's matrix multiplication in a hexagonal mesh [KL78] and also Kosaraju and Flynn's earlier one [FK76] for square meshes) are, *in large part*, conceptualized in terms of the *motion of numerical data in space*. It just seems to us to be more natural and efficient to try to exploit the inherent parallelism of individual particle motion directly, and that is how our project is proceeding.

It also occurred to us that, if we could represent the inherent parallelism in particle motion directly, this should eventually lead to an ergonomic soundness for the design phase of associated algorithms. This contrasts with most current approaches to parallel computation which require a lot of pain in algorithm design to exploit that parallelism [She91].

The point about ergonomic soundness is justified, in part, by the considerable literature in experimental psychology [SC82, Kos80, Kos83, RN74] (discussed above briefly in Section 2 and further discussed in Section 5.1 below) suggesting that *human* mental imagery is analogical and approximately real-time, not analytical. For example, the time it takes people to mentally rotate 3-dimensional objects is *linear* in the angle through which the objects are to be rotated [SM71, SC82] (of course the time it takes to *analytically* simulate rotation by standard matrix operations is *not* linear in the angle).

4 Our Approach and Lattice Computers

Our approach can be roughly described as one *representing space by space and time by time*. We will first explain our approach by an example. Although this example does not quite accurately present what we really do, it provides a good way to begin explaining our approach. Additionally, it helps in precipitating some issues that need to be resolved.

Consider the problem of simulating the uniform motion of a 2-dimensional object, O, in a finite, convex region, R, of a copy of euclidean 2-space (we are actually much more interested in dimensions three and above). For simplicity, assume that O is the only object in R.

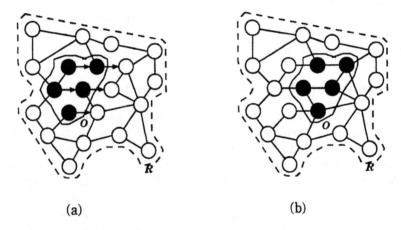

(a)   (b)

Fig. 1. Analogical Representation of the Motion of O in R

We *choose* a finite set of points from R. We place identical, synchronized computer processors at each of the points in this set, and connect some of these processors by bi-directional communication channels with delay time proportional to length. Our choices could produce the mesh-work of computer processors representing R shown in Fig. 1(a). The circles (filled and unfilled) stand for the processors, and the solid lines for connections. Note that we did make some (possibly peculiar) choices to arrive at this particular mesh-works—we will refer to this matter below. Imagine that somehow each of the processors in this mesh-works is programmed to "behave" like the point of R it is placed on. So, we would have some processors programmed to behave like empty space (these are the unfilled ones in Fig. 1(a)), and others (the filled ones in Fig. 1(a)) programmed to behave as particles of O. Motion is represented, then, by the synchronized passage of messages, across direct communication channels, from one processor to another. Imagine that a processor that represents a particle of O instructs a directly connected processor in the direction of motion, to start representing that particle. In the example shown in Fig. 1(a) each neighboring processor in the direction of motion happens to be a constant length away from the particles of O, and, since all the processors in the mesh-works execute in synchrony (or in parallel), after one message passing, O would effectively have moved in the direction of motion. The arrows in Fig. 1(a) indicate the direction of motion of O. Fig. 1(b) shows the state of the mesh-works, as far as what each processor represents, after one message passing. Repeating this process over and over again, *if it were possible*, would result in the mesh-works simulating the uniform motion of O in R; moreover, the simulation time could come out *linearly proportional* to the actual time O would take to move in R.

Generalization of this description to higher dimensions should be fairly clear, but it should also be clear that our choice of discrete points and connections to represent R is fairly higgledy-piggledy except for enabling us to cleanly present the example, one step only motion depicted in Fig. 1. About this one step motion example, the reader may even suspect (correctly it turns out) that we "cheated". Early on in our project we worried a lot about *which* set of points and interconnections to use to represent a region and, for that choice, how to deal with motions not so cleanly representable as the example in Fig. 1. For example, for a mesh-works of points arranged and connected in squares, but without diagonal connections, we had to deal with the question of how to handle diagonal motion at roughly the same *speed* as motion along the edge of a square. The example from Fig. 1 doesn't deal with this and related problems, but our algorithms, discussed briefly below, do.

First we'll discuss how we've actually dealt with the selection of points and interconnections [CRS90a, CRS91a]. Then we'll say a little about our algorithms to date [She91, CRS91c, CRS91b].

Of course, if real physical space is discrete (instead of continuous like euclidean spaces), it is not clear whether the points and interconnections of real space are regular, and if so with what regularity, whether it is irregular, whether it changes with time, ... [Min82, Fredkin]. It could be rather a mess. Also, if real space is discrete, its resolution is likely to be much finer than we could hope to precisely represent with a mesh-works computer for macroscopic level phenomena; furthermore, real space may have no minimal distance between points. We simply adopted for the points and interconnections in our computer meshes very regular schemes which have *very nice properties*, including, of course, a minimal distance between points. Unlike for the approach of Funt [Fun80, RN74] and for the numerical finite element method [CB91], we decided that we didn't want our discrete version of a region of euclidean space to have its points having thiner and thiner density as one moves outward from a area of high interest in the region. Very much unlike Funt (see the further discussion in Section 5.3 below), we chose to have our arrangements of points to be (for the infinite extension of a bounded region) invariant under translations. Roughly, these design decisions of ours are provably mathematically equivalent [CRS90a, CRS91a] to having the set of points which represent all of a copy of euclidean n-space be an *n-dimensional lattice* [CN88, GL87]. An n-dimensional *lattice* is a set of points, from some copy of euclidean n-space, providing a discrete variant of an n-dimensional vector space [Her64] in euclidean n-space in which the scalar multipliers for magnifying vectors are restricted to being integers. For example,

$\mathbf{Z}^n$, the set of n-tuples of integers, and $\mathbf{A}_n$, the set of $(n + 1)$-tuples of integers that add up to 0, are both n-dimensional lattices [CN88]. For $\mathbf{A}_n$, the associated copy of euclidean n-space is the set of $(n + 1)$-tuples of *reals* that add to 0. Clearly, for example, the set of 3-tuples of *reals* that add to 0 is just a plane, a copy of 2-dimensional space.

In [CRS90a, CRS91a] we define an n-dimensional lattice to be *regular* iff it can be generated from integer linear combinations of some set $\boldsymbol{B}$ of n vectors which are minimal length for the lattice and such that any two distinct vectors in $\boldsymbol{B}$ are a constant angle apart. Regularity is a powerful symmetry condition to the effect that with respect to some set of n generating vectors one dimension is not to be preferred to another; it also considerably simplifies vector computations. Both $\mathbf{Z}^n$ and $\mathbf{A}_n$ are regular n-dimensional lattices. $\mathbf{D}_n$, the set of all n-tuples of integers which sum to an even number, [CN88] is an n-dimensional lattice generated by its set of vectors of minimal length but, for $n > 3$, is not regular.

We associate any bounded region of a copy of euclidean n-space and an n-dimensional regular lattice embedded in that copy of n-space with a meshworks computer having identical, synchronized processors on each lattice point in the region and processors immediately connected (by identical, bi-directional communication channels) iff they are the *lattice minimal distance* apart. We call such a mesh computer, a *lattice computer*. We represent bounded regions of euclidean n-space by particular lattice computers.

We prove in [CRS90a, CRS91a] that $\mathbf{A}_n$ is the unique (up to angle-preserving isomorphism) regular n-dimensional lattice with the *maximum* number of nearest-neighbors among the n-dimensional *regular* lattices. Each point in $\mathbf{A}_n$ has $n(n + 1)$ nearest-neighbors; each point in $\mathbf{Z}^n$ has but $2n$ nearest-neighbors. We chose, then, to base our lattice computer [CRS90b] on the lattice $\mathbf{A}_n$. [CRS90b] also contains a top level design for the individual processors and a feasible scheme for embedding our n-dimensional lattice computers, $n > 3$, in real physical 3-space. (We mean feasible with respect to wire length and crowding [Vit88]. We expect that it would be too expensive to build one of our lattice computers for dimension much bigger than 3 if there are to be on the order of 10^2 processors along each of at least 3 dimensions.) For $n > 3$, an embedding into physical 3-space of a lattice computer based on $\mathbf{A}_n$ would involve having to "bend" some connections; however, simulated objects traveling in a machine so embedded would, of course, be insensitive to the bends.

Fig. 2 shows a picture (with opaque processors) of a lattice computer based on $\mathbf{A}_3$ representing a small parallelepiped region of euclidean 3-space.

In [She91, CRS91c, CRS91b] we present algorithms associated with the euclidean transformations. The algorithms include discrete versions of constant speed particle translation, non-dissipating spherical wave-front motion and circular revolution of a particle about a point, all in n-space and for a wide class of n-dimensional lattice computers, including ours. (We recently discovered [Koc91] which presents an algorithm for the energy *dissipation* of light in 3-dimensional cubic lattice computers—essentially lattice computers based on $\mathbf{Z}^3$.) The lattice computers for which most of our algorithms work are based on a class of lattices recently characterized in [RS91] as the well-known root lattices [CN88], and we now believe all our algorithms can be extended to root lattice computers.

Our discrete, constant speed particle translation and (circular) revolution algo-

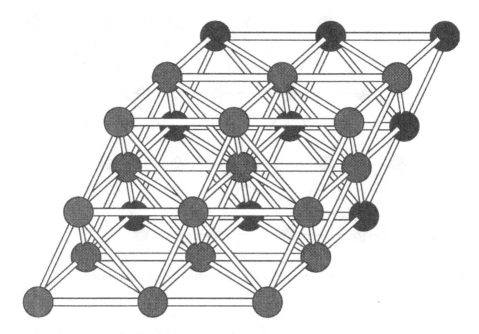

Fig. 2. A Small Lattice Computer Based on $\mathbf{A}_3$

rithms are instances of an algorithm schemata, CURVE [She91, CRS91b]. CURVE analogically simulates the constant speed motion of a particle moving along any one of a large class of curves. Straight lines and circles are among this class of curves, and the corresponding two instances of the schemata CURVE simulate, approximately in real–time, the constant speed translation and the constant angular speed circular revolution of a particle, respectively. Processors running algorithm schemata CURVE are in one of two states: *active* or *passive*. Active processors track the motion of the particle being simulated. Unlike, say, spherical wavefronts, where every processor is eventually on some simulated wavefront, curves could pass through the empty space in between processors, not hitting any processor for long stretches. Hence, we have each processor represent a whole region of n-space around it. Suppose $\boldsymbol{X}$ is a point in an n-dimensional lattice. Consider the points in n-space that are at least as close to $\boldsymbol{X}$ as to any other point in the lattice. This set of points forms a convex, n-dimensional body around $\boldsymbol{X}$ called the *Voronoi cell around* $\boldsymbol{X}$ [CN88, Aur90]. Voronoi cells have $(n-1)$-dimensional faces, the Voronoi cells around individual lattice points are congruent to one another, and they tessellate n-space.

Figure 3 shows a lattice computer based on $\mathbf{A}_2$, and a curve $\boldsymbol{C}$ in 2-space traced by a moving particle starting at the point/processor, $\boldsymbol{S}$, in the lattice computer. Figure 3 shows the Voronoi cell (with a dashed-line boundary) around the point/processor labeled $\boldsymbol{P}$ in the lattice computer based on $\mathbf{A}_2$. In algorithm schemata CURVE, each point/processor is "responsible" for points in its Voronoi cell. Algorithm schemata CURVE actually treats the curve $\boldsymbol{C}$ as a sequence of small, equal length straight line segments. The *length s* of these segments is, essentially, a parameter to CURVE [She91]. To minimize the number of different Voronoi cells a

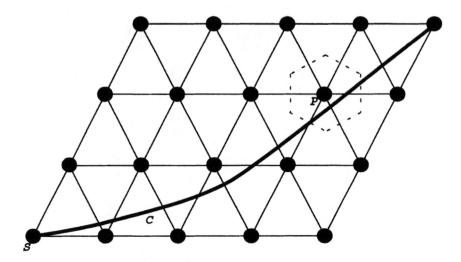

Fig. 3. A Curve C and a Voronoi Cell in a Lattice Computer Based on $\mathbf{A}_2$

segment of length s can intersect, s should be chosen less than an upper bound that depends on the lattice; however, in practice, one chooses s much smaller than this upper bound. For $\mathbf{A}_n$, the upper bound is one-half the lattice minimal distance.

Henceforth, by C we will mean the corresponding curve made up of the tiny straight line segments. As the particle moves along the curve C, it enters and exits Voronoi cells around some of the points/processors in the lattice computer. Algorithm schemata CURVE ensures that the point/processor S is initially active at simulation time 0, and, afterward, that each point/processor P is active exactly in a duration of simulation time uniformly approximately linear in the real–time duration that the particle spends inside, or on the boundary of, the Voronoi cell around P. Each point/processor P receives a message stating approximately when and where the particle entered the Voronoi cell surrounding it and any additional information it needs to compute the motion of the particle within that Voronoi cell. P then computes approximately when and where the particle will leave the Voronoi cell and, at the appropriate time, sends a message to each neighboring processor into whose Voronoi cell the particle might enter next. Again, a point/processor becomes active if and only if the particle actually enters the Voronoi cell around it.

It is beyond the scope of the present paper to present in detail any of our algorithms, but intuitively they perform delicate calculations of (i) the *time* a processor must wait after receiving a message before it can pass a message to a nearest-neighbor processor and (ii) calculations of which nearest-neighbor(s) to send which messages based on which nearest-neighbor(s) sent which messages. Being able to work with integer vector arithmetic is a big help.

Essentially these algorithms discretely simulate the corresponding continuous motions, with simulations approximately real-time, and where the error in the approximation can in most cases be bounded arbitrarily small. Unlike round-off errors in numerical calculations, the errors here are controlled. We should note that we pay a small price regarding circular motion for the design decision of invariance under translations. Circular motion provably [She91] cannot be as perfect as straight line motion. For circular motion in a lattice computer, we define an *angular resolution* which depends on s and the euclidean diameter of the lattice computer. Our algorithm for circular motion requires us to work with an angle that has rational sines and cosines and that *approximates* the resolution angle. This approximation results in a slight drift from perfect constant angular speed. However, the drift can be made so small that it cannot be seen within the angular resolution of the lattice computer until after as many thousands of revolutions as we like. This control of the drift is achieved by tiny and feasible adjustments in the approximating angle [She91]. Funt's [Fun80, RN74] spatial framework handles circular motion (about one axis) better than translations (see the discussion in Section 5.3 below).

Some readers may think we are wasting processors in our simulations: those simulating empty space at any time seem to be doing nothing at that time. We don't look at it that way: they *are* properly simulating empty space. We do *not* subscribe to a parallel computing philosophy that says that almost all processors should be *actively* computing something at any time. That attitude is correct for most other current approaches to parallel computing, but leads to a lot of pain (see Section 3) in the algorithm design phase for those approaches.

We are in the process of extending our algorithms to handle multiple wavefronts, magnification of figures, accelerated motion, and multiple, possibly joined particles. Furthermore, many things are left to decide about hardware and I/O before we can build a prototype of our lattice computers. We expect that the first useful applications will involve discrete analog scientific computing. We hope to develop algorithms to solve, say, classical physics problems, especially fluid flow problems. (See further discussion in Section 5.4 below.) *Thinking Machines* [Mac86, SW86] successfully employed their Connection Machine to *analogically* simulate 2-dimensional fluid flow problems in a similar fashion. (*Thinking Machines*'s video tape of this is impressive.) They *simulated* a hexagonal 2-dimensional mesh with their Connection Machine, essentially an SIMD hypercube that has an interconnection network [Sie85] and a routing algorithm to *simulate* arbitrary connection schemes. Simulation on a Connection Machine likely can't be carried out approximately real-time because of unpredictable delays in the interconnection network.

We expect our lattice computers will be useful in problems involving real-time control.

5 Discussion

5.1 Human Non-Verbal Cognition and Perception

Many dichotomies have been proposed to capture conceptually the essence of the intriguing cognitive differences between the left and right hemispheres of the human brain [SD85, Orn72, Kin82]. We shall not go into all these here. Suffice it to say that some of them, e.g., rational vs intuitive thought, while suggestive, are seemingly a little too operationally ill-defined to admit of testing in experimental and/or clinical settings. Others such as basic language competence vs the simplest spatial skills are much more amenable to clear testing. For example, most human adults (especially right-handed males, the most cognitively lateralized) who suffer *extensive* damage to their left-brain hemispheres (through stroke or other trauma) are thereafter unable to understand or communicate in written or spoken language, but they retain competence to more or less correctly copy simple line drawings of cubes, houses, etc. (they may leave out some details or simplify); furthermore, they retain roughly their prior competence level to solve simple spatial puzzles such as Koh Block Designs [SD85, Gar75, Gar82, Orn72]; just the opposite occurs with extensive damage to the right hemisphere: most language functions will remain intact, but the spatial skills will be severely impaired. Interestingly enough, on tasks such as copying a simple line drawing of a house, those with right-hemisphere damage may copy all the details (windows, corners, and such like), but display these details without connections to one another, strewn all over the paper: the resultant drawings will not resemble a house or capture anything of its 3-dimensional character. (In the case of right-hemisphere damage there may also be neglect of anything in the left visual field, but this curiosity is not so relevant to the points we want to make.) Kinsbourne [Kin82] posits that the left hemisphere handles details and the orderly sequence in which they are to be dealt with; whereas, (as we noted in Section 2 above) the right hemisphere provides a *spatial framework* in which to make entries.

In general it seems that both brain hemispheres in normals must contribute to non-verbal, simple spatial puzzle solving, although, if one hemisphere cannot or is not allowed to participate (as with brain damaged subjects and the split brain patients studied by Sperry and his students), then the right hemisphere is superior. For example, there is right brain superiority at mental rotation tasks [SD85]. Possibly, when one hemisphere alone must work on *most* spatial tasks, the maintenance of a spatial framework is *much* more important than being extremely careful with details and the orderly sequencing of steps. (We said '*most* spatial tasks' because those spatial tasks that are employed clinically do seem to be prototypical of spatial tasks and intuitively seem to require a spatial framework. One can suspect that for the "spatial" task of connectivity recognition, studied by Minsky and Papert [MP69], there would not be right-hemisphere superiority. Minsky and Papert explicitly employed this task to show the severe limitations of simple "holistic" computers (perceptrons), but they showed that machines with cycloptic tunnel vision (Turing machines) could easily handle it.)

A sense in which we are modeling right brain hemisphere computation with lattice computers is that, ostensibly like right brain hemispheres, a lattice computer provides a spatial framework. For other aspects of human spatial cognition, it is not so clear what the contribution of each hemisphere is. We're more interested in modeling spatial cognition than in just modeling the right hemisphere's contribution. Naturally we are talking about high level modeling, not low level, neural net modeling. There is no reason to believe that a portion of the wetware of the brain's architecture *literally* corresponds to, say, a 3-dimensional lattice computer. The cortex of the cerebrum itself, including the visual cortex, is essentially a 2-dimensional surface [Coo86]. We would expect that the reduction, to the neural net level, of high level mental imagery of 3-dimensional transformations is not quite so simplistically straightforward. (There is further discussion of levels of modeling in science in this section.)

Nonetheless, the experimental human reaction time results for a wide variety of tasks apparently requiring dynamic mental imagery, tasks including *mentally* checking congruence of pairs of complex 3-dimensional shapes [SM71, RN74], the *mental solving* of paper folding puzzles [SF72, RN74], etc., invariably produce times linear in the real time to physically carry out actual real world rotation of shapes for matching, the folding of paper shapes, etc. [SC82, Kos80, Kos83, RN74]! Since our simulations so far are approximately real-time, this is an important indicator of the correctness of using our lattice computers to model *at a high level* human non-verbal spatial cognition. N.B. We distinguish, of course, between non-verbal *cognition* and non-verbal *perception*; solving spatial puzzles involves cognition, at least low-level vision does not. However, there does seem to be important sharing of brain "machinery" (at *some* level) between vision and production (if not manipulation) of mental images. Many ingenious experiments show that the same unusual perceptual effects (which effects are unlikely to be known to the subjects in advance) occur with both real images *and imagined ones* [FS77, She78, Fin80, Blo81, Kos83].

There are various known topographic maps in the cerebral cortex, 2-dimensional patterns on the essentially 2-dimensional cortex [Coo86], *some* of which patterns are roughly (with topological and other distortion) pictorially isomorphic to what they represent. It is unknown to what extent 2-dimensional *mental* imagery involving 2-dimensional transformations (only) are mirrored pictorially in corresponding 2-dimensional motions of various roughly pictorially corresponding 2-dimensional retinotopic (or other topographic) maps.[4] In the terminology of Shepard and Chipman [SC70] such an isomorphism of mental rotation and corresponding brain representation is called *first-order*. It very unlikely to exist for 3-dimensional mental imagery if the brain representations are to be confined to the essentially 2-dimensional sheet of brain cortex. Thanks to the reaction time experiments involving 3-dimensional imagery, there must, nonetheless, be a kind of strong, but less literal, isomorphism between the transformations of mental imagery and the corresponding (high level) brain representations (but see three paragraphs below). In the terminology of Shepard and Chipman [SC70] this sort of strong isomorphism that does exist is called *second-order*. Our lattice computer representations of the motions of objects in 3-dimensional space are, then, roughly second-order isomorphic to the corresponding acts of human spatial cognition, but first-order isomorphic to the actual motions of objects in space.

It might be argued that, since human visual images, real and imagined, are continuous, our lattice computers automatically fail to model them. However, there is a lower limit to the resolution of human visual images: they actually have a graininess to them [Kos83]; continuity of images is just a, no doubt extremely useful, illusion. (N.B. Many writers in computer science, cognitive science, philosophy, and psychology seem to think that the operation of *all* analog devices must be continuous, not discrete. Even analog computers which have already been built most likely do not quite operate continuously: electrons are discrete. If real physical space is actually

---

[4] There is some evidence that some retinotopic maps on the brain are complex logarithm transformations of the retinal image [Bar87] so that magnification on the retina corresponds to translation in one direction on the representation and rotation on the retina corresponds to translation in a perpendicular direction on the representation. We also recall reading that an experiment on monkeys showed that rotation of an image in the plane of their retinas actually corresponded to a rotation in at least one of the many retinotopic maps on their brains.

discrete, no analog device can be constructed which operates continuously. There is a fairly widespread, but not quite as widespread, misconception that pictorial manipulation cannot be done by *digital* computers, presumably because pictures are believed to be continuous. Of course every *real* picture we know of is grainy at some level of resolution. Algorithmic processing of grainy pictures does not go beyond Turing machine computability—see, for example, [Cas87].)

The simpler experimental human reaction time results for mental manipulation of objects in space, which yield times linear in the real time to carry out such manipulations on real objects, apply to objects of up to 3-dimensions. There was probably no evolutionary pressure for humans to develop manipulative imagery systems with a corresponding mental spatial framework of higher dimension than three. Our lattice computers can, in principle, be constructed for any finite dimension, and, in this respect too, they go beyond a human limitation.

Kosslyn [Kos83] posits the existence of a mental space in which people carry out mental spatial manipulations and which, in Shepard and Chipman's terminology [SC70], is second-order isomorphic to an essentially discretized, finite, connected, convex region of two or three dimensional euclidean space. He reports many clever experiments designed to determine the nature of this mental space. Some of the cleverness was to make sure that subjects were not (perhaps subconsciously) going along with what the experimenter wanted. Kosslyn [Kos83] describes a series of experiments by various of his students (Pinker, Finke, and Shwartz) to investigate whether the mental space is two or three dimensional. He suggests that, while the mental space has many characteristics of a 3-dimensional space, it is a 2-dimensional medium which can be processed so that, except on especially tricky tasks, it appears to be 3-dimensional. We suspect the final word is not in on this, but, again, we are not interested in closely modeling unfortunate human limitations. We are reminded, though, of Marr's notion for vision (not imagery) of a $2\frac{1}{2}$-dimensional representation of the 3-dimensional world [Mar82]. Perhaps there is a correspondence between this $2\frac{1}{2}$-dimensional representation for *vision* and Kosslyn's more-than-2-but-not-quite-3-dimensional space for *mental imagery*. It would be intriguing for appropriate experimentalists to work out a correspondence.

It has been noted that there are severe memory limitations on human mental imagery and that these images fall apart if manipulated too much [Kos83], but, again, we're not interested in modeling human shortcomings.

In all honesty we should note that there is a philosophical debate about whether human mental imagery might be a mere epiphenomenon [Blo81]. The problem is whether mental imagery is as inessential to those acts of cognition which we believe involve mental imagery as the flashing lights on a computer console are to the computations inside the machine. One can argue that since imagistic transformations are carried out in time linear in the real time to carry out the same operations on real objects, and, since (as noted above) image production shares some unusual "perceptual" effects with vision, imagery is not at all a mere epiphenomenon. Consider the following mental puzzle.

Many socks have an emblem on either the right or left side, but not on both. One sock of a pair will have the emblem on the right, the other will have it on the left. Suppose we try to put on such socks so that these emblems will not face one another when we are standing with our legs together. For example, then, when seated, if we cross one leg over the other, the emblem will not show on the top of the top leg. Suppose one of these socks is turned inside out, but we put it on before we discover that. After we discover the problem, perhaps by noticing the emblem is a little indistinct or that the toe stitching is protruding, we remove the sock, turn it right side out and put it on again. Here's the mental puzzle. When we put the sock on the second time, do we have to put it on the same or a different foot? No fair guessing, trying an experiment with a real sock, remembering the answer stored from having tried that or a related experiment in the past, or jumping to conclusions (perhaps correct) from prior knowledge stored about the mathematics of reflections; furthermore, the solution must come from some form of conscious thought which not only gets the right answer, but justifies it: no fair just having the right answer come to you—that's too hard to tell from guessing.

Some people solve this puzzle quickly and according to the (somewhat cumbersome) rules, but we really doubt if anyone can do that without manipulating a mental image. It seems very unlikely a solution could be obtained, both quickly and, say, in time linear in the real time to try it out with a real sock, by means of analytic manipulations of equations or derivations from *non ad hoc* axioms. Hence, if imagery is a mere epiphenomenon and *all* of human cognition is really (mostly subconscious) manipulation of equations or wffs, people would be very unlikely to solve such puzzles *the first time they encounter them* with the *timing* they do.

Incidentally, consider how (if at all) you checked the mutual consistency of these two sentences from above: "Suppose we try to put on such socks so that these emblems will not face one another when we are standing with our legs together. For example, then, when seated, if we cross one leg over the other, the emblem will not show on the top of the top leg." We bet you did it, if you did it, by consulting a real leg *or a mental image of one.*

Some people are fairly conservative as to what constitutes a proper model of (some fragment of) human cognition. They demand something like a complete reduction to neural nets and/or neural biochemistry; for them, nothing short of that will do. In other parts of science, complex phenomena are modeled *with good predictive power* at various levels. For example, no one would seriously consider modeling in biology how predator-prey population sizes oscillate in dynamic or unstable equilibrium on the basis of reduction to the biochemistry (or worse yet, quantum mechanics) of the separate organisms involved. That example is, of course, rather extreme, but is meant to make a point strongly: scientific modeling of complex phenomena can be done at less than a most reduced level, and sometimes it is good sense to do so.

There has been, as there should, work on connectionistic or neural net modeling of mental imagery, including mental rotation [Bar85b, Bar85a]. Baron notes [Bar85b, Bar85a] that his modeling does not, though, naturally lead to computation times linear in the time for the real world events imaged to unfold.

We should note that Kosslyn's modeling is high level, and he has developed a computer model [Kos83], but, since he employs standard analytic representations, his model does not run in time linear in the real time for the imaged events to unfold.

Our model should suggest further work for experimentalists to tease out the exact nature of the left and right hemisphere's contribution to human non-verbal cognition. Of course there is work to be done (by us for the lattice computers, and by psychologists for human cognition) on how to model the (for humans, many times subconscious) decision making regarding which images to have and which spatial transformations to perform.

Our work may shed some light on possible functions of the *corpus callosum* [Coo86], the most massive bundle of nerve fibers connecting the cerebral hemispheres in placental mammals. (Marsupials, for example, don't have this massive connecting bundle; they have analogs of the other, much smaller, connecting bundles.) The *calloso-bulbar index* of a placental mammal is (by definition [Ant38, BG68], [Coo86, Page 9]) the ratio of the cross-sectional area of nerve fibers in its corpus callosum to that of the ascending and descending nerve fibers in its brain stem. One would expect these cross-sectional areas to be approximately proportional to the number of fibers cut by each cross-section. Intuitively, the number of nerve fibers in the corpus callosum is a rough measure of the brain power devoted to brain cross-talk; the number passing through the brain stem is a rough measure of the brain power for dealing with the body's external (and internal) effectors and sensors; now, *perhaps* the ratio *roughly* quantifies part of the brain power given over to pure thought, or at least part of "thought" not directly related to immediate interaction with the outside world (or body organs). In any case, in humans the calloso-bulbar index is 3.12, in chimpanzees it is a mere 1.79, for polar bears it is 1.06, and for the hippopotamus it is 0.56 [BG68], [Coo86, Page 9].

Here is a possible connection between our work and the corpus callosum. We will want a host computer to help with I/O for our lattice computers. That host could be a powerful, but more standard computing engine in its own right, and the connection between the two machines can be reconceptualized so that each machine is construed as a host to the other: perhaps each brain hemisphere functions as a host computer to the other with the corpus callosum playing the role of principal bundle of host connecting wires.

Regarding cognition in physics we note the following. Analogical thinking is natural for physics and engineering. For example, visual and kinesthetic imagery, not verbal thinking, was the cognitive forte of physicist Albert Einstein [Sch49] and inventor Nikola Tesla [O'N81]. Maxwell's early model of electromagnetic phenomena was quite mechanical/visual complete with rotating cylinders and idle wheels [Niv61]. Once *a lot* more experience is had with our lattice computers, they may become a tool for thinking out new physics and engineering too. It is probably no accident that the words 'imagine' and 'image' have a common root.

5.2 Airplanes Don't Make Nests

For good reasons the Wright brothers didn't design feathered, wing-flapping airplanes. It is one thing to understand how *birds* fly, quite another to *abstract* (and adapt) salient features of that process as the basis for designing an artifact in which people can fly. The abstractions of air-foil based lift and propulsion are principal salient features. For air-foil, the shape of the wing and how a fluid made of tiny particles flows over it are what are important. To *completely* understand *bird* flight, it would no doubt be required to include a quantum mechanical explanation of the biochemistry of both feathers and how energy is generated for flapping. To *understand and apply* the *abstraction* of flight is quite another thing.

We want to understand and apply, with improvements, an abstraction from human spatial cognition.

Organisms (including humans) were mostly "designed" by mindless evolutionary forces to simultaneously satisfy lots of engineering-like constraints (the partial exceptions to the mindless part are those organisms purposefully bred by people to have certain characteristics). Here are some of the constraints. The organism must descend from close ancestors that are not too unlike it, it must survive to successfully reproduce (a big constraint), if it has a brain at all, it must have a brain it can easily carry around and feed, this brain must be good at many tasks especially those related to basic needs, ... Birds, but not airplanes, have to build nests, find mates, etc. Artifacts do not have to satisfy the same or (fortunately) as many constraints as biological organisms. Many times, then, an artifact analog of some biological process can be designed to considerably turn up the gain on some special talent relative to the original biological case. Airplanes fly faster than birds. Ordinary computers do arithmetic faster than people.

The human cerebral cortex is a 2-dimensional sheet, in part, because it is for non-human ancestors quite a ways back. Perhaps originally the cerebral cortex was 2-dimensional, also in part, because the body's principal, *external* sensory surfaces (tactile and visual) are 2-dimensional. In any case, we are not so constrained in the dimensionality of our lattice computers, our lattice computers are not necessarily as limited in memory capacity and resolution for images as people are, and we are not required to make the lattice computers out of slow neural nets.

However, for example, both bird and airplane design are constrained to handle a common problem, the abstraction of propulsion; but, as is well known, they needn't handle it the same way. No doubt biological brain design is somewhat constrained by the need to cool circuits and have access for "wiring". We have to deal with such problems and other feasibility issues for our lattice computers.

5.3 Artificial Intelligence

Sloman [Slo71] pointed out several disadvantages, for certain problem domains, of *Fregean* representations, i.e., ones that use predicate calculus, or some other sentential form of representation, over *analogical* representations. (Henceforth, we will use the terms Fregean, sentential, propositional, and declarative [GN87] interchangeably.) Spatial problems are from such problem domains, and hence these disadvantages apply. We summarize below the disadvantages of Fregean representations and the advantages of analogical representations, partly as seen by Sloman, partly as seen by others including ourselves.

Interpretation of or extracting information from a Fregean representation may involve complex procedures. In a Fregean system, although the structure of the expressive medium need not constrain the variety of structures of configurations which can be so expressed (represented), one needs procedures for dealing with and accessing *efficiently* the representation for any problem domain. Furthermore, changes made to the description, especially in the case of spatial phenomena, are not so usefully/efficiently related to the changes in the structure of the represented configuration. The motion of objects in space can create a severe update propagation problem for a Fregean representation scheme, but not for our scheme.

On the other hand, translations from and into spatio-temporal configurations will, likely, involve less complex, efficient procedures if the internal representations use a medium *analogous* to space-time. In analogical representations, small changes in the representation (syntactic) are likely to correspond to small changes in what is represented (semantic). Changes in a certain direction or dimension in the representation correspond, directly, to similarly related changes in the represented configuration. In an analogical representation, all relationships involving any certain object can be obtained "locally". Here we are especially concerned with motion in the spatial domain. We are concerned that both the *timing* of motion and the spatial placement of objects be strongly vividly analogical. We are reminded here (and in Section 5.1 above) of Shepard's "definition" [Sel88, SC82] of an *analogical process* which seems to capture the essence of this timing requirement: an *analogical process* is one by which the intermediate internal states have a natural one-to-one correspondence to appropriate intermediate states in the external world. We would add that the one-to-one correspondence be computable approximately real-time too as for our strongly vividly analogical representations.

Since we are dealing with spatial/kinematic problems, Sloman's observation that a change in the represented configuration would require many more changes in a Fregean representation than in an analogical representation is of particular importance. This is a severe drawback of Fregean representations for spatial/kinematic problems. Regarding *spatial* (and other) problems, [Slo71, For81, For83, Hin79, Bro81, MD84, LS87, Sel88] also emphasize the computational complexity savings in certain examples resulting from vivid (and non-vivid) analog processing and/or point out the inefficiency of Fregean representations.

Our approach employs both analogical representations, and analogical processes. Such an approach, then, is *vivid* and *pictorial* in the strongest sense from Selman's survey [Sel88] on reasoning in Artificial Intelligence with analogs.

Funt [Fun80, RN74], mentioned above in Section 4, designed a diagrammatic representation scheme for qualitative physics (including "mental" rotation). The scheme admitted of exploiting the natural parallelism inherent in moving a multiparticle object around and was based on a 2-dimensional, foveated retina-like spatial framework. (He actually constructed only a sequential simulation, which sufficed for his purposes.) Funt's framework was designed to be especially good for rotation of an object, but its corresponding limitation was that it had but one center of rotation, the center of the framework, where there was maximal resolution. It was not possible, then, to simulate a non-trivial gear train linear in real-time, but, as is pointed out in [BL85], the importance of Funt's project was, among other things, in showing that Sloman [Slo85] need not have partially recanted his position in [Slo71] that reasoning with analogs is important to Artificial Intelligence. Our lattice computers are designed to have highly desirable translational invariance properties, and to admit of pretty good rotation about any point. Foveated retinas nicely handle many biological engineering constraints for seeing, but our design doesn't need to be bound by these constraints.

As is pointed out many places, e.g, [Min86], a curious discovery of early Artificial Intelligence is that it was fairly easy to simulate esoteric, expert problem solving in such disciplines as calculus, but very difficult to simulate the perfectly commonplace cognition involved in the *common sense* of a child building block structures or a janitor cleaning a room. *Part* of the trouble with those latter problems is the difficult problem of vision, but, and this is important for our project, it also seems to be very difficult to construct the knowledge bases required. If one *abstracts* out the problem of vision from most (or all) examples of common sense tasks hard for Artificial Intelligence and easy for perfectly ordinary people, one is mostly left with *spatial* reasoning/cognition/puzzle-solving/performance tasks! Here is what we think is going on. *Totally* verbal/propositional representation schemes for general spatial tasks are inherently too complex to build and too inefficient to use! It is much easier to build a spatial framework, and move analog objects around in it to see what will happen. Such a system has the perfect infrastructure for spatial *performance* (or procedural) knowledge. Most of the knowledge of space is, then, stored in the spatial framework! We suspect that that is just a vastly more *succinct* representation than any completely verbal/propositional scheme; furthermore, totally verbal/propositional schemes are, many times, too computationally complex to access and update, but, for example, lattice computers naturally and efficiently exploit parallelism and do *not* have an update propagation problem. We further conjecture that these efficiency issues together with the strong biological need for complex animals to handle spatial problems efficiently forced the human brain to evolve so that, for most people, there is a special region of the brain providing a spatial framework.

While Genesereth and Nilsson devoted [GN87] to the study of declarative representations in Artificial Intelligence, they clearly recognize the importance of both declarative and procedural/performance representations. They do claim, though, that procedural knowledge is not as flexible as declarative, that procedurally represented knowledge is harder to change. However, they weren't thinking of examples of spatial tasks employing the infrastructure (spatial framework) of lattice computers, but, on their side, see the next paragraph just below. Lattice computers are general purpose for spatial/kinematic knowledge, hence flexible in that respect. The update propagation problem is severe for declarative representations, but clearly our knowledge bases update quite automatically regarding the positions of objects in space and the like.

We expect that our lattice computers will be very good vehicles for modeling the *learning* of one performance task similar to another one already programmed in. See the discussions below on template pattern matching. We don't know yet if performance learning in our lattice computers will itself suffer an update propagation problem, and this is probably closer to Genesereth and Nilsson's concern.

Genesereth and Nilsson also note that declarative knowledge can be accessed introspectively. It turns out, though, that any computation task in any acceptable programming formalism [Rog58, Rog67, MY78][5] can be handled by an introspective program which explicitly constructs a perfect, quiescent copy of itself to inspect as data. As the first author has pointed out many times (e.g., [Cas86, Roy87, RC86,

---

[5] Case showed the *acceptable* systems are *characterized* as those in which every control structure can be constructed [Ric80, Roy87]. Royer and later Marcoux examined complexity analogs of this characterization [Ric80, Ric81, Roy87, Mar89]. All "naturally" occurring programming systems are essentially acceptable, but non-acceptable systems can be mathematically constructed [Rog58].

RC91, CS83]), various recursion theorems from recursive function theory essentially guarantee this. Our lattice computers essentially constitute such an acceptable programming formalism. In fact, in most instances where the "non-empty" portion of the lattice computer resides in n-dimensions and the lattice computer is at least two processors thick in the $(n + 1)$-st-dimension, a quiescent copy of the active portion can be projected into the extra dimension in one step and then accessed as data for introspection by the active portion. Hence, introspective programs are not limited to programming formalisms featuring only declarative representations.

In a private conversation, Jerry Feldman, a connectionism advocate, suggested that one of his reasons for being such is that he thinks that performance knowledge is crucial to human cognition and that connectionist networks are good for modeling it. Of course, he, as well as other connectionists, are also interested in using connectionist networks to model declarative knowledge. In a sense, our lattice computers might be construed as a special case of a connectionist network, but we believe that does not give the most useful conceptual picture of what our lattice computers are about.

Lattice computers might be helpers for natural language processing: one could use lattice computers to dynamically store and modify a diagrammatic, "concrete" model of (some of) what's being discussed as the discourse comes in. The diagrams could include time lines. Objects, when first introduced with not yet totally definite features and spatial and temporal placement, could be given *generic*, simple features and spatial and temporal placement consistent with the discourse up to their introduction; then, later, as more information comes in, the analogical representation could be updated by changing/adding features, and analogically moving the objects about in time and space. Objects given generic features, temporal and/or spatial placement because the specific information is not available could be tagged as tentative with respect to this information until (if ever) the information becomes specific. Ambiguities could be handled with multiple analogical models. Since half of a metaphor is relatively concrete, building a (generic) analogous model of that half would be useful in metaphor comprehension. For example, Lakoff and Johnson [LJ80] introduce the *conduit metaphor* to explain how we understand the abstraction of *communication*: communication can be viewed (metaphorically) as the process of putting an object in a container, moving that container along a conduit, and then taking out the object at the other end of the conduit when the container arrives. So, for example, to *help* understand sentences about communication, an analog of a physical model of Lakoff and Johnson's conduit with containers could be constructed and manipulated in our lattice computers.

In a private conversation the first author had a few years ago with Michael Gazzaniga (a former Sperry student and, at that time, on the faculty at Stony Brook), it developed that he favored the not uncommon point of view (Marvin Minsky's view too, we believe) that the right-hemisphere is just a retarded left-hemisphere. When the first author pressed him on the point of which hemisphere in split-brain patients (his specialty; Sperry got the Nobel Prize for his ground-breaking work with these patients) is superior for such *spatial* tasks as Koh Block Designs, he admitted that the right-hemisphere was. In "cognitive science" there is an overwhelmingly large preponderance of two kinds of people: those who recognize the existence of non-verbal cognition, but who are working on verbal/propositional cognition, and those who don't seem to recognize the existence of non-verbal cognition. We really can't do anything about this state of affairs except to continue our work and be grateful for the existence of those who work on imagery and such like.

Rosch [MR81, RL78] takes the point of view that those *categories* in which humans naturally think (except, perhaps, in mathematics) are each based, not on a careful verbal description, but on one (or a few) prototypes with membership in the category, then, determined by "closeness" to prototype. For example, for the category of *bird* most people seem to have a wren or robin as prototype bird. Here's some evidence. In reaction time experiments in which people are shown a picture of an animal and asked to respond as quickly as possible to the question, "Is this animal a bird?", their response times are fast on wrens and robins, a little slower on blue jays and cardinals, and very slow on penguins, ostriches, and kiwis. Also they have fast response for elephant and slow response for bat. It is conceivable, but not yet certain, then, that there is an imagistic component to common human conceptualization by categories. The measure of "closeness" may be visual. Perhaps our lattice computers can be a vehicle to model aspects of this usefully. Our lattice computers could be used for template pattern matching. This may, then, eventually be relevant to category testing by approximate matching to prototype. It may also be relevant to prototype formation. Here's how that might work. One overlays (appropriately dimensioned) patterns, each representing an example; prototypes are examples that "best fit" the overlaid pattern of all known examples (see the discussion of Galton's photography experiments below). This sort of thing may be of aid in vision too. Furthermore, regarding vision, it may be helpful, for example, to pattern match a sequence of *projections* from various vantage points of stored 3-dimensional (prototypical?) scenes with (possibly preprocessed) retinal-like images from corresponding vantage points. Of course, there is the following problem for template pattern matching: the patterns must be overlaid just right (perhaps with a topological distortion); expensive trial and error may be required[6] to find a nicely matching overlaying! In some cases, though, there may be a clear way to find points in each pattern to serve as the anchors for overlaying to check matching. For human face patterns, Sir Francis Galton [New61], in his experiments with superimposed photographs, found that it sufficed, for front views, just to anchor on eyes and mouth. If those lined up, the superpositions of faces looked like faces. His superposition of faces of members of families picked out family resemblance. The superposition of faces of (unrelated) women were strikingly beautiful. He did not have the advantage of being able to do matching for dimension > 2 patterns.

Regarding loose or approximate template matching and the learning or *partial* reproduction of performance (e.g., tennis strokes) we are reminded of [Bar32, Pages 201-213].

Perhaps automatic theorem proving (for robotics and math) could be considerably enhanced by connecting up a logic engine to one of our lattice computers and using the lattice computer to do relevant diagram manipulation to cut down on the combinatorial explosion of pure trial and error on the logic engine side [Gel63]. Even mathematicians who work in a specialty neither inherently pictorial nor about (ide-

---

[6] This expense may be reflected in the apparent high computational complexity of the graph isomorphism problem [GJ79].

alized) pictures, say, a specialty quite unlike geometry, nonetheless, work mentally and/or on paper with (possibly moving) diagrams. These diagrams *metaphorically* (metaphor again!) represent abstractions of the specialty. This is very much the case, for example, for recursive function theory. We suspect it is mainly this spatial manipulative cognitive component that enables human mathematicians to considerably surpass *current* automatic theorem proving systems in sophisticated mathematical theorem proving. It seems likely that, theoretically, the speed-up in finding proofs is not significant as measured by $O(\ )$ [CLR90], but does involve some *significantly* large constants, significant relative to, say, human lifetimes.

5.4 Cellular Automata and Physics

We expect that microscopically accurate (discrete, analogical) simulations of the motions of multiple, perhaps totally interacting, objects can be done on our lattice computers, but, some preliminary analysis of simple cases suggests these simulations might be slow (for example, if the forces between them act orders of magnitude more quickly than the bodies can respond), although linear in real time. They shouldn't be much slower, though, for many objects, than for a few. It may also be that simulations of some physical phenomena on our lattice computers may be piecewise (approximately) linear in real-time if simulations have to be stopped once in a while to rescale magnitudes. [CRS90b] cites a feasibility result we obtained suggesting that for modeling closed physical systems with superimposable forces, we should be able to do our lattice computer simulations without swamping the bandwidth of the nearest-neighbor connections, a problem with many numerical analysis simulations.

Real space may not be euclidean; it may, for example, be twisted up a bit. Spaces people have bothered to think up can generally be embedded in n-dimensional euclidean space, for suitably large n. (For example, the surface of a Klein bottle can be embedded in 4-dimensional euclidean space with no self-intersecting surfaces.) Hence, one of our appropriately dimensioned lattice computers would suffice to represent discretized versions of them.

Heisenberg [Hei58, Pages 164-165] argues that there must exist a universal constant in nature—the smallest length. This might mean that the universe, including space, is discrete. Some of the workers in the cellular automata approach to physics [Fey82, Min82, FT82, Tof84, TM87, Mar84, SW86, Mac86, Tof77b, Tof77a, Vic84, Wol83, Svo86, FHP86, Has87] seem to take this idea seriously. The theory of Cellular Automata [Neu66, Bur70, Cod68] is a clean, theoretical model for representing discrete space, especially from the point of view of massively parallel processing. A *cellular automaton* is essentially (by definition) a mesh-work of processors (where each processor is thought of as a finite automaton) [Neu66, Bur70, Cod68]. Several cellular automata based architectures have been proposed and built for problems in discrete physics [TM87], graphics [PF+85], and medical image processing [PD84, Chaps. 10 & 11]. Most of these architectures are 2-dimensional square mesh-works. The philosophy of computing in the cellular automata physics community seems to require that each individual cellular machine (we would say processor) must be extremely simple. To some extent this may be a carry over from the theoretical cellular automata theorists; to some extent this may come from the idea that each point in physical space must be quite simple. *We* are *not* bound by this seeming constraint.

It should be admitted that the cellular automata approach does provide processors that are easy to build. In *our* approach, we decided to trade processor complexity (to a feasible extent) for increased flexibility in programming motion.

The Connection Machine, of the Thinking Machines Corp., a massively parallel computer with simple individual processors, employs a hard-wired interconnection scheme quite different from ours. Also different is the philosophy behind the interconnection scheme (and other design features)—they were interested in designing a *general-purpose* parallel architecture. So, they were necessarily sensitive to the issue of their architecture having a small *diameter*, an issue prevalent among those involved in the design of general-purpose parallel architectures [MS89]. For example, one of the operations that is basic in most people's approach to parallel computing is that of *sorting* data in processors which are widely scattered across the whole architecture. For sorting, the path length in the architecture between any two pieces of data becomes of paramount importance because this length places a lower bound on the amount of time required to compare the data that is scattered in the architecture. Keeping the maximum such path length, i.e., the *diameter* of the architecture, as low as possible is clearly, *then*, an important criterion in designing general-purpose parallel architectures. Our lattice computers, on the other hand, should have a *large* diameter to simulate large chucks of space, and, fortunately, we essentially have no need to use operations which dictate low diameter, e.g., operations such as sorting data scattered across a mesh-works. For a given, large number of processors, we also happen to avoid the physical wiring problems associated with tightly-coupled architectures offering a low diameter [Vit88].

While our lattice computer approach bears a resemblance to that of cellular automata approaches, our philosophy of algorithmic locality is also not subject to the same apparent computational limitations. For example, (as noted in Section 4 above) although 2-dimensional *analogical* fluid flow simulations (based on the lattice A_2) can be carried out quite successfully with the cellular automata approach [SW86, Mac86], there are problems (for example using the lattice A_3) in the 3-dimensional case [FHP86, Has87]. We believe our algorithm [She91, CRS91b], lets call it TRANSLATE, to simulate constant speed, straight line particle motion may serve as another basis for circumventing these problems. [Has87] notes that projecting from a fourth dimension (with two velocities) helps for *some* cases of fluid flow in the cellular automata approach. We expect our approach will be more general purpose for tackling a *variety* of cases computationally. Essentially TRANSLATE enables us to send particles in *any lattice-representable (virtual) direction* at (approximately) constant speed. In a lattice computer based on A_3, while there are (up to) 12 directions given by the local, nearest-neighbor connections, many more *virtual* directions are representable. The limitations of the cellular automata approach pointed out in [FHP86, Has87] are fundamentally tied to the geometric shape and symmetry of the *local* connectedness (e.g., the 12-connectedness of A_3). With TRANSLATE we can, in effect, add more virtual directions to try to circumvent these limitations in new ways and add generality. Much remains to be tested. Our attempts would likely be aided by feasible increases in the resource of communication bandwidth between nearest-neighbors to handle extra directions.

References

[Ant38] R. J. Anthony. Essai de recherche d'une expression anatomique approximative du degré d'organisation cérébrale autre que le poids de l'encephale comparée au poids du corps. *Bulletin de la Societé N' Anthropologie de Paris*, 9:1–67, 1938.

[Aur90] Franz Aurenhammer. Voronoi diagrams—a survey of a fundamental geometric data structure. Technical Report B-90-9, Institute for Computer Science, Dept. of Mathematics, Freie Universität Berlin, November 1990.

[Bar32] F. C. Bartlett. *Remembering — A Study in Experimental and Social Psychology*. Cambridge University Press, Cambridge, 1932. Reprinted, 1977.

[Bar85a] R. Baron. A model of mental imagery. *Int. J. Man–Machine Studies*, 23:313–334, 1985.

[Bar85b] R. Baron. Visual memories and mental images. *Int. J. Man–Machine Studies*, 23:275–311, 1985.

[Bar87] R. Baron. *The Cerebral Computer*. Lawrence Erlbaum, Associates, Hillsdale, NJ, 1987.

[BG68] S. M. Blinkov and I. I. Glezer. *The Human Brain in Figures and Tables*. Plenum Press, NY, 1968.

[BL85] Ronald Brachman and Hector J. Levesque, editors. *Readings in Knowledge Representation*. Morgan Kaufmann Publishers, Inc., 1985.

[Blo81] Ned Block, editor. *Imagery*. MIT Press, Cambridge, MA, 1981.

[Bro81] R. Brooks. Symbolic reasoning among 3–d models and 2–d images. *Artificial Intelligence*, 17:285–348, 1981.

[Bur70] A. W. Burks, editor. *Essays on Cellular Automata*. Univ. of Illinois Press, 1970.

[Cas86] J. Case. Learning machines. In W. Demopoulos and A. Marras, editors, *Language Learning and Concept Acquisition: Foundational Issues*. Ablex Publishing Company, Norwood, NJ, 1986.

[Cas87] J. Case. Turing machine. In Stuart Shapiro, editor, *Encyclopedia of Artificial Intelligence*. John Wiley and Sons, New York, NY, 1987.

[CB91] Tripathi Chandrupatla and Ashok Belegundu. *Introduction to Finite Elements in Engineering*. Prentice-Hall, NJ, 1991.

[CLR90] T. Cormen, C. Leiserson, and R. Rivest. *Introduction to Algorithms*. MIT Press/McGraw Hill, 1990.

[CN88] J. H. Conway and N. J. A. Sloane. *Sphere Packings, Lattices and Groups*. Springer Verlag, 1988.

[Cod68] E. F. Codd. *Cellular Automata*. Academic Press, 1968.

[Coo86] Norman D. Cook. *The Brain Code: Mechanisms of Information Transfer and the Role of the Corpus Callosum*. Methuen, London, 1986.

[CRS90a] J. Case, D. S. Rajan, and A. M. Shende. Optimally representing euclidean space discretely for analogically simulating physical phenomena. In K. V. Nori, editor, *Foundations of Software Technology & Theoretical Computer Science*, volume 472 of *Lecture Notes in Computer Science*, pages 190–203. Springer Verlag, Berlin, 1990. See [CRS91a].

[CRS90b] John Case, Dayanand S. Rajan, and Anil M. Shende. Parallel processor computer, Dec 1990. U.S. Patent Application submitted by SUNY, Research Foundation.

[CRS91a] John Case, Dayanand S. Rajan, and Anil M. Shende. Lattice computers for optimally representing euclidean space. Technical Report 91-15, University of Delaware, June 1991. Expands on and corrects slightly [CRS90a].

[CRS91b] John Case, Dayanand S. Rajan, and Anil M. Shende. Simulating uniform motion in lattice computers I: Constant speed particle translation. Technical Report 91-17, University of Delaware, June 1991.

[CRS91c] John Case, Dayanand S. Rajan, and Anil M. Shende. Spherical wave front generation in lattice computers. Technical Report 91-16, University of Delaware, June 1991.

[CS83] J. Case and C. Smith. Comparison of identification criteria for machine inductive inference. *Theor. Comp. Sci.*, 25:193–220, 1983.

[Fey82] Richard P. Feynman. Simulating physics with computers. *International Journal of Theoretical Physics*, 21(6/7), 1982.

[FHP86]   U. Frisch, B. Hasslacher, and Y. Pomeau. Lattice-gas automata for the Navier Stokes equation. *Physical Review Letters*, 56(14):1505–1508, April 1986.

[Fin80]   R. A. Finke. Levels of equivalence in imagery and perception. *Psychological Review*, 87:113–139, 1980.

[FK76]   M. Flynn and R. Kosaraju. *Kybernetes*, 5:159–163, 1976.

[For81]   K. Forbus. A study of qualitative and geometric knowledge in reasoning about motion. Technical Report AI.TR.615, MIT, AI–Lab, February 1981.

[For83]   K. Forbus. Qualitative reasoning about space and motion. In D. Gentner and A. Stevens, editors, *Mental Models*. Lawrence Erlbaum Associates, Hillsdale, N.J., 1983.

[FS77]   R. A. Finke and M. J. Schmidt. Orientation–specific color after–effects following imagination. *Journal of Experimental Psychology: Human Perception and Performance*, 3:599–606, 1977.

[FT82]   Edward Fredkin and Tommaso Toffoli. Conservative logic. *International Journal of Theoretical Physics*, 21(3/4), 1982.

[Fun80]   Brian V. Funt. Problem–solving with diagrammatic representations. *Artificial Intelligence*, 13:201–230, 1980. Reprinted in [BL85].

[Gar75]   Howard Gardner. *The Shattered Mind: The Person after Brain Damage*. Knopf, New York, 1975.

[Gar82]   Howard Gardner. *Art, Mind, and Brain: A Cognitive Approach to Creativity*. Basic Books, New York, 1982.

[Gel63]   H. Gelernter. Realization of a geometry theorem–proving machine. In E. Feigenbaum and J. Feldman, editors, *Computers and Thought*. McGraw–Hill, NY, 1963.

[GJ79]   M. Garey and D. Johnson. *Computers and Intractability*. Freeman, 1979.

[GL87]   Peter M. Gruber and Gerrit Lekkerkerker. *Geometry of Numbers*. North-Holland Mathematical Library, 1987.

[GN87]   M. Genesereth and N. Nilsson. *Logical Foundations of Artificial Intelligence*. Morgan Kaufmann, Los Altos, CA, 1987.

[Has87]   Brosl Hasslacher. Discrete fluids. *Los Alamos Science*, (15):175–217, 1987. Special Issue.

[Hei58]   Werner Heisenberg. *Physics and Philosophy*. Harper & Brothers Publishers, New York, 1958.

[Her64]   I. N. Herstein. *Topics in Algebra*. Blaisdell Publishing Co., 1964.

[Hin79]   G. Hinton. Some demonstrations of the effects of structural descriptions in mental imagery. *Cognitive Science*, 3:231–250, 1979.

[Kin82]   M. Kinsbourne. Hemispheric specialization and the growth of human understanding. *American Psychologist*, 37(4):411–420, April 1982.

[KL78]   H. T. Kung and C. E. Leiserson. Systolic arrays (for VLSI). In *Proceedings of the Symposium on Sparse Matrix Computing and Their Applications*, pages 245–282, November 1978.

[Koc91]   P. Kochevar. A simple light simulation algorithm for massively parallel machines. *Journal of Parallel and Distributed Computing*, 13(2):193–201, October 1991.

[Kos80]   Stephen M. Kosslyn. *Image and Mind*. Harvard Univ. Press, Cambridge, Massachusetts, 1980.

[Kos83]   Stephen M. Kosslyn. *Ghosts in the Mind's Machine: Creating and Using Images in the Brain*. Harvard Univ. Press, Cambridge, Massachusetts, 1983.

[LJ80]   G. Lakoff and M. Johnson. *Metaphors We Live By*. University of Chicago Press, 1980.

[LS87]   J. Larkin and H. Simon. Why a picture is (sometimes) worth ten thousand words. *Cognitive Science*, 1987.

[Mac86]   Thinking Machines. Introduction to data level parallelism. Technical Report 86.14, Thinking Machines, April 1986.

[Mar82]   David Marr. *Vision: A Computational Investigation into the Human Representation and Processing of Visual Information*. W.H. Freeman, San Francisco, 1982.

[Mar84]   Norman Margolus. Physics–like models of computation. *Physica 10D*, pages 81–95, 1984.

[Mar89]   Y. Marcoux. Composition is almost as good as s-1-1. In *Proceedings, Structure in Complexity Theory–Fourth Annual Conference*. IEEE Computer Society Press, 1989.

[MD84]   D. McDermott and E. Davis. Planning routes through uncertain territory. *Artificial Intelligence*, 22:107–156, 1984.

[Min82]   Marvin Minsky. Cellular vacuum. *International Journal of Theoretical Physics*, 21(6/7), 1982.

[Min86]   M. Minsky. *The Society of Mind*. Simon and Schuster, NY, 1986.

[MP69]   M. Minsky and S. Papert. *Perceptrons: An Introduction to Computational Geometry*. MIT Press, Cambridge, MA, 1969.

[MR81]   C. B. Mervis and E. Rosch. Categorization of natural objects. In M. R. Rosenzweig and L. W. Porter, editors, *Annual Review of Psychology*, volume 32. 1981.

[MS89]   Russ Miller and Quentin F. Stout. Mesh computer algorithms for computational geometry. *IEEE Transactions on Computers*, C-38(3):321–340, March 1989.

[MY78]   M. Machtey and P. Young. *An Introduction to the General Theory of Algorithms*. North Holland, New York, 1978.

[Neu66]   J. Von Neumann. *Theory of Self–Reproducing Automata*. Univ. Illinois Press, 1966. edited and compiled by A. W. Burks.

[New61]   James R. Newman. *Science and Sensibility*. Simon and Schuster, NY, 1961.

[Niv61]   W. D. Nivan, editor. *The Scientific Papers of James Clerk Maxwell*. Dover Publications, Inc., 1961.

[O'N81]   J. O'Neil. *Prodigal Genius: The Life of Nikola Tesla*. Angriff Press, Hollywood, CA, 1981.

[Orn72]   R. Ornstein. *The Psychology of Consciousness*. Freeman, San Francisco, California, 1972.

[PD84]   Kendall Preston and M. J. B. Duff. *Modern Cellular Automata: Theory and Applications*. Plenum Publishers, 1984.

[PF+85]   John Poulton, Henry Fuchs, et al. PIXEL–PLANES: Building a VLSI–based graphic system. In *Chapel Hill Conference on VLSI*, 1985.

[RC86]   J. Royer and J. Case. Progressions of relatively succinct programs in subrecursive hierarchies. Technical Report 86–007, Univ. of Chicago, Computer Science Dept., 1986.

[RC91]   J. Royer and J. Case. *Intensional Subrecursion and Complexity Theory*. Research Notes in Theoretical Science. Pitman Press, in revision, 1991.

[Ric80]   G. Riccardi. *The Independence of Control Structures in Abstract Programming Systems*. PhD thesis, SUNY Buffalo, 1980.

[Ric81]   G. Riccardi. The independence of control structures in abstract programming systems. *Journal of Computer and System Sciences*, 22:107–143, 1981.

[RL78]   E. Rosch and B. Lloyd, editors. *Cognition and Categorization*. Erlbaum Associates, Hillsdale, NJ, 1978.

[RN74]   David Rumelhart and Donald Norman. Representation in memory. In R. Atkinson, R. Herrnstein, G. Lindzey, and D. Luce, editors, *Stevens' Handbook of Experimental Psychology*, volume 2: Learning and Cognition. John Wiley and Sons, NY, second edition, 1974.

[Rog58]   H. Rogers. Gödel numberings of partial recursive functions. *Journal of Symbolic Logic*, 23:331–341, 1958.

[Rog67]   H. Rogers. *Theory of Recursive Functions and Effective Computability*. McGraw Hill, New York, 1967. Reprinted, MIT Press, 1987.

[Roy87]   J. Royer. *A Connotational Theory of Program Structure*. Lecture Notes in Computer Science 273. Springer Verlag, 1987.

[RS91]   Dayanand S. Rajan and Anil M. Shende. Efficiently generated lattices and root lattices. Technical Report 92–02, University of Delaware, August 1991. Journal article under review.

[SC70]   R. N. Shepard and S. Chipman. Second–order isomorphism of internal representations: shapes of states. *Cognitive Psychology*, 1:1–17, 1970.

[SC82]   R. N. Shepard and L. A. Cooper. *Mental Images and Their Transformations*. MIT Press, Cambridge, Massachusetts, 1982.

[Sch49]   P. A. Schilpp, editor. *Albert Einstein: Philosopher–Scientist*. Open Court, La Salle, IL, 1949.

[SD85]   S. Springer and G. Deutsch. *Left Brain, Right Brain*. W.H. Freeman, New York, 1985.

[Sel88]   B. Selman. Analogues. Technical report, University of Toronto, 1988. Technical Note CSRI–47.

[SF72]   R. N. Shepard and C. Feng. A chronometric study of mental paperfolding. *Cognitive Psychology*, 3:228–243, 1972.

[She78]   R. N. Shepard. The mental image. *American Psychologist*, 33:123–137, 1978.

[She91]   Anil M. Shende. *Digital Analog Simulation of Uniform Motion in Representations of Physical n-Space by Lattice-Work MIMD Computer Architectures*. PhD thesis, SUNY at Buffalo, Buffalo, N. Y., 1991. TR 91-14, Department of Computer Science.

[Sie85]   Howard Jay Siegel. *Interconnection Networks for Large-Scale Parallel Processing*. Lexington Books, 1985.

[Slo71]   Aaron Sloman. Interactions between philosophy and A.I.—the role of intuition and non–logical reasoning in intelligence. *Artificial Intelligence*, 2:209–224, 1971.

[Slo85]   Aaron Sloman. Afterthoughts on analogical representations. In Ronald Brachman and Hector J. Levesque, editors, *Readings in Knowledge Representation*. Morgan Kaufmann Publishers, Inc., 1985.

[SM71]   R. N. Shepard and J. Metzler. Mental rotation of three–dimensional objects. *Science*, 171(4):701–703, 1971.

[Spe74]   R. W. Sperry. Lateral specialization in the surgically separated hemispheres. In B. Milner, editor, *Hemispheric Specialization and Interaction*. MIT Press, 1974.

[Svo86]   Karl Svozil. Are quantum fields cellular automata? *Physics Letters A*, 119(4), December 1986.

[SW86]   James B. Salem and S. Wolfram. Thermodynamics and hydrodynamics with cellular automata. In S. Wolfram, editor, *Theory and Applications of Cellular Automata*. World Scientific, 1986.

[TM87]   Tommaso Toffoli and Norman Margolus. *Cellular Automata Machines*. MIT Press, 1987.

[Tof77a]   Tommaso Toffoli. Cellular automata machines. Technical Report 208, Comp. Comm. Sci. Dept., University of Michigan, 1977.

[Tof77b]   Tommaso Toffoli. Computation and construction universality of reversible cellular automata. *Journal of Computer and System Sciences*, 15:213–231, 1977.

[Tof84]   Tommaso Toffoli. CAM: A high–performance cellular–automaton machine. *Physica 10D*, pages 195–204, 1984.

[Vic84]   Gérard Y. Vichniac. Simulating physics with cellular automata. *Physica 10D*, pages 96–116, 1984.

[Vit88]   Paul M. B. Vitányi. Locality, communication and interconnect length in multicomputers. *SIAM J. Comp.*, 17(4):659–672, 1988.

[Wol83]   Stephen Wolfram. Statistical mechanics of cellular automata. *Reviews of Modern Physics*, 55(3):601–644, July 1983.

A Solution of the Credit Assignment Problem in the Case of Learning Rectangles

(Abstract)

Zhixiang Chen *   Wolfgang Maass **

1 Introduction

The *credit assignment problem* may be defined as "the problem of assigning credit or blame to the individual decisions that led to some overall result" (Cohen and Feigenbaum [CF]). Obviously this problem is ubiquitous not just in Artificial Intelligence, but also in the study of adaptive neural networks, where credit or blame for the overall performance of the network has to be distributed to the individual components of the network.

We examine here the credit assignment problem in the case of on-line learning of rectangles $\prod_{i=1}^{d} \{a_i, a_i + 1, \ldots, b_i\}$ over a discrete domain $\{1, \ldots, n\}^d$. In order to learn such rectangle, one has to search for the correct values of the $2d$ parameters $a_1, b_1, \ldots, a_d, b_d$. The credit assignment problem in the case of learning rectangles is the problem to decide, which of the $2d$ local search strategies should be blamed when the global learning algorithm makes an error. We propose here a rather radical solution to this problem: *each* local search strategy that is possibly involved in this global error will be blamed. With this radical solution it is unavoidable that frequently local search strategies will be incorrectly blamed. Therefore we employ as local search strategies for the $2d$ parameters $a_1, b_1, \ldots, a_d, b_d$ suitable *error tolerant* binary search procedures.

More specifically the credit assignment problem in the case of on-line learning of rectangles is the following. When the learner receives a negative counterexample $< x_1, \ldots, x_d >$ to his current hypothesis $\prod_{i=1}^{d} \{a_i, \ldots, b_i\}$, it is clear that the learner

---

*Department of Computer Science, Boston University, MA 02215, USA. E-mail: zchen@cs.bu.edu.

**Institute for Theoretical Computer Science, Technische Universitaet Graz, Klosterwiesgasse 32, A-8010 Graz, Austria; and Department of Mathematics, Statistics, and Computer Science, University of Illinois at Chicago, Chicago, IL 60680, USA. E-mail: maass@igi.tu-graz.ac.at

has to change at least one of the intervals $\{a_i, \ldots, b_i\}$ so that it no longer contains x_i. But it is not clear *which* of the intervals $\{a_i, \ldots, b_i\}$ should be changed. We explore here an approach where the learner attempts to change for *each* $i \in \{1, \ldots, d\}$ the interval $\{a_i, \ldots, b_i\}$ so that it no longer contains x_i.

With this new approach towards on-line learning of rectangles one achieves a positive solution to the open problem, whether arbitrary axis-parallel rectangles over the domain $\{1, \ldots, n\}^d$ can be learnt with a worst case number of counterexamples that is polylogarithmic in the size n^d of the domain (i. e. polynomial in d and $\log n$). One is also able to give an asymptotically optimal on-line learning algorithm for a version of the somewhat more complex problem of learning the *union of two rectangles* in the plane. We refer to [CM] for details to all results in this abstract.

2 Background and Definitions

We consider the concept class

$$BOX_n^d := \left\{ \prod_{i=1}^d \{a_i, \ldots, b_i\} \;\middle|\; 1 \le a_i, b_i \le n \text{ for } i = 1, \ldots, d \right\}$$

over the domain $\{1, \ldots, n\}^d$.

Our learning model is the standard model for on-line learning (see [A], [L], [MTc]). A *learning process* for a concept class $\mathcal{C}$ over a domain X is viewed as a dialogue between a *learner* A and the *environment*. The goal of the learner A is to "learn" an unknown target concept $C_T \in \mathcal{C}$ that has been fixed by the environment. In order to gain information about C_T the learner proposes hypotheses H from a fixed hypothesis space $\mathcal{H}$ with $\mathcal{C} \subseteq \mathcal{H} \subseteq 2^X$. Whenever $H \ne C_T$ for the proposed hypothesis H, the environment responds with some *counterexample* (CE) $g \in H\Delta C_T := (C_T - H) \cup (H - C_T)$. g is called a *positive counterexample* (PCE) if $g \in C_T - H$, and g is called a *negative counterexample* (NCE) if $g \in H - C_T$. Each new hypothesis H_{i+1} of the learner (resp. learning algorithm) A may depend on the earlier hypotheses $H_1, \ldots, H_i$ and the given counterexamples $g_j \in H_j \Delta C_T$ for $j = 1, \ldots, i$.

One defines the resulting *learning complexity of a learning algorithm* A by

$$LC(A) := \max\{i \in \mathbf{N} \mid \quad \text{there is some } C_T \in \mathcal{C} \text{ and a sequence } g_1, \ldots, g_{i-1}$$
$$\text{of counterexamples to the hypotheses } H_1, \ldots, H_{i-1}$$
$$\text{of the learner } A \text{ such that } H_i \ne C_T\}.$$

The *learning complexity of concept class* $\mathcal{C}$ *with hypothesis space* $\mathcal{H}$ is defined by

$$LC^{\mathcal{H}}(\mathcal{C}) := \min\{LC(A) \mid \quad A \text{ is a learning algorithm}$$
$$\text{for } \mathcal{C} \text{ with hypothesis space } \mathcal{H}\}.$$

One sets $LC(\mathcal{C}) := LC^{\mathcal{C}}(\mathcal{C})$ and $LC - ARB(\mathcal{C}) := LC^{2^X}(\mathcal{C})$.

It is known that $LC(BOX_n^d) \geq LC - ARB(BOX_n^d) = \Theta(d \log n)$. The upper bound $O(d \log n)$ for $LC - ARB(BOX_n^d)$ follows by considering the HALVING-algorithm (see [A], [L], [MTc]). The lower bound $\Omega(d \log n)$ is shown by constructing a decision tree for BOX_n^d in which every leaf has depth $\Omega(d \log n)$. This is sufficient by a result of Littlestone [L] (see also [MTc]).

The HALVING-algorithm uses arbitrary subsets of the domain as hypotheses. With regard to learning algorithms for BOX_n^d that use computationally feasible hypotheses there exist two quite different approaches. Both of these algorithms use hypotheses from BOX_n^d. There is a learning algorithm B with $LC(B) = O(d \cdot n)$ that issues as its next hypothesis always the smallest $C \in BOX_n^d$ that is consistent with all preceding counterexamples. This algorithm is frequently considered in the special case $n = 2$ where the concepts $C \in BOX_2^d$ correspond to monomials over d boolean variables (see the algorithm for the complementary class 1-CNF in [V]).

It is less trivial (even for $d = 2$) to design a learning algorithm D for BOX_n^d with computationally feasible hypotheses such that $LC(D) = O(f(d) \log n)$ for some function $f : \mathbf{N} \to \mathbf{N}$. An algorithm D of this type (which uses hypotheses from BOX_n^d) was exhibited in [MTa], [MTb]. However this algorithm D learns separately each of the 2^d corners of the target concept, and hence $LC(D)$ is exponential in d (i.e. $f(d) \geq 2^d$).

The question whether the advantageous features of both learning algorithms B and D can be combined in a single algorithm S with $LC(S) \leq \text{poly}(d, \log n)$ was first brought to our attention by David Haussler ([H], see also [MTb]).

A learning algorithm S which achieves this performance is exhibited in section 4 of this paper. It proceeds in a completely different way than the two previously described learning algorithms for BOX_n^d. We describe the main component of the new algorithm in section 3.

In Section 5 we discuss another application of this design technique: an algorithm for learning the union of two rectangles in the plane. We assume here that the learner knows already that the top left corner of the domain is contained in one rectangle, and the bottom right corner in the other. Nevertheless this learning problem is substantially more complicated than the preceding one: The obvious local search procedures that search for the lengths of the sides of the two rectangles are likely to get not only *false negative counterexamples* (as in the preceding learning problem), but also *false positive counterexamples*. This complication arises from the fact that in general the learner does not know to which one of the two rectangles of C_T a positive counterexample belongs. Nevertheless one can construct for this learning problem an efficient learning algorithm whose learning complexity is asymptotically optimal. Again this algorithm consists of suitable versions of binary search as modules, which will tolerate certain incorrect credit assignments.

This positive result for learning the union of two rectangles provides a contrast to earlier results about efficiently learnable concept classes $\mathcal{C}$ such as half-planes over $\{1, \ldots, n\}^2$, or monomials, for which one has shown that $\mathcal{U} - 2 - \mathcal{C} := \{C_1 \cup C_2 \mid C_1, C_2 \in \mathcal{C}\}$ is not efficiently learnable (see [MTb], [PV]).

3   An Algorithm for Binary Search that Tolerates One-sided Errors

In this section we consider an extension of the notion of a "negative counterexample", and along with it an extension of the previously described learning model.

Assume $C_T \in \mathcal{C}$ is the target concept and H_s is the current hypothesis of the learner. The environment may respond in the extended model with a positive counterexample ("PCE") $g \in C_T - H_s$, with a *true negative counterexample* ("true NCE") $g \in H_s - C_T$, or with a *false negative counterexample* ("false NCE") $g \in H_s \cap C_T$. Note that the environment is allowed to respond with a false NCE even if $H_s = C_T$. We extend the notion of a negative counterexample (NCE) so that it subsumes both true and false NCE's. The environment is not required to tell the learner to which of these categories a counterexample g belongs.

We define a binary search algorithm TBS_n (the "T" stands for error-tolerant) for learning the "head" h of a halfinterval $\{1, \ldots, h\} \subseteq \{1, \ldots, n\}$ in this extended learning model. The new algorithm S for learning rectangles $C_T = \prod_{i=1}^{d} \{a_i, \ldots, b_i\} \in BOX_n^d$ (see section 4) will consist of $2d$ separate copies of the here defined error-tolerant binary search algorithm TBS: in each dimension i it uses separate copies of TBS and its symmetric counterpart TBS^* for learning the "head" b_i and the "tail" a_i of the interval $\{a_i, \ldots, b_i\}$. Although this learning algorithm S for BOX_n^d will receive only true counterexamples, the individual binary search procedures may also receive *false* negative counterexamples. This is a consequence of our quite radical solution to the associated "credit assignment problem", where we blame *each* of the $2d$ subroutines for binary search for any error of the learning algorithm S. In particular a true NCE for S will result in a true NCE for at least one subroutine and false NCE's for up to $d - 1$ other subroutines.

In this section we consider the concept class

$$HEAD_n := \{\{1, \ldots, j\} \mid j \in \{1, \ldots, n\}\}$$

over the domain $\{1, 2, \ldots, n\}$.

At the beginning of each step r of a learning process in the extended learning model the learner issues a hypothesis $H_r := \{1, \ldots, h_r\} \in HEAD_n$. If $H_r \neq C_T$, then the learner will receive at step r the counterexample $g_r \in \{1, \ldots, n\}$. We set

$$p_s \quad := \quad \max(\{1\} \ \cup \ \{g_r \mid 1 \leq r \leq s \text{ and } g_r \text{ was a PCE }\})$$

$$n_s \quad := \quad \min(\{n+1\} \ \cup \ \{g_r \mid 1 \leq r \leq s, \ g_r > p_s, \text{ and } g_r \text{ was a} \\ \text{(true or false) NCE}\})$$

$$n_s^{true} \quad := \quad \min(\{n+1\} \ \cup \ \{g_r \mid 1 \leq r \leq s \text{ and } g_r \text{ was a true NCE}\}).$$

Note that in the definition of n_s we consider exactly those earlier NCE's that are still unrefuted by the end of step s.

Definition of the binary search algorithm TBS_n for learning $HEAD_n$ in the extended learning model:

Set $h_1 := 1$.
For $s \geq 1$ set $h_{s+1} := h_s$ if g_s is a NCE and $g_s \leq p_s$.

Else, we define

$$h_{s+1} := \begin{cases} \min(\{n_s - 1\} \ \cup \ \{h_r \mid 1 \leq r \leq s \text{ and } p_s \leq h_r < n_s\}) \\ \qquad\qquad\qquad\qquad\qquad , \text{ if } g_s \text{ is a PCE.} \\ \\ p_s + \left\lfloor \dfrac{n_s - p_s}{2} \right\rfloor \qquad\qquad , \text{ if } g_s \text{ is a (true or false) NCE.} \end{cases}$$

The algorithm TBS_n issues at step s the hypothesis $\{1, \ldots, h_s\}$.

Theorem 3.1 *Assume that f false NCE's occur in a learning process for $HEAD_n$ with learning algorithm TBS_n. Then at most $\log n$ true NCE's and at most $\log n + 3f + 1$ PCE's occur in this learning process.* ∎

Remark 3.2 *One can construct in the same manner a learning algorithm TBS_n^* for the concept class*

$$TAIL_n := \{\{j, j+1, \ldots, n\} \mid 1 \leq j \leq n\}$$

that satisfies an analogous version of Theorem 3.1 .

Remark 3.3 *There exist already various algorithms for binary search in the presence of two-sided errors, see e.g. [KMRSW], [P], [SW]. These algorithms do not provide sufficiently strong bounds (e.g. on the number of true NCE's) to be useful for our application in section 4.*

4 A Learning Algorithm for BOX_n^d whose Error Bound is Polynomial in d and $\log n$

Theorem 4.1 $LC(BOX_n^d) = O(d^2 \log n)$.

Proof: Consider any target concept $C_T = \prod_{i=1}^{d} \{a_i, \ldots, b_i\} \in BOX_n^d$. The learning algorithm S for BOX_n^d issues $H_1 := \emptyset$ as its first hypothesis. If $H_1 \neq C_T$ then S receives a PCE $u = < u_1, \ldots, u_d > \in C_T$. Henceforth the algorithm S splits the task of learning C_T into $2d$ separate subtasks: The learning of $\{u_i, \ldots, b_i\} \subseteq \{u_i, \ldots, n\}$ (i.e. of a concept from $HEAD_{n-u_i+1}$ over the transformed domain $\{u_i, \ldots, n\}$) and the learning of $\{a_i, \ldots, u_i\} \subseteq \{1, \ldots, u_i\}$ (i.e. of a concept from $TAIL_{u_i}$) for $i = 1, \ldots, d$. For each $i \in \{1, \ldots, d\}$ the algorithm S employs TBS_{n-u_i+1} for the former and $TBS_{u_i}^*$ for the latter subtask.

One sets $H_2 := \{u\}$. Assume that at any step $r \geq 2$ the learning algorithm S for BOX_n^d has issued a hypothesis $H_r := \prod_{i=1}^{d} \{h_i^*, \ldots, h_i\}$. Then the next hypothesis H_{r+1} is determined in the following way by the $2d$ subroutines.

Let $x = < x_1, \ldots, x_d > \in C_T \Delta H_r$ be the counterexample to the hypothesis H_r of algorithm S. Note that we use the notion of a counterexample for algorithm S in the traditional sense (i.e. x is a PCE or a true NCE). If x is a PCE to hypothesis H_r, then for at least one $i \in \{1, \ldots, d\}$ the point x_i is a PCE to the current hypothesis of one of the two subroutines TBS_{n-u_i+1} or $TBS_{u_i}^*$. For each such i one changes the interval in the i-th dimension according to the next hypothesis of the subroutine TBS_{n-u_i+1} resp. $TBS_{u_i}^*$. For other i one has $x_i \in \{h_i^*, \ldots, h_i\}$, and one repeats in these dimensions the same interval $\{h_i^*, \ldots, h_i\}$ in the next hypothesis H_{r+1} of S.

Assume now that $x = < x_1, \ldots, x_d >$ is a NCE to hypothesis H_r. For each $i \in \{1, \ldots, d\}$ with $x_i \neq u_i$ the point x_i provides a (true or false) NCE to the current hypothesis $\{u_i, \ldots, h_i\}$ of subroutine TBS_{n-u_i+1}, or to the current hypothesis $\{h_i^*, \ldots, u_i\}$ of subroutine $TBS_{u_i}^*$. One updates the interval in the i-th dimension of the next hypothesis H_{r+1} of S according to the next hypothesis of TBS_{n-u_i+1} resp. $TBS_{u_i}^*$. For those i with $x_i = u_i$ one leaves the interval in the i-th dimension unchanged.

By Theorem 3.1 each subroutine for learning one of the $2d$ halfintervals encounters at most $\log n$ true NCE's. Since each NCE for algorithm S provides a true NCE for at least one of the $2d$ subroutines, S gets altogether at most $2d \log n$ NCE's. Each of these NCE's may generate false NCE's for up to $d - 1$ subroutines. Hence the sum of false NCE's for all $2d$ subroutines together is $\leq (d - 1)2d \log n$. Thus by Theorem 3.1 the sum of all PCE's that are received by the $2d$ subroutines is bounded by $2d(\log n + 1) + 3(d - 1)2d \log n = (6d^2 - 4d) \log n + 2d$. Since each PCE to algorithm S (exept for the first one) generates a PCE for at least one of its $2d$

subroutines, the total number of PCE's that S receives is $\leq (6d^2 - 4d)\log n + 2d + 1$. Hence $LC(S) \leq 2d\log n + (6d^2 - 4d)\log n + 2d + 1 = 6d^2\log n - 2d\log n + 2d + 1$. $\blacksquare$

5 Learning the Union of Two Boxes in the Plane

The algorithm in the preceding section was based on a solution of the credit assignment problem in which the local search procedures tolerate false negative counterexamples. It was essential for the success of this algorithm that the local search procedures never receive false positive counterexamples.

In this section we examine a more complex learning problem, in which the obvious local search procedures have to tolerate both false negative and false positive counterexamples. For any $m, n \in \mathbf{N}$ let $X_{m,n}$ be the domain

$$X_{m,n} := \{<i,j> \mid i \in \{1,\ldots,m\} \text{ and } j \in \{1,\ldots,n\}\}.$$

Set $BOX_{m,n} := \{\{i,\ldots,j\} \times \{k,\ldots,l\} \mid 1 \leq i, j \leq m \text{ and } 1 \leq k, l \leq n\}$.

We write $a := <1,n>$ for the upper left corner and $b := <m,1>$ for the lower right corner of this domain $X_{m,n}$. We consider the following concept class over the domain $X_{m,n}$:

$$TWO - BOX_{m,n} := \{RA \cup RB \mid RA, RB \in BOX_{m,n}, a \in RA \text{ and } b \in RB\}.$$

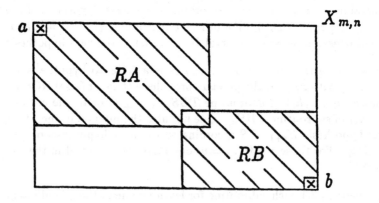

Figure 1

The learning of arbitrary target concepts $RA \cup RB$ from $TWO - BOX_{m,n}$ may be viewed as a combination of 4 search procedures that determine the lengths of the sides of RA and RB. In the same way as in the preceding section these local search procedures will receive *false negative counterexamples*, since it is not clear *which* side of RA (RB) has to be shortened in order to accomodate a NCE $g \in (RA \cup RB) - C_T$. However these local search procedures will in general also receive *false positive counterexamples*, since it is not clear whether a PCE should lie in RA, or in RB (or in both). The following result shows that nevertheless there is an efficient learning algorithm for this learning problem.

Theorem 5.1 $LC(TWO - BOX_{m,n}) = \Theta(log(m + n))$.

The *proof* of Theorem 5.1 is based on the same solution of the credit assignment problem as Theorem 4.1, together with some rather subtle structural results. We refer to [CM] for details.

6   Acknowledgement

We would like to thank David Haussler for drawing our attention to the problem of efficient on-line learning of rectangles in arbitrary dimensions.

References

[A]   D. Angluin, "Queries and concept learning", *Machine Learning*, 2, 1988, 319 - 342.

[CM]   Z. Chen, W. Maass, "On-line learning of rectangles", Proc. of the Fifth Annual ACM Workshop on Computational Learning Theory 1992

[CF]   P. R. Cohen, E. A. Feigenbaum, "The Handbook of Artificial Intelligence" vol. 3, William Kaufmann (Los Altos, 1982).

[H]   D. Haussler, *personal communication*, 1989.

[KMRSW]   D.J. Kleitman, A.R. Meyer, R.L. Rivest, J. Spencer, K. Winklman, "Coping with errors in binary search procedures", *J. Comp. Syst. Sci.*, 1980, 396 - 404.

[L]   N. Littlestone, "Learning quickly when irrelevant attributes abound: a new linear threshold algorithm", *Machine Learning*, 2, 1987, 285 - 318.

[MTa]   W. Maass, G. Turán, "On the complexity of learning from counterexamples (extended abstract)", *Proc of the 30th Annual I.E.E.E. Symposium on Foundations of Computer Science*, 1989, 262 - 267.

[MTb]   W. Maass, G. Turán, "Algorithms and Lower Bounds for On-line Learning of Geometrical Concepts", Report 316 (Oct. 1991), *IIG-Report Series, Technische Universitaet Graz*; to appear in *Machine Learning*.

[MTc]   W. Maass, G. Turán, "Lower bound methods and separation results for on-line learning models", Report 322 (Nov.1991), *IIG-Report Series, Technische Universitaet Graz*; to appear in *Machine Learning* (1992)

[P]   A. Pelc, "Searching with known error probability", *Theoretical Comp. Sci.*, 1989, 185 - 202.

[PV]   L. Pitt, L. G. Valiant, "Computational limitations on learning from examples", *J. of the ACM*, 35, 1988, 965 - 984.

[SW]   J. Spencer, P. Winkler, "Three thresholds for a liar", *DIMACS Tech. Report* 91 - 72 (Oct. 1991).

[V]   L.G. Valiant, "A theory of the learnable", *Comm. of the ACM*, 27, 1984, 1134 - 1142.

Learning Decision Strategies with Genetic Algorithms

John J. Grefenstette

Navy Center for Applied Research in Artificial Intelligence
Naval Research Laboratory
Washington, DC 20375-5000, U.S.A.
Email: GREF@AIC.NRL.NAVY.MIL

Abstract. Machine learning offers the possibility of designing intelligent systems that refine and improve their initial knowledge through their own experience. This article focuses on the problem of learning sequential decision rules for multi-agent environments. We describe the SAMUEL learning system that uses genetic algorithms and other competition based techniques to learn decision strategies for autonomous agents. One of the main themes in this research is that the learning system should be able to take advantage of existing knowledge where available. This article describes some of the mechanisms for expressing existing knowledge in SAMUEL, and explores some of the issues in selecting constraints for the learning system.

1 Introduction

Machine learning offers the possibility of designing intelligent systems through a cooperative effort between humans and machines. The human designers might provide initial guidance to the system in the form of advice obtained through traditional knowledge engineering methods. A learning system might then build upon or refine the initial knowledge through its own experience. That is, the total effort E in designing a system might be described by:

$$E = KA + ML \tag{1}$$

where KA represents the cost of manual knowledge acquisition and ML represents the computational effort by the learning system. With machine costs declining rapidly, it makes good sense to shift as much of the burden as possible onto the ML component of the design equation. This paper describes one approach in this direction. We are investigating the use of genetic algorithms and other competition-based heuristics to evolve high-performance reactive rules for multi-agent environments.

The general class of tasks under study can be characterized as *sequential decision problems*: The decision making agent interacts with a discrete-time dynamical system in an iterative fashion. At the beginning of each time step, the agent observes a representation of the current state and selects one of a finite set of actions, based on the agent's decision rules. As a result, the dynamical system enters a new state (perhaps based on the actions of other agents in the environment) and returns a (perhaps null) *payoff*. This cycle repeats indefinitely. The *reinforcement learning* task is to find a set of decision rules that maximizes the expected payoff (usually discounted as a function of time). For many interesting problems, including those considered here, payoff is delayed in the sense that non-null payoff occurs only at the end of an episode that may span several decision steps.[1] Machine learning methods designed for inducing concepts from

---

[1] Barto, Sutton and Watkins [2] give a good discussion of the broad applicability of the reinforcement

examples are generally not well-suited for sequential decision tasks, because the it is difficult to tell whether a particular decision is a positive or negative example when it occurs within a sequence of other decisions. This is well-known as the *credit assignment problem*. Further complications for learning arise when the environment is only partially modeled, contains other independent agents, and permits only limited sensing of important state variables. In such environments, a complete mathematical analysis is usually impossible, because of the complexity of the multi-agent interactions and the inherent uncertainty about the future actions of other agents. Such features also reduce the utility of traditional projective planning methods from artificial intelligence [3] and favor the use of reactive control rules that respond to current information and suggest useful actions [1], [16].

There have been attempts to learn sequential decision rules with neural networks [2], There are two problems with the neural net approach. First, current learning methods for neural nets work well on smaller problems, but do not scale up well as the problem size increase. Second, because the knowledge representation, that is, the activation levels of nodes and the weights on the connection between nodes, is opaque, it is difficult to initialize neural networks with heuristic knowledge that might serve as a starting point for the learning. The inability to user existing knowledge place a heavy burden on the learning algorithms, and probably limits the approach to relatively simple problems.

An alternative approach to such problems is to develop a policy expressed as a set of decision rules, or *strategy*, that specifies an appropriate response to any given situation. The behavior of a strategy can be monitored in a simulation and incrementally modified on the basis of the simulated experience. One well-known reinforcement-learning method, called *Q-learning* [23], involves constructing a Q-function:

$$Q(state, action) \rightarrow utility$$

that predicts the utility for each state-action pair. The Q-function is typically constructed incrementally using *Temporal Difference* (TD) methods [21]. One apparent shortcoming of Q-learning is that it requires a lookup-table for all state-action pairs. Another problem is that, like neural nets, Q-learning systems are often difficult to initialize using partially correct knowledge, because the knowledge representation is far removed from the sorts of rules that a human expert might use to express his or her knowledge. Tesauro [22] discusses several other important issues in the development of practical TD systems.

This paper describes an alternative method for reinforcement learning based on based on genetic algorithms [12]. Genetic algorithms (GAs) is a class of adaptive search algorithms based on principles derived from biological population genetics. In particular, we describe a system called SAMUEL that uses GA and other competition-based methods to improve strategies for sequential decision problems. An important feature of SAMUEL is that the strategies it learns are expressed in terms of symbolic condition-action rules, enabling the user to easily inject the system with existing knowledge about the task. Furthermore, the methods used by SAMUEL to create new decision rules make it easy to bias the learning by constraining the range of decisions that the learning agent may consider. This enables the application of SAMUEL to problems that are more complex that those that have been investigated to date using other reinforcement learning methods. This article focuses on the use of constraints in SAMUEL.

---

learning model. This model is also closely related to the *animat problem* defined by Wilson [24].

The remainder of the paper is organized as follows: Section 2 presents a general overview of genetic algorithms. Section 3 provides an overview of the SAMUEL learning system. Section 4 discusses the role of constraints in SAMUEL, and illustrates some potential advantages and disadvantages of constrained learning. Section 5 briefly surveys some other studies we have performed with SAMUEL. Section 6 summarizes some current open problems and directions for further research.

2   Genetic Algorithms

Genetic algorithms (GAs) are general purpose adaptive search techniques derived from principles of natural population genetics.[2] This section presents a high-level description of genetic algorithms. See [5],[6], or [12] for a more detailed account. A GA is an adaptive generate-and-test algorithm as follows:

```
procedure GA
begin
        t = 0;
        initialize P(t);
        evaluate structures in P(t);
        while termination condition not satisfied do
        begin
                t = t + 1;
                select P(t) from P(t - 1);
                recombine structures in P(t);
                evaluate structures in P(t);
                mutate structures in P(t);
        end
end.
```

Fig. 1. A Genetic Algorithm

At iteration t, the GA maintains a population of knowledge structures $P(t)$ that represent candidate solutions to the given problem. The population size usually remains fixed for the duration of the search. Each structure is evaluated by a module that assigns the structure a measure of its fitness as a solution to the problem at hand. When each structure in the population has been evaluated, a new population of structures is formed in two steps. First, structures in the current population are selected to be reproduced on the basis of their relative fitness. That is, high performing structures may be chosen several times for replication and poorly performing structures may not be chosen at all. Next the selected structures are recombined using idealized genetic operators to form a new set of structures for evaluation. One of the most important genetic operators is the crossover operator, which combines the features of two "parent" structures to form two similar "offspring". In its simplest form, crossover operates by swapping corresponding segments of a string or list representation of the parents. For example, if the parents are represented by the lists: (A B C D E) and (a b c d e) then crossover might produce the offspring (A B c

---

[2] We will describe Holland's formulation; Rechenberg [15] and Schwefel [19] have independently developed similar algorithms.

d e) and (a b C D E). Even this simple operator has some important properties. First, the offspring share many of the combinations of features exhibited by the parents. In the preceding example, the combination (# # C # E) appears in both the first parent and in the second offspring. (The "#" indicates that the value in this position is irrelevant.) Also, many new combinations of features, such as (a # C # #), are introduced by the crossover operator.

The theoretical properties of GAs have been extensively analyzed. Holland shows that if selection is proportional to a structure's relative performance, then the rate of increase for each combination of features present in the population is proportional to that combination's average relative performance. That is, GAs actually search the space of all feature combinations, quickly identifying and exploiting combinations which are associated with high performance. The ability to perform such a search on the basis of the evaluation of completely specified candidate solutions is called the *implicit parallelism* of GAs. Analysis shows that GAs make much more extensive use of the information provided by the evaluation of candidates than most other heuristic search routines. For example, a hill-climbing algorithm tests several structures and keeps the most promising one. In the process, hill-climbing discards a vast amount of information concerning the combinations of features present in the unsuccessful structures. In GAs, on the other hand, promising combinations of features in unsuccessful structures may still be passed along to other more successful structures.

GAs are general-purpose heuristic optimization algorithms, and have been applied successfully in a variety of domains, including image processing, schedule optimization, engine design, synthesis of neural networks, and machine learning [5],[6]. There have been two main approaches to learning rules with GAs. In one approach, called *classifier systems*, the individual population elements are single rules, or *classifiers*, and each rule is assigned a fitness based on its contribution to the overall success of the strategy. New rules are created by special genetic operators [13]. In an alternative approach developed by Smith [20], each individual in the population represents a strategy, i.e., an entire set of decision rules. Our learning system, described in more detail in the next section, is based on this latter approach.

3   SAMUEL

SAMUEL is a system that uses competition-based machine learning to develop reactive strategies. The overall system design is shown in Figure 2. The operation of SAMUEL has been described in detail in the literature [9], [10]. Space permits us only to mention some of the features that enable the user to bias the learning in SAMUEL.

SAMUEL is specifically designed for reactive agents whose perception facilities are limited to a fixed set of discrete, possibly noisy, sensors. It is assumed that there is a fixed set of control variables that may be set by the decision making agent. The system's decision rules are limited to simple condition/action rules of the form

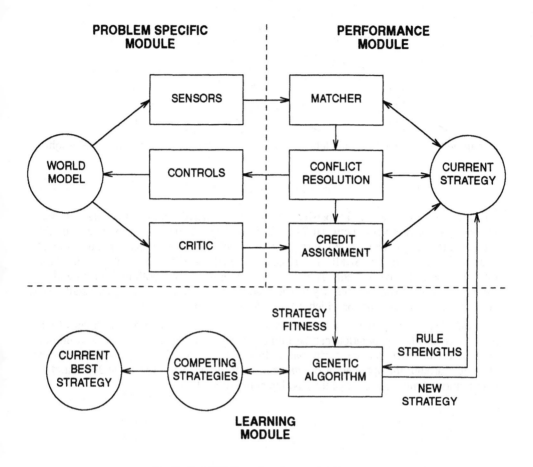

Fig. 2. SAMUEL Learning System Architecture

```
IF    c₁ AND  · · ·  AND cₙ
THEN SET a₁ AND  · · ·  AND aₘ
```

where each c_i is a condition on one of the sensors and each action a_j specifies a setting for one of the control variables. Both conditions and actions can be specified in either numeric or symbolic terms. For example, the symbolic attribute *turn* might assume values from the partial order shown in Figure 3.

Conditions for specify a list of sensor values, and actions specify a set of values for the corresponding control variable. For example, a typical SAMUEL rule might be as follows:

```
RULE 13
IF    last-turn = [left]
AND   time = [6, 19]
AND   heading = [270, 45]
THEN SET turn = [med-left] (0.9)
```

The rule specifies that *last-turn* must match any value in the subtree with root *left*, the

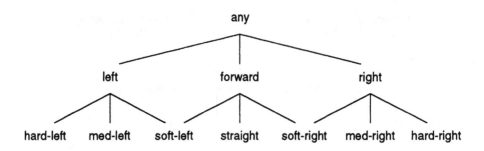

Fig. 3. A Structured Attribute

time sensor must have a value between 6 and 19, inclusive, and the *heading,* (a cyclic sensor), must have a value between 270 and 45 degrees. If these conditions are met, the rule recommends a medium-left turn with high confidence (indicated by the strength value 0.9). Each rule in SAMUEL has an associated *strength* that estimates the rule's utility for the task environment. A high strength rule must have both high mean and low variance in its estimated payoff. By biasing conflict resolution toward high strength rules, we expect to select actions for which we have high confidence of success.

Each member of the population represents a *reactive strategy*, comprising a set of such decision rules. The population can be initialized with strategies that provide a minimal level of competence on the performance tasks [18]. SAMUEL improves its reactive strategies through the application of *competition* at two levels. First, SAMUEL maintains a population of alternative strategies, as shown in Figure 4.

$$\text{Strategy 1: } < (\text{rule}_{1,1}, \text{ rule}_{1,2}, \ldots) \text{ , } \textit{fitness}_1>$$
$$\text{Strategy 2: } < (\text{rule}_{2,2}, \text{ rule}_{2,2}, \ldots) \text{ , } \textit{fitness}_2>$$
$$\vdots$$
$$\text{Strategy } N: < (\text{rule}_{N,1}, \text{ rule}_{N,2}, \ldots) \text{ , } \textit{fitness}_N>$$

Fig. 4. A Population of Strategies.

These strategies compete with one another using a genetic algorithm, as follows: Each strategy in the current population is evaluated on a number of tasks from the problem domain (typically, 20 tasks in the experiments described here). The Critic module provides the evaluation in the form of a scalar payoff at the end of each problem solving episode. As a result of these evaluations, strategies with high performance are selected and recombined using a specialized form called CROSSOVER [11], producing plausible new strategies for the next iteration. The second level of competition occurs at the rule level, where each rule competes with other rules for the right to fire. This competition is based on the rule's strength, which reflects its own payoff history. Rules that are associated with high payoff become stronger and fire more often. Low strength rules are eventually deleted to make room for variants of higher strength rules.

SAMUEL uses a slightly modified form of the standard GA. In particular, the *evaluate* and *mutate* steps in Figure 1 are implemented in four phases:

1. The new offspring strategies are randomly mutated in small ways We can consider these mutations to be those that might occur during the development of an individual.

2. These strategies are then *pre-evaluated* by executing a small number of episodes (default of 20) on the task environment. The experience gathered during this pre-evaluation stage is used in the next phase.

3. In addition to Darwinian principles of survival-of-the-fittest, SAMUEL applies several modification operators that are more Lamarckian in nature, in the sense that they modify the rules within a strategy as a direct result of the strategy's pre-evaluation experience with the task environment. The modification operators include three rule creation operators, SPECIALIZE, GENERALIZE, and MERGE, as well as a DELETE operator The resulting modifications are subsequently passed along to the strategy's offspring.

4. Once the modifications have occurred, the final (adult) strategy is evaluated again: this time to measure its fitness for the task environment.

The rule creation operators in SAMUEL are triggered by successful behavior. For example, the SPECIALIZE operator is triggered when a general rule fires in a high payoff episode. The operator creates a new rule whose left-hand side more closely matches the current sensor values and whose right-hand side more closely matches the current action value.[3] For example, if the original rule is:

```
IF    time = [0, 20] AND speed = [300, 1500]
THEN SET turn = [any]    (0.8)
```

where the *turn* attribute is described by Figure 3. If the sensor readings are:

```
(time = 2,   speed = 500)
```

and the action taken is:

```
turn = soft-left
```

then the new rule would be:

```
IF    time = [1, 11]  AND  speed = [400, 1000]
THEN SET turn = [left, forward] (0.8)
```

This new rule would now compete with the original rule and the other rules within the strategy. If the new rule turns out to be an appropriate specialization, its strength will rise and it will be protected from deletion. On the other hand, if the new rule is an inappropriate specialization, its strength will fall, and it may eventually be deleted.

Clearly, the rules that are created depend on the actual behavior of the agent during its pre-evaluation phase. Thus one way to bias the learning is to restrict the behaviors of the learning agent. The remainder of this section show how this is accomplished in SAMUEL.

---

[3] For numeric conditions, the operator creates a new condition with roughly half the generality of the previous condition by moving each endpoint half way toward the sensor reading. For structured conditions, SPECIALIZE replaces each value in the list by each of its children that covers the current sensor reading.

If SAMUEL is given a task for which its initial rules perform very poorly, the rule creation operators will not have useful experiences upon which to build new rules. More importantly, for many tasks, certain behaviors are clearly counterproductive or dangerous. For example, if SAMUEL is controlling an autonomous airplane, then it should never consider a rule that recommends diving if the altitude is below a certain threshold. One might design such constraints into the payoff function and permit SAMUEL to learn the appropriate behavior, but a more direct solution is for the user to specify a list of constraints using the SAMUEL rule language. Constraints specify conditions under which the specified actions may or may not be considered. For example, if *altitude* is a sensor for an aircraft control task, the user might place the following rule in the constraint file:

> CONSTRAINT 1
> IF altitude = [0, 10000]
> THEN DISABLE action = dive

Constraints are fixed rules and are not modified through learning.[4] They provide a mechanism for bounding the behavior of the strategies learned by SAMUEL. If the user wants to provide additional advice that can be modified by learning, the user may provide initial sets of rules as a starting point [18].

4 A Case Study

This section illustrates the use of constraints on a task involving a two-agent game of cat-and-mouse. The *tracker* agent, playing the role of the cat, must learn to keep the mouse agent, or *target*, within a certain distance, called the tracking distance, as shown in Figure 5. The target (the mouse) follows a random course and speed. The learning agent has a set of sensors, namely: *time* (since the beginning of the episode), *last-turn* (by the agent), *bearing* (direction to target's position), *heading* (relative direction of target's motion), *speed* (of the target), and *range* (to the target). Each sensor has fairly large granularity. That is, the mapping from the true world state to observed world state is many-to-one. The sensors are also noisy, and may report incorrect values. The tracker must learn to control both its speed and its direction. It is assumed that the tracker has sensors that operate at a greater distance than the target's sensors.

The object is to keep the target within range of the tracker's sensors, without being detected by the target. The usual behavior of the target agent is a random walk, occasionally changing its speed and direction. However, if the target detects the tracker, the target immediately flees the area at high speed. The target can only detect the tracker if the tracker is within the *detection range* of the target. Furthermore, when the tracker is within the detection range of the target, the probability of detection depends upon both the tracker's speed and distance from the target. The tracker does not initially have any information concerning the relationship between its behavior and its probability of detection by the target. In particular, the tracker does not know the detection range or the range of speeds that the target might assume. For further details, see [10].

---

[4] All action-values are disabled by default. For an action to be taken, it must be explicitly enabled by one of the constraints and not disabled by any other constraint.

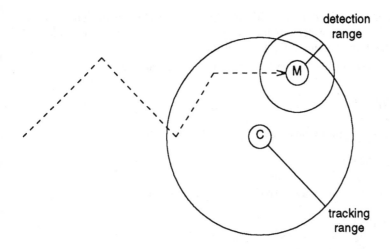

Fig. 5. Cat-and-Mouse Task

The task is broken down into individual tracking *episodes*. Each episode begins with a random placement of the two agents, and lasts for 20 time steps. At the end of each episode, the critic module provides full payoff if the tracker keeps the target within tracking distance for 75% of the episode. Otherwise, the tracker's partial payoff is equal to the portion of time that it tracks the target. While this particular task may be easy enough to yield to traditional analysis, it is representative of the kinds of uncertain environments in which a learning agent might be useful. And in fact, the environment can be made much more complex by adding additional agents on both sides, taking fuel constraints into account, and so on.

Because the behavior required for this task is so constrained, it is necessary to provide some initial knowledge, or the cat will never successfully track the moving mouse. In [9], we showed an example of learning this task from an initial set of rules. Here, we illustrate the use of constraints. We performed three separate learning experiments, varying only the constraints on the behavior of the cat.[5] In all cases, the initial control rule for the cat was a completely general rule of the form:

> IF NULL
> THEN SET turn = any AND speed = any

The null left-hand-side of this rule matches any sensor readings, and the right-hand-side recommends all settings of the control variables equally. The result is a random walk by the cat.

In Experiment 1, no constraints were provided. The episodes in which the cat happens to successfully track a moving object with a random walk are, of course, quite rare. In fact, the cat initially tracks the mouse in about 0.2% of the episodes. As the dotted line in Figure 8 shows, SAMUEL has difficulty in learning the tracking task with this weak

---

[5] Because GAs are probabilistic algorithms, we repeated each experiment for 10 independent runs. In all cases, we used a population of 50 competing strategies, and ran the experiment for 100 generations.

learning bias. The unconstrained case gives the learning system insufficient positive experiences for it to build a high-performance set of control rules. The learned rules are finally able to track the mouse about 20% of the episodes.

In Experiment 2, the constraints in Figure 6 were applied to the cat's behavior.

CONSTRAINT 1
IF range = high
THEN ENABLE turn = any AND speed = high

CONSTRAINT 2
IF range = [close, low, medium]
THEN ENABLE turn = any AND speed = [low, medium]

CONSTRAINT 3
IF range = high AND bearing = right
THEN DISABLE turn = left

CONSTRAINT 4
IF range = high AND bearing = directly-behind
THEN DISABLE turn = forward

CONSTRAINT 5
IF range = high AND bearing = left
THEN DISABLE turn = right

CONSTRAINT 6
IF range = high AND bearing = ahead
THEN DISABLE turn = [hard-right, med-right, med-left, hard-left]

Fig. 6. Constraints on Cat's Behavior

The first constraint forces the cat to consider only high speeds if the mouse is far away (there are several particular speeds that qualify as "high" in this problem). Likewise, the second constraint requires a lesser speed if the mouse is near. The final four constraints prevent the cat from turning away from the direction of the mouse if the mouse is far away. Taken together, these rules constrain the mouse to consider only plausible alternatives, but they are not sufficient to specify highly successful behavior by the mouse. The initial strategy specifies a random walk on the part of the cat, but the actual behavior is limited by the constraints, so the cat successfully tracks the mouse about 15% of the time. The rule creation operators quickly create rules that reflect the successful behaviors in the cat's early experience. After 100 generations, the cat typical performs at a 90% success rate.

Unfortunately, not every bias is equally helpful. It is possible to overconstrain the behavior of a learning system, especially if our prior understanding of the problem is limited. SAMUEL must be given sufficient freedom to explore options. If the initial constraints are too strict, the system may converge to a sub-optimal solution. As an illustration of this problem, for Experiment 3 we selected a set of constraints for the cat-and-mouse task that appear to be plausible, but which actually overconstrain the problem. See Figure 7.

CONSTRAINT 1
IF range = high
THEN ENABLE turn = any AND speed = 500

CONSTRAINT 2
IF range = [close, low, medium]
THEN ENABLE turn = any AND speed = medium

CONSTRAINT 3
IF range = high AND bearing = right
THEN DISABLE turn = [left, forward]

CONSTRAINT 4
IF range = high AND bearing = directly-behind
THEN DISABLE turn = forward

CONSTRAINT 5
IF range = high AND bearing = left
THEN DISABLE turn = [right, forward]

CONSTRAINT 6
IF range = high AND bearing = ahead
THEN DISABLE turn = [hard-right, med-right, med-left, hard-left]

Fig. 7. Stricter Constraints on Cat's Behavior

These constraints are strictly more confining than those in the previous experiment. The first constraint forces the cat to adopt a particular high speed if the mouse is far away. Likewise, the second constraint requires a medium speed if the mouse is near. As before, the final four constraints prevent the cat from turning away from the direction of the mouse if the mouse is far away, but they restrict the range of turns to a smaller subset than the previous set of constraints. Initially, the performance of the cat is approximately same as with the broader constraints, and the cat successfully tracks the mouse about 15% of the time. However, the learning system cannot learn rules that violate these constraints, and it turns out that the best SAMUEL can do within these constraints is to achieve about a 63% success rate.

the three experiments are summarized in Figure 8. The graph represents the mean over ten independent runs of each experiment. The differences between the graphs are all statistically significant and the 0.95 level from generation 10 onward. While it is unknown whether the level of performance for Experiments 1 and 3 would never reach the level of Experiment 2, they do establish that there are significant differences in the time required to achieve a given level of performance in the three cases.

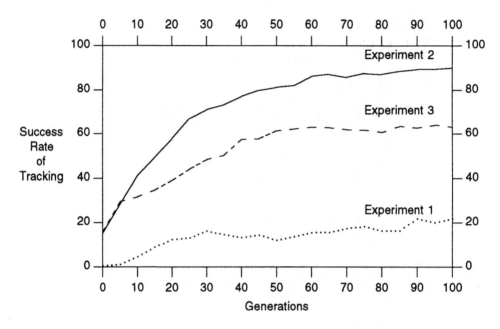

Fig. 8. Learning on Cat-and-Mouse Task

These results illustrate that the use of constraints can enable SAMUEL to learn strategies that it could not have discovered without prior knowledge. This demonstrates a useful paradigm for creating high performance strategies in autonomous systems. The user initially specifies enough knowledge to permit the system to function at a minimal level of competence. The system then refines the initial knowledge to improve its own performance on the task. We believe that this hybrid approach is likely to produce robust, autonomous systems with less total effort than either traditional manual knowledge engineering or machine learning that methods do not exploit existing knowledge.

5   Other Studies of SAMUEL

In this section, we will briefly describe a number of recent studies on this approach. The reader is referred to the published articles for more complete details.

The foundations for SAMUEL can be traced to the analysis of the credit assignment problem in [8]. The credit assignment problem arises when long sequences of rules fire between successive external rewards. It can be shown that the two distinct approaches to rule learning with genetic algorithms each offer a useful solution to a different level of the credit assignment problem. Analytic and experimental results are presented that support the hypothesis that multiple levels of credit assignment, at both the levels of the individual rules and at the level of rule sets, can improve the performance of rule learning systems based on genetic algorithms. These multiple levels are both present in SAMUEL.

One focus of our experimental work has been on the robustness of the rules learned in simulated environments. Robustness can be measured by testing the learned rules in new environments that have been systematically altered from the simulation environment in which the rules were learned. For example, either the learning environment or the target environment may contain noise. Experiments reported in [14] examine the effect of learning tactical plans without noise and then testing the plans in a noisy environment, and the effect of learning plans in a noisy simulator and then testing the plans in a noise-free environment. Empirical results show that, while best results are obtained when the training model closely matches the target environment, using a training environment that is more noisy than the target environment is better than using using a training environment that has less noise than the target environment.

In [18], the use of available heuristic domain knowledge to initialize the population to produce better plans is investigated, and two methods for initialization of the knowledge base are empirically compared. These results provide an interesting contrast with most published work on genetic algorithms, which usually assume *tabula rasa* initial conditions. The results presented here show that genetic algorithms can be used to improve partially correct decision rules, as well as to learn rules from scratch.

The use of a high-level language also facilitates the explanation of the learned rules. Gordon [7] describes a method for improving the comprehensibility, accuracy, and generality of reactive plans learned by genetic algorithms. The method involves two phases: (1) formulate explanations of execution traces, and (2) generate new reactive rules from the explanations. The explanation phase involves translating the execution trace of a reactive planner into an abstract language, and then using Explanation-Based Learning to identify general strategies within the abstract trace. The rule generation phase consists of taking a subset of the explanations and using these explanations to generate a set of new reactive rules to add to the original set for the purpose of performance improvement. The particular subset of the explanations that is chosen yields rules that provide new domain knowledge for handling knowledge gaps in the original rule set. The original rule set, in a complimentary manner, provides expertise to fill the gaps where the domain knowledge provided by the new rules is incomplete.

Cobb and Grefenstette [4] explore the effect of explicitly searching for the persistence of each decision in a time-dependent sequential decision task. Prior studies showed the effectiveness of SAMUEL in solving a simulation problem where an agent learns how to evade a predator that is in pursuit. In the previous work, an agent applies a control action at each time step. This paper examines a reformulation of the problem: the agent learns not only the level of response of a control action, but also how long to apply that control action. By examining this problem, the work shows that it is appropriate to choose a representation of the state space that compresses time information when solving a time-dependent sequential decision problem. By compressing time information, critical events in the decision sequence become apparent.

We have begun to apply the SAMUEL approach to more complex learning environments. In [17], SAMUEL is used to learn high-performance reactive strategies for navigation and collision avoidance. The task requires an autonomous underwater vehicle to navigate through a randomly generated, dense mine field and then rendezvous with a stationary object. The vehicle has a limited set of sensors, including sonar, and can set its speed and direction. The strategy that is learned is expressed as a set of reactive rules that map sensor readings to actions to be performed at each decision time-step. Simulation results demonstrate that an initial, human-designed strategy which has an average success rate of only eight percent on randomly generated mine fields can be improved by this system so that the final strategy can achieve a success rate of 96 percent. This study provides encouraging evidence that this approach to machine learning may scale up to realistic problems.

6 Open Issues

SAMUEL is designed to allow the user to bias its learning with knowledge expressed either as initial strategies or as behavioral constraints. While the ability to improve upon the knowledge that it is provided initially makes SAMUEL an interesting system to study, it is clear that we need more information about the relationship between the initial knowledge and the ultimate level of performance that SAMUEL may attain in its learned strategies. The experiments reported here suggest that, if the initial bias is either too weak or too strong, the performance level of the learning system levels out at some point below the optimal performance. But when does existing knowledge produce too strong a bias? We would like to develop some useful guidelines for selecting the initial bias for the system. One rather conservative principle might be:

> *Include as constraints only knowledge that is absolutely necessary to the minimally acceptable performance of the task.*

This rule should at least avoid undesirable bias based on the user's preconceptions about how to solve the task. In some practical cases, it may be difficult to operationalize this principle.

A theory that relates the initial bias to ultimate performance of a learning system would provide the basis for achieving the cost trade-off suggested by equation (1). That is, we should be able to find the optimal balance between knowledge engineering performed by humans and learning performed by machines.

Acknowledgments

I want to acknowledge the contributions toward the development of SAMUEL by the members of the Machine Learning Group at NRL, especially Alan Schultz, Connie Ramsey, Diana Gordon, Helen Cobb, and Ken De Jong. I also want to thank Bob Daley for his help on the project during his stay at NRL as a Visiting Scientist. This work is supported in part by ONR under Work Request N00014-91-WX24011.

References

1. P. E. Agre and D. Chapman (1987). Pengi: An implementation of a theory of activity. *Proceedings Sixth National Conference on Artificial Intelligence.* (pp. 268-272).

2. A. B. Barto, R. S. Sutton and C. Watkins (1990). Learning and sequential decision making. In *Learning and computational neuroscience,* M. Gabrial and J. W. Moore, eds., Cambridge: MIT Press.

3. J. G. Carbonell, C. A. Knoblock and S. Minton (1990). Prodigy: An integrated architecture for planning and learning. In Van Lehn (ed.), *Architectures for Intelligence.* Hillsdale, NJ: Erlbaum.

4. H. G. Cobb and J. J. Grefenstette (1991). Learning the persistence of actions in reactive control rules. *Proceedings of the Eighth International Machine Learning Workshop* (pp. 293-297). Evanston, IL: Morgan Kaufmann.

5. L. Davis, Ed. (1991). *Handbook of Genetic Algorithms.* New York: Van Nostrand Reinhold.

6. K. A. De Jong (1990). Genetic-algorithm-based learning. In Y. Kodratoff and R. Michalski (eds.), *Machine learning: An artificial intelligence approach* (Vol. 3). Los Altos, CA: Morgan Kaufmann.

7. D. F. Gordon (1991). An enhancer for reactive plans. *Proceedings of the Eighth International Machine Learning Workshop* (pp 505-508). Evanston, IL: Morgan Kaufmann.

8. J. J. Grefenstette (1988). Credit assignment in rule discovery system based on genetic algorithm. *Machine Learning, 3,* (pp 225-245).

9. J. J. Grefenstette (1991). Lamarckian learning in multi-agent environments. *Proceedings of the Fourth International Conference of Genetic Algorithms* (pp. 303-310). San Diego, CA: Morgan Kaufmann.

10. J. J. Grefenstette (1992). The evolution of strategies for multi-agent environments. *Adaptive Behavior, 1(1).*

11. J. J. Grefenstette, C. L. Ramsey, and A. C. Schultz (1990). Learning sequential decision rules using simulation models and competition. *Machine Learning, 5,* (pp. 355-381).

12. J. H. Holland (1975). *Adaptation in natural and artificial systems.* Ann Arbor: University Michigan Press.

13. J. H. Holland (1986). Escaping brittleness: The possibilities of general-purpose learning algorithms applied to parallel rule-based systems. In R.S. Michalski, J. G. Carbonell, & T. M. Mitchell (Eds.), *Machine learning: An artificial intelligence approach* (Vol. 2). Los Altos, CA: Morgan Kaufmann.

14. C. L. Ramsey, A. C.. Schultz and J. J. Grefenstette (1990). Simulation-assisted learning by competition: Effects of noise differences between training model and target environment. *Proceedings of the Seventh International Conference on Machine Learning.* Austin, TX: Morgan Kaufmann (pp. 211-215).

15. I. Rechenberg (1973). *Evolutionsstrategie - Optimierung technischer Systeme nach Prinzipien der biologischen Information.* Fromman Verlag: Freiburg.

16. M. J. Schoppers (1987). Universal plans for reactive robots in unpredictable environments. *Proceedings of the 10th International Joint Conference on Artificial Intelligence.* (pp. 1039-1046).

17. A. C. Schultz (1991). Using a genetic algorithm to learn strategies for collision avoidance and local navigation. *Proceedings of the Seventh International Symposium on Unmanned, Untethered Submersible Technology* (pp. 213-225). Durham, NH.

18. A. C. Schultz and J. J. Grefenstette (1990). Improving tactical plans with genetic algorithms. *Proceeding of IEEE Conference on Tools for AI 90,* Washington, DC: IEEE (pp. 328-334).

19. H.-P. Schwefel (1981). *Numerical Optimization of Computer Models.* Wiley: Chichester.

20. S. F. Smith (1980). *A learning system based on genetic adaptive algorithms,* Doctoral dissertation, Department of Computer Science, University of Pittsburgh.

21. R. S. Sutton (1988). Learning to predict by the method of temporal differences. *Machine Learning, 3,* (pp. 9-44).

22. T. Tesauro (1992). Practical issues in temporal difference learning. *Machine Learning, 8,* (pp. 257-277).

23. C. J. C. H. Watkins (1989). *Learning with delayed rewards.* Ph. D. dissertation, Psychology Department, Cambridge University.

24. S. W. Wilson (1987). Classifier systems and the animat problem. *Machine Learning, 2,* (pp. 199-228).

Background knowledge and declarative bias in inductive concept learning

Nada Lavrač and Sašo Džeroski

Jožef Stefan Institute
Jamova 39, 61000 Ljubljana, Slovenia
Phone: (+38)(61) 159 199, Fax: (+38)(61) 161 029
email: {nada.lavrac,saso.dzeroski}@ijs.ac.mail.yu

Abstract. There are two main limitations of classical inductive learning algorithms: the limited capability of taking into account the available background knowledge and the use of limited knowledge representation formalisms based on propositional logic. The paper presents a method for using background knowledge effectively in learning both attribute and relational descriptions. The method, implemented in the system LINUS, uses propositional learners in a more expressive logic programming framework. This allows for learning of logic programs in the form of constrained deductive hierarchical database clauses. The paper discusses the language bias imposed by the method and shows how a more expressive language of determinate logic programs can be used within the same framework.

1 Introduction

Given a set of training examples $\mathcal{E}$ and background knowledge $\mathcal{B}$, the task of inductive learning is to find a hypothesis $\mathcal{H}$, which explains the examples by using the background knowledge. In *inductive concept learning*, hypotheses are concept definitions, usually expressed in some logic-based language, examples are descriptions of instances and non-instances of the concept to be learned, while background knowledge provides additional information about the examples and the domain under study.

For the representation of training examples, background knowledge and induced hypotheses, most inductive learning algorithms use an attribute-value language which has the same expressive power as the language of propositional logic. This language is limited and does not allow for representing complex structured objects and relations among objects or components of objects. Therefore, background knowledge that can be used in the learning process is of a very restricted form (for example, see [35]). As a consequence, many learning tasks can not be solved by propositional learning algorithms such as the members of the AQ (e.g., [27]) and ID3 [37] families of inductive learning programs.

There are several ways to overcome the problem of a limited description language:

- Methods for *constructive induction* and *predicate invention* enable a learning system to generate new terms (which are not used in the descriptions of examples) to be used in the induced hypotheses (e.g., [16, 31, 33]), thus extending the initial vocabulary.

- New terms can be proposed by the expert based on his/her domain knowledge. This *background knowledge* can be given as functions of attribute values used to describe the training examples, or as relations among attribute values reflecting relations among objects in the problem domain [26].

- A language more expressive than a propositional language can be selected for describing concepts and richer background knowledge used in the learning process. In *inductive logic programming* (ILP, [32]), the selected first-order concept description language is the language of *logic programs*.

The paper presents a method which implements the later two approaches, i.e., which can effectively use background knowledge in the learning process, performed in a logic programming framework. The presented approach allows for building an integrated environment for learning both attribute and relational descriptions using propositional inductive learning algorithms. The method is implemented in the system LINUS which was successfully applied to the problem of learning diagnostic rules in rheumatology [21], to the problem of learning relational descriptions in several domains known from the machine learning literature [20] and to finite element mesh design in CAD [11]. Using attribute-value algorithms, LINUS allows for recent advances in handling imperfect data, developed in propositional algorithms, to be applied easily to real-life, imperfect data. Experiments in a chess endgame domain with a controlled amount of noise [12, 19] showed that LINUS performs well on imperfect, noisy data.

The common logical framework into which LINUS integrates various attribute-value learners is, in fact, the ILP framework. More specifically, in the current implementation, LINUS uses the deductive hierarchical database (DHDB) formalism [23]. LINUS is a descendant of the learning module of QuMAS (Qualitative Model Acquisition System [29]) which was used to learn functions of components of a qualitative model of the heart in the system KARDIO [3].

The paper discusses the potential of the LINUS approach in the following dimensions. First, in Section 2, it gives the intuition of how background knowledge can be used in the propositional and in the ILP learning framework. Section 3 discusses the declarative language bias in LINUS, which is initially set to deductive hierarchical database clauses, and shows how the approach can be extended to solve more complex ILP problems by setting the language bias to determinate logic programs. The extended LINUS algorithm is given in Section 4. Finally, in Section 5 we briefly compare the extended LINUS approach to other ILP approaches and conclude.

2 Using Background Knowledge in Learning

The section shows how background knowledge can be effectively applied to induce more compact hypotheses in a propositional learning setting (Section 2.1), and illustrates how this same approach can be used within the ILP framework (Section 2.2); given is also the complexity of this ILP learning task.

2.1 Attribute-Value Learning

In a propositional learning task, examples are tuples of attribute values labeled with a concept name (e.g., $\oplus$ for positive instances of the concept and $\ominus$ for negative), and the induced hypotheses typically have the form of if-then rules or decision trees.

An Example Learning Problem. Suppose that the learning task is to find a description of friendly and unfriendly robots [44] from given examples. In the original problem, there are 432 examples, described by 6 attributes. In our simplified problem, given in Table 1, robots are described by five attributes: *Is_smiling* $\in$ { *no*, *yes*}, *Holding* ∈ {*sword, balloon, flag*}, *Has_tie* ∈ {*no, yes*}, *Head_shape* ∈ {*round, square, octagon*}, and, *Body_shape* ∈ {*round, square, octagon*}.

Class	Attributes and values				
	Is_smiling	Holding	Has_tie	Head_shape	Body_shape
friendly	yes	balloon	yes	square	square
friendly	yes	flag	yes	octagon	octagon
unfriendly	yes	sword	yes	round	octagon
unfriendly	yes	sword	no	square	octagon
unfriendly	no	sword	no	octagon	round
unfriendly	no	flag	no	round	octagon

Table 1: Examples of friendly and unfriendly robots.

NEWGEM [28], an algorithm from the AQ family, induces the following if-then rules from the above examples:

$$Class = friendly \quad \textbf{if} \quad [Is\_smiling = yes] \wedge$$
$$[Holding = balloon \vee flag]$$
$$Class = unfriendly \quad \textbf{if} \quad [Is\_smiling = no]$$
$$Class = unfriendly \quad \textbf{if} \quad [Is\_smiling = yes] \wedge$$
$$[Holding = sword]$$

Using ASSISTANT [6], an ID3-like learning algorithm which has a number of mechanisms for dealing with noisy data, the decision tree on Figure 1 is induced. When transcribed into if-then rules, the tree produces exactly the same rules as above.

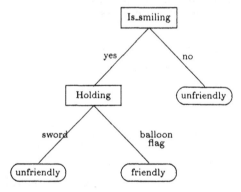

Figure 1: Decision tree for the robot world.

Using Background Knowledge. The induced hypotheses could include new terms, given as background knowledge about the world of robots. Background knowledge can be expressed as *functions* of values of attributes or as *relations* among attribute values. In learning attribute descriptions, these functions/relations can be represented by a new attribute which then needs to be considered in the learning process. If background knowledge is represented with functions, the value of the new attribute is computed as a function of values of existing attributes, in turn for each training example. On the other hand, if background knowledge has the form of relations, the only values the new attribute can have are *true* and *false* (if values of the corresponding attributes of the example do/do not satisfy the relation).

For example, background knowledge can check for the equality of attribute values for pairs of attributes of the same type (i.e., attributes with the same set of values). In the world of robots this would lead to two new attributes that test the equalities $Is\_smiling = Has\_tie$ and $Head\_shape = Body\_shape$. For simplicity, let us consider only the new attribute $Head\_shape = Body\_shape$ and name it $Same\_shape \in \{true, false\}$. Using this idea, initially introduced by [29], an extended set of tuples is generated (Table 2) and used in learning.

Class	Attributes and values					
	Is_smiling	*Holding*	*Has_tie*	*Head_shape*	*Body_shape*	*Same_shape*
friendly	*yes*	*balloon*	*yes*	*square*	*square*	*true*
friendly	*yes*	*flag*	*yes*	*octagon*	*octagon*	*true*
unfriendly	*yes*	*sword*	*yes*	*round*	*octagon*	*false*
unfriendly	*yes*	*sword*	*no*	*square*	*octagon*	*false*
unfriendly	*no*	*sword*	*no*	*octagon*	*round*	*false*
unfriendly	*no*	*flag*	*no*	*round*	*octagon*	*false*

Table 2: Examples of friendly and unfriendly robots. Last column gives the values of the new attribute $Same\_shape$ (i.e., $Head\_shape = Body\_shape$).

Since its two values *true* and *false* distinguish correctly between friendly and unfriendly robots, the new attribute $Same\_shape$ is the only attribute in the induced decision tree. The tree is shown in Figure 2. The example shows that new attributes, expressing functions/relations among the original attributes that describe the examples, can be more informative than the original attributes. Thus, using background knowledge, a learner can build more compact hypotheses, which can potentially have a better classification accuracy on unseen cases.

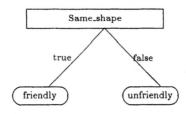

Figure 2: Decision tree built by using background knowledge.

2.2 Inductive Logic Programming

Background knowledge plays a central role in inductive logic programming (ILP), where the task is to define, from given examples, an unknown relation in terms of known relations from the background knowledge.

Definition of ILP. One of the early systems that addressed the problem of learning relational descriptions was INDUCE [25]. Recent inductive learning systems learn descriptions of relations in the form of logic programs and are named *inductive logic programming* (ILP) systems [32]. Shapiro's MIS [41] is their ancestor.

In ILP, one can distinguish between interactive and empirical ILP systems, which can either learn single or multiple predicate definitions. *Empirical* systems require all the training examples as the input to the system while *interactive* systems generate examples in the learning process. Noninteractive *empirical ILP* systems, such as GOLEM [34], FOIL [38] and LINUS [20], induce a single hypothesis from a large collection of examples. MOBAL [45, 17] is basically an empirical system which learns multiple predicate definitions; however, training examples are generated whenever a new predicate definition is induced. CLINT [9] is an interactive multiple predicate learning system.

The task of empirical, single predicate learning in ILP can be formulated as follows:

Given:
- a set of training examples $\mathcal{E}$, consisting of true $\mathcal{E}^+$ and false $\mathcal{E}^-$ facts of an unknown predicate p,
- a description language $\mathcal{L}$, specifying syntactic restrictions on the definition of predicate p,
- background knowledge $\mathcal{B}$, described in language $\mathcal{L}_B$, defining predicates q_i (other than p) which may be used in the definition of p and which provide additional information about the arguments of the examples of predicate p

Find:
- a definition $\mathcal{H}$ for p, expressed in $\mathcal{L}$, such that H is complete, i.e., $\mathcal{B} \wedge \mathcal{H} \models \mathcal{E}^+$, and consistent with respect to the examples, i.e., $\mathcal{B} \wedge \mathcal{H} \not\models \mathcal{E}^-$.

In the following, we refer to the true facts $\mathcal{E}^+$ as *positive examples*, the false facts $\mathcal{E}^-$ as *negative examples* and the definition of p as definition of the *target* relation. When learning from noisy examples, the completeness and consistency criteria need to be relaxed in order to avoid overly specific hypotheses.

The language of concept descriptions $\mathcal{L}$ is usually called the *hypothesis language*. It is typically some subset of the language of definite clauses (Horn clauses) or the language of program clauses (Horn clauses with negated literals, also named *normal clauses*) of the form:

$$p(X_1, \ldots, X_n) \leftarrow L_1, \ldots, L_m.$$

where the body of a clause is a conjunction of positive literals $q_i(Y_1, \ldots, Y_{n_i})$ and/or negative literals *not* $q_j(Y_1, \ldots, Y_{n_j})$.

The complexity of learning grows with the expressiveness of the hypothesis language $\mathcal{L}$. Therefore, to reduce the complexity, various restrictions can be applied to clauses expressed in $\mathcal{L}$. For example, some of the current empirical ILP systems constrain $\mathcal{L}$ to function-free program clauses, as is the case in FOIL, and/or determinate clauses as in GOLEM in FOIL2.0 [39], a later version of FOIL. MOBAL uses rule models which define the form of the induced predicates.

Transforming ILP Problems to Propositional Form. The method of using background knowledge, outlined in Section 2.1, is based on the idea that the use of background knowledge can introduce new attributes in the learning process. This same method can be used within the ILP framework. To do so, the learning problem is transformed from the relational to the attribute-value form and solved by an attribute-value learner. The induced hypothesis is then transformed back into the relational form. This is, of course, feasible only for a restricted class of ILP problems.

This approach allows for a variety of approaches developed for propositional problems, including noise-handling techniques in attribute-value algorithms ASSISTANT or CN2 [7], to be used for learning relations.

Various restrictions on the complexity of the hypothesis language $\mathcal{L}$ and various kinds of information about the background knowledge predicates can be used to further constrain the hypothesis space, which is initially determined by the predicates from background knowledge B. To illustrate our method, let us currently assume the following restrictions on the hypothesis language $\mathcal{L}$:

- A hypothesis is a set of *Datalog clauses* [42], i.e., program clauses with no function symbols in the arguments.

- Clauses are *typed*, i.e., each variable appearing in arguments of literals is associated with a finite set of constant values.

- Clauses are *constrained*, i.e., all variables in the body also appear in the head (there are no new, existentially quantified variables in literals in the body).

- Clauses are *nonrecursive*, i.e., the predicate symbol in the head does not appear in any of the literals in the body.

Let us further assume that background knowledge B is represented by typed Datalog clauses (with no further restrictions) and training examples have the form of ground facts.

In such a setting, we illustrate the ILP task on a simple problem of learning family relationships. The task is to define the target relation $daughter(X, Y)$, which states that person X is a daughter of person Y, in terms of the background knowledge relations $female$ and $parent$. These relations are given in Table 3, where all variables are of type $person$. The type $person$ is defined as $person = \{ann, eve, pat, sue, tom\}$. There are two positive and two negative examples of the target relation.

Training examples		Background knowledge	
daughter(sue, eve).	⊕	parent(eve, sue).	female(ann).
daughter(ann, pat).	⊕	parent(ann, tom).	female(sue).
daughter(tom, ann).	⊖	parent(pat, ann).	female(eve).
daughter(eve, ann).	⊖	parent(tom, sue).	

Table 3: A simple ILP problem: learning the *daughter* relationship.

The transformation of the ILP problem into attribute-value form is performed as follows. The possible applications of the background predicates on the arguments of the target relation are determined, taking into account argument types. Each such application introduces a new attribute. In our example, all variables are of the same type $person$. The corresponding attribute-value learning problem is given in Table 4. The attribute-value tuples are generalizations (relative to the given background knowledge) of the individual facts about the target relation.

Class	Variables		Propositional features			
	X	Y	female(X)	female(Y)	parent(X,Y)	parent(Y,X)
⊕	sue	eve	true	true	false	true
⊕	ann	pat	true	false	false	true
⊖	tom	ann	false	true	false	true
⊖	eve	ann	true	true	false	false

Table 4: Propositional form of the *daughter* relationship problem.

Next, an attribute-value learning program induces, from the tuples in Table 4, the following *if-then* rule:

$$Class = \oplus \quad \textbf{if} \quad [female(X) = true] \quad \bigwedge \quad [parent(Y, X) = true]$$

In Table 4, *variables* stand for the arguments of the target relation, and *propositional features* denote the new attributes. When learning relations, usually only new attributes are considered for learning; however, a learner may use initial attributes (i.e., arguments of the target relation) as well (see Section 3.2 for a more detailed explanation).

Finally, the induced if-then rules are transformed into Datalog clauses. In our example, we get the following clause:

$$daughter(X, Y) \leftarrow female(X), parent(Y, X).$$

Note that the same result can be obtained on a similar learning problem, where the target relation $daughter(X, Y)$ is to be defined in terms of relations *female* and *parent*, given the background knowledge from Table 5. It consists of both facts and rules and not just ground facts as in Table 3.

Background knowledge		
$mother(eve, sue).$	$parent(X, Y) \leftarrow$	$female(ann).$
$mother(ann, tom).$	$mother(X, Y).$	$female(sue).$
$father(pat, ann).$	$parent(X, Y) \leftarrow$	$female(eve).$
$father(tom, sue).$	$father(X, Y).$	

Table 5: Alternative background knowledge for learning the *daughter* relationship.

Complexity of Learning Constrained Logic Programs. To show the complexity of the ILP learning task, obtained by using background knowledge in the learning process, let us consider the number of attributes to be used for learning [20], and then outline some learnability results.

The total number of attributes k_{Attr} equals:

$$k_{Attr} = k_{Arg} + \sum_{i=1}^{l} k_{New, q_i}$$

where $k_{Arg} = n$, i.e., the number of arguments of the target relation p (i.e., *variables* in Table 4), and k_{New, q_i} is the number of new attributes, resulting from the possible (with regard to given types) applications of one of the l background predicates q_i on the arguments of the target relation (i.e., *propositional features* in Table 4).

Suppose that u is the number of distinct types of arguments of target predicate p, u_i is the number of distinct types of arguments of background precidate q_i, $n_{i,s}$ is the number of arguments of q_i that are of type T_s and k_{ArgT_s} is the number of arguments of target predicate p that are of type T_s. Then k_{New, q_i} is computed by the following formula:

$$k_{New, q_i} = \prod_{s=1}^{u_i} (k_{ArgT_s})^{n_{i,s}}$$

We can namely fill $n_{i,s}$ places for arguments of type T_s in $(k_{ArgT_s})^{n_{i,s}}$ ways, independently from choosing the arguments of q_i which are of different types.

Since a relation where two arguments are identical can be represented by a relation of a smaller arity, we can restrict the arguments of a background predicate to be different. In this case the following formula holds:

$$k_{New, q_i} = \prod_{s=1}^{u_i} \binom{k_{ArgT_s}}{n_{i,s}} \cdot n_{i,s}! \tag{1}$$

To illustrate the above formulae on our simple example from Tables 3 and 4, observe that $q_1 = parent$ and $q_2 = female$. As all arguments are of the same type T_1, we have $u_1 = u_2 = 1$ for both q_1 and q_2, and $k_{ArgT_1} = 2$. Since we are dealing with only one type $person$ (thus $s = 1$), we can write n_i instead of $n_{i,s}$ and get rid of the product in Equation (1). In this notation, $n_1 = 2$ and $n_2 = 1$. Thus, according to Equation (1), $k_{New,q_1} = \binom{k_{ArgT_1}}{n_1} \cdot n_1! = \binom{2}{2} \cdot 2! = 2$ $(parent(X,Y), parent(Y,X))$. Similarly, $k_{New,q_2} = \binom{k_{ArgT_2}}{n_2} \cdot n_2! = \binom{2}{1} \cdot 1! = 2$ $(female(X), female(Y))$. Finally, $k_{Attr} = k_{Arg} + k_{New,q_1} + k_{New,q_2} = 2 + 2 + 2 = 6$.

Background predicates can be declared *symmetric* in certain pairs of arguments. In case that q_i is symmetric in all pairs of arguments, each factor in the product of Equation (1) is replaced by the corresponding number of combinations:

$$k_{New,q_i} = \prod_{s=1}^{u_i} \binom{k_{ArgT_s}}{n_{i,s}}$$

For example, the number of possible applications of the symmetric background predicate *equality* $(= /2)$ equals to:

$$k_{New,=} = \sum_{s=1}^{u} \binom{k_{ArgT_s}}{2} = \sum_{s=1}^{u} \frac{k_{ArgT_s} \cdot (k_{ArgT_s} - 1)}{2}$$

where k_{ArgT_s} denotes the number of arguments of the same type T_s, and u is the number of distinct types of arguments of the target relation; from the arguments of type T_s, $\binom{k_{ArgT_s}}{2}$ different attributes of the form $X = Y$ can be constructed.

Assuming a constant upper bound j on the arity of background knowledge predicates, the largest number of attributes that can be obtained in case all variables are of the same type is of the order $\mathcal{O}(ln^j)$, where l is the number of predicates in the background knowledge and n is the arity of the target predicate. This allows us to use PAC-learnability results for the propositional case in an ILP framework [15].

3 Declarative Language Bias

Any mechanism employed by a learning system to constrain the search for concept descriptions is named *bias* [43]. *Declarative bias* denotes explicit, user-specified bias which can preferably be formulated as a modifiable parameter of the system. Bias can either determine how the hypothesis space is searched (*search bias*) or determine the hypothesis space itself (*language bias*). This paper is only concerned with the language bias. By selecting a stronger language bias (a less expressive hypothesis language) the search space becomes smaller and learning more efficient; however, this may prevent the system from finding a solution if it is not expressible in the language. This expressiveness/tractability tradeoff underlies much of the current research in inductive learning.

As outlined in [5], various forms of language bias have been employed by existing ILP learners, including types and symmetry of predicates in pairs of arguments [20], input/output modes and ij-determinacy [34], program schemata [45], predicate sets [2], parametrized languages [8], integrity constraints [10] and determinations [40].

In this section we first give a hierarchy of hypothesis languages (language biases) which can be used in inductive learning. We then describe the syntactic language bias which is currently used in LINUS [20], a system which implements the learning method outlined in Section 2.2. Next, we present a weaker bias that can be used within the same approach, extending it to solve more complex ILP problems which require a more expressive hypothesis language.

3.1 Expressiveness Hierarchy of Hypothesis Languages

In inductive learning, one can distinguish between systems which learn attribute descriptions, and systems which learn first-order relational descriptions. In *attribute descriptions*, objects are described with their global features in terms of a fixed collection of *attributes*. There can only be a finite number of objects in the universe of discourse. In *first-order relational descriptions*, objects and relations among objects can be described in terms of their components. Objects and their relationships are described by quantified first-order logical expressions.

Different hypothesis languages can be ordered into a hierarchy according to their *expressiveness*. We use the term expressiveness to capture two different dimensions in the same word. The first dimension is the expressive power of a formalism; in its standard meaning, *stronger expressive power* means that there are concepts that can be represented in the stronger formalism which can not be represented in the weaker formalism. The other dimension is the *compactness* of the concept representation. For example, it is possible to state that two Boolean attributes have the same value in both an attribute-value language and a first-order language. But, whereas in the former we have to say $(A = 0 \land B = 0) \lor (A = 1 \land B = 1)$, we can simply say $A = B$ in the latter.

Below is a list and a brief overview of some of the potential hypothesis languages [30], ordered according to increasing expressiveness.

1. In a *propositional language*, propositions are 0-ary predicates. There are no variables and function symbols, and thus no terms.

2. In an *attribute-value language*, attributes can be considered as unary predicates and their values as their arguments. Predicates are typed. No variables and no function symbols, except for constants, are used.

3. In the *relational database form*, clauses are restricted to ground atoms. Relations can be represented by n-ary predicates. Variables, function symbols of arity greater than zero, and rules are not allowed.

4. In the *deductive hierarchical database (DHDB) form*, variables, function symbols and rules are used. The DHDB form is substantially more expressive than the relational database form since it does not only contain ground facts but also nonground facts and rules from which new facts can be deduced. In the DHDB form only nonrecursive predicate definitions are allowed. The language is typed; only nonrecursive types are allowed.

5. The *deductive database (DDB) form* allows for recursive predicate definitions and recursive types as well. On the one hand, compared to Horn clauses, database clauses are more expressive since they allow for negated literals (negations of atoms under the negation as failure rule) to be used in the body of a clause. On the other hand, using a typed language, the DDB form is less expressive than the Horn clause form and the logic program form used in Prolog programming.

6. In the *logic program form*,[1] the language is not typed. Variables in program clauses are implicitly universally quantified. Negated literals in the body of a clause are allowed.

7. In the *clausal form*, clauses have the form of a disjunction of positive/negative literals. In contrast to *normal program clauses*, the head of a general clause is a (possibly empty) conjunction of literals. All variables are still implicitly universally quantified.

---

[1] Under the *logic program form* we understand *normal programs* as defined by Lloyd [23].

8. The *full first-order form*[2] allows for existential quantification of variables.

As mentioned before, one distinction between languages is according to the use of *attribute* or *relational* descriptions. Form (1) uses attribute descriptions, while (3)-(8) use relational descriptions. Another distinction can be made according to the use of variables. In (1)-(3) no variables are used in the descriptions, while (4)-(8) *are first-order formalisms* which allow for the use of variables. The grouping of the formalisms according to these two aspects nearly overlaps; the exception is (3) which uses relational descriptions, but without variables. More details on individual first-order languages can be found in Lloyd [23].

Among the languages we would also need to mention the Horn clause form and the Datalog form; they are not included since they do not fit into the proposed linear ordering of languages. Horn clauses (called *definite clauses* in logic programming) do not allow for negative literals in the body; more general (normal) program clauses allow also for negative literals in the body. Datalog clauses mainly differ from program clauses by not allowing for function symbols of non-zero arity in the arguments.

In the above hierarchy, several languages are *typed*. Although standard logic makes no distinction in the interpretation of non-logical symbols (except for dividing them into three sorts: constants, function symbols, and predicate symbols), constants may be further divided into different *sorts* or *types*. Typing provides a simple syntactic way of specifying semantic information and can substantially decrease the search space of hypotheses. Having in mind the above hierarchy of logical languages, our goal is to find the most expressive language (the weakest language bias) which still allows for using the learning method outlined in Section 2.2.

3.2 Language Bias in LINUS

The learning method which transforms an ILP problem to a propositional learning problem (Section 2.2) is implemented in the system LINUS [20]. Before giving the restrictions imposed by the hypothesis language $\mathcal{L}$ of deductive hierarchical database clauses in LINUS, it is important to consider the form of training examples $\mathcal{E}$ and, in particular, predicates in $\mathcal{B}$ which actually determine the search space of hypotheses. Training examples have the form of ground facts (which may contain structured, but nonrecursive terms) and background knowledge has the form of deductive database clauses (possibly recursive). Variables are typed. Structured terms are flattened before the learning process.

Background Knowledge. In LINUS, predicate definitions in background knowledge $\mathcal{B}$ are of two types:

- *Utility functions* are annotated predicates; mode declarations specify the *input* and *output* arguments, similar to mode declarations in GOLEM and FOIL2.0. When applied to ground input arguments from the training examples, the utility functions compute the unique ground values of their output arguments. When used in an induced clause, output variables must be bound to constants. This corresponds to introducing new variables, which have a uniquely determined value, say X, immediately followed by the use of literals of the form $X = a$, where a is a constant of the appropriate type.

- *Utility predicates* have only *input* arguments and can be regarded as boolean utility functions having values *true* or *false* only.

---

[2]Our scope is limited to first-order languages in which variables and quantified expressions refer to objects of a universe of discourse, not to functions or relations. We do not consider second-order languages, which have function and relation variables as well.

A reduction of the hypothesis space is achieved by taking into account the pre-specified types of predicate arguments and by exploiting the fact that some utility predicates are symmetric in certain pairs of arguments:

- *Symmetric predicates.* Utility predicates can be declared *symmetric* in certain pairs of arguments of the same type. For example, a binary predicate $q(X, Y)$ is symmetric in X and Y if X and Y are of the same type, and $q(X, Y) = q(Y, X)$ for every value of X and Y. A built-in symmetric utility predicate *equality* ($=/2$) is defined by default on arguments of the same type.

Hypothesis Language. In the current implementation of LINUS, the selected hypothesis language $\mathcal{L}$ is restricted to constrained deductive hierarchical database (DHDB) clauses. In DHDB, variables are typed and recursive predicate definitions are not allowed. In addition, all variables that appear in the body of a clause have to appear in the head as well, i.e., only constrained clauses are induced.

To be specific, the body of an induced clause in LINUS is a conjunction of literals, each having one of the following four forms:

1. a binding of a variable to a value, e.g., $X = a$,

2. an equality of pairs of variables, e.g., $X = Y$,

3. an atom with a predicate symbol (utility predicate) and input arguments which are variables occurring in the head of the clause, e.g., $q_i(X, Y)$, and

4. an atom with a predicate symbol (utility function) having as input arguments variables which occur in the head of the clause, and output arguments with an instantiated (computed) variable value, e.g., $q_j(X, Y, a)$.

In the above, X and Y are variables from the head of the clause, and a is a constant of the appropriate type. Literals of the second and third form can be either positive or negative.

To guide induction, LINUS uses meta-level knowledge which can exclude any of the above four cases, thus reducing the search space. For example, if only case (1) is retained, the hypothesis language is restricted to an attribute-value language. This can be achieved by only using the arguments of the target relation as attributes for learning. Cases (2)-(4), on the other hand, result from the use of preficates/functions from $\mathcal{B}$ as attributes for learning (see also Section 2.2). The equality predicate ($= /2$), which generates literals of the form (2), is built-in in LINUS.

Complexity of the LINUS learning task. Note that the complexity of learning with LINUS is in fact already analysed in Section 2. The analysis shows the number of new attributes, leading to literals of the form (1)-(3) above. Similar complexity analysis can be made for the use of utility functions which results in literals of the form (4). A detailed analysis of the actual hypothesis space, i.e., space of all possible literals, can be found in [13].

Language Biases for Three Typical Learning Tasks. As mentioned above, meta-level knowledge can be used to shift the language bias in LINUS, which is done by the user according to the type of learning task at hand. Below we list three types of tasks with the appropriate settings of the language bias:

1. *Propositional learning.* LINUS can be used as a propositional learner for learning individual classes ('class learning mode'), using any of the incorporated attribute-value learning algorithms. The induced clauses have the form

$$class(Class) \leftarrow L_1, \ldots, L_m.$$

where all literals L_i are of the form (1) above, i.e., binding a variable to a value. In this case, the class of the training examples can be different than just $\oplus$ and $\ominus$ and is determined by the values of an argument (or a set of arguments) of the target relation.

2. *Propositional learning using relational background knowledge.* Again, in the 'class learning mode', the induced clauses have the form

$$class(Class) \leftarrow L_1, \ldots, L_m.$$

but literals L_i have any of the forms (1)-(4) above.

3. *Inductive logic programming.* In the so-called 'relation learning mode', the induced clauses have the form

$$p(X_1, \ldots, X_n) \leftarrow L_1, \ldots, L_m.$$

where p is the name of the target predicate and literals L_i have any of the forms (1)-(4) above. In most of the experiments with LINUS reported elsewhere [20, 19], only literals of form (2) and (3) have been used.

The language bias in LINUS is declarative. The user can shift the language bias to any of the above forms, depending on the learning task at hand, the most expresive language being that of constrained DHDB clauses.

3.3   Weakening the Language Bias in LINUS

For simplicity, from here on we treat LINUS as an ILP learner, using only background knowledge in the form of utility predicates and disregard the fact that the language is typed. We first describe the language bias of ij-determinacy and then illustrate it on a simple example.

The ij-Determinacy Bias. To weaken the language bias in LINUS and allow for more expressiveness, we borrow an idea from GOLEM, which was later also used in FOIL2.0 to reduce search. The idea of determinacy allows for a restricted form of new variables to be introduced into the learned clauses. The very type of restriction (determinacy) allows the LINUS approach to this case as well.

We first define two syntactic restrictions on the hypothesis language. The syntactic complexity of $\mathcal{B}$ can be limited by restricting it to be of bounded arity. $\mathcal{B}$ is of *bounded arity* if the maximum arity of the predicates in $\mathcal{B}$ is bounded by some constant j. We next define the notion of *variable depth*. Consider a clause $p(X_1, X_2, \ldots, X_n) \leftarrow L_1, L_2, \ldots, L_r, \ldots$. Variables that appear in the head of the clause have depth zero. Let a variable V appear first in literal L_r. Let d be the maximum depth of any of the other variables in L_r that appear in the clause $p(X_1, X_2, \ldots, X_n) \leftarrow L_1, L_2, \ldots, L_{r-1}$. Then the depth of V is $d + 1$. By setting a maximum variable depth i, the syntactic complexity of clauses is restricted.

The following definition of *determinacy*, adapted to the case of function-free clauses, is taken from [14]. A predicate definition is determinate if all of its clauses are determinate. A clause is determinate if each of its literals is determinate. A literal is determinate if each of its variables that do not appear in preceding literals has only one possible binding given the bindings of its variables that appear in preceding literals.

This restriction is called $ij - determinacy$ for a given *maximum variable depth* i and *maximum arity j* of predicates from $\mathcal{B}$. Note that while i and j restrict the syntactic complexity of clauses, the notion of determinacy is essentially a semantic restriction.

If we set the hypothesis language to the language of ij-determinate clauses, the transformation approach of LINUS is still applicable, as demonstrated in Section 4. Dealing with nonrecursive clauses is easier, as the recursive case may require querying the user (oracle), in order to complete the transformation process. The transformation of propositional concept descriptions to the logic program form adds in the necessary determinate literals, ensuring that clauses are *linked* [3] and that the values of new variables can be computed from the values of old variables. Note that determinate literals are a natural extension of the utility functions used presently in LINUS. In the light of the above definitions we can say that, in the current implementation of LINUS, only variables of depth 0 and 1 are allowed, that variables of depth 1 must be bound to constants and may not be used in other literals.

Given background knowledge $\mathcal{B}$, the parameter j is fixed to the maximum arity of the predicates in $\mathcal{B}$. On the other hand, the parameter i can be increased to increase the expressiveness of the hypothesis language. For a fixed j, the user can consider the following series of languages:

$$\mathcal{L}_{0j} - \mathcal{L}_{1j} - \mathcal{L}_{2j} - \ldots$$

where the expressiveness (and thus the complexity of the search space) grows with i. The language $\mathcal{L}_{0j}$ is the language of constrained function-free DHDB clauses. If a solution for the ILP problem can not be found in the selected language, the next language in the series may be chosen, and the learning process repeated until a complete and consistent solution is found. Along these lines, LINUS could even shift its bias dynamically, similarly to CLINT [9] and NINA [1].

However, there are several problems with shifting bias dynamically. First of all, the series of languages considered has to be in some sense complete. Consider, for example, the case where the target definition is not determinate (is not in any of the languages in the series). In this case the system may continue to shift its bias forever without finding a satisfactory definition. Next, the learning process is repeated for each language in the series, up to the appropriate one. This leads to less efficient learning, although some improvements are possible. The most important problem, however, is when and how to shift the bias if learning data is imperfect, which can easily be the case in empirical ILP. Therefore, we will rather assume a fixed language bias $\mathcal{L}_{ij}$.

An Example Determinate Definition. Let us illustrate the notion of ij-determinacy on a simple ILP problem. The task is to define the predicate *grandmother*, where $grandmother(X, Y)$ states that person X is a grandmother of person Y, in terms of background knowledge predicates *father* and *mother*. The training examples and background knowledge are given in Table 6.

Training examples		Background knowledge		
$grandmother(ann, bob)$.	$\oplus$	$father(zak, tom)$.	$father(pat, ann)$.	$father(zak, jim)$.
$grandmother(ann, sue)$.	$\oplus$	$mother(ann, tom)$.	$mother(liz, ann)$.	$mother(ann, jim)$.
$grandmother(bob, sue)$.	$\ominus$	$father(tom, sue)$.	$father(tom, bob)$.	$father(jim, dave)$.
$grandmother(tom, bob)$.	$\ominus$	$mother(eve, sue)$.	$mother(eve, bob)$.	$mother(jean, dave)$.

Table 6: A simple ILP problem: Learning the *grandmother* relationship.

The induced target predicate definition is:

$$grandmother(X, Y) \leftarrow father(Z, Y), mother(X, Z).$$
$$grandmother(X, Y) \leftarrow mother(U, Y), mother(X, U).$$

---

[3] A clause is linked if all variables are linked. Variable v is *linked* if it occurs in the head of a clause or if there is a literal with distinct variables v and w such that w is linked.

This hypothesis can be induced in a language which is at least as expressive as $\mathcal{L}_{12}$. The clauses are *determinate* (but not *constrained*), because each occurrence of a new variable (Z in $father(Z, Y)$ and U in $mother(U, Y)$) has only one possible binding given particular values of the other (old) variables in the literal (Y in this case); this is the case since each person has exactly one mother and father. The hypothesis is function-free, the maximum depth of any variable is 1, and the maximum arity of background knowledge predicates is 2 ($i = 1, j = 2$).

However, the logically equivalent hypothesis:

$$grandmother(X, Y) \leftarrow mother(X, Z), father(Z, Y).$$
$$grandmother(X, Y) \leftarrow mother(X, U), mother(U, Y).$$

is not determinate, since the new variable Z in the literal $mother(X, Z)$ can have more than one binding for a fixed value of X ($X = ann$, $Z = tom$ or $Z = jim$); each person can namely have several children.

4 Learning Determinate Clauses with LINUS

In this section we present the algorithm which transforms the problem of learning nonrecursive function-free ij-determinate clauses into a propositional form and then illustrate its operation on the example from Section 3.3. We then discuss how this algorithm could be extended to learn recursive clauses.

4.1 The Transformation Algorithm

For the moment, we consider only the problem of learning nonrecursive clauses. The transformation of the ILP problem of constructing an ij-determinate definition for target predicate $p(X_1, X_2, ..., X_n)$ from examples $\mathcal{E}$ and from l predicate definitions in $\mathcal{B}$ proceeds as follows. First, construct a list F of all literals that use predicates from the background knowledge and contain variables of depth at most i. The determinate literals that introduce new variables are excluded from this list, as they do not distinguish between positive and negative examples (note that the new variables have a unique binding for any example, due to the determinacy restriction). The resulting list is the list of features (attributes) used for propositional learning. Next, transform the examples to propositional form. For each example, the truth value of each of the propositional features is determined by calls to the background knowledge $\mathcal{B}$. This is done by Algorithm 1. Finally, after applying a propositional learning algorithm, transform the output propositional concept definition to Horn clause form. This conversion is fairly straightforward (see example in Section 4.2 below).

Algorithm 1

1. $V_0 = \{X_1, X_2, ..., X_n\}$
2. $L = \{\}$
3. *for* $r = 1$ *to* i *do*
   - $D_r = \{q_s(Y_1, Y_2, ...) \mid q_s \in \{q_1, q_2, ..., q_l\},\ q_s(Y_1, Y_2, ...)$ *is determinate and contains exactly one new variable not in* V_{r-1}[4] $\}$
   - *add literals from* D_r *to the end of list* L
   - $V_r = V_{r-1} \cup \{Y \mid Y$ *appears in a literal from* $D_r\}$
4. $F = \{q_s(Y_1, Y_2, ..., Y_{j_s}) \mid q_s \in \{q_1, q_2, ..., q_l\},\ Y_1, Y_2, ..., Y_{j_s} \in V_i\} - (D_1 \cup D_2 ... \cup D_i)$

---

[4]The restriction to one new variable is for the purpose of simplicity and does not affect the applicability of the approach.

$g(X,Y)$	Variables		New variables				...	Propositional features		...
	X	Y	$f(U,X)$	$f(V,Y)$	$m(W,X)$	$m(Z,Y)$		$m(X,V)$	$m(X,Z)$	
Class	X	Y	U	V	W	Z		A_1	A_2	
$\oplus$	ann	bob	pat	tom	liz	eve		true	false	
$\oplus$	ann	sue	pat	tom	liz	eve		true	false	
$\ominus$	bob	sue	tom	tom	eve	eve		false	false	
$\ominus$	tom	bob	zak	tom	ann	eve		false	false	

Table 7: Propositional form of the *grandmother* learning problem.

5. *for each* $p(a_1, a_2, ..., a_n) \in \mathcal{E}^+$
and each $p(a_1, a_2, ..., a_n) \in \mathcal{E}^-$ *do*

- *determine the values of variables in* V_i *by executing the body of the clause* $p(X_1, X_2, ..., X_n) \leftarrow L$ *with variables* $X_1, ..., X_n$ *bound to* $a_1, ..., a_n$.
- *given the values of the variables in* V_i, *determine* f, *the vector of truth values of the literals in* F, *by querying the background knowledge*
- f *is an example of a propositional concept* c *(positive if* $p(a_1, a_2, ..., a_n) \in \mathcal{E}^+$ *or negative if* $p(a_1, a_2, ..., a_n) \in \mathcal{E}^-$ *)*

The knowledge base of background predicates may take the form of a (normal) logic program. The only additional requirement we make concerning the background knowledge is that it is in some sense efficient, so that the transformation process can be completed in polynomial time [14]. Two types of queries have to be posed to this knowledge base.[5] The first type are *existential* queries, which are used to determine the values of the new variables. Given a partially instantiated goal (literal containing variables that do not appear in previous literals), an existential query returns the set (possibly empty) of all bindings for the unbound variables which make the literal true. For example, the query $mother(X, A)$, where $X = ann$ and A is a new variable would return the set of answers $\{A = tom, A = jim\}$. The other type of queries are ground (*membership*) queries about background knowledge predicates, where the goal is completely bound. These are used to determine the truth values of the propositional features.

In an actual implementation of Algorithm 1, steps (3) and (5) should be interleaved, i.e., the values of the new variables and the propositional features should be calculated for each example as they are introduced. In this way, the determinacy of literals in step (3) is automatically tested when the existential query determining the values of the new variables in a literal is posed. A literal is determinate if the set of answers to the existential query is singleton for all the examples. If the set of answers for some example is not singleton, the literal is not determinate.

The extension of the algorithm to typed variables is straightforward and will be illustrated in the example in Section 4.3.

4.2 The Transformation Algorithm at Work: An Example

For our grandmother example, given in Table 6, we have $j = 2$, $i = 1$, $l = 2$, and $n = 2$. A literal $father(X, A)$, where X is old and A is new is not determinate, (e.g., $X = tom$, $A = sue$ or $A = bob$). However, if A is old and X is new, the literal is determinate. As the target predicate is $grandmother(X, Y)$, we have $V_0 = \{X, Y\}$ and $D_1 = \{f(U, X), f(V, Y), m(W, X), m(Z, Y)\}$, where f and m stand for *father* and *mother*, respectively.

---

[5]These are not queries to the example distribution!

This gives $L = D_1$, $V_1 = \{X, Y, U, V, W, Z\}$. F includes literals such as $f(X, X)$, $f(X, Y)$, $f(Z, Y)$, $f(W, X)$ and similarly $m(Z, Z)$, $m(V, Y)$, $m(W, W)$, $m(U, X)$. In fact, the pairs of arguments of f and m are all the pairs from the Cartesian product $V_1 \times V_1$, excluding the pairs that produce literals from D_1.

To illustrate the transformation process, Table 7 gives two propositional features and their values, as well as the values of the variables introduced by the determinate literals, generated for the ILP problem as defined by the training examples and background knowledge from Table 6.

To illustrate the transformation from a propositional concept description to a set of program clauses we again use our simple example. Suppose that a propositional learner induces the concept description in a DNF form and that the description $c \leftrightarrow x_1 \vee x_2$ is induced from the examples in Table 7. Note that c stands for $Class = \oplus$, x_1 for $A_1 = true$ and x_2 for $A_2 = true$.[6] The literals $m(X, V)$ and $m(X, Z)$ correspond to features A_1 and A_2. As these literals use new variables, we must include the determinate literals that introduced the new variables in the corresponding first-order form. The corresponding logic program form would then be:

$$grandmother(X, Y) \leftarrow father(V, Y), mother(X, V).$$
$$grandmother(X, Y) \leftarrow mother(Z, Y), mother(X, Z).$$

Expressed in logic, this program stands for:

$$\forall X \forall Y : grandmother(X, Y) \leftrightarrow [\exists V : f(V, Y) \wedge m(X, V)] \vee [\exists Z : m(Z, Y) \wedge m(X, Z)]$$

or more precisely for:

$$\forall X \forall Y : grandmother(X, Y) \leftrightarrow [\exists! V : f(V, Y) \wedge m(X, V)] \vee [\exists! Z : m(Z, Y) \wedge m(X, Z)]$$

as the value of each of the new variables is uniquely determined.

4.3 Learning Recursive Determinate Clauses

To learn recursive determinate definitions, we will need to slightly modify Algorithm 1. Let us first distinguish between the case of recursive literals which do not and recursive literals which do introduce new variables. For the first case we will need membership queries and for the second both membership and existential queries about the target relation.

For the first case only steps (4) and (5) of the algorithm need to be modified. In step (4) we treat the target predicate p as any of the other background knowledge predicates and form all possible literals with it and the variables available, excluding the literal $p(X_1, X_2, ..., X_n)$. However, in step (5), we cannot evaluate features involving p by querying the background knowledge. In that case we first check whether the ground query is among the training examples for p, in which case we can determine its truth value (*true*, if the example is positive, *false* if negative). If, however, the query cannot be found among the examples, we have to resort to a *membership* query, that is, we must ask the user whether the answer to the query involved is true or false.

An example learning problem. To illustrate the above modification to Algorithm 1, consider the task of learning the relation $member(X, Y)$, where X is of type *element* and Y is of type *list*. The background knowledge given includes the

---

[6]This description is consistent with the examples, i.e., does not cover any negative example; however, it is not too probable that any propositional learner would actually induce this description, since $c \leftrightarrow x_1$ would suffice for discriminating between the positive and negative examples.

	Vars		New vars		Propositional features					
m(X,Y)	X	Y	c(Y,A,B)	c(Y,X,B)	X = A	Y = B	m(X,B)	m(A,Y)	m(A,B)
Class	X	Y	A	B	A_1	A_2	A_3	A_4	A_5	A_6
⊕	1	[1,2]	1	[2]	true	true	false	false	true	false
⊕	1	[2,1]	2	[1]	false	false	false	true*	true*	false*
⊕	2	[2]	2	[]	true	true	false	false*	true	false*
⊖	1	[2]	2	[]	false	false	false	false*	true	false*

Table 8: Propositional form of a recursive ILP problem.

predicate $components(X, Y, Z)$, where X and Z are of type *list* and Y is of type *element*. This predicate is defined as $components([A|B], A, B)$ and decomposes a list $[A|B]$ into its head A and tail B. It is a flattened version of the *cons* function symbol. The equality predicate which works on arguments of the same type is also given. In this case $j = 3$. We set the maximum depth of variables to $i = 1$.

Table 8 gives four training examples and their transformation into the propositional form. From the table we can see that the only determinate literal is $c(Y, A, B)$ (c and m stand for *components* and *member*, respectively), and $V_1 = \{X, Y, A, B\}$, where X and A are of type *element* and Y and B are of type *list*. Taking into account the types of arguments, the modified algorithm produces the list of features in the table. The literals $c(Y, X, Y)$, $c(Y, A, Y)$, $c(B, X, B)$, $c(B, A, B)$, $c(B, X, Y)$ and $c(B, A, Y)$ are also on the list of features, but have been excluded for the sake of readability (they always have the value false). Consider the propositional feature A_4 which corresponds to the recursive call $member(X, B)$. The value of this feature can be determined for the first example, since the ground query is in this case $member(1, [2])$, which can be found as a negative training example. However, for the other three examples, membership queries have to be posed (the answers are marked with an asterisk '*'). Similar observation holds for features A_5 and A_6.

A propositional learner might generate the Boolean formula $c \leftrightarrow x_2 \lor x_4$ from the given propositional examples. Again, c is $Class = \oplus$, x_2 stands for $A_2 = true$ and x_4 for $A_4 = true$. This would be eventually transformed to the following definition:

$$member(X, Y) \quad \leftarrow \quad components(Y, A, B), \ = (X, A).$$
$$member(X, Y) \quad \leftarrow \quad components(Y, A, B), \ member(X, B).$$

which is the correct definition of the concept $member(X, Y)$. Again, the literal $components(Y, A, b)$ is introduced in order to ensure linked variables.

Finally, let us conclude by noting that, in addition to the changes outlined above, step 3 of the algorithm has also to be changed if we want to allow for recursive literals with new variables, which are, for example, necessary for learning the *quicksort* program. In this step, the target predicate p is treated exactly as the other predicates. Determining the values of the new variables in literals involving the target predicate requires in this case the use of *existential* queries about the target concept.

Complexity of Learning Determinate Clauses. Given l predicates in $\mathcal{B}$ with arity bounded by a constant j, a target predicate of arity n, and a constant bound i on variable depth, Algorithm 1 generates at most $l((jl + 1)n)^{j^{i+1}}$ features [14]. The LINUS approach uses propositional learning for which PAC-learnability results have been proved for simple distributions [22]. Simple distributions assign higher probabilities to simpler examples; for instance, the example $member(1, [1])$ should be much more likely than $member(3, [7, 1, 4, 3, 2, 8])$ under a simple distribution. Given the simple distribution assumption and the restrictions for the language bias $\mathcal{L}_{ij}$, LINUS can guarantee that the learned concept definitions are probably approximately correct. For more details, we refer the reader to [14].

The above upper bound of features (attributes) is fortunately not realistic for computing the actual number of attributes to be used for learning. Due to typing restrictions, symmetry of predicates and determinacy, the actual number of attributes is substantially smaller, as can be seen in the *member* example above. However, one has to be aware of the drastical increase in the complexity with the increased depth i in language bias $\mathcal{L}_{ij}$. The proposed approach can therefore be used only for a limited class of ILP problems.

5 Conclusions

To conclude, we have presented a method which allows for the effective use of background knowledge in inductive concept learning. For the constrained DHDB clauses bias, the method has already been implemented in the LINUS learning system. We have analysed the declarative bias in LINUS and showed how it can be weakened to learn more expressive concept definitions.

It is important to emphasize that, by incorporating state-of-the-art propositional learners, LINUS allows for learning from imperfect, noisy data, both in the propositional and the ILP framework. Compared to propositional attribute-value learners, however, its advantage is the effective use of background knowledge and the incorporation of attribute-value learners into the more expressive logic programming framework.

Compared to empirical ILP systems GOLEM and FOIL, the proposed extension to LINUS has the following advantages. The concept description language based on ij-determinate clauses is more expressive than the one used in GOLEM. Namely, negated literals may be used in LINUS, thus allowing for learning determinate normal program clauses, whereas only (definite) Horn clauses can be induced by GOLEM. Furthermore, unlike in FOIL and GOLEM, nonground background knowledge may be used directly. In FOIL and GOLEM nonground background knowledge may be used, but has to be converted to a ground model, i.e., a set of ground unit clauses, by carrying out all h-easy derivations starting from the constant symbols in the observations. Bratko et al. [4] report serious problems resulting from this requirement, due to the enormous number of ground facts generated.

Acknowledgements

This work was supported by the Slovenian Ministry of Science and Technology. The scholarschip for Sašo Džeroski, who is currently visiting The Turing Institute Limited, Glasgow, Scotland, was provided both by the British Council and the Slovenian Ministry of Science and Technology. The authors are grateful to Igor Mozetič and Marko Grobelnik for their constribution to the development of LINUS and to Peter Flach and Irma Sutlič for their comments on the paper.

References

1. H. Ade and M. Bruynooghe. A comparative study of declarative and dynamically adjustable language bias in concept learning. In *Proc. Workshop on Logical Approaches to Machine Learning, Tenth European Conference on Artificial Intelligence*, Vienna, Austria, 1992. To appear.

2. F. Bergadano, A. Giordana and S. Ponsero. Deduction in top-down inductive learning. In *Proc. Sixth International Workshop on Machine Learning*, pages 23–25, Morgan Kaufmann, San Mateo, CA, 1989.

3. I. Bratko, I. Mozetič and N. Lavrač. *KARDIO: a study in deep and qualitative knowledge for expert systems*, MIT Press, Cambridge, MA, 1989.

4. I. Bratko, S.H. Muggleton and A. Varšek. Learning qualitative models of dynamic systems. In S. H. Muggleton, editor, *Inductive Logic Programming*, Academic Press, London, 1992. In press.

5. M. Bruynooghe and L. De Raedt. Technical annex of the ESPRIT BRA 6020 Inductive Logic Programming.

6. B. Cestnik, I. Kononenko and I. Bratko. ASSISTANT 86: A knowledge elicitation tool for sophisticated users. In I. Bratko and N. Lavrač, editors, *Progress in Machine Learning*, pages 31–45, Sigma Press, Wilmslow, 1987.

7. P. Clark and T. Niblett. The CN2 induction algorithm. *Machine Learning*, 3(4): 261–283, 1989.

8. L. De Raedt and M. Bruynooghe. Indirect relevance and bias in inductive concept-learning. *Knowledge Acquisition*, 2: 365–390, 1990.

9. L. De Raedt and M. Bruynooghe. Interactive concept learning and constructive induction by analogy. *Machine Learning*, 8(2): 107–150, 1992.

10. L. De Raedt, M. Bruynooghe and B. Martens. Integrity constraints in interactive concept learning. In *Proc. Eighth International Workshop on Machine Learning*, pages 394–398, Morgan Kaufmann, San Mateo, CA, 1991.

11. S. Džeroski. Handling noise in inductive logic programming. MSc Thesis, Faculty of Electrical Engineering and Computer Science, University of Ljubljana, Slovenia, 1991.

12. S. Džeroski and N. Lavrač. Learning relations from noisy examples: an empirical comparison of LINUS and FOIL. In *Proc. Eighth International Workshop on Machine Learning*, pages 399–402, Morgan Kaufmann, San Mateo, CA, 1991.

13. S. Džeroski and N. Lavrač. Refinement graphs for FOIL and LINUS. In S.H. Muggleton, editor, *Inductive Logic Programming*, Academic Press, London, 1992. In press.

14. S. Džeroski, S. Muggleton and S. Russell. PAC-learnability of determinate logic programs. In *Proc. Fifth ACM Workshop on Computational Learning Theory*, Pittsburgh, PA, 1992. To appear.

15. S. Džeroski, S. Muggleton and S. Russell. PAC-learnability of constrained non-recursive logic programs. Submitted for publication.

16. L. M. Fu and B. G. Buchanan. Learning intermediate concepts in constructing a hierarchical knowledge base. In *Proc. Ninth International Joint Conference on Artificial Intelligence*, pages 659–666, Morgan Kaufmann, Los Altos, CA, 1985.

17. J.U. Kietz and S. Wrobel. Controlling the complexity of learning in logic through syntactic and task-oriented models. In S.H. Muggleton, editor, *Inductive Logic Programming*, Academic Press, London, 1992. In press.

18. R. Kowalski. *Logic for problem solving*, North Holland, New York, 1979.

19. N. Lavrač and S. Džeroski. Inductive learning of relations from noisy examples. In S.H. Muggleton, editor, *Inductive Logic Programming*, Academic Press, London, 1992. In press.

20. N. Lavrač, S. Džeroski and M. Grobelnik. Learning nonrecursive definitions of relations with LINUS. In *Proc. Fifth European Working Session on Learning*, pages 265–281, Springer, Berlin, 1991.

21. N. Lavrač, S. Džeroski, V. Pirnat and V. Križman. Learning rules for early diagnosis of rheumatic diseases. In *Proc. Third Scandinavian Conference on Artificial Intelligence*, pages 138–149, IOS Press, Amsterdam, 1991.

22. M. Li and P. Vitányi. Learning simple concepts under simple distributions. *SIAM Journal of Computing*, 20(5): 911–935, 1991.

23. J.W. Lloyd. *Foundations of Logic Programming* (2nd edn), Springer, Berlin, 1987.

24. R. S. Michalski. Discovering classification rules using variable-valued logic system VL1. In *Proc. Third International Joint Conference on Artificial Intelligence*, pages 162–172, Stanford Research Institute, Menlo Park, CA, 1973.

25. R.S. Michalski. Pattern recognition as rule-guided inductive inference. *IEEE Transactions on Pattern Analysis and Machine Intelligence*, 2(4): 349–361, 1980.

26. R.S. Michalski. A theory and methodology of inductive learning. In R.S. Michalski, J.G. Carbonell and T.M. Mitchell, editors, *Machine learning: an artificial intelligence approach, Vol. 1*, pages 83–134, Tioga, Palo Alto, CA, 1983.

27. R.S. Michalski, I. Mozetič, J. Hong and N. Lavrač. The multi-purpose incremental learning system AQ15 and its testing application on three medical domains. In *Proc. National Conference on Artificial Intelligence*, pages 1041–1045, Morgan Kaufmann, San Mateo, CA, 1986.

28. I. Mozetič. NEWGEM: Program for learning from examples, technical documentation and user's guide. *Reports of Intelligent Systems Group*, No. UIUCDCS-F-85-949, Department of Computer Science, University of Illinois at Urbana Champaign, 1985. Also *Technical Report IJS-DP-4390*, Jožef Stefan Institute, Ljubljana, Slovenia.

29. I. Mozetič. Learning of qualitative models. In I. Bratko and N. Lavrač, editors, *Progress in Machine Learning*, pages 201–217, Sigma Press, Wilmslow, 1987.

30. I. Mozetič and N. Lavrač. Incremental learning from examples in a logic-based formalism. In P. Brazdil, editor, *Proc. Workshop on Machine Learning, Meta-Reasoning and Logics*, pages 109–127, Sesimbra, Portugal, 1988.

31. S.H. Muggleton. Duce, an oracle-based approach to constructive induction. In *Proc. Tenth International Joint Conference on Artificial Intelligence*, pages 287–292, Morgan Kaufmann, San Mateo, CA, 1989.

32. S.H. Muggleton. Inductive logic programming. *New Generation Computing*, 8(4): 295–318, 1991.

33. S.H. Muggleton and W. Buntine. Machine invention of first-order predicates. In *Proc. Fifth International Conference on Machine Learning*, pages 339–352, Morgan Kaufmann, San Mateo, CA, 1988.

34. S.H. Muggleton and C. Feng. Efficient induction of logic programs. In *Proc. First Conference on Algorithmic Learning Theory*, pages 368–381, Ohmsha, Tokyo, 1990.

35. M. Nunez. The use of background knowledge in decision tree induction. *Machine learning*, 6(3): 231–250, 1991.

36. G. Pagallo and D. Haussler. Boolean feature discovery in empirical learning. *Machine Learning* 5(1): 71–99, 1990.

37. J.R. Quinlan. Induction of decision trees. *Machine Learning*, 1(1): 81–106, 1986.

38. J.R. Quinlan. Learning logical definitions from relations. *Machine Learning*, 5(3): 239–266, 1990.

39. J.R. Quinlan. Knowledge acquisition from structured data - using determinate literals to assist search. *IEEE Expert* 6(6): 32–37, 1991.

40. S. Russell. *The use of knowledge in analogy and induction*, Pitman, London, 1989.

41. E.Y. Shapiro. *Algorithmic Program Debugging*, MIT Press, Cambridge, MA, 1983.

42. J.D. Ullman. *Principles of database and knowledge base systems (Volume I)*, Computer Science Press, Rockville, MA, 1988.

43. P.E. Utgoff and T. M. Mitchell. Acquisition of appropriate bias for inductive concept learning. In *Proc. National Conference on Artificial Intelligence*, pages 414–417, Kaufmann, Los Altos, CA, 1982.

44. J. Wnek, J. Sarma, A. A. Wahab, and R. S. Michalski. Comparing learning paradigms via diagrammatic visualization: A case study in single concept learning using symbolic, neural net and genetic algorithm methods. In *Proc. Fifth International Symposium on Methodologies for Intelligent Systems*, Knoxville, TN, 1990.

45. S. Wrobel. Automatic representation adjustment in an observational discovery system. In *Proc. Third European Working Session on Learning*, pages 253–262, Pitmann, London, 1988.

Too Much Information Can be Too Much for Learning Efficiently

Rolf Wiehagen*

Humboldt–Universität

Institut für Theoretische Informatik

PSF 1297

O–1086 Berlin

wiehagen@hubinf.uucp

Thomas Zeugmann

TH Darmstadt

Institut für Theoretische Informatik

Alexanderstr. 10

W–6100 Darmstadt

zeugmann@iti.informatik.th-darmstadt.de

Abstract

In designing learning algorithms it seems quite reasonable to construct them in a way such that all data the algorithm already has obtained are correctly and completely reflected in the description the algorithm outputs on these data. However, this approach may totally fail, i.e., it may lead to the unsolvability of the learning problem, or it may exclude any efficient solution of it. In particular, we present a natural learning problem and prove that it can be solved in polynomial time if and only if the algorithm is allowed to ignore data.

1 Introduction

The phenomenon of learning has attracted much attention of researchers in various fields. When dealing with learning computer scientists are mainly interested in studying the question whether or not learning problems may be solved algorithmically. Nowadays, algorithmic learning theory is a rapidly emerging science (cf. Angluin and Smith (1983, 1987), Osherson, Stob and Weinstein (1986) and the references therein). Nevertheless, despite the enormous progress having been made since the pioneering papers of Solomonoff (1965) and of Gold (1965, 1967), there are still many problems that deserve special attention. The global question we shall deal with may be posed as follows: Are all data of equal importance a learning algorithm is fed with?

First we study this question in the setting of inductive inference. Then we ask whether the insight obtained may be important when one has to solve learning problems that are somehow closer to potential applications. But let us explain all these things in some more detail.

---

*On leave at TH Darmstadt

One main problem of algorithmic learning theory consists in synthesizing "global descriptions" for the objects to be learnt from examples. Thus, one goal is the following. Let f be any computable function from N into N. Given more and more examples $f(0), f(1), ..., f(n), ...$ a learning strategy is required to produce a sequence of hypotheses $h_0, h_1, ..., h_n, ...$ the limit of which is a correct global description of the function f, i.e., a program that computes f. Since at any stage n of this learning process the strategy knows exclusively the examples $f(0), f(1), ..., f(n)$, it seems reasonable to construct the hypothesis h_n in a way such that for any $x \leq n$ the "hypothesis function" g described by h_n is defined and computes the value $f(x)$. Such a hypothesis is called *consistent*. In other words, a hypothesis is consistent if and only if all information obtained so far about the unknown object is completely and correctly encoded in this hypothesis. Otherwise, a hypothesis is said to be *inconsistent*. Consequently, if the hypothesis h_n above is inconsistent, then there must be an $x \leq n$ such that $g(x) \neq f(x)$. Note that there are two possible reasons for g to differ from f on argument x; namely, $g(x)$ may be not defined, or the value $g(x)$ is defined and does not equal $f(x)$. Hence, if a hypothesis is inconsistent then it is not only wrong at all but it is wrong on an argument for which the learning strategy does already know the correct value. At first glance we are tempted to totally exclude strategies producing inconsistent hypotheses from our considerations. It might seem that *consistent strategies*, i.e., strategies that produce always consistent hypotheses, are the only reasonable learning devices.

Surprisingly enough this is a misleading impression. As it turns out, in a sense learning seems to be *the art of knowing what to overlook*. Barzdin (1974) first announced that there are classes of recursive functions that can be inferred in the limit but only by strategies working inconsistently. This result directly yields the following questions:

(1) Why does it make sense to output inconsistent hypotheses?
(2) What kind of data, if any, the strategy should overlook?

As we shall see below the first question finds its preliminary answer in the fact that, roughly speaking, there is no algorithm detecting whether or not a hypothesis is consistent. Consequently, in general a strategy has no chance to effectively verify the consistency of its previous guess with the new data it has been fed with. On the other hand, a strategy cannot overcome this drawback by simply searching any consistent hypothesis, since it has to converge in the limit, too. Therefore, in order to be really successful, intuitively speaking, a strategy cannot take care whether all the information it is provided with is actually correctly reflected by its current hypotheses. Answering the second question is more complicated. However, an intuitively satisfying answer is provided by a characterization of identification in the limit in terms of computable numberings (cf. Wiehagen (1978b), Theorem 8). This theorem actually states that a class U of recursive functions can be learnt in the limit iff there are a space of hypotheses containing for each function at least one program, and a computable "discrimination" function d such that for any two programs i and j the value $d(i,j)$ is an upper bound for an argument x on which program i behaves different than program j does. The key observation used in constructing the strategy that infers any function from U is the following. Let i be the strategy's last guess and let $f(0), ..., f(n)$ be the data now fed to it. If the strategy finds a program j such that for all inputs $x \leq d(i,j)$ its output equals $f(x)$, then program i

cannot be a correct one for function f. Then the strategy changes its mind from i to $i+1$. In other words, the strategy uses the data it receives for the purpose to find a *proof* for the *incorrectness* of its actual hypothesis via some global property the space of all hypotheses possesses.

Summarizing the above discussion we see that the main reason for the superiority of inconsistent strategies in the setting of inductive inference of recursive functions is caused by the undecidability of consistency. However, it remained open whether this phenomenon is of fundamental epistemological importance but of almost no pratical relevance. Dealing with the latter problem requires a different approach. It might be well conceivable that consistency is always decidable if one restricts itself to learning problems that are of interest with respect to potential applications. Consequently, the superiority of inconsistent strategies in this setting, if any, can only be established in terms of complexity theory. What we present in the sequel is a partial solution to this problem. As it turned out, there are "natural" learning problems having the following properties: First, consistency is decidable, and second, they can be solved by a polynomial–time strategy if and only if the strategy may work inconsistently.

Hence the inconsistency phenomenon does survive also in domains where consistency *is* decidable. Moreover, the reason for the eventual superiority of inconsistent strategies is in both settings in some sense the same. In both cases the learning algorithms cannot handle the consistency problem. On the one hand this inability has been caused by the provable absense of any algorithm solving it, while, on the other hand, the consistency problem is computationally intractable, provided $\mathcal{P} \neq \mathcal{NP}$. As far as we know the result above is the first one proving the existence of learning problems that cannot be solved in polynomial time by any consistent strategy in a setting where consistency is decidable. Moreover, in our opinion it strongly recommends to take seriously inconsistent learning strategies into consideration. This requires both, the elaboration of "intelligent" inconsistent techniques as well as finding criteria with the help of which one can decide whether or not inconsistent strategies are appropriate. The inconsistent technique we have applied consists in overlooking or ignoring data unnecessary for the strategy in order to fulfil its learning task. Of course, this might not be the only such technique.

The paper is structured as follows. Section 2 presents notation and definitions. Section 3 deals with the inconsistency phenomenon in the setting of inductive inference of recursive functions. The problem whether the inconsistency phenomenon is of any relevance in the world of polynomial time computability is affirmatively exemplified in Section 4. In Section 5 we discuss the results obtained and present open problems. All references are given in Section 6.

2 Preliminaries

Unspecified notations follow Rogers (1967). $N = \{0, 1, 2, ...\}$ denotes the set of all natural numbers. The set of all finite sequences of natural numbers is denoted by N^*. The classes of all partial recursive and recursive functions of one, two arguments over N are denoted by P, P^2, R, and R^2, respectively. $R_{0,1}$ denotes the set of all $0-1$ valued recursive functions. Sometimes it will be suitable to identify a recursive function with the sequence of its values, e.g., let $\alpha = (a_0, ..., a_k) \in N^*$, $j \in N$, and $p \in R_{0,1}$; then we write $\alpha j p$ to denote the function f for which $f(x) = a_x$, if $x \leq k$, $f(k+1) = j$, and $f(x) = p(x - k - 1)$, if $x \geq k+2$. Furthermore, let $g \in P$; we write $\alpha \sqsubset$ iff α is a prefix of the sequence of values associated with g, i.e., for any $x \leq k$, $g(x)$ is defined and $g(x) = a_x$. If $U \subseteq R$, then we denote by $[U]$ the set of all finite prefixes of functions from U.

Any function $\psi \in P^2$ is called a numbering. Moreover, let $\psi \in P^2$, then we write ψ_i instead of $\lambda x \psi(i, x)$ and set $P_\psi = \{\psi_i \mid i \in N\}$ as well as $R_\psi = P_\psi \cap R$. Consequently, if $f \in P_\psi$, then there is a number i such that $f = \psi_i$. A numbering $\varphi \in P^2$ is called a Gödel numbering (cf. Rogers (1967)) iff $P_\varphi = P$, and for any numbering $\psi \in P^2$, there is a $c \in R$ such that $\psi_i = \varphi_{c(i)}$ for all $i \in N$. *Göd* denotes the set of all Gödel numberings.

Using a fixed encoding $\langle ... \rangle$ of N^* onto N we write f^n instead of $\langle (f(o), ..., f(n)) \rangle$, for any $n \in N$, $f \in R$. Now we define some concepts of learning.

Definition 1. (Gold, 1965)
Let $U \subseteq R$ and let $\psi \in P^2$. The class U is said to be learnable in the limit with respect to ψ iff there is a strategy $S \in P$ such that for any function $f \in U$,

(1) for any $n \in N$, $S(f^n)$ is defined,

(2) there is a $j \in N$ such that $\psi_j = f$ and, for almost all n, $S(f^n) = j$.

If U is learnable in the limit with respect to ψ by strategy S we write $U \in LIM_\psi(S)$. Let $LIM_\psi = \{U \mid U$ is learnable in the limit w.r.t. $\psi\}$, and let $LIM = \bigcup_{\psi \in P^2} LIM_\psi$.

Note that $LIM_\varphi = LIM$ for any Gödel numbering φ. Next we formally define consistent learning.

Definition 2. (Barzdin, 1974)
Let $U \subseteq R$ and let $\psi \in P^2$. The class U is called consistently learnable in the limit with respect to ψ iff there is a strategy $S \in P$ such that

(1) $U \in LIM_\psi(S)$

(2) $\psi_{S(f^n)}(x) = f(x)$ for all $n \in N$ and $x \leq n$.

$CONS_\psi(S)$, $CONS_\psi$ and $CONS$ are defined analogously as above.

Intuitively speaking, a consistent strategy does correctly reflect all the data it has already seen. Note that $CONS_\varphi = CONS$ for any Gödel numbering φ. If a strategy does not always work consistently, we call it inconsistent.

3 The Inconsistency Phenomenon

The inconsistency phenomenon has been discovered independently by Barzdin (1974) and the Blums (1975). They observed that there are classes of recursive functions that are inferrable in the limit but which cannot be learnt by any consistent strategy. Since both papers do not contain a proof of this assertion, we present here a proof from Wiehagen (1976) actually showing a somewhat stronger result than the one formulated in the next theorem. We shall discuss this issue below.

Theorem 1. (Barzdin, 1974)

$CONS \subset LIM$

Proof. Let $U_\varphi = \{f \in R \mid f = \alpha j p,\ \alpha \in N^*,\ j \geq 2,\ p \in R_{0,1},\ \varphi_j = f\}$, where $\varphi \in G\ddot{o}d$. Obviously, $U_\varphi \in LIM(S)$, where $S(f^n)$ is equal to the last value $f(x) \geq 2$ from $(f(0),...,f(n))$ and 0, if no such value exists. For the purpose to prove that $U_\varphi \notin CONS$ we need the following claim.

Claim: Let $\varphi \in G\ddot{o}d$. For any $\alpha \in N^*$, there is a $f \in U_\varphi$ such that $\alpha \sqsubseteq f$.

Indeed, by an implicit use of the Recursion Theorem (cf. Rogers (1967)) it is easy to see that for any $\alpha \in N^*$ and any $p \in R_{0,1}$ there is a $j \geq 2$ such that $\varphi_j = \alpha j p$.

Now, suppose the converse, i.e., there is a strategy $S \in P$ such that $U_\varphi \in CONS_\varphi(S)$. By the claim we get that $S \in R$ and that for any $\alpha \in N^*$, $\alpha \sqsubseteq \varphi_{S(\alpha)}$. Thus, on any $\alpha \in N^*$, S always produces a consistent guess. Then, again by an implicit use of the Recursion Theorem, let $j \geq 2$ be any φ–number of the function f defined as follows: $f(0) = j$, and for any $n \in N$,

$$f(n+1) = \begin{cases} 0 & , \quad if \quad S(f^n 0) \neq S(f^n) \\ 1 & , \quad if \quad S(f^n 0) = S(f^n)\ and S(f^n 1) \neq S(f^n) \end{cases}$$

In accordance with the claim and the assumption that S works consistently one straightforwardly verifies that $S(f^n 0) \neq S(f^n)$ or $S(f^n 1) \neq S(f^n)$ for any $n \in N$. Therefore the function f is everywhere defined and we have $f \in U_\varphi$. On the other hand, the strategy S changes its mind infinitely often when successively fed with f, a contradiction to $U_\varphi \in CONS_\varphi(S)$.

q.e.d.

Note that the class U_φ from the proof of Theorem 1 is even *iteratively* learnable in the limit. We call a class U of recursive functions iteratively learnable iff there is a strategy that learns any $f \in U$ as follows: In step n the strategy exclusively gets its previous guess produced in step $n-1$ as well as the new value $f(n)$. By IT we denote the collection of all classes U which can be learnt iteratively. In Wiehagen (1976) $CONS \subset IT \subset LIM$ has been proved. Recent papers give new evidence for the power of iterative learning (cf. e.g. Porat and Feldman (1988), Lange and Wiehagen (1991), Lange and Zeugmann (1992)).

A closer look to the proof above shows that, in general, a strategy attempting to consistently learn functions has to overcome two difficulties. First, it should avoid to change too often its current guess that is eventually no longer consistent, to a definitely consistent hypothesis, since this behavior may force the strategy to diverge. Second, trusting that its current guess is consistent may eventually lead to an actually inconsistent hypothesis, since the strategy cannot effectively prove consistency. Indeed, it turns out that a class U is consistently learnable iff there is a suitable space of hypotheses ψ such that the consistency problem restricted to U and ψ is effectively decidable. More precisely, let $U \subseteq R$ and let ψ be any numbering. We say that U–consistency is decidable with respect to ψ iff there is a predicate $cons \in P^2$ such that for any $\alpha \sqsubseteq U$ and any $i \in N$, $cons(\alpha, i)$ is defined and $cons(\alpha, i) = 1$ if and only if $\alpha \sqsubseteq \psi_i$.

We say that consistency with respect to ψ is decidable iff there is a predicate $cons \in R^2$ such that for any $\alpha \in N^*$ and for any $i \in N$, $cons(\alpha, i) = 1$ if and only if $\alpha \sqsubseteq \psi_i$.

Theorem 2. $U \in CONS$ *iff there is a numbering* $\psi \in P^2$ *such that*

(1) $U \subseteq P_\psi$

(2) U*-consistency with respect to* ψ *is decidable.*

Theorem 2 is a consequence of Theorem 9 from Wiehagen (1978b). Note that for an arbitrary Gödel numbering, U-consistency is undecidable for any non–empty class $U \subseteq R$.

Furthermore, for many classes $U \in CONS$, the halting problem with respect to the numbering ψ from Theorem 2 is *undecidable*. More exactly, let $NUM = \{U \mid U \subseteq R$ and there is $\psi \in R^2$ such that $U \subseteq P_\psi\}$ denote the family of all classes of recursive functions that are contained in some recursively enumerable class of recursive functions. Then we know that $NUM \subset CONS$ (cf. Wiehagen (1976)). Furthermore, it turns out that for any class $U \notin NUM$, there are only spaces of hypotheses ψ such that $U \subseteq P_\psi$ implies the undecidabilty of the halting problem with respect to ψ (cf. Lemma 3 below). Moreover, it is justified to call the latter property a "bad" one, since conversely the decidability of the halting problem easily implies the consistent learnability in the limit of *all* functions from R_ψ with respect to ψ.

Lemma 3. *Let* $U \subseteq R$ *and let* $U \notin NUM$. *Then, for any numbering* $\psi \in P^2$ *satisfying* $U \subseteq P_\psi$, *the halting problem with respect to* ψ *is undecidable.*

Proof. Let $U \subseteq R$ and let $U \notin NUM$. Furthermore, let $\psi \in P^2$ be any numbering such that $U \subseteq P_\psi$. Suppose, the halting problem with respect to ψ is decidable. Hence there is a function $h \in R^2$ such that for any $i, x \in N$, $h(i, x) = 1$ iff $\psi_i(x)$ is defined. Then define a numbering $\tilde{\psi}$ by effectively filling out the "gaps" in ψ as follows:

$$\tilde{\psi}_i(x) = \begin{cases} \psi_i(x) & , \quad if \quad h(i, x) = 1 \\ 0 & , \quad otherwise \end{cases}$$

Obviously, for any $i \in N$, if $\psi_i \in R$ then $\tilde{\psi}_i = \psi_i$. Hence $U \subseteq P_{\tilde{\psi}}$. However, $\tilde{\psi} \in R^2$ and consequently, $U \subseteq P_{\tilde{\psi}}$ does imply $U \in NUM$, a contradiction.

$$\text{q.e.d.}$$

Therefore, Theorem 2 offers a possibility to compensate the undecidability of the halting problem with respect to ψ by the decidability of U–consistency. One can even show that there are classes $U \in CONS \setminus NUM$ such that $[U] = N^*$. By Theorem 2 and Lemma 3 this yields the existence of numberings ψ with undecidable halting problem and decidable consistency problem. Note that the latter assertion is a pure numbering theoretical result proved by learning theoretical observations (though it can also be proved directly).

Lemma 4. *There is a class* $U \subseteq R$ *such that*

(1) $U \in CONS$

(2) $U \notin NUM$

(3) $[U] = N^*$

Sketch of proof. Let (φ, Φ) be any complexity measure (cf. Blum (1967)). We modify Φ to $\hat{\Phi}$ in a way such that

1. $(\varphi, \hat{\Phi})$ is again a complexity measure,

2. for any $\alpha \in N^*$, there is an $i \in N$ such that $\varphi_i \in R$ and $\alpha \sqsubseteq \hat{\Phi}_i$.

Now let $U = \{\hat{\Phi}_i \mid \varphi_i \in R\}$. Then $U \in CONS_{\hat{\Phi}}$, since for any $i, x, y \in N$ the predicate "$\hat{\Phi}_i(x) = y$" is uniformly decidable. Furthermore, $U \notin NUM$, since otherwise $R \in NUM$. Finally, $[U] = N^*$ by construction.

q.e.d.

Corollary 5. *There is a numbering ψ with $[R_\psi] = N^*$ such that*

(1) The halting problem with respect to ψ is undecidable.

(2) The consistency problem with respect to ψ is decidable.

Proof. Let $U \subseteq R$ be a class in accordance with Lemma 4. Furthermore, let ψ be a numbering chosen accordingly to Theorem 2. Then (1) is an immediate consequence of Lemma 3, and (2) follows from Theorem 2, assertion (2), taking into account that, by construction, $[R_\psi] = N^*$.

q.e.d.

Finally in this section we want to point out that a natural weakening of consistency does not suffice to learn any class inferrable in the limit.

Definition 3. (Wiehagen, 1978a)
Let $U \in R$, $\psi \in P^2$. U is called conformly learnable in the limit with respect to ψ iff there is a strategy $S \in P$ such that

(1) $U \in LIM_\psi(S)$,

(2) for any function $f \in U$, any $n, x \in N$ such that $x \leq n$, either $\psi_{S(f^n)}(x) = f(x)$ or $\psi_{S(f^n)}(x)$ is not defined.

Intuitively speaking, a conform strategy is never allowed to output a hypothesis that indeed computes a wrong value at an argument x which is less than the length of the initial segment seen so far. By $CONF_\psi$ we denote the collection of classes $U \subseteq R$ that are conformly identifiable with respect to ψ. Finally, let $CONF$ denote the union of all families $CONF_\psi$ where $\psi \in P^2$. The following theorem is due to Wiehagen (1978a).

Theorem 6.
$$CONS \subset CONF \subset LIM$$

The reader is encouraged to consult Jantke and Beick (1981), Zeugmann (1983) and Fulk (1989) for further investigation concerning consistent and conform identification.

4 Inconsistency and Polynomial Time

The results presented in the previous section may lead to the impression that the inconsistency phenomenon may be far beyond any practical relevance, since it has been established in a setting where both, the halting and the consistency problem are undecidable in general. Therefore now we ask whether the inconsistency phenomenon does survive in more realistic settings, i.e., in settings where consistency is decidable. Moreover, in order to be consequently realistic we additionally restrict ourselves to deal exclusively with learning strategies that are polynomial time computable. Then, of course, the superiority of inconsistent strategies, if any, has to be established in terms of complexity theory. We present a learning problem in a realistic setting which is generally consistently solvable but which *cannot be solved consistently in polynomial time*, unless $\mathcal{P} \neq \mathcal{NP}$. The desired goal is achieved by elaborating an algorithm *inconsistently* solving the same learning problem in *polynomial time*. As far as we know this is the first learning problem for which the announced properties are rigorously proved. In our opinion, this result gives strong evidence of taking seriously inconsistent learning strategies into consideration.

The setting we want to deal with is the learnability of pattern languages introduced by Angluin (1980). Subsequently, Shinohara (1982) dealt with polynomial time learnability of subclasses of pattern languages. Nix (1983) outlined interesting applications of pattern inference algorithms. Recently, Kearns and Pitt (1989) as well as Ko, Marron and Tzeng (1990) studied intensively the learnabilty of pattern languages in the PAC–learning model.

So let us define what are a pattern and a pattern language. Let $\Sigma = \{a, b, ..\}$ be any non–empty finite alphabet containing at least two elements. Furthermore, let $X = \{x_i \mid i \in N\}$ be an infinite set of variables such that $\Sigma \cap X = \emptyset$. *Patterns* are non–empty strings from $\Sigma \cup X$, e.g., ab, ax_1ccc, $bx_1x_1cx_2x_2$ are patterns. $L(p)$, the language generated by pattern p is the set of strings which can be obtained by substituting non–null strings from Σ^* for the variables of the pattern p. Thus $aabbb$ is generable from pattern ax_1x_2b, while $aabba$ is not. *Pat* and *PAT* denote the set of all patterns and of all pattern languagues, respectively. In order to deal with the learnability of pattern languages we have to specify from what information the learning strategies should do their task. Following Gold (1967) we distinguish between learning from text and from informant. Formally, let $L \subseteq \Sigma^*$; we call a mapping $I : N \rightarrow \Sigma^* \times \{+, -\}$ *informant* of L iff

(1) For any $w \in \Sigma^*$, there are an $n \in N$ and $\lambda \in \{+, -\}$ such that $I(n) = (w, \lambda)$.

(2) For any $n \in N$, $w \in \Sigma^*$, and $\lambda \in \{+, -\}$, if $I(n) = (w, \lambda)$ then $w \in L$ iff $\lambda = +$.

Let *Info(L)* denote the set of all informants of L. Furthermore, for $I \in Info(L)$ and $n \in N$ let $I^n = cod(I(0), ..., I(n))$, where *cod* denotes an effective and bijective mapping from the set of all finite sequences of elements from $\Sigma^* \times \{+, -\}$ onto N. Finally, we set $I_n = \{w \in \Sigma^* \mid \text{there are } i \leq n, \lambda \in \{+, -\} \text{ s.t. } I(n) = (w, \lambda)\}$, and $I_n^+ = I_n \cap L$, $I_n^- = I_n \setminus I_n^+$.

Any mapping T from N onto L is called a *text* for L. By *Text(L)* we denote the set of all texts for L. The sets T_n, T_n^+ as well as T_n^- are defined analogously as above.

Intuitively, a text for L generates the language $L-$ without any information concerning the complement of L, whereas an informant of L decides L by informing the strategy whether or not any word from Σ^* belongs to L. Note that we allow a text and an informant to be non–effective.

Definition 4. *PAT is called learnable in the limit from informant (abbr. PAT $\in$ LIM $-$ INF) iff there is an effective strategy S from N into Pat such that for any*

$L \in PAT$ and any $I \in Info(L)$,

(1) for any $n \in N$, $S(I^n)$ is defined, and

(2) there is a $p \in PAT$ such that $L(p) = L$ and for almost all $n \in N$, $S(I^n) = p$.

Definition 5. *PAT is called consistently learnable in the limit from informant (abbr. $PAT \in CONS - INF$) iff there is an effective strategy S from N into Pat such that*

(1) $PAT \in LIM - INF$ by S

(2) for any $L \in PAT$, $I \in Info(L)$ and $n \in N$, $I_n^+ \subseteq L(S(I^n))$ and $I_n^- \cap L(S(I^n)) = \emptyset$.

Note that a consistent learning strategy is required to correctly reflect both, the positive as well as the negative data it has already seen. Next we sharpen Definition 5 by additionally requiring polynomial time computability of S.

Definition 6. *PAT is called (consistently) learnable in the limit from informant in polynomial time (abbr. $PAT \in Poly - LIM - INF$ ($PAT \in Poly - CONS - INF$)) iff there are a strategy S and a polynomial pol such that*

(1) $PAT \in LIM - INF$ ($PAT \in CONS - INF$) by S, and

(2) for any $L \in PAT$, $I \in Info(L)$ and any $n \in N$, time to compute $S(I^n) \leq pol(length(I^n))$.

Learning from text is analogously defined in replacing everywhere "informant" by "text". However, one point should be stated more precisely, i.e., consistent learning on text does only require consistency with the data contained in the text. In order to have an example illuminating the difference we could define a strategy that initially outputs x_1. Since $L(x_1)$ contains any string over Σ but the empty one, this hypothesis is consistent on text for any finite input. However, since the strategy has to converge, it cannot maintain this hypothesis ad infinitum. Finally, we use $LIM - TXT$, $CONS - TXT$ as well as $Poly - CONS - TXT$ to denote the corresponding learning types on text.

Now we can precisely state the result mentioned above.

Theorem 7.

(1) $PAT \in CONS - INF$

(2) If $P \neq NP$, then $PAT \notin Poly - CONS - INF$.

(3) $PAT \in Poly - LIM - INF$

Sketch of proof. Assertion (1) is proved in applying Gold's (1967) enumeration technique. Therefore, let $(p_i)_{i \in N}$ be any fixed effective enumeration of *Pat*. Let $L \in PAT$, let $I \in Info(L)$ be any informant, and let $n \in N$. Define $S(I^n)$ to be the first pattern p in the enumeration of *Pat* satisfying $I_n^+ \subseteq L(p)$ and $I_n^- \cap L(p) = \emptyset$. Since membership for pattern languages is uniformly decidable (cf. Angluin (1980)), S is computable. Due to the definition of S, consistency is obvious. Moreover, the strategy converges to the first pattern in the enumeration that generates the language L to be learnt. Note that S cannot be computed in polynomial time, unless $\mathcal{P} = \mathcal{NP}$, since membership for pattern languages is $\mathcal{NP}$-complete (cf. Angluin (1980)).

Next we have to show that there is no strategy at all consistently learning PAT that is computable in polynomial time, if $\mathcal{P} \neq \mathcal{NP}$. This part of the proof is done by showing the $\mathcal{NP}$-hardness of an appropriate problem defined below. For any information concerning reducibility as well as $\mathcal{NP}$-complete problems the reader is referred to Garey and Johnson (1979). First we define the following decision problem SEP. Let W^+, $W^- \subseteq \Sigma^*$. We say that W^+, W^- are *separable* iff there is a pattern p such that $W^+ \subseteq L(p)$ and $W^- \cap L(p) = \emptyset$. SEP denotes the problem of *deciding* whether any W^+, $W^- \subseteq \Sigma^*$ are separable. Moreover, by $CSEP$ we denote the problem of *constructing* a separating pattern p for any given W^+, W^- that are separable. The proof of assertion (2) is completed via the following lemmata.

Lemma A. (Ko, Marron, Tzeng, 1990)
$3 - SAT$ *is polynomial time reducible to* SEP.

Lemma B. $CSEP$ *is* $\mathcal{NP}$-*hard.*

Proof of Lemma B. Let $C3 - SAT$ denote the problem to construct a satisfying assignment to any satisfiable instance from $3 - SAT$.
Claim 1. $C3 - SAT \in \mathcal{P}$ implies $3 - SAT \in \mathcal{P}$

Assume there is an algorithm $\mathcal{A}$ having a running time that is bounded by some polynomial *pol* in the length of its input, and that, moreover, on input C returns a satisfying assignment of C, if C is satisfiable. Now let C be any instance of $3 - SAT$. Start $\mathcal{A}$ on input C. Since any polynomial is time constructable, we we may combine $\mathcal{A}$ with a clock, i.e., we can efficiently stop $\mathcal{A}$ on input C after at most $length(C)$ steps of computation. Then two cases are possible. Either $\mathcal{A}$ returns nothing. Consequently, C cannot be satisfiable. Otherwise $\mathcal{A}$ outputs an assignment *ass* within the given time bound. Then one can check in polynomial time whether or not *ass* indeed satisfies C. In case it does, we know that C is satisfiable. In case it does not C is again not satisfiable, since otherwise $\mathcal{A}$ fails.

Note that we *cannot* prove the $\mathcal{NP}$-hardness of $CSEP$ in the same manner as in showing claim 1, since membership for pattern languages is $\mathcal{NP}$-complete, i.e., one cannot check in polynomial time whether a pattern eventually returned on input (W^+, W^-) does indeed separate these sets. However, we overcome this difficulty in showing the following claim.
Claim 2. $CSEP \in \mathcal{P}$ implies $C3 - SAT \in \mathcal{P}$

In accordance with Lemma A let *red* be any polynomial time reduction of $3 - SAT$ to SEP. Suppose, there is an algorithm $\mathcal{B}$ solving $CSEP$ in polynomial time. Now let C be any satisfiable instance of $3 - SAT$. The wanted satisfying assignment may be computed as follows. First, compute $red(C) = (W^+, W^-)$. Since C is satisfiable, we get that (W^+, W^-) are separable. Next compute $p = \mathcal{B}(W^+, W^-)$. Finally, let *ass* be the assignment contructed to p in the proof of the "only-if" direction of Lemma A. Since *red* is computable in time bounded by a polynomial in the length of C, the length of

(W^+, W^-) is bounded by a polynomial in the length of C, too. Consequently, ass is polynomial time computable. Hence, $C3 - SAT \in \mathcal{P}$, if $CSEP \in \mathcal{P}$.

Finally, Claim 1 and 2 directly yield Lemma B.

The proof of assertion (2) is completed by showing the next claim.

Claim 3. $PAT \in Poly - CONS - INF$ implies $CSEP \in \mathcal{P}$.

Suppose $PAT \in Poly - CONS - INF$ by some strategy S. Let W^+, W^- be any two separable sets, and let p be any pattern separating them. Let $I \in Info(L(p))$ be an arbitrary informant such that, for some n, $I_n^+ = W^+$ and $I_n^- = W^-$. In accordance with the definition of separabilty, I obviously exists. Consequently, $S(I^n)$ has to be defined, and furthermore, $q = S(I^n)$ has to be a pattern separating W^+, W^-, too. Finally, S is polynomial time computable. Hence we get $CSEP \in \mathcal{P}$.

It remains to prove assertion (3). In Lange and Wiehagen (1991) $PAT \in Poly - LIM - TXT$ has been shown. The corresponding strategy witnessing $PAT \in Poly - LIM - TXT$ works by "overlooking" data, i.e., it ignores all but the actually shortest strings of the language to be learnt. It turns out that sufficiently many really shortest strings of a pattern language do suffice to learn it. From these remaining strings a hypothesis is generated in time that is even polynomial in the length of these strings. However, it is most of the time inconsistent, while being correct in the limit. Let S denote the strategy from Lange and Wiehagen (1991) proving $PAT \in Poly - LIM - TXT$. We define a strategy $\tilde{S}$ witnessing $PAT \in Poly - LIM - INF$ as follws: On any input I^n we set $\tilde{S}(I^n) = S(I_n^+)$. This proves the theorem.

Note that $\tilde{S}$ even works semi–consistently, since $I_n^- \cap L(\tilde{S}(I^n)) = \emptyset$ is valid for all $n \in N$. Moreover, $\tilde{S}$ works iteratively as S does.

q.e.d.

At this point some remarks are mandatory. It should be mentioned that any consistent strategy S, independently of how complex it is, may be trivially converted into an inconsistent one that works in quadratic time. This is done as follows. On input I^n, one simulates S on input I^1, I^2,...,I^n no more than n steps, and outputs $S(I^k)$, where k is the largest number $y \leq n$ for which $S(I^y)$ is computable within at most n steps.

However, it is obvious that this simulation technique does not yield any advantage. It does neither increase the efficiency of the learning algorithm, if one sums up all steps of computation until the learning task is successfully solved; nor does it enlarge the learning power. What we are looking for are "intelligent" inconsistent techniques. In our opinion, Lange and Wiehagen's (1991) refined strategy behaves thus by the following reasons. First, it avoids membership tests at all. Second, it computes its current hypothesis iteratively. Third, the test whether or not it should eventually change its mind is extremely simple and may be executed in linear time. Moreover, the algorithm yielding an eventually new hypothesis performs exclusively syntactical or formal manipulations over strings.

Finally, let $Poly - CONS - LEXINF$ ($Poly - CONS - LEXTXT$) be the learning type obtained from $Poly - CONS - INF$ ($Poly - CONS - TXT$) by restricting the information presentation from any informant $I \in Info(L)$ (any text $T \in Text(L)$) to the lexicographically ordered one (cf. Definition 6). Furthermore, let S be a strategy such that $PAT \in LIM - INF\ (LIM - TXT)$ by S. Then, for any $L \in PAT$ and $D \in Info(L) \cup Text(L)$, let

$$Conv(S, D) = \text{the least number } m \text{ such that for all } n \geq m,\ S(D^n) = S(D^m)$$

denote the *stage of convergence* of S on D.

We have been surprised to obtain the following theorem. It actually states that the inconsistent learning strategy of Lange and Wiehagen (1991) may behave both, i.e., consistently and efficiently, if it receives the crucial information on the language to be learnt in an appropriate order.

Theorem 8

(1) There are a strategy $\tilde{S}$ and a polynomial pol such that

    (i) $PAT \in Poly - CONS - LEXINF$ by $\tilde{S}$,

    (ii) for any $p \in Pat$, there is an $I_p \in Info(L(p))$ such that

        – $\tilde{S}$ works consistently on I_p,

        – $\sum_{n=0}^{Conv(S, I_p)}$ time to compute $\tilde{S}(I_p^n) \leq pol(length(p))$.

(2) There are a strategy S and a polynomial pol such that

    (i) $PAT \in Poly - CONS - LEXTXT$ by S,

    (ii) for any $p \in Pat$, there is a $T_p \in Text(L(p))$ such that

        – S works consistently on T_p,

        – $\sum_{n=0}^{Conv(S, T_p)}$ time to compute $S(T_p^n)) \leq pol(length(p))$.

Sketch of proof. Assertion (1), part (i) is proved using the strategy $\tilde{S}$ from the proof of Theorem 7, assertion (3) above. Then part (i) follows by Lemma 2 of Lange and Wiehagen (1991). Part (ii) directly follows from Theorem 2, assertion (3) of Lange and Wiehagen (1991).

The first part of assertion (2) is an immediate consequence of the proof of Theorem 1 in Lange and Wiehagen (1991), while the second follows as above.

                                    q.e.d.

We conjecture that Theorem 7 remains valid for $CONS - TXT$. Assertion (1) has been proved by Angluin (1980). As already mentioned above, the strategy from Lange and Wiehagen (1991) directly yields (3). Consequently, the only part not yet proved is (2). One reason why (2) seems to be easier provable for informant than for text is the following. A strategy working consistently on informant has to work "hard" at any step of the learning process, while a consistent strategy on text may output x_1 for a while.

5 Conclusions

We have investigated the problem of consistent versus inconsistent learning. In spite of the remarkable power of consistent learning it turns out that this power is not universal.

There are learning problems which can be exclusively solved by inconsistent strategies, i.e., by strategies that do temporarily incorrectly reflect the behavior of the unknown object on data for which the correct behavior of the object is already known at the current stage of the learning process. This phenomenon has been investigated in a "highly theoretical" setting, namely in inductive inference of recursive functions. In this setting the seemingly senseless work of inconsistent strategies could be completely explained by the undecidability of consistency.

However, it turned out that the inconsistency phenomenon is also valid in more realistic situations, namely in domains where consistency is always decidable and the learning strategies have to work in polynomial time. The reason is quite anologous to that in the setting of arbitrary recursive functions. Providing $\mathcal{P} \neq \mathcal{NP}$, the $\mathcal{NP}$-hardness of problems can prevent learning strategies to produce consistent hypotheses in polynomial time.

Moreover, we conjecture that an analogous effect can be shown for incremental learning of *finite* classes of *finite* objects such as Boolean functions.

In any case, we regard the results obtained as giving strong evidence to take fast *inconsistent* strategies seriously into account.

Finally, the presented results do suggest directions of further research such as

1. finding fast inconsistent learning techniques

2. deriving conditions yielding that a given learning problem has no fast consistent solution, but a fast inconsistent one.

Acknowledgement

Substantial part of this work has been performed while the first author was visiting TH Darmstadt. He is grateful indebted to Rüdiger Reischuk and Wolfgang Bibel for providing inspiring working conditions.

Furthermore, both authors would like to acknowledge fruitful discussions with Andreas Jakoby and Christian Schindelhauer.

6 References

[1] Angluin, D., (1980), Finding Patterns Common to a Set of Strings, Journal of Computer and System Sciences 21, 46 - 62

[2] Angluin, D. and C.H. Smith, (1983), Inductive Inference: Theory and Methods, Computing Surveys 15, 3, 237 - 269

[3] Angluin, D. and C.H. Smith, (1987), Formal Inductive Inference, In Encyclopedia of Artificial Intelligence, St.C. Shapiro (Ed.), Vol. 1, pp. 409 - 418, Wiley-Interscience Publication, New York

[4] Barzdin, Ya.M., (1974), Inductive Inference of Automata, Functions and Programs, Proc. Int. Congress of Math., Vancouver, pp. 455 - 460

[5] Blum, M., (1967), Machine Independent Theory of Complexity of Recursive Functions, Journal of the ACM 14, 322 -336

[6] Blum, L. and M. Blum, (1975), Toward a Mathematical Theory of Inductive Inference, Information and Control 28, 122 - 155

[7] Fulk, M.,(1988), Saving the Phenomena: Requirements that Inductive Inference Machines Not Contradict Known Data, Information and Computation 79, 193 - 209

[8] Garey, M.R. and D.S. Johnson, (1979), Computers and Intractability, A Guide to the Theory of $\mathcal{NP}$-completness, Freeman and Company, San Francisco

[9] Gold, M.E., (1965), Limiting Recursion, Journal of Symbolic Logic 30, 28 - 48

[10] Gold, M.E., (1967), Language Identification in the Limit, Information and Control 10, 447 - 474

[11] Jantke, K.P. and H.R. Beick, (1981), Combining Postulates of Naturalness in Inductive Inference, Journal of Information Processing and Cybernetics (EIK) 17, 465 - 484

[12] Kearns, M. and L. Pitt, (1989), A Polynomial-time Algorithm for Learning k-variable Pattern Languages From Examples. In Proc. 2nd Annual Workshop on Computational Learning Theory, R. Rivest, D. Haussler, and M.K. Warmuth (Eds.), pp. 57 - 70, Morgan Kaufmann Publishers Inc.

[13] Ko, Ker-I, Marron, A. and W.G. Tzeng, (1990), Learning String Patterns and Tree Patterns From Examples, Proc. 7th Conference on Machine Learning, pp. 384 - 391

[14] Lange, S. and R. Wiehagen, (1991), Polynomial-Time Inference of Arbitrary Pattern Languages, New Generation Computing 8, 361 - 370

[15] Lange, S. and T. Zeugmann, (1991), Monotonic versus Non-monotonic Language Learning, in Proc. 2nd International Workshop on Nonmonotonic and Inductive Logic, December 1991, Reinhardsbrunn, to appear in Lecture Notes in Artificial Intelligence

[16] Lange, S. and T. Zeugmann, (1992), Types of Monotonic Language Learning and Their Characterization, Proc. 5th Annual Workshop on Computational Learning Theory, Morgan Kaufmann Publishers Inc.

[17] Nix, R.P., (1983), Editing by Examples, Yale University, Dept. Computer Science, Technical Report 280

[18] Osherson, D., Stob, M. and S. Weinstein, (1986), Systems that Learn. An Introduction to Learning Theory for Cognitive and Computer Scientists, MIT-Press, Cambridge, Massachusetts

[19] Porat, S. and J.A. Feldman, (1988), Learning Automata from Ordered Examples, in Proc. First Workshop on Computational Learning Theory, D. Haussler and L. Pitt (Eds.), pp. 386 - 396, Morgan Kaufmann Publishers Inc.

[20] Rogers, H.Jr., (1967), Theory of Recursive Functions and Effective Computability, Mc Graw–Hill, New York

[21] Shinohara, T., (1982), Polynomial Time Inference of Extended Regular Pattern Languages, RIMS Symposia on Software Science and Engineering, Kyoto, Lecture Notes in Computer Science 147, pp. 115 - 127, Springer–Verlag

[22] Solomonoff, R., (1964), A Formal Theory of Inductive Inference, Information and Control 7, 1 - 22, 234 - 254

[23] Wiehagen, R., (1976), Limes–Erkennung rekursiver Funktionen durch spezielle Strategien, Journal of Information Processing and Cybernetics (EIK) 12, 93 - 99

[24] Wiehagen, R., (1978a), Zur Theorie der algorithmischen Erkennung, Dissertation B, Humboldt–Universität zu Berlin

[25] Wiehagen, R., (1978b), Characterization Problems in the Theory of Inductive Inference, Proc. 5th Colloquium on Automata, Languages and Programming, Udine, July 17 - 21, G. Ausiello and C. Böhm (Eds.), Lecture Notes in Computer Science 62, pp. 494 - 508, Springer-Verlag

[26] Zeugmann, T., (1983), A–posteriori Characterizations in Inductive Inference of Recursive Functions, Journal of Information Processing and Cybernetics (EIK) 19, 559 - 594

Some Experiments With a Learning Procedure[*]

Kurt Ammon[†]

Windmühlenweg 27, W-2000 Hamburg 52
Germany

Abstract

The input of the learning procedure is a set of data and a set of axioms giving the domains and ranges of elementary functions including predicates. It repeatedly applies these axioms to the input data which yields more and more complex compositions of functions. These compositions are used to form quantified propositions, set constructors, and programs which are composed of the elementary functions in the input. The procedure is controlled by the input data and by partial results such as partial programs which were previously produced. In computer experiments, the procedure classified structured objects such as trains, generated mathematical conjectures such as Goldbach's conjecture, rediscovered laws of physics such as Ohm's law, constructed polygon concepts from line drawings, and developed powerful theorem provers from simple proofs.

1   Introduction

Goldbach's conjecture says that every even number is the sum of two prime numbers, i.e., for every even number n, there are two prime numbers p and q such that $n = p+q$ holds. For example, the natural number 8 is the sum of the prime numbers 3 and 5. The conjecture is composed of the function "+" and the predicates "*is-even*" and "=" whose domains and ranges are natural numbers. A simple procedure to construct the conjecture is to introduce variables for natural numbers and prime numbers, to produce compositions of the functions and predicates "+", "*is-even*", and "=" by means of their domains and ranges, and to bind the variables in the compositions by quantifiers. For example, let n be a variable for a natural number and let p and q be variables for prime numbers. The application of the function "+" to the numbers p and q yields the number "$p + q$". The application of the predicates "*is-even*", and "=" to the numbers n and $p + q$ yields the propositions "*is-even*(n)" and "$n = p + q$". Goldbach's conjecture can be produced from these propositions by binding the variable n by a universal quantifier and the variables p and q by existential quantifiers. These considerations formed a starting point for the development of a learning procedure for the construction of new knowledge which is

---

[*]This work, in whole or in part, describes components of machines or processes protected by one or more patents or patent applications in Europe, the United States of America, or elsewhere. Further information is available from the author.

[†]This work was supported in part by the German Science Foundation (DFG).

described in Section 3. This knowledge is represented in the language CL which is introduced in Section 2. Section 4 describes how the procedure developed a powerful theorem prover from a simple proof. Section 5 discusses further applications of the procedure.

2 Knowledge Representation

Propositions, set constructors, and programs are represented in the knowledge representation language CL. We describe essential aspects of the interpreter of CL which efficiently evaluates quantified propositions and set constructors whose variables refer to finite sets.

Let S be a finite set and p be a unary predicate defined on S. A universal proposition

$$\forall x(x \in S \rightarrow p(x)), \tag{1}$$

i.e., the proposition $p(x)$ holds for all elements $x \in S$, is evaluated by successively substituting each element of S for the variable x in $p(x)$ and evaluating the resulting propositions. If all propositions yield true, the universal proposition (1) is true. Otherwise, it is false. Existential propositions

$$\exists x(x \in S \wedge p(x)), \tag{2}$$

i.e., there is an element $x \in S$ such that $p(x)$ holds, are also evaluated by successively substituting each element of S for the variable x in $p(x)$ and evaluating the resulting propositions. If all propositions yield false, the existential proposition (2) is false. Otherwise, it is true. Furthermore, the interpreter of the language CL processes set constructors

$$\{f(x) : x \in S \wedge p(x)\}, \tag{3}$$

where S is a finite set, f is a function on S, and p is a predicate on S. Such a set constructor is evaluated by applying the function f to the elements of S for which $p(x)$ holds. This yields the set represented by the set constructor (3). Quantified propositions and set constructors may contain several variables that refer to finite sets. They are evaluated by processing the variables and their sets successively in the same manner as a single variable and its set are processed.

An example of a program in the language CL is the automatic theorem prover in Table 1 which is represented by two set constructors. The theorem prover produces proofs of theorems in group theory. A group is a set with a binary associative operation such that the axioms $1x = x = x1$ and $x^{-1}x = 1 = xx^{-1}$ hold for all elements x of the group. A very simple theorem in group theory is $1^{-1} = 1$, i.e., the inverse of the identity 1 of a group is equal to the identity 1 itself. Table 2 gives a proof of this theorem which was generated by the theorem prover in Table 1. The proof consists of two proof steps. The first proof step substitutes the term 1^{-1} for the variable x in the axiom $x = x1$ which yields the equation $1^{-1} = 1^{-1}1$. The second proof step substitutes the indentity 1 for the variable x in the axiom $x^{-1}x = 1$ which yields the equation $1^{-1}1 = 1$. The first proof step is generated by the first set constructor in Table 1. The first three lines in this set constructor say that the left side t_1 of an equation $t_1 = t_2$ in a proof step is the left side of

$\{(t_1 = t_2, a, s)\ :$	$\textit{is-a-proof-step}(t_1 = t_2, a, s) \wedge$
	$t_1 = \textit{left-side}(\textit{THEOREM}) \vee$
	$\qquad t_1 \in \textit{right-sides}(\textit{equations-in}(\textit{PREC.-STEPS})) \wedge$
	$\textit{substituents}(s) \subseteq \textit{subterms}(\textit{left-side}(\textit{THEOREM}))\,\}$
$\{(t_1 = t_2, a, s)\ :$	$\textit{is-a-proof-step}(t_1 = t_2, a, s) \wedge$
	$t_1 \in \textit{right-sides}(\textit{equations-in}(\textit{PREC.-STEPS})) \wedge$
	$t_2 \neq \textit{left-side}(\textit{THEOREM}) \wedge$
	$\textit{variables}(\textit{left-side}(a)) \supseteq \textit{variables}(\textit{right-side}(a)) \wedge$
	$\textit{number-of-symbols}(\textit{left-side}(a)) \geq$
	$\qquad\qquad \textit{number-of-symbols}(\textit{right-side}(a))\,\}$

Table 1: The two set constructors in the theorem prover

Equation $(t_1 = t_2)$	Axiom (a)	Substitution (s)
$1^{-1} = 1^{-1}1$	$x = x1$	$1^{-1}/x$
$1^{-1}1 = 1$	$x^{-1}x = 1$	$1/x$

Table 2: A proof of the $THEOREM$ $1^{-1} = 1$

the $THEOREM$ or the right side of an equation in a preceding proof step: The left side 1^{-1} of the equation in the first proof step is the left side of the $THEOREM$ $1^{-1} = 1$. The last line of the first set constructor says that the substituents of the substitution s are subterms of the left side of the $THEOREM$: The substituent 1^{-1} in the first proof step in Table 2 is a subterm of the left side 1^{-1} of the $THEOREM$ $1^{-1} = 1$. The second set constructor in Table 1 produces the second proof step. The last three lines of the second set constructor say that the variables in the right side of an axiom are contained in its left side and that the number of symbols in the right side of an axiom is less than or equal to the number of symbols in its left side. This entails a simplification of right side $1^{-1}1$ of the first equation which yields the equation $1^{-1}1 = 1$ in the second proof step. The equations in the first and the second proof step immediately imply the $THEOREM$ $1^{-1} = 1$ to be proved.

An optimizing compiler translates the theorem prover in Table 1, which is represented by two set constructors, into efficient procedural code. In an experiment, the translated theorem prover produced proofs of nine theorems in group theory without any human intervention. The first five theorems said that the inverse of the identity is the identity itself (see Table 2), that the identity of a group is unique, that the inverse of each element is unique, that a left identity is a right identity, and that a left inverse is a right inverse. The sixth theorem said that $x^{-1}y^{-1}yx = 1$ holds for all elements x and y of a group, the seventh theorem that $x^2 = x$ implies $x = 1$, the eighth theorem that linear equation solvability implies the existence of an identity, and the ninth theorem that $x^2 = 1$ implies group commutativity. The ninth theorem is the "limit of the capability" of the heuristic theorem prover ADEPT developed at MIT in the mid-sixties (Loveland, 1984, p. 13). Table 3 compares the run times of the theorem prover in Table 1 and McCune's (1990, 1991) theorem prover OTTER 2.2 for proving these theorems on an IBM PC AT. OTTER is often regarded as the most powerful and fastest resolution-based theorem prover. Table 3 shows that

Theorem	Theorem prover in Table 1	OTTER 2.2
1	1.93 sec	3.41 sec
2	.66 sec	3.46 sec
3	9.06 sec	10.88 sec
4	2.69 sec	6.26 sec
5	8.01 sec	9.51 sec
6	9.45 sec	31.92 sec
7	6.70 sec	9.62 sec
8	11.46 sec	98.41 sec
9	29.27 sec	10.16 sec

Table 3: A run time comparison between the theorem prover in Table 1 and OTTER 2.2

the theorem prover in Table 1 is faster than OTTER in all theorems but the last one. OTTER 2.2 takes 8 minutes and 22.03 seconds to generate a proof of SAM's Lemma on an IBM PC AT from the axioms for a modular lattice in McCharen *et al.* (1976, p. 779). This set of axioms is not complete because it does not contain the ordinary lattice operations "join" and "meet", i.e., the existence of a minimum and a maximum in McCharen *et al.'s* (1976, p. 779) representation. A variant of the theorem prover in Table 1 generated a proof of SAM's Lemma from a complete set of axioms in ordinary representation in 3 minutes and 43.66 seconds.

Section 4 will describe how the theorem prover in Table 1 was automatically constructed by a learning procedure which is introduced in the next section.

3   Learning Procedure

The learning procedure constructs propositions and programs in the language CL from data and axioms giving the domains and ranges of elementary functions including predicates. It repeatedly applies these axioms to the input data which yields more and more complex compositions of functions. These compositions are used to form quantified propositions and set constructors which are composed of the elementary functions in the input. The set constructors are used to represent programs. The procedure is controlled by the input data and by partial results such as partial programs which were previously produced. This section describes a simple specific embodiment of the procedure which constructs quantified propositions by means of three operators. The *initial operator* initializes the construction of propositions by introducing variables. The *proposition operator* applies axioms giving the domains and ranges of functions including predicates to the initial variables which yields propositions. The *quantifier operator* binds variables in these propositions by quantifiers which yields quantified propositions. The procedure, which is implemented in a program called SHUNYATA, is illustrated by a detailed description of the construction of Goldbach's conjecture.

1.	$n \in N$	variable n for an element of N
2.	$p \in P$	variable p for an element of P
3.	$q \in P$	additional variable q
4.	$n \in \mathbf{N}$	step 1 and axiom (4)
5.	$p \in \mathbf{N}$	step 2 and axiom (5)
6.	$q \in \mathbf{N}$	step 3 and axiom (5)
7.	$is\text{-}a\text{-}proposition(is\text{-}even(n))$	step 4 and axiom (6)
8.	$p + q \in \mathbf{N}$	steps 5, 6 and axiom (7)
9.	$is\text{-}a\text{-}proposition(n = p + q)$	steps 4, 8 and axiom (8)

Table 4: The construction of the proposition $n = p + q$

3.1 Initialization

The *initial operator* of the learning procedure initializes the construction of propositions by introducing variables for elements of the sets in the input data. Examples of input data are the set of natural numbers $N = \{1, 2, ..., 10\}$ and the set of $P = \{1, 2, 3, 5, 7\}$ which contains the natural number 1 and the prime numbers 2, 3, 4, 5 and 7. The initial operator introduces a variable $n \in N$ and a variable $p \in P$ for elements of the sets N and P which yields the first two steps in Table 4. Furthermore, an additional variable $q \in P$ for another element of P is introduced which yields the third step in Table 4. The operator also initializes another set of variables for the construction of propositions which introduces an additional variable for an element of the set N. The subsequent operators of the learning procedure, i.e., the proposition and the quantifier operator, process this set of variables separately.

3.2 Propositions

The *proposition operator* of the learning procedure applies axioms giving the domains of functions including predicates to the initial variables which yields propositions. Examples of axioms with regard to the sets N and P in Section 3.1 are

$$\forall x (x \in N \rightarrow x \in \mathbf{N}), \tag{4}$$

which says that the elements of N are elements of the set of natural numbers $\mathbf{N}$,

$$\forall x (x \in P \rightarrow x \in \mathbf{N}), \tag{5}$$

which says that the elements of P are natural numbers,

$$\forall x (x \in \mathbf{N} \rightarrow is\text{-}a\text{-}proposition(is\text{-}even(x))), \tag{6}$$

which says that "$is\text{-}even(x)$" is a proposition if x is a natural number,

$$\forall x, y (x \in \mathbf{N} \wedge y \in \mathbf{N} \rightarrow x + y \in \mathbf{N}), \tag{7}$$

which says that $x + y$ is a natural number if x and y are natural numbers, and

$$\forall x, y (x \in \mathbf{N} \wedge y \in \mathbf{N} \rightarrow is\text{-}a\text{-}proposition(x = y)), \tag{8}$$

which says that "$x = y$" is a proposition if x and y are natural numbers. The repeated application of the axioms (4), (5), (6), (7), and (8) to the initial variables in Table 4 yields steps 4–9 in Table 4.

3.3 Quantified Propositions

The *quantifier operator* of the learning procedure produces quantified propositions, i.e., existential and universal propositions. First, it binds the free variables of propositions by existential quantifiers which yields existential propositions. For example, it binds the variables n, p, and q in the proposition $n = p + q$ in step 9 in Table 1 by an existential quantifier which yields the existential proposition

$$\exists n, p, q(n \in N \wedge p \in P \wedge q \in P \wedge n = p + q). \tag{9}$$

If an existential proposition such as (9) is true, the operator attempts to generalize it by replacing existential quantifiers by universal quantifiers. For example, the replacement of the existential quantifier containing the variable n in (9) by a universal quantifier yields the universal proposition

$$\forall n(n \in N \rightarrow \exists p, q(p \in P \wedge q \in P \wedge n = p + q)). \tag{10}$$

Because the proposition (10) is false and thus too general, a proposition in Table 4 containing the variable n such as " *is-even(n)*" is added to its antecedent $n \in N$. This yields the universal proposition

$$\forall n(n \in N \wedge \text{is-even}(n) \rightarrow \exists p, q(p \in P \wedge q \in P \wedge n = p + q)) \tag{11}$$

which is true. It says that for every even number $n \in N$, there are two prime numbers $p \in P$ and $q \in P$ such that $n = p + q$ holds. This is Goldbach's conjecture with regard to the sets N and P. SHUNYATA constructed the proposition (11) and six further conjectures in some six minutes. Four further conjectures were trivial. For example, one of these conjectures said that for all prime numbers $p \in P$, there is a natural number $n \in N$ and a prime number $q \in P$ such that $p+n = 2q$ holds. This conjecture is trivial because you can choose $n = p$ and $q = p$. The sixth conjecture said that for every prime number p, there is a prime number q and a natural number n such that $p+q = 3n$ holds. The seventh conjecture said that for every prime number p, there is a prime number q and a natural number n such that $p+q = 4n$ holds. The sixth and the seventh conjecture came as a surprise to me because I could not easily find proofs or refutations of these conjectures. Even a specialist in number theory of the mathematics department of the University of Hamburg could not immediately tell whether the conjectures were known or provable. After some days he told me that they were true and related to the theory of arithmetic progressions. A proof of the sixth conjecture, which was discovered with the assistance of the SHUNYATA program, is: For $p = 3$, you can choose $q = 3$ and $n = 2$. For any prime number $p \neq 3$, you can choose $q = 2$ or $q = 7$. Any sequence of three consecutive natural numbers such as 7, 8, and 9 contains one number that is divisible by 3 such as 9. In particular, the sequence p, $p + 1$, and $p + 2$ contains a number that is divisible by 3. Therefore, either $p+1$ or $p+2$ is divisible by 3 because p is a prime number. If $p + 1$ is divisible by 3, $p + 7$ is also divisible by 3 because the difference 6 between $p+1$ and $p+7$ is divisible by 3. It follows that either $p+7$ or $p+2$ is divisible by 3, i.e., either $p+7 = 3n$ or $p+2 = 3n$ holds with a natural number n. This completes the proof of the sixth conjecture. The seventh conjecture can analogously be proved if one chooses $q = 2$, $q = 3$, or $q = 5$.

Equation ($t_1 = t_2$)	Axiom (a)	Substitution (s)
$(x^{-1})^{-1} = 1(x^{-1})^{-1}$	$x = 1x$	$(x^{-1})^{-1}/x$
$1(x^{-1})^{-1} = xx^{-1}(x^{-1})^{-1}$	$1 = xx^{-1}$	x/x
$xx^{-1}(x^{-1})^{-1} = x1$	$xx^{-1} = 1$	x^{-1}/x
$x1 = x$	$x1 = x$	x/x

Table 5: A proof of the theorem $(x^{-1})^{-1} = x$

$$\{ (t_1 = t_2, a, s) : \quad \text{is-a-proof-step}(t_1 = t_2, a, s) \land$$
$$t_1 = \text{left-side}(THEOREM) \land$$
$$\text{substituents}(s) \subseteq \text{subterms}(\text{left-side}(THEOREM)) \}$$

Table 6: The set constructor for the first proof step

The construction of the proposition (10) is controlled by the fact that the proposition (9) is true and the construction of the Goldbach's conjecture (11) is controlled by the fact that the proposition (10) is false, i.e., the construction of the propositions (10) and (11) is controlled by more elementary partial results which are fed back into the construction process and the structure of Goldbach's conjecture (11) is a successive extension of the structure of the partial results (9) and (10). This "structural feedback" principle, which feeds back more elementary partial results into the construction process, is an essential feature of the learning procedure. It makes an efficient construction of complex propositions and programs possible.

4 Theorem Prover

In another experiment which was more complex than the preceding experiment, SHUNYATA developed the theorem prover in Table 1 from a proof of a simple theorem in group theory in some three hours on an IBM PC AT. The theorem was that $(x^{-1})^{-1} = x$ holds for all elements x of a group. Its proof is given in Table 5. The input of SHUNYATA contained sixteen axioms. The first two axioms say that the proof consists of proof steps and that the axioms of group theory are equations. The remaining axioms give the domains and ranges of the elementary functions and relations the theorem prover in Table 1 is composed of. In this experiment, the third operator of the learning procedure produced set constructors instead of quantified propositions (see Section 3.3). SHUNYATA analyzed the proof steps of the proof in Table 5 one by one, produced a set constructor for each step, and attempted to unify the set constructor for the current proof step and the preceding proof step. The analysis of the first proof step yielded the set constructor in Table 6. We describe the construction of the proposition

$$t_1 = \text{left-side}(THEOREM) \tag{12}$$

in the set constructor in Table 6 in detail. The construction is initialized by introducing the name $THEOREM$ for the theorem $(x^{-1})^{-1} = 1$ and variables t_1, t_2, a, and s for the left and the right side of the equation, the axiom, and the substitution in a proof step. This yields the first two steps in Table 7. The name $THEOREM$ in

1.	is-an-equation($THEOREM$)	name for the theorem
2.	is-a-proof-step($t_1 = t_2, a, s$)	variables for a proof step
3.	is-a-term(left-side($THEOREM$))	step 1 and axiom (13)
4.	is-a-term(t_1)	step 2 and axiom (14)
5.	is-a-proposition(P)[1]	steps 3, 4 and axiom (15)

[1]P denotes the proposition $t_1 = $ left-side($THEOREM$)

Table 7: The construction of the proposition $t_1 = $ left-side($THEOREM$)

$$\{\,(t_1 = t_2, a, s) : \quad \text{is-a-proof-step}(t_1 = t_2, a, s) \land$$
$$t_1 \in \text{right-sides}(\text{equations-in}(PREC.\text{-}STEPS)) \land$$
$$\text{substituents}(s) \subseteq \text{variables}(\text{left-side}(THEOREM))\,\}$$

Table 8: The set constructor for the second proof step

the first step is later used in propositions representing properties of proof steps such as the proposition (12). The variables t_1, t_2, a, and s in the second step are later bound by a set constructor. The input of SHUNYATA contained the axiom

$$\forall x(\text{is-an-equation}(x) \rightarrow \text{is-a-term}(\text{left-side}(x))), \tag{13}$$

which says that the left side of an equation is a term, the axiom

$$\forall t_1, t_2, a, s(\text{is-a-proof-step}(t_1 = t_2, a, s) \rightarrow \text{is-a-term}(t_1) \land ...), \tag{14}$$

which defines the concept of proof steps, and the axiom

$$\forall x, y(\text{is-a-term}(x) \land \text{is-a-term}(y) \rightarrow \text{is-a-proposition}(x = y)), \tag{15}$$

which says that "$x = y$" is a proposition for all terms x and y. The application of the axioms (13), (14), and (15) to the initial variables in steps 1 and 2 in Table 7 yields steps 3, 4, and 5. Because the proposition in step 5, which says that the left side t_1 of the equation $t_1 = t_2$ in the proof step is equal to the left side of the $THEOREM$, is true, it is used as a property of the first proof step in the set constructor in Table 6. The learning procedure generates many properties of a proof step which are used to form a set constructor. It deletes superfluous properties as follows: It tentatively deletes each property and evaluates the modified set constructor. If the evaluation produces the proof step as efficiently as the original set constructor, the property is deleted definitively. This mechanism deleted all properties of the first proof step but the two properties in Table 6. The analysis of the second proof step in Table 5 produced the set constructor in Table 8. Then, the learning procedure attempted to unify the set constructors in Tables 6 and 8 for the first and the second proof step which yielded the first set constructor in Table 1. The unification is not contained in the special embodiment of the procedure in Section 3. The unification tests whether the properties in the set constructors in Tables 6 and 8 are valid for the first two proof steps in Table 5. The valid properties such as the last property in the set constructor in Table 6 are used in the unified set constructor. The unification forms disjunctions of the other properties in the two constructors in Tables 6 and 8 and tests whether they are valid for the two proof steps. This yields the disjunction in the first set constructor in Table 1. The unification also produces superfluous properties of the proof steps which are deleted in the same manner as superfluous properties of a single proof step are deleted. Analogously to the construction of Goldbach's conjecture (11) in Section 3.3, the construction of the unified set constructor is thus achieved by "structural feedback" because the unified set constructor is a structural revision and extension of the set constructors in Tables 6 and 8. The analysis of the third proof step in Table 5 produced the second set constructor in Table 1. This set constructor also generates the fourth proof step. Thus, the construction of the theorem prover in Table 1 is complete. It came as a surprise to me that the theorem prover produced proofs of nine further theorems in group theory without any human intervention (see Section 2). The "ideas" in the theorem prover were not antcipated by me. Rather, I believed that the generation of such a lot of proofs can only be achieved by several variations of the theorem prover whose set constructors contain various properties of the proof steps (see Ammon, 1988, p. 561). By means of a simple heuristic, the theorem prover developed by SHUNYATA even generated a proof of SAM's Lemma which is a theorem in modular lattice theory and a difficult problem for conventional theorem provers (see Antoniou and Ohlbach, 1983, p. 919; and Ohlbach and Siekmann, 1989, p. 58). The heuristic is required because one of the axioms of modular lattice theory is an implication. Roughly speaking, the heuristic says: If an axiom is an implication, the theorem prover should only use its consequent if it can prove its antecedent within a time limit. Ammon (1988) describes an earlier comparable experiment which also applied the learning procedure to a simple proof. The proofs of SAM's Lemma generated in the two experiments are equivalent. They are simpler than any other proof of SAM's Lemma known to me.

5 Related Work

AM rediscovered mathematical conjectures such as Goldbach's conjecture on the basis of more than 100 initial concepts and some 250 sophisticated heuristics (Lenat, 1982). AM uses a frame-like representation for its concepts. In contrast, SHUN-YATA's concepts are represented in the language CL which models the ordinary representation of concepts in mathematics textbooks. SHUNYATA generates mathematical conjectures on the basis of elementary knowledge about elementary functions such as knowledge about their domains and ranges (see Section 3). The functions, which form the building blocks of the conjectures, might be compared with AM's initial concepts. AM contains a large number of sophisticated heuristics which were developed manually. In contrast, SHUNYATA does not contain heuristics in the beginning but constructs conjectures by "structural feedback", i.e., it repeatedly produces partial results which are fed back into the construction process until a conjecture is achieved. Examples of such partial results for the construction of Goldbach's conjecture (11) in Section 3 are the propositions (9) and (10). The partial results produced by SHUNYATA can be regarded as heuristics which control the construction of conjectures.

   SHUNYATA was also applied to other tasks, for example, the classification of structured objects such as trains (see Stepp and Michalski, 1986), the rediscovery of Ohm's law from the experimental data for nine electric circuits in Langley *et al.* (1983), and the development of programs such as an infimum program from input-output pairs (Ammon, 1991). All these tasks, which more or less represent the limit of the capabilities of complex and very different conventional systems or which are even "beyond the present capabilities of AI" such as the construction of an infimum program (Amarel, 1986), are trivial applications of the learning procedure in SHUNYATA which which took from three up to six minutes to achieve these results. This illustrates the generality and the power of the learning procedure. SHUNYATA can also be used to construct Prolog programs from specific facts. For example, it constructed a Prolog program for list-membership in some five seconds (see Muggleton and Buntine, 1988). The construction of a Prolog program for insertion sort is also a simple task for SHUNYATA (see Shapiro, 1983). In another experiment, SHUNYATA constructed polygon concepts from line drawings in some fourteen minutes (Ammon and Stier, 1988). The development of the theorem prover in Table 1 in Section 2 was more complex than the preceding experiments (see Section 4). Its automatic generation took some three hours. The theorem prover produced proofs of nine further theorems in group theory (see Section 2) and a proof of SAM's Lemma without any human intervention. Table 3 in Section 2 shows that the theorem prover in Table 1 is faster than McCune's (1990, 1991) theorem prover OTTER 2.2 which is often regarded as the most powerful and fastest resolution-based theorem prover. The Markgraf Karl Refutation Procedure is one of the largest software projects in the history of automatic theorem proving (see Bläsius *et al.*, 1981, p. 516; and Loveland, 1984, p. 22). After some fifteen years of development, Ohlbach and Siekmann (1989, p. 58) give SAM's Lemma as the only "more difficult" theorem that their theorem prover has proved. OTTER 2.2 and the Markgraf Karl Refutation Procedure were developed manually. In contrast, SHUNYATA automatically developed the "ideas" for the theorem prover on the basis of elementary knowledge, implemented them in a program in the language CL, and applied the resulting theorem prover to the new theorems without any human intervention (see Ammon, 1992a, 1992b).

6 Conclusion

We have described a learning procedure whose input is a set of data and a set of simple axioms giving the domains and the ranges of elementary functions including predicates. The procedure repeatedly applies these axioms to the input data which yields more and more complex compositions of these functions. Special operators use these compositions to form quantified propositions and set constructors of the language CL which are composed of the elementary functions in the input. The generality and the power of the learning procedure is illustrated by experiments such as the generation of Goldbach's conjecture, the rediscovery of Ohm's law from experimental data, the construction of polygon concepts from line drawings, and the development of an automatic theorem prover which can compete with and even surpass theorem provers whose manual development took many years.

References

Amarel, S. 1986. Program synthesis as a theory formation task: Problem representations and solution methods. In R. S. Michalski, J. G. Carbonell, and T. M. Mitchell (Eds.), *Machine Learning: An Artificial Intelligence Approach* (Vol. 2). San Mateo, Calif.: Morgan Kaufmann.

Ammon, K. 1988. The automatic acquisition of proof methods. *Proceedings of the Seventh National Conference on Artificial Intelligence*, August 21–26, St. Paul, Minnesota, pp. 558–563.

Ammon, K. 1991. Constructing programs from input-output pairs. *Proceedings of the Fifteenth German Workshop on Artificial Intelligence*, September 15–20, Bonn. Berlin: Springer.

Ammon, K. 1992a. Automatic proofs in mathematical logic and analysis. *11th International Conference on Automated Deduction*, Saratoga Springs, U.S.A., Juni 1992. Berlin: Springer.

Ammon, K. 1992b. The SHUNYATA system. *11th International Conference on Automated Deduction*, Saratoga Springs, U.S.A., Juni 1992. Berlin: Springer.

Ammon, K., and Stier, S. 1988. Constructing polygon concepts from line drawings. *Proceedings of the Eighth European Conference on Artificial Intelligence*, August 1–5, Munich, Germany.

Antoniou, G., and Ohlbach, H. J. 1983. Terminator. *Proceedings of the Eighth International Joint Conference on Artificial Intelligence*, August 8–12, Karlsruhe.

Birkhoff, G., and MacLane, S. 1953. *A Survey of Modern Algebra*. New York: Macmillan.

Bläsius, K., Eisinger, N., Siekmann, J., Smolka, G., Herold, A., and Walther, C. 1981. The Markgraf Karl Refutation Procedure. *Proceedings of the Seventh International Joint Conference on Artificial Intelligence*, August, Vancouver.

Langley, P., Bradshaw, G. L., and Simon, H. A. 1983. Rediscovering chemistry with the BACON system. In R. S. Michalski, J. G. Carbonell, and T. M. Mitchell, eds., *Machine Learning: An Artificial Intelligence Approach*, San Mateo, Calif.: Morgan Kaufmann.

Lenat, D. B. 1982. AM: Discovery in mathematics as heuristic search. In R. Davis and D. B. Lenat, *Knowledge-Based Systems in Artificial Intelligence*, McGraw-Hill, New York, 1982.

Loveland, D. W. 1984. Automated theorem proving: a quarter century review. In W. W. Bledsoe and D. W. Loveland, *Automated Theorem Proving: After 25 Years*. Providence, R.I.: American Mathematical Society.

McCharen, J. D., Overbeek, R. A., and Wos, L. A. 1976. Problems and experiments for and with automated theorem-proving programs. *IEEE Transactions on Computers*, Vol. C-25, No. 8, pp. 773–782.

McCune, W. W. 1990. OTTER 2.0 Users Guide. Report ANL-90/9, Argonne National Laboratory, Argonne, Illinois.

McCune, W. W. 1991. What's new in OTTER 2.2. Report ANL/MCS-TM-153, Argonne National Laboratory, Argonne, Illinois.

Muggleton, S., and Buntine, W. 1988. Machine Invention of First-Order Predicates by Inverting Resolution. *Proceedings of the Fifth International Conference on Machine Learning*, June 12–14, Ann Arbor, Michigan. San Mateo, Calif.: Morgan Kaufmann.

Ohlbach, H. J., and Siekmann, J. 1989. The Markgraf Karl Refutation Procedure. University of Kaiserslautern, Department of Computer Science, SEKI Report SR-89-19.

Shapiro, E. Y. 1983. Algorithmic Program Debugging. Cambridge, Mass.: MIT Press.

Stepp, R. S., and Michalski, R. S. 1986. Conceptual clustering: Inventing goal-oriented classifications of structured objects. In R. S. Michalski, J. G. Carbonell, and T. M. Mitchell, eds., *Machine Learning: An Artificial Intelligence Approach*, Vol. II, Morgan Kaufmann, Los Altos, California.

Unions of identifiable classes
of total recursive functions

Kalvis Apsītis*
Rūsiņš Freivalds*
Mārtiņš Kriķis**
Raimonds Simanovskis*
Juris Smotrovs*

ABSTRACT

J.Barzdin [Bar74] has proved that there are classes of total recursive functions which are EX–identifiable but their union is not. We prove that there are no 3 classes U_1, U_2, U_3 such that $U_1 \cup U_2$, $U_1 \cup U_3$, and $U_2 \cup U_3$ would be in EX but $U_1 \cup U_2 \cup U_3 \notin$ EX. For FIN–identification there are 3 classes with the above–mentioned property and there are no 4 classes U_1, U_2, U_3, U_4 such that all 4 unions of triples of these classes would be identifiable but the union of all 4 classes would not. For identification with no more than p minchanges a $(2^{p+2}-1)$–tuple of such classes do exist but there is no (2^{p+2})–tuple with the above–mentioned property.

1 Introduction

Inductive inference is the term coined for developing an algorithm from sample computations. We restrict ourselves to the case in which a total recursive function is to be identified. The first paper in this area was [Gold 67]. For more complete information see surveys [Wie 77, AS 83, Fre 91].

The inductive inference strategy tries to use the initial fragments of the function to develop the algorithm computing it. Hence, from the recursion theory point of view, the strategy is a functional mapping the class R of all total recursive functions into the set N of nonnegative integers. The theory of recursive functions [Rog 67] has developed a precise notion for such a functional. Informally, a recursive functional is computed by a Turing machine with an input tape containing the graph of function f and a work tape. The machine works for some time, then stops after a finite number of steps (decided by the machine itself) and produces the result needed.

Unfortunately, only rather simple classes of functions are identifiable in this sense. (We denote this type of identification by FIN and call these clases of functions to be *finitely*

---

*Institute of Mathematics and Computer Science, University of Latvia, Raiņa bulvāris 29, Riga, Latvia
**Computer Science Department, Yale University, New Haven, CT 06520, U.S.A.

identifiable.) Indeed, in a finite number steps only a finite number of values of the function can be observed. If two functions differ only by the value on a later value of the argument the machine, nevertheless, produces the same output.

A more interesting type of identification is *identification in the limit* (usually denoted by EX) considered in [Gold 67]. Instead of being printed once forever, the output (*hypothesis*) is shown on a *screenboard* and, if there is a need, it may be changed later. The strategy has resulted in y if at some moment it has produced the output y and after that moment the output is never changed.

In [CS 83] and in other papers restricted types of EX–identification (the identification with no more than p mindchanges) and generalized types of EX–identification (the identification where the final output is a program correct but for p values of the argument) are considered.

Many results in the theory of inductive inference merely prove or disprove equality of different types of identification. Of course, the theory contain more mightful results on properties of the identification. One of the first results of such type was the theorem proved by J.Barzdin [Bar 74]: there are two classes of total recursive functions which are EX–identifiable but their union is not.

Since the classes used in [Bar 74] were very different (the class of self–referential functions and the class of the functions of finite support), we were interested to find out whether or not it is possible to generalize this theorem to unions of many classes.

We found that the properties of the union–operation for identifiable classes of total recursive functions are more complicated than it was expected after the paper [Bar 74]. It seems that there is a relationship to the properties of probabilistic inductive inference.

2. EX–identification

Theorem 2.1. Let U_1, U_2, U_3 be classes of total recursive functions. If $U_1 \cup U_2 \in$ EX, $U_1 \cup U_3 \in$ EX and $U_2 \cup U_3 \in$ EX, then $U_1 \cup U_2 \cup U_3 \in$ EX.

Proof. By F_1, F_2, F_3 we denote the strategies EX–identifying the classes $U_1 \cup U_2$, $U_1 \cup U_3$, $U_2 \cup U_3$, respectively. (We assume that the strategies output a hypothesis for arbitrary initial fragment of the function to be identified). For arbitrary function $f \in U_1 \cup U_2 \cup U_3$, at least two strategies out of $\{F_1, F_2, F_3\}$ identify f in the limit correctly.

We construct a new strategy F for EX–identification of $U_1 \cup U_2 \cup U_3$. The strategy F uses the strategies F_1, F_2, F_3 as subroutines.

1^0. We describe the output of the strategy F at the moment of mind–change. (We will describe below in 2^0, at which moments the mind–change takes place.)

The new hypothesis is always based on two strategies $G_1, G_2 \in \{F_1, F_2, F_3\}$, explicitly pointed at the moment of mind–change. If G_1 and G_2 are the two strategies and at the moment of mind–change our strategy F has observed the initial fragment $<f(0), f(1), ..., f(n)>$ of the function f, the current output of F is a program h such that, for every x, the value $\varphi_h(x)$ equals that particular value $\varphi_{G1(<f(0), f(1), ..., f(n)>)}(x)$ or $\varphi_{G2(<f(0), f(1), ..., f(n)>)}(x)$ which is computed first.

2^0. Now we describe the moment when the strategy F decides to have a mind–change. Assume that the preceding hypothesis of F on f was produced on the initial fragment $<f(0), f(1), ..., f(n)>$ and it was based on the $G_1, G_2 \in \{F_1, F_2, F_3\}$.

A mind–change is performed at an m>n such that on the initial fragment $<f(0), f(1), ..., f(m)>$ for the first time one of the following 4 events takes place:

a) the strategy G_1 has a mind–change,

b) the strategy G_2 has a mind–change,

c) the strategy G_1 turns out to be such that $\varphi_{G1(<f(0), f(1), ..., f(n)>)}(y)$ is computed in no more than m steps, it differs from f(y), and y≤m,

d) the strategy G_2 turns out to be such that $\varphi_{G2(<f(0), f(1), ..., f(n)>)}(y)$ is computed in no more than m steps, it differs from f(y), and y≤m.

The new hypothesis produced in the result of the current mind–change is based on the strategies from the set

$$\begin{cases} \{F_1, F_2, F_3\} \setminus \{G_1\} \text{ in the cases a) and c),} \\ \{F_1, F_2, F_3\} \setminus \{G_2\} \text{ in the cases b) and d).} \end{cases}$$

$3.^0$ Now we prove the correctness of F. Namely, we prove that if $f \in U_1 \cup U_2 \cup U_3$ (i.e. if at least two of the strategies F_1, F_2, F_3 correctly identify f), then F identifies f correctly.

First, the strategy F cannot stabilize its output on a hypothesis h producing a value $\varphi_h(x)$ different from f(x). Otherwise either the case c) or d) would take place.

Second, the strategy F stabilizes its output on a hypothesis h which is not a total function, because it would follow from 1^0 that the strategy G_1 and G_2 produce an index of non–total function in the limit.

Third, the strategy F cannot have identifely many mind–changes because otherwise ifinitely many mind–changes of F would be performed after the stabilization of two out of three strategies F_1, F_2, F_3 but this contradicts to the simple observation saying us that after this moment one of cases c) or d) is impossible, the other one can take place at most once and other that no more mind–changes are possible. ∎

Another proof of Theorem 2.1. Let F_1, F_2, F_3 be the strategies for identification of the classes $U_1 \cup U_2$, $U_1 \cup U_3$, $U_2 \cup U_3$, respectively. We consider the following probabilistic algorithm. For arbitrary target function, the probabilistic algorithm acts as F_1, F_2, F_3 with probabilities $1/3$, respectively. If the target function is in $U_1 \cup U_2 \cup U_3$, then it is identified by this probabilistic algorithm with probability at least $2/3$ (since arbitrary U_i belongs to at least 2 unions $U_1 \cup U_2$, $U_1 \cup U_3$, $U_2 \cup U_3$ out of the three). Since $2/3$ strictly exceeds $1/2$, it follows from Assertion 2 in [Fre 79'] that the class $U_1 \cup U_2 \cup U_3$ is identifiable in the limit by a deterministic strategy as well. $\square$

After [Bar 74] it was easy to assume that whatever requirements about the EX–identifiability are considered (e.g. $U_1 \in EX$, $U_2 \in EX$, $U_1 \cup U_2 \notin EX$), they are satisfiable. However, Theorem 2.1 shows that there are non–satisfiable requirements as well (e.g. $U_1 \cup U_2 \in EX$, $U_1 \cup U_3 \in EX$, $U_2 \cup U_3 \in EX$, $U_1 \cup U_2 \cup U_3 \notin EX$). We are interested in the problem how to distinguish between satisfiable and non–satisfiable requirements.

One limitation on the requirements is immediate. If a class of recursive functions is identifiable, then every subclass of it is also identifiable.

For the sequel, we consider only lists of requirements which contain a finite number of classes U_1, U_2, ... , U_n and the requirements are expressed in terms of unions of classes. Every list of this kind can be described by a monotone Boolean function taking values 1 on vectors of the values of the arguments expressing requirement «$\notin EX$» and taking values 0 on vectors expressing requirement «$\in EX$». For instance, the two above–mentioned lists of requirements are described by the Boolean functions $x_1 \& x_2$ and $x_1 \& x_2 \& x_3$, respectively.

We remind that a Boolean function f is called monotone if for arbitrary vectors $(\partial_1,...,\partial_n)$, $(\tau_1,...,\tau_n)$ such that $\partial_1 \leq \tau_1,...,\partial_n \leq \tau_n$, there holds $f((\partial_1,...,\partial_n) \leq f(\tau_1,...,\tau_n)$.

We say that a Boolean function f is EX–satisfiable if there are classes U_1, U_2, ... , U_n of total recursive functions such that for arbitrary vector $(\partial_1,...,\partial_n) \in \{0, 1\}^n$, the union of all the U_i ($i \in \{1,2,...,n\}$), such that $\partial_i = 1$, is in EX if and only if $f(\partial_1,...,\partial_n) = 0$.

We say that a Boolean function f is 3–convolutional if:

1) it is monotone,

2) it equals 0 for all the vectors $(\partial_1,...,\partial_n)$ containing at most one 1,

3) if, for an arbitrary vector $(\partial_1,...,\partial_n)$ and arbitrary three distinct $i,j,k \in \{1,2,...,n\}$, such that the function takes values

$$f(\partial_1, ..., \partial_{i-1}, 0, \partial_{i+1}, ..., \partial_{j-1}, 1, \partial_{j+1}, ..., \partial_{k-1}, 1, \partial_{k+1}, ..., \partial_n) = 0,$$
$$f(\partial_1, ..., \partial_{i-1}, 1, \partial_{i+1}, ..., \partial_{j-1}, 0, \partial_{j+1}, ..., \partial_{k-1}, 1, \partial_{k+1}, ..., \partial_n) = 0,$$
$$f(\partial_1, ..., \partial_{i-1}, 1, \partial_{i+1}, ..., \partial_{j-1}, 1, \partial_{j+1}, ..., \partial_{k-1}, 0, \partial_{k+1}, ..., \partial_n) = 0,$$

then

$$f(\partial_1, ..., \partial_{i-1}, 1, \partial_{i+1}, ..., \partial_{j-1}, 1, \partial_{j+1}, ..., \partial_{k-1}, 1, \partial_{k+1}, ..., \partial_n) = 0.$$

Theorem 2.2. A Boolean function is EX—satisfiable if and only if it is 3—convolutional.

Proof. $\Rightarrow$ Let f be an EX—satisfiable Boolean function and $U_1, \ldots, U_n$ be the classes of total recursive functions from the definition of its EX—satisfiability. Let V_1, V_2, V_3 be the unions of $U_1, \ldots, U_n$ corresponding to the vectors

$$(\partial_1, \ldots, \partial_{i-1}, 0, \partial_{i+1}, \ldots, \partial_{j-1}, 0, \partial_{j+1}, \ldots, \partial_{k-1}, 1, \partial_{k+1}, \ldots, \partial_n),$$
$$(\partial_1, \ldots, \partial_{i-1}, 0, \partial_{i+1}, \ldots, \partial_{j-1}, 1, \partial_{j+1}, \ldots, \partial_{k-1}, 0, \partial_{k+1}, \ldots, \partial_n),$$
$$(\partial_1, \ldots, \partial_{i-1}, 1, \partial_{i+1}, \ldots, \partial_{j-1}, 0, \partial_{j+1}, \ldots, \partial_{k-1}, 0, \partial_{k+1}, \ldots, \partial_n).$$

Then $V_1 \cup V_2$, $V_1 \cup V_3$, $V_2 \cup V_3$, correspond to the vectors

$$(\partial_1, \ldots, \partial_{i-1}, 0, \partial_{i+1}, \ldots, \partial_{j-1}, 1, \partial_{j+1}, \ldots, \partial_{k-1}, 1, \partial_{k+1}, \ldots, \partial_n),$$
$$(\partial_1, \ldots, \partial_{i-1}, 1, \partial_{i+1}, \ldots, \partial_{j-1}, 0, \partial_{j+1}, \ldots, \partial_{k-1}, 1, \partial_{k+1}, \ldots, \partial_n),$$
$$(\partial_1, \ldots, \partial_{i-1}, 1, \partial_{i+1}, \ldots, \partial_{j-1}, 1, \partial_{j+1}, \ldots, \partial_{k-1}, 0, \partial_{k+1}, \ldots, \partial_n).$$

It follows from Theorem 2.1 that if the function f takes values 0 on the 3 latter vectors, then $f(\partial_1, \ldots, \partial_{i-1}, 1, \partial_{i+1}, \ldots, \partial_{j-1}, 1, \partial_{j+1}, \ldots, \partial_{k-1}, 1, \partial_{k+1}, \ldots, \partial_n)=0$ as well.

$\Leftarrow$ We say that the vector $(\partial_1, \ldots, \partial_n)$ is a minimal 1—vector for the Boolean function f, if:

1) $f(\partial_1, \ldots, \partial_n)=1$,

2) $f(\tau_1, \ldots, \tau_n)=0$ for arbitrary $(\tau_1, \ldots, \tau_n)$ such that $\tau_1 \le \partial_1, \ldots, \tau_n \le \partial_n$.

Let f be an arbitrary 3—convolutional Boolean function. Let $(\partial_1{}^1, \ldots, \partial_n{}^1), \ldots (\partial_1{}^2, \ldots, \partial_n{}^2),$ $(\partial_1{}^m, \ldots, \partial_n{}^m)$ be list of all the minimal 1—vectors for f. By the definition of 3—convolutionality, every $(\partial_1{}^s, \ldots, \partial_n{}^s)$ contains precisely 2 components $\partial_i{}^s$ and $\partial_j{}^s$ equaling 1. The class U_t ($t \in \{1, \ldots, n\}$) is defined to consist of all total recursive functions g(x) such that:

1) $g(0) \in \{1, \ldots, m\}$,

2) $\partial_t{}^{g(0)}=1$,

3) if $u \ne t$, $\partial_u{}^{g(0)}=1$, and $u>t$, then $g(x)=\varphi_{g(1)}(x)$ for all $x \ge 1$,

4) if $u \ne t$, $\partial_u{}^{g(0)}=1$, and $u<t$, then $g(x)=0$ for all but a finite number of values of x.

We start to prove that $U_1, \ldots, U_n$ satisfy the requirements for the EX—satisfiability of the function f. Let $(\partial_1{}^s, \ldots, \partial_n{}^s)$ be a minimal 1—vector for f, and $\partial_i{}^s=\partial_j{}^s=1$, i<j. Then U_j contains all the total recursive functions g such that g(0)=s and $g(x)=\varphi_{g(1)}(x)$ for all $x \ge 1$. U_i contains all total recursive functions g such that g(0)=s and g(x)=0 for all but a finite number of values of x. The union $U_i \cup U_j$ contains simultanously the two above-mentioned types of functions. Hence it is not EX—identifiable (by the argument used in [Bar 74]).

On the other hand, if a union $U_i \cup U_j \cup \ldots \cup U_k$ corresponding to a $(\partial_1, \ldots, \partial_n)$ such that $f(\partial_1, \ldots, \partial_n)=0$ then for arbitrary $a \in \{1, \ldots, m\}$ all the functions g in $U_i \cup U_j \cup \ldots \cup U_k$, such that g(0)=a, are defined either by the condition 3) or by the condition 4) but they are never defined by the two conditions simultaneously. Hence the union $U_i \cup U_j \cup \ldots \cup U_k$ is EX—identifiable. $\square$

3 FIN–identification

Finite identification seems to be very similar to the identification in the limit. However, the properties of the unions of FIN–identifiable classes are very much dissimilar.

Theorem 3.1. There are classes of total recursive functions U_1, U_2, U_3 such that $U_1 \cup U_2 \in$ FIN, $U_1 \cup U_3 \in$ FIN, $U_2 \cup U_3 \in$ FIN, but $U_1 \cup U_2 \cup U_3 \notin$ FIN.

Proof. We define the class $U = U_1 \cup U_2 \cup U_3$ as a class consisting of total recursive functions such that:

1) $f(x) \geq 2$ may be true for at most 3 values of x, and
2) there are at least 2 values of x such that $f(x) = y + 2$ and $\varphi_y = f$.

The classes U_1, U_2, U_3 are defined as subclasses of U. Namely, U_1 is the class of all $f \in U$ such that $\varphi_y = f$ for the first and the second x such that $f(x) \geq 2$. U_2 is the class of all $f \in U$ such that $\varphi_y = f$ for the first and the third x such that $f(x) \geq 2$. U_3 is the class of all $f \in U$ such that $\varphi_y = f$ for the second and the third x such that $f(x) \geq 2$.

$1.^0$ For all functions $f \in U_1 \cup U_2$ the first x_1, such that $f(x_1) \geq 2$, provides us with correct program for f, namely, $f(x_1) - 2$. Similary, for $f \in U_1 \cup U_3$ a correct program for f is $f(x_1) - 2$ where x_2 is the second x_1, such that $f(x_1) \geq 2$. Hence these unions are in FIN.

$2.^0$ $U = U_1 \cup U_2 \cup U_3$ is not FIN–identifiable, as proved in [Fre 79]. □

Theorem 3.1. Let U_1, U_2, U_3, U_4 be classes of total recursive functions. If $U_1 \cup U_2 \cup U_3 \in$ FIN, $U_1 \cup U_2 \cup U_4 \in$ FIN, $U_1 \cup U_3 \cup U_4 \in$ FIN, and $U_2 \cup U_3 \cup U_4 \in$ FIN, then $U_1 \cup U_2 \cup U_3 \cup U_4 \in$ FIN.

Proof. By F_1, F_2, F_3, F_4 we denote the strategies FIN–identifying the classes $U_1 \cup U_2 \cup U_3$, $U_1 \cup U_2 \cup U_4$, $U_1 \cup U_3 \cup U_4$, and $U_2 \cup U_3 \cup U_4$, respectively. For arbitrary function $f \in \{F_1 \cup F_2 \cup F_3 \cup F_4\}$ at least three strategies out of $\{F_1, F_2, F_3, F_4\}$ identify f.

We construct a new strategy F for FIN–identification of $U_1 \cup U_2 \cup U_3 \cup U_4$. The strategy F uses the strategies F_1, F_2, F_3, F_4 as subroutines.

F produces the output after the moment when three strategies out of four have produced their outputs. Let G_1, G_2, $G_3 \in \{F_1 \cup F_2 \cup F_3 \cup F_4\}$ be these three strategies and let a, b, c be their outputs on the function f to be identified. We know that at most one of them may be an incorrect output. The output h by F based on a, b, c is a program such that, for every x, the value $\varphi_h(x)$ equals an integer y such that at least two of the following three equalities are true:

$$\varphi_a(x) = y,$$
$$\varphi_b(x) = y,$$
$$\varphi_c(x) = y.$$ □

We say that a Boolean function f is 4-convolutional if:

1) it is monotone,

2) it equals 0 for all the vectors $(\partial_1, ..., \partial_n)$ containing at most one 1,

3) if for an arbitrary vector $(\partial_1, ..., \partial_n)$ and arbitrary four distinct i, j, k, m $\in \{1, 2, ...,$ m}, such that the function takes values

$$f(\partial_1, ..., \partial_{i-1}, 0, \partial_{i+1}, ..., \partial_{j-1}, 1, \partial_{j+1}, ..., \partial_{k-1}, 1, \partial_{k+1}, ..., \partial_{m-1}, 1, \partial_{m+1}, ..., \partial_n)=0,$$
$$f(\partial_1, ..., \partial_{i-1}, 1, \partial_{i+1}, ..., \partial_{j-1}, 0, \partial_{j+1}, ..., \partial_{k-1}, 1, \partial_{k+1}, ..., \partial_{m-1}, 1, \partial_{m+1}, ..., \partial_n)=0,$$
$$f(\partial_1, ..., \partial_{i-1}, 1, \partial_{i+1}, ..., \partial_{j-1}, 1, \partial_{j+1}, ..., \partial_{k-1}, 0, \partial_{k+1}, ..., \partial_{m-1}, 1, \partial_{m+1}, ..., \partial_n)=0,$$
$$f(\partial_1, ..., \partial_{i-1}, 1, \partial_{i+1}, ..., \partial_{j-1}, 1, \partial_{j+1}, ..., \partial_{k-1}, 1, \partial_{k+1}, ..., \partial_{m-1}, 0, \partial_{m+1}, ..., \partial_n)=0,$$

then

$$f(\partial_1, ..., \partial_{i-1}, 1, \partial_{i+1}, ..., \partial_{j-1}, 1, \partial_{j+1}, ..., \partial_{k-1}, 1, \partial_{k+1}, ..., \partial_{m-1}, 1, \partial_{m+1}, ..., \partial_n)=0.$$

Theorem 3.3. A Boolean function is FIN-satisfiable if and only if it is 4-convolutional.

4 EX-identification

Theorem 4.1. For arbitrary positive integer p, there are classes of total recursive functions $U_1, U_2, ..., U_m$ (where $m=2^{p+2}-1$) such that every union of m—1 classes out of $\{U_1, U_2, ..., U_m\}$ is identifiable with at most p mind-changes (is in EX_p), but the union $U_1, U_2, ..., U_m$ of all m classes is not identifiable with at most p mind-changes.

Theorem 4.2. Let p be arbitrary positive integer, m exceed $2^{p+2}-1$, and every union of m—1 classes out of $\{U_1, U_2, ..., U_m\}$ be identifiable with at most p mind-changes. Then the union $U_1, U_2, ..., U_m$ is also identifiable with at most p mind-changes.

Theorem 4.3. A Boolean function is EX_p-satisfiable if and only if it is 2^{p+2}-convolutional.

5 Identification with a bound on errors

Theorem 5.1. There are classes of total recursive functions $\{U_1, U_2, ..., U_8\}$ such that every union of seven classes out of $\{U_1, U_2, ..., U_8\}$ is finitely identifiable with at most 1 error (is in EX_0^1) but the union $U_1, U_2, ..., U_8$ is not in EX_0^1.

Theorem 5.2. Let $U_1, U_2, ..., U_9$ be classes of total recursive functions. If every union of eight classes out of $\{U_1, U_2, ..., U_9\}$ is in $EX_0{}^1$ then the union $U_1 \cup U_2, ... \cup U_9\}$ is also in $EX_0{}^1$.

Theorem 5.3. A Boolean function is $EX_0{}^1$–satisfiable if and only if it is 9–convolutional.

6 Conclusions

We did not expect the effect found in this paper (for small numbers m, identifiability of the union of m classes is not implied by the identifiability of given classes, but for large numbers m it is). Even less expected, was the numerical value $m = 2^{p+2} - 1$ for the crucial amount of the unions (Theorems 4.1 and 4.2).

On the other hand, the formulation of Theorems 3.1 and 4.1 does not reflect all the content of the proofs found. We wish to underline that the classes used for these proofs have very special properties.

It was found in [KF 81] (see the survey [Fre 91] for an English version) that, like the notion of NP–completeness in the complexity theory, a notion of M–complete classes of functions can be considered for *natural* types of identification. An M–complete class is *the most difficult* class for the identification type M. Instead of proving that every class identifiable in sense M_1 is also identifiable in the sense M_2, it suffices to prove that the M_1–complete class is M_2–identifiable.

We wish to turn the readers' attention to the fact that the class in $U_1 \cup U_2 \cup U_3$ in Theorem 3.1 is complete for the probabilistic finite identification with probabilistic finite identifiability does not simply the deterministic finite identifiability). The same can be said about the classes used in Theorem 4.1 about identifiability with no more than p mind–changes.

Most probably, this ability to use the complete classes for probabilistic inference in solution of a problem where no probabilities are in sight, reflects some fundamental relationship between these two problems.

References

[AS 83] Angluin, D. and Smith, C.H. Inductive inference: theory and methods. Computing Surveys 15 (1983), 237—269.

[Bar 74] Barzdin, J. Two theorems on the limiting synthesis of functions. In *Theory of Algorithms and Programs*. Barzdin, Ed., 1, Latvian State University, Riga, 1974, 82—88 (Russian).

[CS 83] Case J. and Smith, C. Comparison of identification criteria for machine inductive inference. Theoretical Computer Science 25, 2 (1983), 193—220.

[Fre 79] Freivalds R. Finite identification of general recursive functions by probabilistic strategies. In *Proc. 2nd Interm. Conf. Fundamentals of Computation Theory*, Berlin, Akademie, 1979, 138—145.

[Fre 79'] Freivalds R. On principal capabilities of probabilistic algorithms in inductive inference. — Semiotika i informatika, Moscow, VINITI, 12 (1979), 137—140 (Russian).

[Fre91] Freivalds R. Inductive inference of recursive functions: qualitative theory. Lecture Notes in Computer Science 502 (1991) 77—110.

[Gold 67] Gold, E.M. Language identification in the limit. *Information and Control* 10 (1967), 447—474.

[KF 81] Kinber, E. and Freivalds R. A distinction criterion for types of limiting synthesis. In *Procedings USSR National Conference of Synthesis. Testing, Verification and Debugging of Programs*, Latvian State University, Riga, 1981 (Russian)

[Rog 67] Rogers, H.J. Theory of Recursive Functions and Effective Computability. McGraw Hill, 1967. Reprinted. MIT Press. 1987.

[Smi 82] Smith, C.H. The power of pluralism for automatic program synthesis. — Journal of the ACM, 29, 4 (1982), 1144 — 1165

[Wie 77] Wiehagen, R. Identification of formal languages. *Lecture Notes in Computer Science*, 53 (1977), 571 — 579.

Learning from Multiple Sources of Inaccurate Data

Ganesh Baliga[1], Sanjay Jain[1] and Arun Sharma[2]

[1] Department of Computer and Information Sciences
University of Delaware
Newark, Delaware 19716
USA

[2] School of Computer Science and Engineering
The University of New South Wales
Sydney, NSW, 2033
Australia

Abstract. Most theoretical studies of inductive inference model a situation involving a machine M learning its environment E on following lines. M, placed in E, receives data about E, and simultaneously conjectures a sequence of hypotheses. M is said to learn E just in case the sequence of hypotheses conjectured by M stabilizes to a final hypothesis which correctly represents E.

The above model makes the idealized assumption that the data about E that M receives is from a *single* and *accurate* source. An argument is made in favor of a more realistic learning model which accounts for data emanating from *multiple* sources, some or all of which may be *inaccurate*. Motivated by this argument, the present paper introduces and theoretically analyzes a number of inference criteria in which a machine is fed data from multiple sources, some of which could be infected with inaccuracies. The main parameters of the investigation are the number of data sources, the number of faulty data sources, and the kind of inaccuracies.

1 Introduction

A situation involving an *algorithmic* learner attempting to learn its environment could be described thus. At any given time, some finite data about the environment is made available to the learner. The learner reacts to this finite information by conjecturing a hypothesis concerning the behavior of his/her environment. Availability of additional data may cause the learner to revise its old hypotheses. A criterion of success for the learner is that the sequence of conjectured hypotheses stabilizes to a final hypothesis which correctly represents the environment.

The above model of learning, generally referred to as *identification in the limit*, originated in the pioneering works of Putnam [Put73], Gold [Gol67] and Solomonoff [Sol64a, Sol64b]. More recently, this model has been the subject of numerous studies in the area called Computational Learning Theory (see, e.g., [HPe88, RHWe89, FCe90, VWe91]). A problem with this model is the idealized assumption that the data available to the learner is from a *single* and *accurate* source. The present paper argues that in realistic learning situations the data available to a learner is from *multiple* sources, some of which may be *inaccurate*. Below, we discuss this problem for a specific learning situation, viz., scientific inquiry. Although we present our results in the context of this particular learning task, we note that similar arguments and techniques apply to other learning situations also.

Consider a scientist S investigating a real world phenomenon F. S performs experiments on F, noting the result of each experiment, while simultaneously conjecturing a succession of candidate explanations for F. A criterion of success is for S to eventually conjecture an explanation which S never gives up and which correctly explains F. Since we never measure a continuum of possibilities, we could treat S as performing discrete experiments x on F and receiving back experimental results $f(x)$. By using a suitable Gödel numbering we may treat the f associated with F as a function from N, the set of natural numbers, into N. Then, a complete and predictive explanation of F is just a computer program for computing f. Thus, replacing the ever experimenting S with a machine yields a plausible model for scientific inquiry—algorithmic identification in the limit of programs for computable functions from their graphs.

Now, let us look at some common facts of scientific life. Data is collected using different instruments, possibly at different places (for example, astronomers use data gathered from different telescopes situated at different locations). In many cases there are experimental errors and in some cases the instruments are just faulty. In some extreme cases, the same instrument gives different readings at different times. Also, it is infeasible to perform certain experiments (for example, taste of cyanide). Moreover, experimental findings of one scientist are generally available to others. All this tends to suggest that often a scientist receives data from multiple sources, many of which are likely to be inaccurate. Thus, there is a strong case for incorporating this observation in the standard learning model. This is the subject of this investigation. We now proceed formally.

Section 2 presents the notation; readers familiar with inductive inference literature may skip it. Section 3 presents the preliminary notions about identification in the limit and inaccurate data. Section 4 introduces the main subject of this paper, viz., learning in the presence of multiple sources of inaccurate data. Section 5 contains representative results of this investigation.

2 Notation

Recursion-theoretic concepts not explained below are treated in [Rog67]. N denotes the set of natural numbers, $\{0, 1, 2, 3, \ldots\}$, and N^+ denotes the set of positive integers, $\{1, 2, 3, \ldots\}$. $\in$, $\subseteq$, and $\subset$ denote, respectively, membership, containment, and proper containment for sets.

$*$ denotes *unbounded* but *finite*. We let $(\forall n \in N)[n < * < \infty]$. $e, i, j, k, l, m, n, r, s, t, u, v, w, x, y, z$ with or without decorations, range over N. a, b, c with or without decorations range over $N \cup \{*\}$.

$[m, n]$ denotes the set $\{x \in N \mid m \leq x \leq n\}$. We let S, with or without decorations, range over subsets of N and we let A, B, C, and D, with or without decorations, range over finite subsets of N. $\mathrm{card}(S)$ denotes the cardinality of S. So then, 'card$(S) \leq *$' means that card(S) is finite. min(S) and max(S) respectively denote the minimum and maximum element in S (max(S) is undefined if S contains infinitely many elements). We take min$(\emptyset)$ to be ∞ and max$(\emptyset)$ to be 0.

Let $\lambda x, y . \langle x, y \rangle$ denote a fixed pairing function (a recursive, bijective mapping: $N \times N \rightarrow N$) [Rog67]. $\lambda x, y . \langle x, y \rangle$ and its inverses are useful to simulate the effect of having multiple argument functions. π_1 and π_2 are corresponding projection functions, i.e., $(\forall x, y)[\pi_1(\langle x, y \rangle) = x \wedge \pi_2(\langle x, y \rangle) = y]$.

η and ξ range over partial functions. For $a \in (N \cup \{*\})$, we say that η_1 is an a-variant of η_2 (written $\eta_1 =^a \eta_2$) iff card$(\{x \mid \eta_1(x) \neq \eta_2(x)\}) \leq a$. Otherwise we say that η_1 is not an a-variant of η_2 (written $\eta_1 \neq^a \eta_2$). domain(η) and range(η) respectively denote the domain and range of partial function η. Let $A \subseteq N$, $c \in N$. We say that $\eta(A) = c$ iff for all $x \in A$, $\eta(x) = c$. If S_1, S_2 are two sets, then $S_1 \triangle S_2$ denotes $(S_1 - S_2) \cup (S_2 - S_1)$.

$\mathcal{R}$ denotes the class of all *recursive* functions of one variable, i.e., total computable functions with arguments and values from N. f, g, and h, with or without decorations, range over $\mathcal{R}$. $\mathcal{C}$ and $\mathcal{S}$, with or without decorations, range over subsets of $\mathcal{R}$.

We fix φ to be an *acceptable programming system* [Rog58, Rog67, MY78] for the partial recursive functions: $N \rightarrow N$. φ_i denotes the partial recursive function computed by φ-program i. W_i denotes domain(φ_i). W_i is, then, the r.e. set/language ($\subseteq N$) accepted (or equivalently, generated) by the φ-program i. We let Φ be an arbitrary Blum complexity measure [Blu67] associated with acceptable programming system φ; such measures exist for any acceptable programming system [Blu67]. $W_{i,s}$ denotes the set $\{x \mid x < s \wedge \Phi_i(x) \leq s\}$.

In some contexts p, q with or without decorations range over programs. In other contexts p, q range over total recursive functions, with the range of p, q being viewed as programs. In some contexts P, with or without decorations ranges over programs. In other contexts, P ranges over sets of programs.

For any predicate Q, $\mu n . Q(n)$ denotes the minimum integer n such that $Q(n)$ is true if such an n exists; it is undefined otherwise. For any set A, 2^A denotes the power set of A. A^k denotes the cartesian product of A with itself k times. The quantifiers $\stackrel{\infty}{\forall}$, $\exists!$ and '$\stackrel{\infty}{\exists}$' mean 'for all but finitely many', 'there exists a unique' and 'there exist infinitely many' respectively.

3 Preliminaries

The kind of data a scientist handles in the investigation of a phenomenon F is an ordered pair $\langle x, f(x) \rangle$, where f is the function associated with F and $f(x)$ is the result of experiment x on F. At any given time, a scientist conjectures a hypothesis after seeing a finite sequence of such ordered pairs. We let SEQ denote the set of all finite sequences of ordered pairs. Finite sequences are also referred to as initial segments. As already mentioned, a hypothesis is simply a computer program which could be identified by its index in a given fixed acceptable programming system. Based on these observations, we describe a learning machine in Definition 1 below. We let σ and τ, with or without decorations, range over SEQ. content(σ) denotes the set of pairs appearing in σ. The length of σ, denoted by $|\sigma|$, is the number of elements in σ. $\sigma \diamond k$ denotes the *concatenation* of k at the end of sequence σ.

Definition 1. A *learning machine* is an algorithmic device that computes a mapping from SEQ into N. We let $\mathbf{M}$, with or without decorations, range over learning machines.

Scientific inquiry is a limiting process. There is no fixed order in which experiments may be performed, and a scientist is never sure if any new experimental evidence would cause a revision of the currently held hypothesis. The notion of a *text* is described in Definition 2 to model the infinite sequence of experimental data a scientist could encounter in the course of investigating a phenomenon.

Definition 2.
(a) A *text* is any infinite sequence of ordered pairs. We let T, with or without decorations, range over texts.
(b) The set of pairs appearing in a text T is denoted by content(T).
(c) Let a total function $f : N \to N$, and a text T be given. T is for f iff content$(T) = \{\langle x, y \rangle \mid f(x) = y\}$.
(d) The initial finite sequence of T of length n is denoted by $T[n]$.

Definition 3 below describes what it means for a learning machine to converge on a text.

Definition 3. Suppose $\mathbf{M}$ is a learning machine and T is a text. $\mathbf{M}(T)\downarrow$ (read: $\mathbf{M}(T)$*converges*) $\Leftrightarrow (\exists p)(\overset{\infty}{\forall} n)[\mathbf{M}(T[n]) = p]$. If $\mathbf{M}(T)\downarrow$, then $\mathbf{M}(T)$ is defined $=$ the unique p such that $(\overset{\infty}{\forall} n)[\mathbf{M}(T[n]) = p]$; otherwise $\mathbf{M}(T)$ is said to diverge (written: $\mathbf{M}(T)\uparrow$).

Definition 4 below describes what it means for a learning machine to successfully learn a function.

Definition 4. [Gol67, BB75, CS83]
(a) $\mathbf{M}$ **Ex**^{a}-*identifies* f (written: $f \in \mathbf{Ex}^a(\mathbf{M})$) $\Leftrightarrow (\forall$ texts T for $f)(\exists p \mid \varphi_p =^a f)[\mathbf{M}(T)\downarrow = p]$.
(b) $\mathbf{Ex}^a = \{ \mathcal{S} \mid (\exists \mathbf{M})[\mathcal{S} \subseteq \mathbf{Ex}^a(\mathbf{M})] \}$.

Definition 4 above models the situation in which a scientist has access to an *accurate* source of data. Since accurate experimental data is seldom available, models of scientific inquiry should attempt to take inaccuracies into consideration. In the paradigm under discussion, inaccurate data is modeled by inaccurate texts. First, we briefly consider the kinds of inaccuracies that could arise in experimentation. The subject of inaccuracies in the data available to a learning machine has been previously studied by Schäfer-Richter [SR86], Fulk and Jain [FJ89], Osherson, Stob and Weinstein [OSW86] and Jain [Jai90].

- **Noisy Data:** Experimental error caused by equipment or otherwise could result in spurious data that is not representative of the phenomenon under investigation.

- **Incomplete Data:** Certain experiments cannot be performed either due to technological limitations or due to ethical considerations. Such situations result in incomplete data.
- **Imperfect Data:** In most experimental investigations, the inaccuracies are a mixture of both noisy and incomplete data. Such situations are said to result in imperfect data.

The three kinds of inaccuracies in data discussed above result in three kinds of inaccurate texts described in Definition 5 below.

Definition 5. [FJ89, OSW86, Jai90] (also see [SR86]) Let a text T and a function $f \in \mathcal{R}$ be given. Let $a \in N \cup \{*\}$. Then,

- We say that a text T is *a-noisy* for f iff
$$\{\langle x, y \rangle \mid f(x) = y\} \subseteq \text{content}(T) \text{ and}$$
$$\text{card}(\text{content}(T) - \{\langle x, y \rangle \mid f(x) = y\}) \leq a.$$
- We say that a text T is *a-incomplete* for f iff
$$\text{content}(T) \subseteq \{\langle x, y \rangle \mid f(x) = y\} \text{ and}$$
$$\text{card}(\{\langle x, y \rangle \mid f(x) = y\} - \text{content}(T)) \leq a.$$
- We say that a text T is *a-imperfect* for f iff $\text{card}(\{\langle x, y \rangle \mid f(x) = y\} \triangle \text{content}(T)) \leq a.$

Definition 6 below describes what it means for a learning machine to learn a function from inaccurate texts. We give the definition for noisy texts; the corresponding notions for incomplete and imperfect texts (respectively called, $\mathbf{In}^a\mathbf{Ex}^b$ and $\mathbf{Im}^a\mathbf{Ex}^b$) could be defined similarly.

Definition 6. [FJ89, OSW86, Jai90] (also see [SR86]) Let $a, b \in N \cup \{*\}$.
(a) $\mathbf{M}$ $\mathbf{N}^a\mathbf{Ex}^b$-*identifies* f (written: $f \in \mathbf{N}^a\mathbf{Ex}^b(\mathbf{M})$) $\Leftrightarrow$ ($\forall$ a-noisy texts T for f)($\exists p \mid \varphi_p =^b f$)[$\mathbf{M}(T)\downarrow = p$].
(b) $\mathbf{N}^a\mathbf{Ex}^b = \{\mathcal{S} \mid (\exists \mathbf{M})[\mathcal{S} \subseteq \mathbf{N}^a\mathbf{Ex}^b(\mathbf{M})]\}$.

4   Multiple Inaccurate Texts

We ended the previous section by describing a paradigm that models situations in which a scientist receives data from a *single*, albeit possibly inaccurate source. In actual scientific practice, a phenomenon is investigated by a number of different scientists, each performing their own experiments. In due course of time, the data of one scientist becomes available to another through scientific journals, word of mouth, personal communications, etc. Thus, a scientist conjectures hypotheses based on data coming from a number of different sources. This situation could be modeled in the present paradigm as a learning machine receiving multiple texts, some or all of which are inaccurate. It should be noted that presence of inaccuracies in at least some of the texts is essential because learning from multiple texts, each of which are accurate, is the same thing as learning from a single accurate text.

Before we define learning from multiple inaccurate texts, we need to tinker with our definition of learning machine to account for data coming from more than one source. Definition 7 below describes learning machines that receive multiple streams of data.

Definition 7. Let $k \in N^+$. A *learning machine with k streams* is an algorithmic device that computes a mapping from SEQ^k into N.

Again, we let **M**, with or without decorations, range over learning machines with multiple streams; it will be clear from context if we mean a learning machine with a single stream. Definition 8 below describes what it means for a learning machine to converge on multiple texts.

Definition 8. Let $k \in N^+$. Suppose **M** is a learning machine and $T_1, T_2, \ldots, T_k$ are k texts. $\mathbf{M}(T_1, T_2, \ldots, T_k))\!\downarrow$ (read: $\mathbf{M}(T_1, T_2, \ldots, T_k)$ converges) $\Leftrightarrow$ $(\exists p)(\exists n)(\forall n_1, n_2, \ldots, n_k \mid n_1 \geq n, n_2 \geq n, \ldots, n_k \geq n)[\mathbf{M}(T_1[n_1], T_2[n_2], \ldots, T_k[n_k]) = p]$. If $\mathbf{M}(T_1, T_2, \ldots, T_k)\!\downarrow$, then $\mathbf{M}(T_1, T_2, \ldots, T_k)$ is defined $=$ the unique p such that $(\exists n)(\forall n_1, n_2, \ldots, n_k \mid n_1 \geq n, n_2 \geq n, \ldots, n_k \geq n)[\mathbf{M}(T_1[n_1], T_2, \ldots, T_k[n_k]) = p]$; otherwise $\mathbf{M}(T_1, T_2, \ldots, T_k)$ is said to diverge (written: $\mathbf{M}(T_1, T_2, \ldots, T_k)\!\uparrow$).

Definition 9 below describes what it means for a learning machine to learn a function from multiple number of inaccurate texts. We give the definition for noisy texts; the corresponding notions for incomplete and imperfect texts could be defined similarly.

Definition 9. Let $j, k \in N^+$.

Let $a, b \in N \cup \{*\}$.

(a) A learning machine **M** $\mathbf{MUL}_k^j \mathbf{N}^a \mathbf{Ex}^b$-*identifies* f (written: $f \in \mathbf{MUL}_k^j \mathbf{N}^a \mathbf{Ex}^b(\mathbf{M})$) $\Leftrightarrow$ $(\forall\, T_1, T_2, \ldots, T_k$ such that at least j of the k texts are a-noisy for $f)(\exists p \mid \varphi_p =^b f)[\mathbf{M}(T_1, T_2, \ldots, T_k)\!\downarrow = p]$.

(b) $\mathbf{MUL}_k^j \mathbf{N}^a \mathbf{Ex}^b = \{\mathcal{S} \mid (\exists \mathbf{M})[\mathcal{S} \subseteq \mathbf{MUL}_k^j \mathbf{N}^a \mathbf{Ex}^b(\mathbf{M})]\}$.

The aim of the present paper is to investigate characteristics of $\mathbf{MUL}_k^j \mathbf{N}^a \mathbf{Ex}^b$, $\mathbf{MUL}_k^j \mathbf{In}^a \mathbf{Ex}^b$, and $\mathbf{MUL}_k^j \mathbf{Im}^a \mathbf{Ex}^b$ for various values of a, b, j, and k.

Before we begin our investigation, we end this section on a speculatory note pointing to future research directions. Scientific success is often not limited to the success of a single scientist receiving data from multiple, possibly inaccurate, sources. In actual practice, a number of scientists are simultaneously investigating a phenomenon, each receiving data from multiple, possibly inaccurate, sources. Scientific success is achieved if any one of these scientists is successful. This scenario could be modeled as a 'team' of learning machines; each member of the team receiving multiple inaccurate texts. The team is successful whenever at least one member of the team converges to a correct program for the function being learned (see Smith [Smi82] for discussion of team identification from a *single* and *accurate* text).

5 Results

A machine $\mathbf{MUL}_k^j \mathbf{N}^a \mathbf{Ex}^b$-identifying a function f is fed k texts, at least j of which are a-noisy for f. Similar observations hold for $\mathbf{MUL}_k^j \mathbf{In}^a \mathbf{Ex}^b$ and $\mathbf{MUL}_k^j \mathbf{Im}^a \mathbf{Ex}^b$-

identification. Henceforth, we refer to text(s) for which the inaccuracy is within the required bound as "good" text(s).

Let $f_1, f_2 \in \mathcal{C}$ be such that $f_1 \neq^{2a} f_2$. Then, for all k, we have $\mathcal{C} \notin \mathbf{MUL}_k^{\lfloor \frac{k}{2} \rfloor} \mathbf{N}^0 \mathbf{Ex}^a$. This is because among the k texts there may be $\lfloor \frac{k}{2} \rfloor$ accurate texts for both f_1 and f_2. Thus, we only consider the cases in which a strict majority of the texts are "good." Clearly, learning from k texts, j out of which are "good," is at least as hard as learning from a single "good" text.

We now present results relating various criteria of inference introduced in Section 4. Most of the results in the present paper deal with the case when the learning machine is receiving data from three sources at least two of which are "good." Section 5.1 presents the cases where learning from multiple texts is not a restriction on learning power. Section 5.3 presents the results where learning from multiple texts is a restriction on learning power. Section 5.2 presents the hierarchy results and Section 5.4 presents results relating different types of inaccuracies. From a purely technical point of view, results presented in Section 5.3 are the most difficult results of this paper.

5.1 Cases where Identification from Multiple Texts is not a Restriction

In this section we study cases when learning from multiple inaccurate texts is equivalent to learning from a single inaccurate text.

Theorem 10. *Let $j, k \in N$, $j > \lfloor \frac{k}{2} \rfloor$. Let $a \in N \cup \{*\}$.*

(I) $\mathbf{MUL}_k^j \mathbf{N}^* \mathbf{Ex}^a = \mathbf{N}^* \mathbf{Ex}^a$.

(II) $\mathbf{MUL}_k^j \mathbf{In}^* \mathbf{Ex}^a = \mathbf{In}^* \mathbf{Ex}^a$.

(III) $\mathbf{MUL}_k^j \mathbf{Im}^* \mathbf{Ex}^a = \mathbf{Im}^* \mathbf{Ex}^a$.

(IV) $\mathbf{MUL}_k^j \mathbf{N}^0 \mathbf{Ex}^a = \mathbf{MUL}_k^j \mathbf{In}^0 \mathbf{Ex}^a = \mathbf{MUL}_k^j \mathbf{Im}^0 \mathbf{Ex}^a = \mathbf{Ex}^a$.

Proof. Given k texts $T_1, T_2, \ldots, T_k$, form a text T such that $x \in \text{content}(T) \Leftrightarrow \text{card}(\{i \mid x \in \text{content}(T_i)\}) \geq \lfloor \frac{k}{2} \rfloor + 1$. It is easy to see that if at least $\lfloor \frac{k}{2} \rfloor + 1$ of the k texts are *-noisy (*-incomplete, *-imperfect, accurate) for f then so is T. The theorem follows. □

Let P be a finite set of programs. Define program **Unify**(P) as follows:

$\varphi_{\mathbf{Unify}(P)}(x)$

   Search for $i \in P$ such that $\varphi_i(x)\!\downarrow$.

   If and when such i is found output $\varphi_i(x)$ (for the first such i found).

End

Theorem 11. *Let $j, k \in N$, $j > \lfloor \frac{k}{2} \rfloor$. Let $a \in N \cup \{*\}$.*

(I) $\mathbf{MUL}_k^j \mathbf{N}^a \mathbf{Ex} = \mathbf{N}^a \mathbf{Ex}$.

(II) $\mathbf{MUL}_k^j \mathbf{In}^a \mathbf{Ex} = \mathbf{In}^a \mathbf{Ex}$.

(III) $\mathbf{MUL}_k^j \mathbf{Im}^a \mathbf{Ex} = \mathbf{Im}^a \mathbf{Ex}$.

Proof. (I) Let $\mathbf{M}$ $\mathbf{N}^a \mathbf{Ex}$-identify $\mathcal{C}$. We show how to **Ex**-identify $f \in \mathcal{C}$ from k texts at least j of which are a-noisy for f. Let n, $S = \{i_1, i_2, \ldots, i_j\} \subseteq \{1, 2, \ldots, k\}$, $P = \{p_{i_1}, p_{i_2}, \ldots, p_{i_j}\}$, be such that,

(i) For all $l \in S$, $\mathbf{M}$ on T_l converges after seeing the first n inputs to p_l.

(ii) If $p, q \in P$, then $\text{card}(\{x | \varphi_p(x)\downarrow \neq \varphi_q(x)\downarrow\}) = 0$.

(iii) $\text{card}(S) = j$.

Clearly, such n, S, P exist (let $S \subseteq \{i | T_i \text{ is } a\text{-noisy for } f\}$ be a set of cardinality j; let n be such that for all $l \in S$, $\mathbf{M}$ converges on T_l after seeing at most n inputs; let $P = \{\mathbf{M}(T_l) | l \in S\}$. Then n, S, P satisfy (i), (ii) and (iii)). Clearly, a machine $\mathbf{M}'$, given texts $T_1, \ldots, T_k$, can find such an n, S, P in the limit. Now since $\mathbf{M}$ on $T_l, l \in S$ converges to p_l, and $\text{card}(S) > k - j$, there exists an $l \in S$ such that $\varphi_{p_l} = f$. This along with (ii) above implies that $\mathbf{Unify}(P)$ is a program for f. This proves (I).

(II) and (III) can be proved similarly. $\square$

Theorem 12. *Let* $j, k \in N$, $j > \lfloor \frac{k}{2} \rfloor$. *Let* $a \in N \cup \{*\}$.

(I) $\mathbf{MUL}_k^j \mathbf{N}^a \mathbf{Ex}^* = \mathbf{N}^a \mathbf{Ex}^*$.

(II) $\mathbf{MUL}_k^j \mathbf{In}^a \mathbf{Ex}^* = \mathbf{In}^a \mathbf{Ex}^*$.

(III) $\mathbf{MUL}_k^j \mathbf{Im}^a \mathbf{Ex}^* = \mathbf{Im}^a \mathbf{Ex}^*$.

Proof. (I) Let $\mathbf{M}$ $\mathbf{N}^a \mathbf{Ex}^*$-identify $\mathcal{C}$. We show how to $\mathbf{Ex}^*$-identify $f \in \mathcal{C}$ from k texts at least j of which are a-noisy for f. Let $n, S = \{i_1, i_2, \ldots, i_j\} \subseteq \{1, 2, \ldots, k\}, P = \{p_{i_1}, p_{i_2}, \ldots, p_{i_j}\}$, be such that,

(i) For all $l \in S$, $\mathbf{M}$ on T_l converges after seeing the first n inputs to p_l.

(ii) If $p, q \in P$ then $\text{card}(\{x | \varphi_p(x)\downarrow \neq \varphi_q(x)\downarrow\}) \leq n$.

(iii) $\text{card}(S) = j$.

Clearly, such n, S, P exist (let $S \subseteq \{i | T_i \text{ is } a\text{-noisy for } f\}$ be a set of cardinality j; let $P = \{\mathbf{M}(T_l) | l \in S\}$; let n be so large that for all $l \in S$, $\mathbf{M}$ converges on T_l after seeing at most n inputs and $f =^{n/2} \varphi_p$ for all $p \in P$; Then n, S, P satisfy (i), (ii) and (iii)). Clearly, a machine $\mathbf{M}'$, given texts $T_1, \ldots, T_k$, can find such an n, S, P in the limit. Now since $\mathbf{M}$ on $T_l, l \in S$ converges to p_l, and $\text{card}(S) > k - j$, there exists an $l \in S$ such that $\varphi_{p_l} =^* f$. This along with (ii) above implies that $\mathbf{Unify}(P)$ is a program for a finite variant of f. This proves (I).

(II) and (III) can be proved similarly. $\square$

5.2 Hierarchy Results

In this section we present results which show that decreasing the number of allowed errors in the final program or increasing the number of inaccuracies in the input decreases the learning capability of the inductive inference machines.

Theorem 13. *Let* $b, j, k \in N$, $j > \lfloor \frac{k}{2} \rfloor$.

(I) $\mathbf{MUL}_k^j \mathbf{Im}^* \mathbf{Ex}^{b+1} - \mathbf{Ex}^b \neq \emptyset$.

(II) $\mathbf{MUL}_k^j \mathbf{Im}^* \mathbf{Ex}^* - \bigcup_{b \in N} \mathbf{Ex}^b \neq \emptyset$.

Proof. Follows from Theorem 1 in [FJ89] and Theorem 10. $\square$

Theorem 14. $(\forall b, j, k \in N \mid j > \lfloor \frac{k}{2} \rfloor)$ $[\mathbf{MUL}_k^j \mathbf{Im}^b \mathbf{Ex} - [\mathbf{N}^{b+1} \mathbf{Ex}^* \cup \mathbf{In}^{b+1} \mathbf{Ex}^*] \neq \emptyset]$.

Proof. Follows from Theorem 6 in [FJ89] and Theorem 11. $\square$

5.3 Disadvantages of Learning from Multiple Texts for the Same Type of Inaccuracy

In this section we show that in certain cases learning from multiple texts is a restriction on learning power. Technically these are the most difficult results in the paper.

Theorem 15. *Let $a, b, c \in N$ be given. If there exist $r, \alpha \in N$ such that,*

$r - b \leq \alpha \leq \min(\{b, r\})$

$r \leq c$

$2r > a$

$d < \max(\{b + \alpha - \frac{r}{2}, b + \frac{\alpha}{3}\})$.

then $\mathbf{N^a Ex^b} - \mathbf{MUL_3^2 N^c Ex^d} \neq \emptyset$.

Proof. Assume the hypothesis. Fix r, α satisfying the hypothesis.

Let $A = \{\langle 0, x \rangle \mid 0 \leq x < r\}$.

Consider the following class of functions

$\mathcal{C} = \{f \in \mathcal{R} \mid$ following conditions are satisfied.

    (1) $f(A) = f(\langle 0, 0 \rangle) \in \{1, 2, 3\}$;

    (2) $(\forall i \in \{1, 2, 3\} - \{f(\langle 0, 0 \rangle)\})[(\max(\{f(\langle i, \langle x, 0 \rangle \rangle)) \mid x \in N\})$exists$) \wedge$
$(\varphi_{\max(\{f(\langle i, \langle x, 0 \rangle \rangle)) \mid x \in N\})} =^b f)]$;

    (3) $(\forall i \in \{1, 2, 3\})(\forall x, y, z)[f(\langle i, \langle x, y \rangle \rangle) = f(\langle i, \langle x, z \rangle \rangle)]$

}

It is easy to show that $\mathcal{C} \in \mathbf{N^a Ex^b}$ (since $2r > a$). We now show that $\mathcal{C} \notin \mathbf{MUL_3^2 N^c Ex^d}$.

Suppose by way of contradiction that machine **M** $\mathbf{MUL_3^2 N^c Ex^d}$ identifies $\mathcal{C}$. Then by the *Operator Recursion Theorem*[Cas74], there exists a recursive, 1-1 and increasing p, with $p(0) > 1$, such that the following holds :

We define $\varphi_{p(i)}$ in stages $s \geq 3$. Let x_3^s denote the least x such that for all y, $\varphi_{p(1)}(\langle 3, \langle x, y \rangle \rangle)$ is not defined before stage s.

For $x < \alpha$, let $\varphi_{p(1)}(\langle 0, x \rangle) = 2$. For $\alpha \leq x < r$, let $\varphi_{p(1)}(\langle 0, x \rangle) = 3$. Let $\varphi_{p(1)}(\langle 1, \langle 0, 0 \rangle \rangle) = p(1)$, and $\varphi_{p(1)}(\langle 2, \langle 0, 0 \rangle \rangle) = p(2)$.

For $x < \alpha$, let $\varphi_{p(2)}(\langle 0, x \rangle) = 1$. For $\alpha \leq x < r$, let $\varphi_{p(2)}(\langle 0, x \rangle) = 3$. Let $\varphi_{p(2)}(\langle 1, \langle 0, 0 \rangle \rangle) = p(1)$, and $\varphi_{p(2)}(\langle 2, \langle 0, 0 \rangle \rangle) = p(2)$.

Let σ_1^3, σ_2^3 and σ_3^3 be such that

content$(\sigma_1^3) = \{\langle x, 2 \rangle \mid x \in A\} \cup \{\langle x, 3 \rangle \mid x \in A\} \cup \{\langle\langle 1, \langle 0, 0 \rangle \rangle, p(1)\rangle, \langle\langle 2, \langle 0, 0 \rangle \rangle, p(2)\rangle\}$,

content$(\sigma_2^3) = \{\langle x, 1 \rangle \mid x \in A\} \cup \{\langle x, 3 \rangle \mid x \in A\} \cup \{\langle\langle 1, \langle 0, 0 \rangle \rangle, p(1)\rangle, \langle\langle 2, \langle 0, 0 \rangle \rangle, p(2)\rangle\}$,

content$(\sigma_3^3) = \{\langle x, 1 \rangle \mid x \in A\} \cup \{\langle x, 2 \rangle \mid x \in A\} \cup \{\langle\langle 1, \langle 0, 0 \rangle \rangle, p(1)\rangle, \langle\langle 2, \langle 0, 0 \rangle \rangle, p(2)\rangle\}$.

Go to stage 3.

    Begin stage s

        1. Let $q = \mathbf{M}(\sigma_1^s, \sigma_2^s, \sigma_3^s)$.

        2. Let $D_1 = \{x \mid x \in A \wedge \Phi_q(x) \leq s \wedge \varphi_q(x) = 1\}$.
        Let $D_2 = \{x \mid x \in A \wedge \Phi_q(x) \leq s \wedge \varphi_q(x) = 2\}$.
        Let $D_3 = \{x \mid x \in A \wedge \Phi_q(x) \leq s \wedge \varphi_q(x) \in N - \{1, 2\}\}$.
        Let $err_{1,2} = r - \text{card}(D_3) + b - \alpha$.

Let $err_{2,3} = r - \text{card}(D_1) + b - r + \alpha$.
Let $err_{1,3} = r - \text{card}(D_2) + b - r + \alpha$.
If $err_{1,2} \leq \max(\{err_{1,3}, err_{2,3}\})$, then let $extra\_err = b - r + \alpha$; otherwise let $extra\_err = b - \alpha$. If $err_{1,3} > err_{2,3}$, then let $l = 1$ and $l' = 2$; otherwise let $l = 2$ and $l' = 1$.
Let $X^s \subset \{\langle 4, x \rangle \mid x \geq s\}$ denote the (lexicographically least) set of $extra\_err$ elements such that for all $x \in X^s$, $\varphi_{p(1)}(x)$ is not defined before stage s.
(Note: Let $T_i = \bigcup_s \sigma_i^s$. D_1 (D_2 and D_3) denote the points in A for which φ_q seems to be correct if T_2 and T_3 (T_1 and T_3, T_1 and T_2) are the valid texts for the function being learned and $err_{i,j}$ denotes the error we can force if we chose a function such that T_i, T_j are correct texts for the function. Informally, an attempt is made at every stage to try and make those two texts correct so as to maximize the number of errors made by **M**'s current output program.)

3. Let $\varphi_{p(s)}(x) = l'$ for $x \in A$; Let $\varphi_{p(s)}(\langle 3, \langle x_3^s, 0 \rangle \rangle) = \varphi_{p(1)}(\langle 3, \langle x_3^s, 0 \rangle \rangle) = \varphi_{p(2)}(\langle 3, \langle x_3^s, 0 \rangle \rangle) = p(s)$. For $x \in \text{domain}(\varphi_{p(1)}^s) - A$, let $\varphi_{p(s)}(x) = \varphi_{p(1)}(x)$.

4. For $i \in \{1, 2, 3\}$ let σ_i' be an extension of σ_i^s such that $\text{content}(\sigma_i') = \text{content}(\sigma_i^s) \cup \{\langle \langle 3, \langle x_3^s, 0 \rangle \rangle, p(s) \rangle\}$.
5. Dovetail steps 5a, 5b and 5c until (if ever) one of steps 5a, 5b succeeds and at least one iteration of the loop at step 5c is completed. If step 5a succeeds (before step 5b (if ever) succeeds) then go to step 6a. If step 5b succeeds (before step 5a (if ever) succeeds) then go to step 6b.

5a. Search for $\sigma_i'' \supseteq \sigma_i'$, $i \in \{1, 2, 3\}$ such that $\mathbf{M}(\sigma_1^s, \sigma_2^s, \sigma_3^s) \neq \mathbf{M}(\sigma_1'', \sigma_2'', \sigma_3'')$ and for all $j, j' \in \{1, 2, 3\}$, for all $x, y, z \in N$, following three conditions hold:

  - $\text{content}(\sigma_j'') - \text{content}(\sigma_j') = \text{content}(\sigma_{j'}'') - \text{content}(\sigma_{j'}')$
  - If $\langle \langle j, \langle x, y \rangle \rangle, v \rangle \in \text{content}(\sigma_1'')$ and $\langle \langle j, \langle x, z \rangle \rangle, w \rangle \in \text{content}(\sigma_1'')$, then $v = w$.
  - If $\langle x, y \rangle \in (\text{content}(\sigma_1'') - \text{content}(\sigma_1'))$ then $[y = 0 \text{ OR } x \in X^s \text{ OR } [\text{For some } i \in \{1, 2, 3\}, u, v \in N: x = \langle i, \langle u, v \rangle \rangle \text{ and } \varphi_{p(1)}(\langle i, \langle u, 0 \rangle \rangle)$ has been defined till now and $\varphi_{p(1)}(\langle i, \langle u, 0 \rangle \rangle) = y]]$.

(Note: this substep looked for one set of suitable extensions of the currently defined initial segments of the three texts which makes **M** change its mind.)

5b. Search for $x \in A - (D_1 \cup D_2 \cup D_3)$ such that $\varphi_q(x){\downarrow}$.

5c. Let $Addednew = \emptyset$.
(Note: We use $Addednew$ in order to identify the set of elements for

which we extend $\varphi_{p(1)}$ in step 5c. *Addednew* will be used (in steps 6a and 6b) provided at least one of steps 5a or 5b succeeds).

Repeat

Let x be the least point not in X^s such that $\varphi_{p(1)}(x)$ is not defined till now. If for some $i \in \{1, 2, 3\}$, x is of the form $\langle i, \langle u, v \rangle \rangle$ and $\varphi_{p(1)}(\langle i, \langle u, 0 \rangle \rangle)$ is defined till now, then let $\varphi_{p(1)}(x) = \varphi_{p(2)}(x) = \varphi_{p(s)}(x) = \varphi_{p(1)}(\langle i, \langle u, 0 \rangle \rangle)$. Else let $\varphi_{p(1)}(x) = \varphi_{p(2)}(x) = \varphi_{p(s)}(x) = 0$.

Let *Addednew* = *Addednew* $\cup \{x\}$.

Forever

6a. For all x, y such that $\langle x, y \rangle \in$ content$(\sigma_1'') - $ content(σ_1^s), let $\varphi_{p(1)}(x) = \varphi_{p(2)}(x) = y$. Let σ_i^{s+1} be an extension of σ_i'' such that content$(\sigma_1^{s+1}) - $ content$(\sigma_1'') = \{\langle x, \varphi_{p(1)}(x) \rangle \mid x \in$ *Addednew*$\}$. Go to stage $s + 1$.

6b. Let σ_i^{s+1} be an extension of σ_i' such that content$(\sigma_1^{s+1}) - $ content$(\sigma_1') = \{\langle x, \varphi_{p(1)}(x) \rangle \mid x \in$ *Addednew*$\}$. Go to stage $s + 1$.

End stage s

Now consider the following cases:

Case 1: All stages terminate.

Let
$$f(x) = \begin{cases} 3, & \text{if } x \in A; \\ \varphi_{p(1)}(x), & \text{otherwise.} \end{cases}$$

Clearly $f \in \mathcal{C}$ (since $\alpha \leq b$, $\varphi_{p(1)} =^b f$ and $\varphi_{p(2)} =^b f$). Also $\mathbf{M}$ on f makes infinitely many mind changes since step 5b can succeed at most r times before step 5a succeeds.

Case 2: Stage $s (\geq 3)$ is the least stage which starts but never terminates.

Let $err_{1,2}, err_{2,3}, err_{1,3}, D_1, D_2, D_3$ be as defined in step 2 in stage s. Now $\max(\{err_{1,2}, err_{2,3}, err_{1,3}\}) \geq \frac{err_{1,2} + err_{2,3} + err_{1,3}}{3} \geq \frac{3b + \alpha}{3}$. Thus $\max(\{err_{1,2}, err_{2,3}, err_{1,3}\}) \geq b + \frac{\alpha}{3}$. Also since $err_{1,2} \leq r + b - \alpha$, we have $\max(\{err_{1,3}, err_{2,3}\}) \geq \frac{2b - r + 2\alpha}{2}$. Thus $\max(\{err_{1,2}, err_{2,3}, err_{1,3}\}) \geq \max(\{b + \alpha - \frac{r}{2}, b + \frac{\alpha}{3}\})$.

Case 2a: In step 2 in stage s it was found that $err_{1,2} \leq \max(\{err_{1,3}, err_{2,3}\})$.

Let l, l' be as found in step 2. In this case domain$(\varphi_{p(s)}) = N - X^s$. Let f be any fixed total extension of $\varphi_{p(s)}$ such that for all $x \in X^s$, we have $f(x) \neq \varphi_q(x)$. Clearly $f \in \mathcal{C}$ (since $\varphi_{p(l)} =^b f$ and $\varphi_{p(s)} =^b f$ and $f(\langle 0, 0 \rangle) = l'$). Let T_1, T_2, T_3 be extensions of $\sigma_1', \sigma_2', \sigma_3'$ (as defined in step 4 in stage s) respectively such that content$(T_1) - $ content$(\sigma_1^s) = \{\langle x, y \rangle \mid f(x) = y \wedge (\forall z)[\langle x, z \rangle \notin$ content$(\sigma_1^s)]\}$ and for all j, $[|\sigma_1'| + j]^{th}$ element of T_1, $[|\sigma_2'| + j]^{th}$ element of T_2 and $[|\sigma_3'| + j]^{th}$ element of T_3 are all same. Clearly $\mathbf{M}(T_1, T_2, T_3) = q$ (otherwise step 5a would succeed).

Now for all $x \in A - D_{l'}$, $f(x) \neq \varphi_q(x)$. (since that was the way $D_{l'}$ was chosen in step 2 of stage s). Thus $\varphi_q \neq^{\max(\{err_{1,3}, err_{2,3}\}) - 1} f$.

Case 2b: In step 2 in stage s it was found that $err_{1,2} > \max(\{err_{1,3}, err_{2,3}\})$.

In this case domain$(\varphi_{p(1)}) = N - X^s$. Let f be a fixed total function such that the following three conditions hold:

- $f(A) = 3$
- $f(x) = \varphi_{p(1)}(x)$, for $x \in$ domain$(\varphi_{p(1)}) - A$
- $(\forall x \in X^s)[f(x) \neq \varphi_q(x)]$

Clearly $f \in \mathcal{C}$ (since $\varphi_{p(1)} =^b f$, $\varphi_{p(2)} =^b f$ and $f(\langle 0, 0 \rangle) = 3$). Let T_1, T_2, T_3 be extensions of $\sigma_1', \sigma_2', \sigma_3'$ respectively such that content$(T_1) -$ content$(\sigma_1^s) = \{\langle x, y \rangle \mid f(x) = y \wedge (\forall z)[\langle x, z \rangle \notin$ content$(\sigma_1^s)]\}$ and for all j, $[|\sigma_1'| + j]^{th}$ element of T_1, $[|\sigma_2'| + j]^{th}$ element of T_2 and $[|\sigma_3'| + j]^{th}$ element of T_3 are all same. Also it is clear that $\mathbf{M}(T_1, T_2, T_3) = q$ (otherwise step 5a would succeed). Now for all $x \in A - D_3$, $f(x) \neq \varphi_q(x)$. (since that was the way D_3 was chosen in step 2 of stage s). Thus $\varphi_q \neq^{err_{1,2}-1} f$.

From the above cases it follows that $\mathcal{C} \notin \mathbf{MUL}_3^2 \mathbf{N}^c \mathbf{Ex}^d$. □

Corollary 16. *Let $a, b, c \in N$ be such that $c \leq a \leq 2c - 1$, $\frac{c}{2} \leq b \leq \frac{3}{4}\lceil \frac{a+1}{2} \rceil$. Then $\mathbf{N}^a \mathbf{Ex}^b - \mathbf{MUL}_3^2 \mathbf{N}^c \mathbf{Ex}^{\lceil \frac{4b}{3} \rceil - 1} \neq \emptyset$.*

Proof. Take $r = c, \alpha = b$ in the above theorem. □

Corollary 17. *Let $a, b, c \in N$ be such that $c \leq a \leq 2c - 1$, $c \leq b$. Then $\mathbf{N}^a \mathbf{Ex}^b - \mathbf{MUL}_3^2 \mathbf{N}^c \mathbf{Ex}^{b + \lceil \frac{c}{2} \rceil - 1} \neq \emptyset$.*

Proof. Take $r = \alpha = c$ in the above theorem. □

Corollary 18. *Let $a, b, c \in N$ be such that $c \leq a \leq 2c - 1$, $\frac{a}{2} < b \leq c$. Then $\mathbf{N}^a \mathbf{Ex}^b - \mathbf{MUL}_3^2 \mathbf{N}^c \mathbf{Ex}^{\lceil \frac{3b}{2} \rceil - 1} \neq \emptyset$.*

Proof. Take $r = \alpha = b$ in the above theorem. □

Corollary 19. *Let $a, b, c \in N$ be such that $c \leq a \leq 2c - 1$, $\max(\{\frac{c}{2}, \frac{3}{4}\lceil \frac{a+1}{2} \rceil\}) \leq b \leq \frac{a}{2}$. Then $\mathbf{N}^a \mathbf{Ex}^b - \mathbf{MUL}_3^2 \mathbf{N}^c \mathbf{Ex}^{\lceil 2b - \frac{a+2}{4} \rceil - 1} \neq \emptyset$.*

Proof. Take $r = \lceil \frac{a+1}{2} \rceil, \alpha = b$ in the above theorem. □

For Theorems 20 to 26 we give the proofs in a slightly informal manner. For Theorems 20 to 26 we need to define certain sets and texts. We also need certain assumptions about the sets which can be assumed *without loss of generality* for the following theorems. We thus use the following definitions and assumptions in the proofs without explicitly stating them in the proofs. Suppose a machine is trying to $\mathbf{MUL}_3^2 \mathbf{N}^c \mathbf{Ex}^d$-identify f. Suppose the three texts provided as input to the machine are T_1, T_2 and T_3, such that at least of two of these texts are c-noisy for f.

Definitions:

Let T_{UNION} be a text such that content$(T_{UNION}) = \{\langle x, y \rangle \mid \langle x, y \rangle \in$ content$(T_1) \vee \langle x, y \rangle \in$ content$(T_2) \vee \langle x, y \rangle \in$ content$(T_3)\}$.

$NOISE\_POINTS = \{x \mid (\exists y, z)[y \neq z \wedge \langle x, y \rangle \in$ content$(T_{UNION}) \wedge \langle x, z \rangle \in$ content$(T_{UNION})]\}$.

$NOISE_{1,2} = \{x \mid$ card$(\{y \mid \langle x, y \rangle \in T_1\}) =$ card$(\{y \mid \langle x, y \rangle \in T_2\}) \geq 2 \wedge$ card$(\{y \mid \langle x, y \rangle \in T_3\}) = 1\}$.

$NOISE_{1,3} = \{x \mid$ card$(\{y \mid \langle x, y \rangle \in T_1\}) =$ card$(\{y \mid \langle x, y \rangle \in T_3\}) \geq 2 \wedge$ card$(\{y \mid \langle x, y \rangle \in T_2\}) = 1\}$.

$NOISE_{2,3} = \{x \mid$ card$(\{y \mid \langle x, y \rangle \in T_2\}) =$ card$(\{y \mid \langle x, y \rangle \in T_3\}) \geq 2 \wedge$ card$(\{y \mid \langle x, y \rangle \in T_1\}) = 1\}$.

$NOISE_{1,2,3} = NOISE\_POINTS - (NOISE_{1,2} \cup NOISE_{1,3} \cup NOISE_{2,3})$.

Assumptions

For all $i \in \{1, 2, 3\}$, card$(\{x \mid (\exists y, z)[y \neq z \wedge \langle x, y \rangle \in$ content$(T_i) \wedge \langle x, z \rangle \in$ content$(T_i)]\}) \leq c$ (since if the cardinality of noisy points is greater than c, then we know which two texts are c-noisy texts for f).

For all $i, j \in \{1, 2, 3\}$ and for all $x \in NOISE\_POINTS$ card$(\{y \mid \langle x, y \rangle \in$ content$(T_i) \cap$ content$(T_j)\}) \geq 1$ (this is so because otherwise at least one of T_i, T_j is not a c-noisy text for f, which implies that the remaining text is a c-noisy text for f).

For all x, y, card$(\{i \mid \langle x, y \rangle \in$ content$(T_i)\}) \neq 1$ (otherwise, surely $f(x) \neq y$ and we can thus drop $\langle x, y \rangle$ from consideration).

Note that if the above assumptions do not hold then we can convert the texts (in the limit) to T_1', T_2' and T_3' such that at least two of these texts are c-noisy for f and T_1', T_2', T_3' satisfy the assumptions given above.

Theorem 20. *Let $b, c \in N$. Then $\mathbf{N}^c\mathbf{Ex}^b \subseteq \mathbf{MUL}_3^2\mathbf{N}^c\mathbf{Ex}^{b + \lceil \frac{c}{2} \rceil}$.*

Proof. Suppose machine $\mathbf{M}$ $\mathbf{N}^c\mathbf{Ex}^b$-identifies $\mathcal{C}$. We construct $\mathbf{M}'$ such that $\mathbf{M}'$ $\mathbf{MUL}_3^2\mathbf{N}^c\mathbf{Ex}^{b + \lceil \frac{c}{2} \rceil}$-identifies $\mathcal{C}$. Let T_1, T_2, T_3 be three texts given for a function $f \in \mathcal{C}$, such that at least two of the three texts are c-noisy for f. Let $m = \min(\{$card$(NOISE_{1,2})$, card$(NOISE_{1,3})$, card$(NOISE_{2,3})\})$.

Let S be a set of cardinality $3m$ such that card$(S \cap NOISE_{1,2}) =$ card$(S \cap NOISE_{1,3}) =$ card$(S \cap NOISE_{2,3})$.

Let $X \subseteq NOISE\_POINTS - S$ be a set of cardinality $\lceil \frac{\text{card}(NOISE\_POINTS) - 3m}{2} \rceil$.

Let i, j be distinct and such that: $\mathbf{M}(T_i)\downarrow$ and $\mathbf{M}(T_j)\downarrow$, $P_i = \mathbf{M}(T_i)$ and $P_j = \mathbf{M}(T_j)$ and card$(\{x \mid \varphi_{P_i}(x)\downarrow \neq \varphi_{P_j}(x)\downarrow \wedge x \notin NOISE\_POINTS\}) \leq 2b$. Let $CLASH = \{x \mid \varphi_{P_i}(x)\downarrow \neq \varphi_{P_j}(x)\downarrow \wedge x \notin NOISE\_POINTS\}$.

Note that we can easily determine all the sets defined above and P_i, P_j as above in the limit from the given texts. $\mathbf{M}'$ in the limit outputs a program p such that:

$$\varphi_p(x) = \begin{cases} \varphi_{P_i}(x), & \text{if } x \in X; \\ \varphi_{P_j}(x), & \text{if } x \in NOISE\_POINTS - (X \cup S); \\ y, & \text{if } x \in CLASH \wedge \langle x, y \rangle \in \text{content}(T_{UNION}); \\ \varphi_{P_i}(x), & \text{if } x \in N - (NOISE\_POINTS \cup CLASH) \wedge x \in \text{domain}(\varphi_{P_i}); \\ \varphi_{P_j}(x), & \text{if } x \in N - (NOISE\_POINTS \cup CLASH) \wedge x \in \text{domain}(\varphi_{P_j}); \\ y, & \text{if } x \in S \wedge \langle x, y \rangle \in \text{content}(T_1) \cap \text{content}(T_2) \cap \text{content}(T_3); \\ \uparrow, & \text{otherwise.} \end{cases}$$

Since at least one of P_i, P_j computes a b-variant of f, the number of errors committed by $\varphi_p \leq b + m + \lceil \frac{\text{card}(NOISE\_POINTS - S)}{2} \rceil$, which is at most $b + \lceil \frac{c}{2} \rceil$. $\square$

Theorem 21. *Let $c, b \in N, \frac{c}{2} \leq b \leq c$ be given. Then $\mathbf{N}^{2c-1}\mathbf{Ex}^b \subseteq \mathbf{MUL}_3^2\mathbf{N}^c\mathbf{Ex}^d$ if $d \geq \max(\{\frac{4b}{3}, 2b - \frac{c}{2}\})$.*

Proof. Suppose machine $\mathbf{M}$ $\mathbf{N}^{2c-1}\mathbf{Ex}^b$-identifies $\mathcal{C}$. We construct machine $\mathbf{M}'$ such that $\mathbf{M}'$ $\mathbf{MUL}_3^2\mathbf{N}^c\mathbf{Ex}^d$-identifies $\mathcal{C}$. Let T_1, T_2, T_3 be three texts given for a function $f \in \mathcal{C}$, such that at least two of the three texts are c-noisy for f.

Note that T_{UNION} is a noisy text for f. If T_{UNION} is a $(2c-1)$-noisy text for f, then $\mathbf{M}'$ can just output the programs output by $\mathbf{M}$ on T_{UNION} to identify f with at most d errors. Thus assume that T_{UNION} so formed contains more than $2c - 1$ noisy elements. A simple calculation shows that the amount of noise in T_{UNION} is bounded by $\frac{3c + \text{card}(NOISE_{1,2,3})}{2}$. If $\text{card}(NOISE_{1,2,3}) < c$ then T_{UNION} is a $(2c-1)$-noisy text for f. Thus $\text{card}(NOISE_{1,2,3}) = c$. Also for all $x \in NOISE_{1,2,3}$, we can assume that there exist distinct y_1^x, y_2^x, y_3^x such that $\langle x, y_1^x \rangle \in \text{content}(T_2) \cap \text{content}(T_3)$, $\langle x, y_2^x \rangle \in \text{content}(T_1) \cap \text{content}(T_2)$ and $\langle x, y_3^x \rangle \in \text{content}(T_1) \cap \text{content}(T_3)$ (otherwise T_{UNION} contains at most $2c - 1$ noisy elements).

Let i, j be distinct and such that: $\mathbf{M}(T_i)\downarrow$ and $\mathbf{M}(T_j)\downarrow$, $P_i = \mathbf{M}(T_i)$ and $P_j = \mathbf{M}(T_j)$ and $\text{card}(\{x \mid \varphi_{P_i}(x)\downarrow \neq \varphi_{P_j}(x)\downarrow \wedge x \notin NOISE\_POINTS\}) \leq 2b$. Let $CLASH = \{x \mid [\varphi_{P_i}(x)\downarrow \neq \varphi_{P_j}(x)\downarrow] \wedge [x \notin NOISE\_POINTS]\}$. For $m \in \{i, j\}$, let $\delta_m = \text{card}(\{x \mid x \in NOISE\_POINTS \wedge [\langle x, \varphi_{P_m}(x) \rangle \in \text{content}(T_i) \cap \text{content}(T_j)]\})$. Let $\delta = \min(\delta_i, \delta_j)$. We can suppose without loss of generality that $c - b \leq \delta \leq b$ (otherwise we can determine a text which is guaranteed to be c-noisy for f. For suppose that $\delta = \delta_i < c - b$, then clearly one of T_i and T_j is not a c-noisy text for f. This implies that the remaining text is a c-noisy text for f. Other cases are similar. In any of these cases, $\mathbf{M}'$ can simply input the correct c-noisy text obtained by the above analysis into $\mathbf{M}$ and arrive (in the limit) at a program which is at most b ($\leq d$) variant of f).

We will pick a $\mu \in N, \mu \leq c$ depending on δ. Let $S \subseteq NOISE\_POINTS$ be a set of cardinality μ. Let $X \subseteq NOISE\_POINTS - S$ be a set of cardinality $\lceil \frac{c - \mu}{2} \rceil$.

$\mathbf{M}'$ in the limit outputs a program p_μ such that the following holds:

$$\varphi_{p_\mu}(x) = \begin{cases} y_k^x, & \text{if } x \in S \wedge k \in \{1,2,3\} - \{i,j\}; \\ y_i^x, & \text{if } x \in X; \\ y_j^x, & \text{if } x \in NOISE\_POINTS - (X \cup S); \\ y, & \text{if } x \in CLASH \wedge \langle x,y \rangle \in \text{content}(T_{UNION}); \\ \varphi_{P_i}(x), & \text{if } x \in N - (NOISE\_POINTS \cup CLASH) \wedge x \in \text{domain}(\varphi_{P_i}); \\ \varphi_{P_j}(x), & \text{if } x \in N - (NOISE\_POINTS \cup CLASH) \wedge x \in \text{domain}(\varphi_{P_j}); \\ \uparrow, & \text{otherwise.} \end{cases}$$

Now the number of errors committed by $\mathbf{M}'$ on f is bounded by $maxerr = \max(\{b - \mu + \delta, b - \delta + \mu + \lceil \frac{c-\mu}{2} \rceil\}) = \lceil \max(\{b - \mu + \delta, b - \delta + \mu + \frac{c-\mu}{2}\}) \rceil$. By choosing an $\mu = \max(\{0, \lfloor \frac{4\delta-c}{3} \rfloor\})$ we have $maxerr = \lceil \max(\{b + \frac{c-\delta}{3}, b - \delta + \frac{c}{2}\}) \rceil$. The value of $maxerr$ is maximized for $\delta = c - b$. Thus $maxerr = \lceil \max(\{\frac{4b}{3}, 2b - \frac{c}{2}\}) \rceil$. Thus if $d \geq \lceil \max(\{\frac{4b}{3}, 2b - \frac{c}{2}\}) \rceil$ then $\mathbf{N}^{2c-1}\mathbf{Ex}^b \subseteq \mathbf{MUL}_3^2\mathbf{N}^c\mathbf{Ex}^d$. $\square$

Theorem 22. *For $b < \lceil \frac{c}{2} \rceil$, $\mathbf{N}^{2c-1}\mathbf{Ex}^b \subseteq \mathbf{MUL}_3^2\mathbf{N}^c\mathbf{Ex}^b$.*

Proof. Suppose machine $\mathbf{M}$ $\mathbf{N}^{2c-1}\mathbf{Ex}^b$-identifies $\mathcal{C}$. We describe $\mathbf{M}'$ such that $\mathbf{M}'$ $\mathbf{MUL}_3^2\mathbf{N}^c\mathbf{Ex}^b$-identifies $\mathcal{C}$. Let T_1, T_2, T_3 be the three texts given such that at least two of these are c-noisy for $f \in \mathcal{C}$.

As in Theorem 21, it can be shown that either T_{UNION}, is a $(2c-1)$-noisy for f or else there exists a set X of cardinality c and distinct y_1^x, y_2^x, y_3^x, for each $x \in X$, such that $(\forall x \in X)(\forall i \in \{1,2,3\})(\forall y \in \{y_1^x, y_2^x, y_3^x\} - \{y_i^x\})[\langle x,y \rangle \in \text{content}(T_i)]$. Now let $i \in \{1,2,3\}$ be such that $\mathbf{M}(T_i)\downarrow$. Let $\mathbf{M}(T_i) = P_i$. For $j \in \{1,2,3\} - \{i\}$, let $D_j = \{x \in X \mid \varphi_{P_i}(x) = y_j^x\}$. Let $j \in \{1,2,3\} - \{i\}$ be such that $\text{card}(D_j) \leq \frac{c}{2}$. Note that such a j exists. Now for all $x \in X$, $f(x) \neq y_j^x$ (since otherwise T_i is a c-noisy text for f and thus φ_{P_i} should be a b-variant of f). Thus T_j is a c-noisy text for f. Thus $\mathbf{M}(T_j)\downarrow$ and $\varphi_{\mathbf{M}(T_j)}$ is a b-variant of f. Clearly in all the above cases $\mathbf{M}'$ can in the limit easily output a program which is a b-variant of f. $\square$

Theorem 23. *Let $b, c \in N$.*
(I) $\mathbf{N}^{2c}\mathbf{Ex}^b \subseteq \mathbf{MUL}_3^2\mathbf{N}^c\mathbf{Ex}^b$.
(II) $\mathbf{In}^{c+\lfloor \frac{c}{2} \rfloor}\mathbf{Ex}^b \subseteq \mathbf{MUL}_3^2\mathbf{In}^c\mathbf{Ex}^b$.

Proof. (I) Suppose machine $\mathbf{M}$ $\mathbf{N}^{2c}\mathbf{Ex}^b$-identifies $\mathcal{C}$. We construct $\mathbf{M}'$ such that $\mathbf{M}'$ $\mathbf{MUL}_3^2\mathbf{N}^c\mathbf{Ex}^b$-identifies $\mathcal{C}$.

Let T_1, T_2, T_3 be three texts given for a function $f \in \mathcal{C}$, such that at least two of the three texts are c-noisy for f. A simple calculation shows that the amount of noise in T_{UNION} (with respect to the graph of f) is bounded by $\frac{3c + \text{card}(NOISE_{1,2,3})}{2}$. Noting that $\text{card}(NOISE_{1,2,3})$ is bounded by c, it follows that T_{UNION} is a $2c$-noisy text for f. $\mathbf{M}'$ outputs in the limit whatever is output by $\mathbf{M}$, in the limit, on the text T_{UNION}. Thus $\mathbf{M}'$ $\mathbf{MUL}_3^2\mathbf{N}^c\mathbf{Ex}^b$-identifies f. This proves (I).

(II) (sketch) For this we need the notion of stabilizing sequence.

Definition 24. [Ful85] σ is said to be a stabilizing sequence for $\mathbf{M}$ on L iff $[\text{content}(\sigma) \subseteq L$ and $(\forall \tau \mid \sigma \subset \tau \wedge \text{content}(\tau) \subseteq L)[\mathbf{M}(\tau) = \mathbf{M}(\sigma)]]$.

Lemma 25. (Based on similar lemma in [BB75, OW82]) *Suppose* **M** **In**^{a}**Ex**^{b}- *identifies* f. *Let* L *be such that* $L \subseteq \{\langle x, y \rangle \mid f(x) = y\} \wedge \mathrm{card}(\{\{\langle x, y \rangle \mid f(x) = y\} - L) \leq a$. *Then there exists a stabilizing sequence for* **M** *on* L. *Moreover if* σ *is a stabilizing sequence for* **M** *on* L *then* $\varphi_{\mathbf{M}(\sigma)} =^b f$.

Suppose machine **M** **In**$^{c + \lfloor \frac{c}{2} \rfloor}$**Ex**^{b}-identifies $\mathcal{C}$. We construct **M**$'$ such that **M**$'$ **MUL**$^2_3$**In**^{c}**Ex**^{b}-identifies $\mathcal{C}$.

Let T_1, T_2, T_3 be three texts given for a function $f \in \mathcal{C}$, such that at least two of the three texts are c-incomplete for f. Let T_{UNION} be a text such that $\mathrm{content}(T_{UNION}) = \mathrm{content}(T_1) \cup \mathrm{content}(T_2) \cup \mathrm{content}(T_3)$. Without loss of generality we assume that $(\forall x)[\mathrm{card}(\{y \mid \langle x, y \rangle \in \mathrm{content}(T_{UNION})\}) \leq 1]$ (for if there is such an x and y, z, i, j such that $\langle x, y \rangle \in \mathrm{content}(T_i), \langle x, z \rangle \in \mathrm{content}(T_j)$ and $y \neq z$, then at least one of T_i, T_j is not a c-incomplete text for f. Thus the third text is a c-incomplete text for f). We can also assume without loss of generality that $(\forall x)[\mathrm{card}(i \in \{1, 2, 3\} \mid (\exists y)[\langle x, y \rangle \in \mathrm{content}(T_i)]) \neq 2]$ (otherwise for such x's the value of $f(x)$ is known and thus without loss of generality we can put $\langle x, y \rangle$ in the content of all three texts).

In the following, we try to locate a stabilizing sequence for **M** on an appropriate subset of $\{\langle x, f(x) \rangle \mid x \in N\}$. If one of the texts has a high amount of incompleteness then this may not be possible (see condition (iii) below); however in this case it is possible to determine the text which has a high amount of incompleteness.

Let $n', n'' \in N$, $X \subset \{0, 1, \ldots, n'\}$ and $\sigma \in \mathrm{SEQ}$ be such that:

(i) $(\forall i \in \{1, 2, 3\})(\forall y \in N)(\forall x \in \{0, 1, \ldots, n'\})[\langle x, y \rangle \in \mathrm{content}(T_i) \Rightarrow \langle x, y \rangle \in \mathrm{content}(T_i[n''])]$.

(ii) $(\forall x \in X)(\forall y \in N)[\mathrm{card}(\{i \mid \langle x, y \rangle \in \mathrm{content}(T_i)\}) \leq 1]$.

(iii)

(A) $[(\exists j \in \{1, 2, 3\})[\mathrm{card}(\{x \mid (x \in X) \wedge (\forall y \in N)[\langle x, y \rangle \notin \mathrm{content}(T_j)]\}) > c]]$

OR

(B) $[[[\mathrm{content}(\sigma) \subseteq [\mathrm{content}(T_{UNION}) \cap \{\langle x, y \rangle \mid (y \in N) \wedge (x \leq n')\}] - [\{\langle x, y \rangle \mid (x \in X) \wedge (y \in N)\}]]$ and σ is a stabilizing sequence for **M** on $L = [\mathrm{content}(T_{UNION}) - \{\langle x, y \rangle \mid (x \in X) \wedge (y \in N)\}]]$ AND $[(\forall x \leq n')[x \notin X \Rightarrow (\exists y)[\mathrm{card}(\{i \mid \langle x, y \rangle \in T_i\}) = 3]]]]]$.

It is easy to see that if such n', n'', X, σ exist then **M**$'$ can find them in the limit. If in (iii) (A) holds then clearly **M**$'$ can know the two texts which are c-incomplete for f, and thus output in the limit a b error program for f. If in (iii) (B) holds then we claim that $\mathbf{M}(\sigma)$ is a b-error program for f. This would be so if $\mathrm{card}(\{\langle x, y \rangle \mid f(x) = y\} - L) \leq c + \lfloor \frac{c}{2} \rfloor$. To prove this, let $\delta_i = \mathrm{card}(\{x \in X \mid (\exists y)[\langle x, y \rangle \in \mathrm{content}(T_i)]\})$. Let δ be the median of $\delta_1, \delta_2, \delta_3$. Now $\mathrm{card}(\{\langle x, y \rangle \mid f(x) = y\} - L) \leq c - (\mathrm{card}(X) - \delta) + \mathrm{card}(X) \leq c + \delta$ and $\delta \leq \frac{c}{2}$.

To complete the proof we have to show that such n', n'', X, σ indeed exist.

Case 1: There exists an $i \in \{1, 2, 3\}$ such that $\mathrm{card}(\{x \mid (\forall y)[\langle x, y \rangle \notin \mathrm{content}(T_i)]\}) > c$.

Let n' be such that there exists an i, $\mathrm{card}(\{x \leq n' \mid (\forall y)[\langle x, y \rangle \notin \mathrm{content}(T_i)]\}) = c + 1$. Let n'' be such that (i) above is satisfied. Let $X = \{x \leq n' \mid \mathrm{card}(\{i \mid$

$(\exists y)[\langle x, y\rangle \in \text{content}(T_i)]\}) \leq 1\}$. Then it is easy to see that (i), (ii) and (iii) above are satisfied.

Case 2: There does not exist an $i \in \{1, 2, 3\}$ such that $\text{card}(\{x \mid (\forall y)[\langle x, y\rangle \notin \text{content}(T_i)]\}) > c$.

Let $X = \{x \mid \text{card}(\{i \mid (\exists y)[\langle x, y\rangle \in \text{content}(T_i)]\}) \leq 1\}$. Now let $L = \{\langle x, y\rangle \mid f(x) = y \wedge x \notin X\}$, let $\delta_i = \text{card}(\{x \in X \mid (\exists y)[\langle x, y\rangle \in \text{content}(T_i)]\})$. Let δ be the median of $\delta_1, \delta_2, \delta_3$. Now $\text{card}(\{\langle x, y\rangle \mid f(x) = y\} - L) \leq c - (\text{card}(X) - \delta) + \text{card}(X) \leq c + \delta$ and $\delta \leq \frac{c}{2}$. Thus there exists a stabilizing sequence σ for $\mathbf{M}$ on L. Let $n' = 1 + \max(X \cup \{x \mid (\exists y)[\langle x, y\rangle \in \text{content}(\sigma)]\})$. Let n'' be chosen so as to satisfy (i) above. Clearly, n', n'', X and σ satisfy (i), (ii) and (iii).

The above cases prove the existence of σ, X, n', n'' satisfying (i),(ii) and (iii). $\square$

Using the idea of (I) in the above theorem we can also show that:

Theorem 26. *Let* $b, c \in N$. *Then* $\mathbf{N}^{\frac{3c+2b}{2}}\mathbf{Ex}^b \subseteq \mathbf{MUL}_3^2\mathbf{N}^c\mathbf{Ex}^b$.

Theorem 27. *Let* $b, c \in N, b \geq c > 1$. *Then* $\mathbf{In}^{\lfloor\frac{3c}{2}\rfloor-1}\mathbf{Ex}^b - \mathbf{MUL}_3^2\mathbf{In}^c\mathbf{Ex}^{b+\lceil\frac{c}{2}\rceil-1} \neq \emptyset$.

The above theorem can be proved using ideas similar to those used to prove Theorem 15. We omit the details.

Theorem 28. *Let* $b, c \in N, b \geq c$ *be given. Then* $\mathbf{In}^c\mathbf{Ex}^b \subseteq \mathbf{MUL}_3^2\mathbf{In}^c\mathbf{Ex}^{b+\lceil\frac{c}{2}\rceil}$.

Proof. Suppose hypothesis. Suppose machine $\mathbf{M}$ $\mathbf{In}^c\mathbf{Ex}^b$-identifies $\mathcal{C}$. We construct $\mathbf{M}'$ such that $\mathbf{M}'$ $\mathbf{MUL}_3^2\mathbf{In}^c\mathbf{Ex}^{b+\lceil\frac{c}{2}\rceil}$-identifies $\mathcal{C}$.

Let T_1, T_2, T_3 be three texts given for a function $f \in \mathcal{C}$, such that at least two of the three texts are c-incomplete for f. Without loss of generality we can assume that $(\forall x)[\text{card}(\{y \mid \langle x, y\rangle \in \text{content}(T_1) \cup \text{content}(T_2) \cup \text{content}(T_3)\}) \leq 1]$ (for if there is such a x then let y, z, i, j be such that $\langle x, y\rangle \in \text{content}(T_i), \langle x, z\rangle \in \text{content}(T_j)$ and $y \neq z$, then at least one of T_i, T_j is not a c-incomplete text for f. Thus the third text is a c-incomplete text for f).

Let T_{UNION} be a text such that $\text{content}(T_{UNION}) = \{\langle x, y\rangle \mid \langle x, y\rangle \in \text{content}(T_1) \vee \langle x, y\rangle \in \text{content}(T_2) \vee \langle x, y\rangle \in \text{content}(T_3)\}$. Let i, j be distinct and such that: $\mathbf{M}(T_i)\downarrow$ and $\mathbf{M}(T_j)\downarrow$, $P_i = \mathbf{M}(T_i)$ and $P_j = \mathbf{M}(T_j)$ and $\text{card}(CLASH = \{x \mid [\varphi_{P_i}(x)\downarrow \neq \varphi_{P_j}(x)\downarrow] \vee (\exists y)[[\langle x, y\rangle \in \text{content}(T_{UNION})] \wedge [[\varphi_{P_i}(x)\downarrow \neq y] \vee [\varphi_{P_j}(x)\downarrow \neq y]]]\}) \leq 3b$.

Let $VIS\_IN = CLASH \cap \{x \mid \text{card}(\{i \mid (\exists y)\langle x, y\rangle \in \text{content}(T_i)\}) \leq 1\}$. For $i \in \{1, 2, 3\}$, let $IN_i = VIS\_IN \cap \{x \mid (\exists y)[\langle x, y\rangle \in \text{content}(T_i)]\}$. Let $m = \min(\text{card}(IN_1), \text{card}(IN_2), \text{card}(IN_3))$. Let $S \subseteq VIS\_IN$ be a set of cardinality $3m$ such that $\text{card}(S \cap IN_1) = \text{card}(S \cap IN_2) = \text{card}(S \cap IN_3)$. Let $X \subseteq VIS\_IN - S$ be a set of cardinality $\lceil\frac{\text{card}(VIS\_IN-S)}{2}\rceil$.

Machine $\mathbf{M}'$ outputs (in the limit) program p as follows :

$$\varphi_p(x) = \begin{cases} \varphi_{P_i}(x), & \text{if } x \notin CLASH \wedge x \in \text{domain}(\varphi_{P_i}); \\ \varphi_{P_j}(x), & \text{if } x \notin CLASH \wedge x \in \text{domain}(\varphi_{P_j}); \\ y, & \text{if } x \in ((CLASH - VIS\_IN) \cup S) \wedge \langle x, y \rangle \in \text{content}(T_{UNION}) ; \\ \varphi_{P_i}(x), & \text{if } x \in X; \\ \varphi_{P_j}(x), & \text{if } x \in VIS\_IN - (S \cup X); \\ \uparrow, & \text{otherwise.} \end{cases}$$

Now the number of errors committed by $\mathbf{M}'$ on f is bounded by $m + \lceil \frac{\text{card}(VIS\_IN - S)}{2} \rceil + b$. Observing that $c \geq \text{card}(VIS\_IN) - m$, it follows that $\mathbf{M}'$ $\mathbf{MUL}_3^2\mathbf{In}^c\mathbf{Ex}^{b + \lceil \frac{c}{2} \rceil}$-identifies C. $\square$

Theorem 29. *Let* $b, c \in N$.
(I) $\mathbf{N}^c\mathbf{Ex}^b \subseteq \mathbf{MUL}_3^2\mathbf{N}^c\mathbf{Ex}^{2b}$.
(II) $\mathbf{In}^c\mathbf{Ex}^b \subseteq \mathbf{MUL}_3^2\mathbf{In}^c\mathbf{Ex}^{2b}$.
(III) $\mathbf{Im}^c\mathbf{Ex}^b \subseteq \mathbf{MUL}_3^2\mathbf{Im}^c\mathbf{Ex}^{2b}$.

Proof. (I) Suppose machine $\mathbf{M}$ $\mathbf{N}^c\mathbf{Ex}^b$-identifies C. We construct $\mathbf{M}'$ such that $\mathbf{M}'$ $\mathbf{MUL}_3^2\mathbf{N}^c\mathbf{Ex}^{2b}$-identifies C.

Let T_1, T_2, T_3 be three texts given for a function $f \in C$, such that at least two of the three texts are c-noisy for f. Let i, j be distinct and such that: $\mathbf{M}(T_i)\downarrow$ and $\mathbf{M}(T_j)\downarrow$, $P_i = \mathbf{M}(T_i)$ and $P_j = \mathbf{M}(T_j)$ and $\text{card}(\{x \mid \varphi_{P_i}(x)\downarrow \neq \varphi_{P_j}(x)\downarrow\}) \leq 2b$. Let $CLASH = \{x \mid \varphi_{P_i}(x)\downarrow \neq \varphi_{P_j}(x)\downarrow\}$. Let $S \subseteq CLASH$ be a set of cardinality $\lfloor \frac{\text{card}(CLASH)}{2} \rfloor$.

Note that we can easily determine all the sets defined above and P_i, P_j as above in the limit from the given texts.

$\mathbf{M}'$ in the limit outputs a program p such that:

$$\varphi_p(x) = \begin{cases} \varphi_{P_i}(x), & \text{if } x \in S; \\ \varphi_{P_j}(x), & \text{if } x \in CLASH - S; \\ \varphi_{P_i}(x), & x \in N - CLASH \wedge x \in \text{domain}(\varphi_{P_i}); \\ \varphi_{P_j}(x), & x \in N - CLASH \wedge x \in \text{domain}(\varphi_{P_j}); \\ \uparrow, & \text{otherwise.} \end{cases}$$

Since at least one of P_i, P_j computes a b-variant of f, it is clear that program p computes a $2b$-variant of f. Thus $\mathbf{M}'$ $\mathbf{MUL}_3^2\mathbf{N}^c\mathbf{Ex}^{2b}$-identifies f.

(II) and (III) can be proved similarly. $\square$

Theorem 30. *Let* $a \in N$. *Then* $\mathbf{In}^a\mathbf{Ex}^1 = \mathbf{MUL}_3^2\mathbf{In}^a\mathbf{Ex}^1$.

We omit the proof of the above theorem.

5.4 Comparison of Different Types of Inaccuracies

Finally, we present results which shed light on how learning from one kind of inaccuracy compares with learning from another kind of inaccuracy.

Theorem 31. *Let* $j, k \in N$, $j > \lfloor \frac{k}{2} \rfloor$. *Then* $\mathbf{MUL}_k^j\mathbf{N}^*\mathbf{Ex} - \mathbf{In}^1\mathbf{Ex}^* \neq \emptyset$.

Proof. Follows from Theorem 10 in [FJ89] and Theorem 10. $\square$

Theorem 32. *Let* $a, b \in N \cup \{*\}$, *and* $j, k \in N$, $j > \lfloor \frac{k}{2} \rfloor$. *Then* $\mathbf{MUL}_k^j \mathbf{In}^a \mathbf{Ex}^b \subseteq \mathbf{MUL}_k^j \mathbf{N}^a \mathbf{Ex}^b$.

Proof. Let $T_1, T_2, \ldots, T_k$ be the k input texts for f, such that at least j of the texts are a-noisy for f. Note that if $f(x) = y$ then at least j of the k texts contain $\langle x, y \rangle$. Let T_i' be the text formed from T_i such that content$(T_i') = \{\langle x, y \rangle \mid \text{card}(\{l \mid \langle x, y \rangle \in \text{content}(T_i)\}) \geq j \wedge \text{card}(\{y \mid \langle x, y \rangle \in \text{content}(T_i)\}) \leq 1 \wedge \langle x, y \rangle \in \text{content}(T_i)\}$. Thus we can easily obtain T_i's from T_is in the limit. Also if T_i was a-noisy for f then T_i' is a-incomplete for f. The theorem follows. $\square$

Theorem 33. *Let* $j, k \in N, j > \lfloor \frac{k}{2} \rfloor$. *Then* $(\forall i \in N)[\mathbf{MUL}_k^j \mathbf{In}^{3i-1} \mathbf{Ex} - \mathbf{Im}^{2i} \mathbf{Ex}^* \neq \emptyset]$.

Proof. Follows from Theorem 58 in [Jai90] and Theorem 11. $\square$

Theorem 34. *Let* $j, k \in N, j > \lfloor \frac{k}{2} \rfloor$. *Then* $\mathbf{MUL}_k^j \mathbf{In}^* \mathbf{Ex} - \mathbf{Im}^* \mathbf{Ex}^* \neq \emptyset$.

Proof. Follows from Theorem 60 in [Jai90] and Theorem 11. $\square$

6 Conclusion

We presented arguments against the idealized assumption in Gold's paradigm that a learning agent receives data from a single and accurate source. Gold's paradigm was suitably extended to account for the possibility that a learning agent may receive data from multiple sources, some of which may be inaccurate. Results were presented for the learning task of scientific inquiry modeled as identification in the limit of computer programs for computable functions from their graphs. In particular, these results shed light on when learning from multiple data sources, some possibly inaccurate, is a restriction on learning power compared to learning from a single data source which could be inaccurate. Some of the results presented could be used to construct hierarchies of learnable classes of computable functions. We also proved results that compared learning from multiple texts with different kinds of inaccuracies.

It should be noted that several of the results presented in Section 5.3 can be easily generalized to the case in which a machine is fed k texts and for at least j of these texts the inaccuracies are "good." Also, results in the present manuscript are about a simple criterion of success, viz., **Ex**-identification. We can also prove corresponding results for a more general criterion of learning, viz., **Bc**-identification (see [CS83] for definition; also known as GN$^\infty$ [Bar74] in the Russian literature). Additionally, we would like to note that similar results can also be shown to hold for another learning task, viz., first language acquisition modeled as identification in the limit of grammars for recursively enumerable languages from a text of these languages. The criterion of success for language acquisition is known as **TxtEx**-identification (see [CL82] for definition).

As already noted in Section 4, the model of scientific inquiry in which a scientist is receiving data from multiple, but possibly inaccurate, sources is still not faithful in modeling the practice of science. A phenomenon is generally investigated by a 'team' of scientists, each member of the team, sooner or later, has access to data, possibly inaccurate, from everyone else. Scientific success is said to take place just in case at least one member of the team is successful[3]. The study of this model is the subject of future research; the results and techniques of the present paper, we feel, would be a necessary resource for such an investigation.

7 Acknowledgements

We would like to thank John Case, Mark Fulk, and Errol Lloyd for encouragement and advice. Helpful discussions were provided by Rajeev Raman, Lata Narayanan and Sudhir K. Jha. We would like to thank Andrea Lobo for careful reading of the paper. We would also like to express our gratitude to Prof. S. N. Maheshwari of the Department of Computer Science and Engineering at IIT–Delhi for making the facilities of his department available to us.

References

[Bar74]   J. M. Barzdin. Two theorems on the limiting synthesis of functions. *In Theory of Algorithms and Programs, Latvian State University, Riga*, 210:82–88, 1974. In Russian.

[BB75]   L. Blum and M. Blum. Toward a mathematical theory of inductive inference. *Information and Control*, 28:125–155, 1975.

[Blu67]   M. Blum. A machine independent theory of the complexity of recursive functions. *Journal of the ACM*, 14:322–336, 1967.

[Cas74]   J. Case. Periodicity in generations of automata. *Mathematical Systems Theory*, 8:15–32, 1974.

[CL82]   J. Case and C. Lynes. Machine inductive inference and language identification. *Lecture Notes in Computer Science*, 140:107–115, 1982.

[CS83]   J. Case and C. Smith. Comparison of identification criteria for machine inductive inference. *Theoretical Computer Science*, 25:193–220, 1983.

[FCe90]   M. Fulk and J. Case (editors). *Proceedings of the Third Annual Workshop on Computational Learning Theory*. Morgan Kaufmann Publishers, Inc., August 1990.

[FJ89]   M. A. Fulk and S. Jain. Learning in the presence of inaccurate information. In R. Rivest, D. Haussler, and M. K. Warmuth, editors, *Proceedings of the Second Annual Workshop on Computational Learning Theory, Santa Cruz, California*, pages 175–188. Morgan Kaufmann Publishers, Inc., August 1989.

[Ful85]   M. Fulk. *A Study of Inductive Inference machines*. PhD thesis, SUNY at Buffalo, 1985.

[Gol67]   E. M. Gold. Language identification in the limit. *Information and Control*, 10:447–474, 1967.

[HPe88]   D. Haussler and L. Pitt (editors). *Proceedings of the 1988 Workshop on Computational Learning Theory*. Morgan Kaufmann Publishers, Inc., August 1988.

[Jai90]   S. Jain. *Learning in the Presence of Additional Information and Inaccurate Information*. PhD thesis, University of Rochester, 1990.

[MY78]   M. Machtey and P. Young. *An Introduction to the General Theory of Algorithms*. North Holland, New York, 1978.

[OSW86]   D. Osherson, M. Stob, and S. Weinstein. *Systems that Learn, An Introduction to Learning Theory for Cognitive and Computer Scientists*. MIT Press, Cambridge, Mass., 1986.

[OW82]   D. Osherson and S. Weinstein. A note on formal learning theory. *Cognition*, 11:77–88, 1982.

---

[3] See Smith [Smi82] for study of team identification from a single and accurate text.

[Put73]   H. Putnam. Reductionism and the nature of psychology. *Cognition*, 2:131–146, 1973.

[RHWe89] R. Rivest, D. Haussler, and M. K. Warmuth (editors). *Proceedings of the Second Annual Workshop on Computational Learning Theory*. Morgan Kaufmann Publishers, Inc., August 1989.

[Rog58]   H. Rogers. Gödel numberings of partial recursive functions. *Journal of Symbolic Logic*, 23:331–341, 1958.

[Rog67]   H. Rogers. *Theory of Recursive Functions and Effective Computability*. McGraw Hill, New York, 1967. Reprinted. MIT Press. 1987.

[Smi82]   C. Smith. The power of pluralism for automatic program synthesis. *Journal of the ACM*, 29:1144–1165, 1982.

[Sol64a]   R. J. Solomonoff. A formal theory of inductive inference, Part I. *Information and Control*, 7:1–22, 1964.

[Sol64b]   R. J. Solomonoff. A formal theory of inductive inference, Part II. *Information and Control*, 7:224–254, 1964.

[SR86]   G. Schäfer-Richter. Some results in the theory of effective program synthesis - learning by defective information. *Lecture Notes in Computer Science*, 215:219–225, 1986.

[VWe91]   L. G. Valiant and M. K. Warmuth (editors). *Proceedings of the Fourth Annual Workshop on Computational Learning Theory*. Morgan Kaufmann Publishers, Inc., August 1991.

Strong Separation of Learning Classes

John Case[1], Keh-Jiann Chen[2] and Sanjay Jain[1]

[1] Department of Computer and Information Sciences
University of Delaware
Newark, DE 19716, USA

[2] Institute for Information Sciences
Academica Sinica
Taipei, 15, Taiwan
Republic of China

Abstract. Suppose LC_1 and LC_2 are two machine learning classes each based on a criterion of success. Suppose, for every machine which learns a class of functions according to the LC_1 criterion of success, there is a machine which learns this class according to the LC_2 criterion. In the case where the converse does *not* hold LC_1 is said to be *separated* from LC_2. It is shown that for many such separated learning classes from the literature a much *stronger* separation holds: $(\forall \mathcal{C} \in LC_1)(\exists \mathcal{C}' \in (LC_2 - LC_1))[\mathcal{C}' \supset \mathcal{C}]$. It is also shown that there is a pair of separated learning classes from the literature for which the stronger separation just above does not hold. A philosophical heuristic toward the design of artificially intelligent learning programs is presented with each strong separation result.

1 Introduction

Technically the present paper presents a strengthening of some of the formal learning class hierarchy results mostly from [CS83]. It is hoped that the particular technical results presented herein can provide one of many possible vehicles to suggest a few philosophical heuristics toward the design of learning programs in artificial intelligence. To that end, we present, with most of our results, brief, corresponding interpretations.

In the present section we'll briefly overview some of the technical results and corresponding interpretations, but first it is helpful to explain what learning classes are and why they are interesting.

We are concerned with the algorithmic learning of programs for functions. The reader may find it interesting that the learning of programs for functions is interpreted in [BB75], [CS83] and [Ful85] as being about inductively inferring explanations for scientific phenomena. The present paper mostly does not pursue further that interpretation.

We consider learning programs for functions each of whose possible inputs and outputs admits of a finite computer representation. Such inputs and outputs clearly can be numerically coded by numbers in N ($\stackrel{\text{def}}{=} \{0, 1, 2, 3, \ldots\}$). We will, then, consider the learning of programs for functions which map N into N. We could also consider the learning of programs for *partial* functions ([Rog67]) mapping N into N (functions with domain a *subset* of N), but, in the present paper, we do not.

Imagine, if you will, an algorithmic device or machine **M** receiving as input *all and only* the ordered pairs from the graph of a total function f mapping N into N. Lets say **M** receives the ordered pairs in the order

$$(0, f(0)), (1, f(1)), (2, f(2)), \dots . \tag{1}$$

The ordered pairs from the graph of f in any other order could be algorithmically preprocessed into the order in (1), so it will suffice for consideration of mere algorithmicity to consider the order in (1). Further imagine, again if you will, that **M** may, as it's receiving the data about f in (1), output, from time to time, a computer program (in some programming system) that **M**, at each such time, conjectures is a possible program for f. The quality of these conjectures may be expected to depend on the cleverness of **M** and the difficulty of f. One way to *define* the *success* of such an **M** on such an f ([BB75, Gol67]) is to require for success that at *some* time **M** receiving the data in (1) about f conjectures some program i such that

$$\text{\textbf{M} receiving \textit{subsequent} data re } f \text{ never conjectures a program} \neq i, \tag{2}$$

and

$$i \text{ \textit{does} compute } f. \tag{3}$$

We say, following the terminology in [CS83], that in (and only in) this case **M** **Ex**-*identifies* f. It is interesting to consider the extent to which a machine **M** can be a general purpose learner, to what extent it can, say, **Ex**-identify each function f in a large class of functions. It is easy to argue, for example, that a suitable machine **M** employing standard interpolation techniques ([Kop61]) can **Ex**-identify each polynomial (of one variable with coefficients in N). It is known ([Gol67, BB75]) that *no* single machine **M**, however clever, can **Ex**-identify *each* computable function f. **Ex** is defined to be the class of all classes $\mathcal{C}$ of computable functions such that *some* machine **M** **Ex**-identifies *each* function in $\mathcal{C}$. **Ex** provides a convenient set theoretic summary of the power of learning (programs for functions) according to the criterion of success, **Ex**-identification. For example, the class of all polynomials (of one variable and with coefficients in N) is in **Ex**, and the class of all computable functions is not.

Ex is our first example of a *learning class*.

We sometimes refer to i conjectured by **M** on f after receiving some data about f and satisfying (2) above as the *final program* of **M** on f. [BB75] and [CS83] in effect introduce the idea that perhaps suitably clever single machines could learn larger classes of functions if the criterion of success were loosened to allow final programs to be slightly erroneous. For $a \in N$, **M** is said ([CS83]) to **Ex**^{a}-*identify* f if and only if **M** on f conjectures a final program i and this i computes f correctly except on up to a arguments to f; on these arguments it may be incorrect. **Ex**^{a} is defined to be the class of all classes $\mathcal{C}$ of computable functions such that *some* machine **M** **Ex**^{a}-identifies *each* function in $\mathcal{C}$. For each $a \in N$, **Ex**^{a} is a *learning class*. Clearly **Ex**$^0 = $ **Ex**. Also, clearly **Ex**$^a \subseteq$ **Ex**$^{a+1}$. It is shown in [CS83] that

$$\textbf{Ex}^{a+1} - \textbf{Ex}^a \neq \emptyset. \tag{4}$$

This means that, for each $a \in N$, there is a class of computable functions $\mathcal{C}$ that *some* **M** can **Ex**$^{a+1}$-identify, but which *no* **M** can **Ex**^{a}-identify. Allowing the possibility of even one extra error in final programs enables the learning of a class that cannot be learned otherwise. An apparent philosophical heuristic toward the design of learning programs in artificial intelligence already from this result is that one should not be too perfectionistic about final programs and consider allowing errors in them since *each* error allowed may increase learning power. There is a possible problem with this heuristic. What if we care about learning all the functions in a particular class C known to be in, say, $\mathbf{Ex}^a$, but then we want to learn all the functions in C *together with even more functions besides* by the device of allowing an error in the final programs. (4) above does *not* guarantee the existence of a class $C' \supseteq C$ such that $C' \in (\mathbf{Ex}^{a+1} - \mathbf{Ex}^a)$. In fact, it might be that, to get the extra learning power from (4) above, we have to give up learning a class C that we started with in $\mathbf{Ex}$. We may not want to adopt the apparent philosophical heuristic above if the cost of increasing learning power in one direction is a loss in another. Fortunately, in the present paper, for a wide variety of learning classes $\mathbf{LC}_1, \mathbf{LC}_2$ such that $\mathbf{LC}_1 \subseteq \mathbf{LC}_2$ *and* $(\mathbf{LC}_2 - \mathbf{LC}_1) \neq \emptyset$, we show the *strong separation* result that

$$(\forall C \in \mathbf{LC}_1)(\exists C' \in (\mathbf{LC}_2 - \mathbf{LC}_1))[C' \supset C], \tag{5}$$

where '$\supset$' denotes proper superset. $\mathbf{LC}_1 = \mathbf{Ex}^a$ and $\mathbf{LC}_2 = \mathbf{Ex}^{a+1}$ is an example.

For learning classes $\mathbf{LC}_1$ and $\mathbf{LC}_2$, from the literature, shown to be strongly separated in the present paper, we can and do propose a corresponding philosophical heuristic recommending loosening ones criterion of successful learning in a "direction" given by passing from the definition of $\mathbf{LC}_1$ to that of $\mathbf{LC}_2$.

Here is another example of a criterion of success we consider, this one first introduced in [Bar74] based on a remark in [Fel72] and later introduced in [CS83]. This criterion does *not* require a final program. We say, following the terminology in [CS83], that $\mathbf{M}$ $\mathbf{Bc}$-*identifies* f if and only if at *some* time $\mathbf{M}$ receiving the data in (1) about f conjectures some program i such that

$$i \text{ computes } f \tag{6}$$

and

$\mathbf{M}$ receiving subsequent data re f never conjectures a program not computing f.

$$\tag{7}$$

Note that (7) permits $\mathbf{M}$, receiving subsequent data re f, to conjecture lots of programs different from i, *but these programs must also compute f*. $\mathbf{Bc}$ is defined to be the class of all classes C of computable functions such that *some* machine $\mathbf{M}$ $\mathbf{Bc}$-identifies *each* function in C. '$\subset$' denotes *proper* subset. In [CS83] it is shown that, for $\mathbf{LC}_1 = \cup_{a \in N} \mathbf{Ex}^a$ and $\mathbf{LC}_2 = \mathbf{Bc}$, $\mathbf{LC}_1 \subset \mathbf{LC}_2$. In the present paper we, in effect, show that, for this choice of $\mathbf{LC}_1$ and $\mathbf{LC}_2$, the strong separation result (5) above actually holds. In this paper we also consider variants of $\mathbf{Bc}$-identification in which errors are allowed and show strong separation results, each accompanied by a corresponding philosophical heuristic. We also show that a particular pair of learning classes, $\mathbf{LC}_1 = \mathbf{Pex}$ and $\mathbf{LC}_2 = \mathbf{Tex}$, defined below and known to be separated ([CNM79]), is *not* strongly separated as in (5).

The reader may have noticed that the example heuristics explicitly given or hinted at above do not really tell the designer of learning programs in artificial intelligence exactly what to put in his or her design to achieve the resultant increase in learning power. It is not at all clear from the above what to actually *do* so as to make sure one is not being too narrow about what constitutes success. It turns out that each of our proofs of a strong separation result of the form (5) essentially presents an algorithm for passing from any machine $\mathbf{M}$ which $\mathbf{LC}_1$-identifies a class $\mathcal{C}$ to a machine $\mathbf{M}'$ which $\mathbf{LC}_2$-identifies a class $\mathcal{C}' \supset \mathcal{C}$, where $\mathcal{C}' \notin \mathbf{LC}_1$. Hence, we present algorithms for *example* ways to explicitly strictly improve any design in the direction of the advice from the corresponding philosophical heuristic. We also present some discussion about the potential eventual practicality of such algorithms (just before Proposition 15 below).

2 Preliminaries

2.1 Notation

N denotes the set of natural numbers, $\{0, 1, 2, 3, \ldots\}$. Unless otherwise specified, $e, i, j, m, n, r, s, t, x, y, z$, with or without decorations (decorations are subscripts, superscripts and the like) range over N. $*$ denotes a non-member of N and is assumed to satisfy $(\forall n)[n < * < \infty]$. a and b with or without decorations, range over $N \cup \{*\}$. $\uparrow$ denotes undefined. S, with or without decorations, ranges over subsets of N. $\mathrm{card}(S)$ denotes the cardinality of the set S. $\max(\cdot), \min(\cdot)$ denote the maximum and minimum of their respective set arguments. We assume that $\max(\emptyset) = 0$ and $\min(\emptyset) = \uparrow$.

η and θ range over *partial* functions with arguments and values from N. $\eta(x)\downarrow$ denotes that $\eta(x)$ is defined; $\eta(x)\uparrow$ denotes that $\eta(x)$ is undefined. f, g, p and q with or without decorations range over *total* functions with arguments and values from N. For $n \in N$ and partial functions η and θ, $\eta =^n \theta$ means that $\mathrm{card}(\{x \mid \eta(x) \neq \theta(x)\}) \leq n$; $\eta =^* \theta$ means that $\mathrm{card}(\{x \mid \eta(x) \neq \theta(x)\})$ is finite. $\mathrm{domain}(\eta)$ and $\mathrm{range}(\eta)$ denote the domain and range of the function η, respectively.

$\langle i, j \rangle$ stands for an arbitrary, computable, one to one encoding of all pairs of natural numbers onto N ([Rog67]) (we assume that $\langle i, j \rangle \geq \max(\{i, j\})$ and that $\langle \cdot, \cdot \rangle$ is increasing in both its arguments). π_1 and π_2 denote the corresponding inverses: for all x, y, $\pi_1(\langle x, y \rangle) = x$ and $\pi_2(\langle x, y \rangle) = y$.

φ denotes a fixed *acceptable* programming system for the partial computable functions: $N \to N$ ([Rog58, Rog67, MY78]). (Case showed the acceptable systems are *characterized* as those in which every control structure can be constructed ([Ric80, Roy87]); Royer and later Marcoux examined complexity analogs of this characterization ([Ric80, Ric81, Roy87, Mar89]). Essentially all "naturally" occurring programming systems are acceptable, but non-acceptable systems can be mathematically constructed ([Rog58]).) φ_i denotes the partial computable function: $N \to N$ computed by program i in the φ-system. Thanks to the numerical coding of programs onto N, we identify φ-programs with natural numbers. Φ denotes an arbitrary Blum complexity measure ([Blu67a, HU79]) for the φ-system. Intuitively, $\Phi_i(x)$ is a measure of the resource (for example, time) used by φ-program i on input x. The set of all total recursive functions of one variable is denoted by $\mathcal{R}$. $\mathcal{C}$, with or without decorations, ranges over subsets of $\mathcal{R}$.

A function f is said to be *zero-extension of η* $\overset{\text{def}}{\Leftrightarrow}$

$$f(x) = \begin{cases} \eta(x) & x \in \text{domain}(\eta); \\ 0 & \text{otherwise.} \end{cases}$$

ZERO* denotes the set $\{f \mid (\overset{\infty}{\forall} x)[f(x) = 0]\}$.

The quantifiers '$\overset{\infty}{\forall}$' and '$\overset{\infty}{\exists}$', essentially from [Blu67a], mean 'for all but finitely many' and 'there exist infinitely many', respectively.

2.2 Fundamental Function Inference Paradigms

Let $f[n]$ denote the finite initial segment $((0, f(0)), (1, f(1)), \ldots, (n-1, f(n-1)))$. Let $\text{INIT} = \{f[n] \mid f \in \mathcal{R} \wedge n \in N\}$. We let $\mathbf{M}$, with or without decorations, range over learning machines (also called *Inductive Inference Machines*, IIMs ([BB75])).

IIMs have been used in the study of machine identification of programs for recursive functions as well as for algorithmic learning of grammars for languages ([BB75, CS83, Che81, Ful85, Gol67, OSW86, Wie78, AS83, KW80, Cas86]). For language learning, direct analogs of the strong separations of the present paper provably do not hold. Whether suitably and interestingly amended versions do hold remains to be investigated.

For any IIM $\mathbf{M}$, behaving as described in Section 1, we define an associated function $\mathbf{M}_F$: $\text{INIT} \to N$ as follows. Consider $\mathbf{M}$ receiving the graph of f as input, in the order given in (1). Let prog_0 be a program for everywhere 0 function. Let $\mathbf{M}_F(f[n]) \overset{\text{def}}{=} \text{prog}_0$ if $\mathbf{M}$ has not output any program by the time it receives $(n, f(n))$; otherwise let $\mathbf{M}_F(f[n]) \overset{\text{def}}{=}$ the last program output by $\mathbf{M}$ by the time it receives $(n, f(n))$.

From now on, for expository convenience, we will use the '$\mathbf{M}$' to mean either '$\mathbf{M}$' itself or '$\mathbf{M}_F$' with context dictating which is intended.

We now extend the domain of $\mathbf{M}$, the function.

$\mathbf{M}(f)$ is defined to have the value i (written: $\mathbf{M}(f){\downarrow} = i$) $\Leftrightarrow (\overset{\infty}{\forall} n)[\mathbf{M}(f[n]) = i]$. $\mathbf{M}(f)$ *is undefined* (written: $\mathbf{M}(f){\uparrow}$) $\overset{\text{def}}{\Leftrightarrow}$ no such i exists.

By means of the next five definitions we *formally* specify all the learning classes mentioned or hinted at in Section 1.

Definition 1. ([Gol67, BB75, CS83]) Recall that a ranges over $N \cup \{*\}$. For all a,
 (a) $\mathbf{M}$ $\mathbf{Ex}^a$-*identifies* a recursive function f (written: $f \in \mathbf{Ex}^a(\mathbf{M})$) iff both $\mathbf{M}(f){\downarrow}$ and $\varphi_{\mathbf{M}(f)} =^a f$.
 (b) $\mathbf{Ex}^a = \{\mathcal{C} \subseteq \mathcal{R} \mid (\exists \mathbf{M})[\mathcal{C} \subseteq \mathbf{Ex}^a(\mathbf{M})]\}$.

Definition 2. ([CS83]) For all a,
 (a) $\mathbf{M}$ $\mathbf{Bc}^a$-*identifies* a recursive function f (written: $f \in \mathbf{Bc}^a(\mathbf{M})$) iff $(\overset{\infty}{\forall} n)[\varphi_{\mathbf{M}(f[n])} =^a f]$.
 (b) $\mathbf{Bc}^a = \{\mathcal{C} \subseteq \mathcal{R} \mid (\exists \mathbf{M})[\mathcal{C} \subseteq \mathbf{Bc}^a(\mathbf{M})]\}$.

We usually write $\mathbf{Ex}$ for $\mathbf{Ex}^0$ and $\mathbf{Bc}$ for $\mathbf{Bc}^0$. ([Bar74]) essentially introduced the notion of $\mathbf{Bc}^0$. Theorem 3 just below states some of the basic hierarchy results about the $\mathbf{Ex}^a$ and $\mathbf{Bc}^a$ classes.

Theorem 3. *For all n,*
(a) $\mathbf{Ex}^n \subset \mathbf{Ex}^{n+1}$;
(b) $\bigcup_{n \in N} \mathbf{Ex}^n \subset \mathbf{Ex}^*$;
(c) $\mathbf{Ex}^* \subset \mathbf{Bc}$;
(d) $\mathbf{Bc}^n \subset \mathbf{Bc}^{n+1}$;
(e) $\bigcup_{n \in N} \mathbf{Bc}^n \subset \mathbf{Bc}^*$; *and*
(f) $\mathcal{R} \in \mathbf{Bc}^*$.

Parts (a), (b), (d), and (e) are due to [CS83]. John Steel first observed that $\mathbf{Ex}^* \subseteq \mathbf{Bc}$ and the diagonalization in part (c) is due to Harrington and Case ([CS83]). Part (f) is due to Harrington ([CS83]). [BB75] first showed that $\mathbf{Ex} \subset \mathbf{Ex}^*$. [Bar74] first showed $\mathbf{Ex} \subset \mathbf{Bc}$.

The following definition was based on Popper's principle ([Pop68]) that scientific conjectures should be refutable.

Definition 4. ([CNM79]) M is *Popperian* iff for all f and n, $\varphi_{\mathbf{M}(f[n])}$ is a total function.

We write $f \in \mathbf{Pex(M)}$ to denote the fact that $f \in \mathbf{Ex(M)}$ and M is Popperian.

Definition 5. ([CNM79]) $\mathbf{Pex} = \{\mathcal{C} \subseteq \mathcal{R} \mid (\exists M)[\mathcal{C} \subseteq \mathbf{Ex(M)} \wedge M \text{ is Popperian }]\}$.

The following definition requires M to output programs for total functions on the initial segments of functions it identifies, but not necessarily otherwise.

Definition 6. ([CNM79])
(a) M **Tex**-*identifies* f (written: $f \in \mathbf{Tex(M)}$) iff M **Ex**-identifies f and $(\forall n)[\varphi_{\mathbf{M}(f[n])}$ is total].
(b) $\mathbf{Tex} = \{\mathcal{C} \subseteq \mathcal{R} \mid (\exists M)[\mathcal{C} \subseteq \mathbf{Tex(M)}]\}$.

Theorem 7. ([CNM79]) $\mathbf{Pex} \subset \mathbf{Tex} \subset \mathbf{Ex}$.

3   Strong Separation

First we consider the **Ex** hierarchy.

Theorem 8. $(\forall n)(\exists \mathcal{C})(\forall M)(\exists M')[[\mathcal{C} \not\subseteq \mathbf{Ex}^n] \wedge [\mathcal{C} \subseteq \mathbf{Ex}^{n+1}(M')] \wedge [(\mathbf{Ex}^n(M) - \mathcal{C}) \subseteq \mathbf{Ex}^n(M')]]$.

Corollary 9. $(\forall n)(\forall \mathcal{C} \in \mathbf{Ex}^n)(\exists \mathcal{C'} \supseteq \mathcal{C})[\mathcal{C'} \in \mathbf{Ex}^{n+1} - \mathbf{Ex}^n]$.

As mentioned in Section 1, the advice suggested by Corollary 9 is to consider allowing even one (more) error in final programs. The proof of Theorem 8 provides one way to algorithmically augment any learning machine to take advantage of this advice.

Proof. (of Theorem 8) Fix n. Let $M_1, M_2, \ldots$ denote a recursive enumeration of all inductive inference machines. The idea is to construct a recursive sequence of programs, $p(0), p(1), p(2), \ldots$ such that, for all i, $\varphi_{p(i)}(0) = i$ and $\mathrm{card}(\{x \mid \varphi_{p(i)}(x)\uparrow\}) \leq n+1$, and, moreover, $\{f \mid \varphi_{p(i)} \subseteq f\} \not\subseteq \mathbf{Ex}^n(M_i)$. We take $\mathcal{C} = \{f \mid (\exists i)[\varphi_{p(i)} \subseteq f]\}$ (thus $\mathcal{C} \not\subseteq \mathbf{Ex}^n$). Given M we first show how to construct M' satisfying the statement of the theorem (assuming the existence of p and $\mathcal{C}$ as defined above). Let $M'(f[0]) = 0$. For $m > 0$, let $M'(f[m]) = p(f(0))$ if $\neg[(\exists x < m)[\Phi_{p(f(0))}(x) \leq m \wedge \varphi_{p(f(0))}(x) \neq f(x)]]$; $M'(f[m]) = M(f[m])$ otherwise. It is easy to see that M' satisfies the statement of the theorem. It remains now to construct p as claimed above. The construction of p is a variant of the construction in [CS83] proving that $(\mathbf{Ex}^{n+1} - \mathbf{Ex}^n \neq \emptyset)$, and we omit here the details. $\qquad\square$

Similarly it can be shown that

Theorem 10. $(\exists \mathcal{C})(\forall M)(\exists M')[[\mathcal{C} \not\subseteq \bigcup_i \mathbf{Ex}^i] \wedge [\mathcal{C} \subseteq \mathbf{Ex}^*(M')] \wedge [(\forall n)[(\mathbf{Ex}^n(M) - \mathcal{C}) \subseteq \mathbf{Ex}^n(M')]]]$.

Corollary 11. $(\forall \mathcal{C} \in \bigcup_i \mathbf{Ex}^i)(\exists \mathcal{C}' \supseteq \mathcal{C})[\mathcal{C}' \in \mathbf{Ex}^* - \bigcup_i \mathbf{Ex}^i]$.

The advice suggested by Corollary 11 is to consider allowing an unbounded, finite number of errors in final programs. A worked out proof of Theorem 10 would provide one way to algorithmically augment any learning machine to take advantage of this advice. We should caution the reader that not every learning application would be able to tolerate an *unbounded*, finite number of errors.

Theorem 12 below can be proved using a combination of the idea used to prove Theorem 13 below and the proof in [CS83] to show that $\mathbf{Bc} - \mathbf{Ex}^* \neq \emptyset$.

Theorem 12. $(\forall \mathcal{C} \in \mathbf{Ex}^*)(\exists \mathcal{C}' \supseteq \mathcal{C})[\mathcal{C}' \in \mathbf{Bc} - \mathbf{Ex}^*]$.

The advice suggested by Theorem 12 is to not necessarily require a final program. Furthermore, this is more powerful advice than that given after Corollary 11 above. A worked out proof of Theorem 12 would provide one way to algorithmically augment any learning machine to take advantage of this advice. We should caution the reader that in some cases the increased learning power *must* come from the improved machine outputting infinitely many different programs ([CS83]), and, hence, in such cases, the *size* of these programs ([Blu67b]) will grow without bound. There are two answers to this. One is that the human race may go extinct before the program sizes get too large to handle, so it might not matter. The other is that, while requiring the number of different programs output to be *finite* does *not* increase learning power ([BP73, CS83]), it *does* increase learning power if one also bounds a suitably sensitive measure of the computational complexity of the learning machine itself ([CJS91]).

We now turn to the $\mathbf{Bc}$ hierarchy. Corollary 14 solves an open problem in [Che81].

Theorem 13. $(\forall n)(\exists \mathcal{C})(\forall M)(\exists M')[[\mathcal{C} \not\subseteq \mathbf{Bc}^n] \wedge [\mathcal{C} \subseteq \mathbf{Bc}^{n+1}(M')] \wedge [(\mathbf{Bc}^n(M) - \mathcal{C}) \subseteq \mathbf{Bc}^n(M')]]$.

Corollary 14. $(\forall n)(\forall \mathcal{C} \in \mathbf{Bc}^n)(\exists \mathcal{C}' \supseteq \mathcal{C})[\mathcal{C}' \in \mathbf{Bc}^{n+1} - \mathbf{Bc}^n]$.

The advice suggested by Corollary 14 is similar to that suggested by Corollary 9: consider allowing even one (more) error in programs conjectured. The proof of Theorem 13 provides one way to algorithmically augment any learning machine to take advantage of this advice.

Proof. (of Theorem 13) Fix n. Let $\mathbf{M}_0, \mathbf{M}_1, \ldots$ denote a recursive sequence of all inductive inference machines. We will construct a recursive sequence of pairwise distinct programs $p(0), p(1), \ldots$ such that, for each i, the following three conditions are satisfied.

(A) $(\exists j)[\varphi_{p(\langle i,j \rangle)}$ is total].
(B) $(\forall j, k \mid j \leq k)[\operatorname{domain}(\varphi_{p(\langle i,k \rangle)}) = \emptyset \vee \operatorname{domain}(\varphi_{p(\langle i,j \rangle)}) \subseteq \operatorname{domain}(\varphi_{p(\langle i,k \rangle)})]$.
(C) $\{f \in \mathcal{R} \mid f(0) = i \wedge (\forall j)[\operatorname{card}(\{x \mid \varphi_{p(\langle i,j \rangle)}(x){\downarrow} \neq f(x)\}) \leq n + 1]\} \not\subseteq \mathbf{Bc}^n(\mathbf{M}_i)$.

Let $\mathcal{C}_i = \{f \in \mathcal{R} \mid f(0) = i \wedge (\forall j)[\operatorname{card}(\{x \mid \varphi_{p(\langle i,j \rangle)}(x){\downarrow} \neq f(x)\}) \leq n + 1]\}$. Note that conditions (A) and (B) imply that, for each i,

$[(\overset{\infty}{\forall} k)[\operatorname{domain}(\varphi_{p(\langle i,k \rangle)}) = \emptyset \vee \varphi_{p(\langle i,k \rangle)}$ is total $] \wedge$
$[\operatorname{card}(\{k \mid \operatorname{domain}(\varphi_{p(\langle i,k \rangle)}) \neq \emptyset\}) < \infty \Rightarrow \varphi_{p(\langle i,\max(\{k \mid \operatorname{domain}(\varphi_{p(i,k)}) \neq \emptyset\}) \rangle)}$ is total $]]$.

Thus, for all f,

$$f \in \mathcal{C}_i \Rightarrow (\overset{\infty}{\forall} m)[\varphi_{p(i,\max(\{k < m \mid \Phi_{p(\langle i,k \rangle)}(0) < m\}))} =^{n+1} f]. \tag{8}$$

We take $\mathcal{C} = \bigcup_{i \in N} \mathcal{C}_i$. We will construct p as claimed above later. Given $\mathbf{M}$, we first construct $\mathbf{M}'$ as claimed in the statement of the theorem. Define $\mathbf{M}'$ as follows. Let

$Sat(m, f) =$
$\quad (\exists k < m)[\operatorname{card}(\{x < m \mid \Phi_{p(\langle f(0),k \rangle)}(x) < m \wedge \varphi_{p(\langle f(0),k \rangle)}(x) \neq f(x)\}) > n + 1]$
$\mathbf{M}'(f[0]) = 0$. For $m > 0$, if $\neg Sat(m, f)$, then $\mathbf{M}'(f[m]) = p(\langle f(0), r \rangle)$, where $r = \max(\{k < m \mid \Phi_{p(\langle i,k \rangle)}(0) < m\})$; $\mathbf{M}'(f[m]) = \mathbf{M}(f[m])$ otherwise.

Note that, if $f \in \mathcal{C}$, then by (8), for all but finitely many m, $\mathbf{M}'(f[m])$ is a program for an $n + 1$ variant of f. Thus $\mathcal{C} \subseteq \mathbf{Bc}^{n+1}(\mathbf{M}')$. If $f \notin \mathcal{C}$, then, for all but finitely many m, $Sat(m, f)$ is true, and thus, for all but finitely many m, $\mathbf{M}'(f[m]) = \mathbf{M}(f[m])$. It follows that $\mathbf{Bc}^n(\mathbf{M}) - \mathcal{C} \subseteq \mathbf{Bc}^n(\mathbf{M}')$.

We now construct p as claimed above. p can be constructed by easy modification of the construction used in the proof in [CS83] of the fact that $\mathbf{Bc}^{n+1} - \mathbf{Bc}^n \neq \emptyset$. For completeness we give the details of the construction. Our construction of p, in addition to satisfying conditions (A) and (C) above also satisfies a strengthened version of (B).

(B') $(\forall k)[\varphi_{p(\langle i,k \rangle)}$ is total $] \vee$
$\quad (\exists k)[\varphi_{p(\langle i,k \rangle)}$ is total $\wedge (\forall k' < k)[\operatorname{domain}(\varphi_{p(\langle i,k' \rangle)}) = \operatorname{domain}(\varphi_{p(\langle i,0 \rangle)})] \wedge (\forall k' > k)[\operatorname{domain}(\varphi_{p(\langle i,k' \rangle)}) = \emptyset]]$.

We now proceed to construct p, as claimed above. By the operator recursion theorem ([Cas74]) there exists a recursive, one-to-one, p, such that, for each i, the (partial) function $\varphi_{p(\langle i, \cdot \rangle)}$ may be described as follows.

Let $\varphi_{p(\langle i,0 \rangle)}(0) = i$. Let x_s denote the least x such that $\varphi_{p(\langle i,0 \rangle)}(x)$ has not been defined before stage s. Go to stage 1.

Begin stage s

1. For each $x < x_s$, let $\varphi_{p(\langle i,s \rangle)}(x) = \varphi_{p(\langle i,0 \rangle)}(x)$.

2. Dovetail steps 3 and 4 until, if ever, step 3 succeeds. If and when step 3 succeeds, complete the then *current* iteration of the repeat loop in step 4, and then, go to step 5.

3. Let g be the zero extension of $\varphi_{p(\langle i,0 \rangle)}[x_s]$. Search for $m > x_s$, and for a $y > m$ such that, for all $r \leq n$, $\varphi_{M_i(g[m])}(y+r)\!\downarrow = 0$.

4. Let $x = x_s$.

   repeat

   $$\varphi_{p(\langle i,s \rangle)}(x) = 0.$$
   $$x = x + 1.$$

   forever

5. If and when step 3 succeeds, let y be as found in step 3.

   5.1 Let $\varphi_{p(\langle i,0 \rangle)}(y+r) = 1$, for $r \leq n$.

   5.2 Let $m' = \max(y+n, x)$.

   5.3 For each $z \leq m'$ such that $\varphi_{p(\langle i,0 \rangle)}(z)$ has not been defined till now, let $\varphi_{p(\langle i,0 \rangle)}(z) = 0$.

   5.4 For each $z \leq m'$ such that $\varphi_{p(\langle i,s \rangle)}(z)$ has not been defined till now, let $\varphi_{p(\langle i,s \rangle)}(z) = 0$.

   5.5 For $z > m'$, make $\varphi_{p(\langle i,s \rangle)}(z) = \varphi_{p(\langle i,0 \rangle)}(z)$ whenever $\varphi_{p(\langle i,0 \rangle)}(z)$ gets defined (i.e. $\varphi_{p(\langle i,s \rangle)}$ "follows" $\varphi_{p(\langle i,0 \rangle)}$ from now on).

   (Note that, because of step 5, $\varphi_{p(\langle i,s \rangle)} =^{n+1} \varphi_{p(\langle i,0 \rangle)}$ and domain$(\varphi_{p(\langle i,0 \rangle)}) = $ domain$(\varphi_{p(\langle i,s \rangle)})$.)

6. Go to stage $s+1$.

End stage s

Case 1: Infinitely many stages are executed.

In this case, for all s, $\varphi_{p(\langle i,s \rangle)}$ is total. Also, for all s, $\varphi_{p(\langle i,s \rangle)} =^{n+1} \varphi_{p(\langle i,0 \rangle)}$ (see comment at the end of step 5). Thus $\varphi_{p(\langle i,0 \rangle)} \in \mathcal{C}_i$. Also $\varphi_{p(\langle i,0 \rangle)} \notin \mathbf{Bc}^n(\mathbf{M}_i)$, since because of the success, in each stage s, of step 3 and the diagonalization in step 5.1, for infinitely many m, $\varphi_{M_i(\varphi_{p(\langle i,0 \rangle)}[m])} \neq^n \varphi_{p(\langle i,0 \rangle)}$. Thus conditions (A)–(C) as stated above are satisfied.

Case 2: Some stage s starts but never finishes.

Clearly, $\varphi_{p(\langle i,s \rangle)}$ is total. Properties (A) and (B) are immediate from the construction (see comment at the end of step 5). Clearly, $\varphi_{p(\langle i,s \rangle)} \in \mathcal{C}_i$. (C) follows from the fact that, for all but finitely many m, for infinitely many x, $\varphi_{M_i(\varphi_{p(\langle i,s \rangle)}[m])}(x) \neq 0$ (otherwise step 3 would succeed). □

It is useful at this juncture to consider the particular ways presented in the proofs so far to algorithmically improve learning. It would be easy to argue that *these* ways to achieve improvement provide mathematical existence proofs but do not necessarily provide improvement on a class of functions that is likely to come up in a natural learning scenario. The proof of Theorem 13 involves a complex self (and other) reference argument. With minor changes we could recast the proof of Theorem 8 as a self-reference argument based on some form of the Kleene recursion theorem ([Rog67, Page 214]). The proof of Theorem 17 below involves a self-reference argument based on the Kleene recursion theorem. In each case the existence of the means for improvement depends on a self-reference argument (or something close enough for our purposes). It is plausibly argued in [Cas88] that self-referential examples witnessing existence are harbingers of natural examples witnessing same. Hence, there is some reason to expect that a search to find natural ways to improve learning along the lines suggested in the present paper would be fruitful.

From Theorem 3, $\mathcal{R} \in \mathbf{Bc}^*$; hence, we have

Proposition 15. $(\forall \mathcal{C} \in \bigcup_i \mathbf{Bc}^i)(\exists \mathcal{C}' \supseteq \mathcal{C})[\mathcal{C}' \in \mathbf{Bc}^* - \bigcup_i \mathbf{Bc}^i]$.

4 Some More Results on Strong Separation

Here is a case where strong separation does not hold.

Theorem 16. $\neg[(\forall \mathcal{C} \in \mathbf{Pex})(\exists \mathcal{C}' \supseteq \mathcal{C})[\mathcal{C}' \in \mathbf{Tex} - \mathbf{Pex}]]$.

Proof. Let $\mathcal{C} = \mathbf{ZERO}^* \in \mathbf{Pex}$. Any machine which $\mathbf{Tex}$-identifies $\mathbf{ZERO}^*$ is a Popperian machine. □

Theorem 17. $(\exists \mathcal{C})(\forall \mathbf{M})(\exists \mathbf{M}')[[\mathcal{C} \not\subseteq \mathbf{Tex}] \wedge [\mathcal{C} \cup \mathbf{Tex}(\mathbf{M}) \subseteq \mathbf{Ex}(\mathbf{M}')]]$.

The advice suggested by the two corollaries just below to Theorem 17 is to not necessarily require that all the conjectures along the way to a final program compute total functions. The proof of Theorem 17 provides one way to algorithmically augment any learning machine to take advantage of this advice, but here we omit its proof.

Corollary 18. $(\forall \mathcal{C} \in \mathbf{Tex})(\exists \mathcal{C}' \supseteq \mathcal{C})[\mathcal{C}' \in \mathbf{Ex} - \mathbf{Tex}]$.

Corollary 19. $(\forall \mathcal{C} \in \mathbf{Pex})(\exists \mathcal{C}' \supseteq \mathcal{C})[\mathcal{C}' \in \mathbf{Ex} - \mathbf{Pex}]$.

5 Acknowledgements

This work was supported by NSF grants MCS 8010728 and CCR 8713846. We would like to thank the anonymous referees for several helpful comments.

References

[AS83]   D. Angluin and C. Smith. A survey of inductive inference: Theory and methods. *Computing Surveys*, 15:237–289, 1983.

[Bar74] J. M. Barzdin. Two theorems on the limiting synthesis of functions. *In Theory of Algorithms and Programs, Latvian State University, Riga*, 210:82–88, 1974. In Russian.

[BB75]   L. Blum and M. Blum. Toward a mathematical theory of inductive inference. *Information and Control*, 28:125–155, 1975.

[Blu67a] M. Blum. A machine independent theory of the complexity of recursive functions. *Journal of the ACM*, 14:322–336, 1967.

[Blu67b] M. Blum. On the size of machines. *Information and Control*, 11:257–265, 1967.

[BP73]   J. M. Barzdin and K. Podnieks. The theory of inductive inference. In *Mathematical Foundations of Computer Science*, 1973.

[Cas74]   J. Case. Periodicity in generations of automata. *Mathematical Systems Theory*, 8:15–32, 1974.

[Cas86]   J. Case. Learning machines. In W. Demopoulos and A. Marras, editors, *Language Learning and Concept Acquisition*. Ablex Publishing Company, 1986.

[Cas88]   J. Case. The power of vacillation. In D. Haussler and L. Pitt, editors, *Proceedings of the Workshop on Computational Learning Theory*, pages 133–142. Morgan Kaufmann Publishers, Inc., 1988.

[Che81]   K. Chen. *Tradeoffs in Machine Inductive Inference*. PhD thesis, SUNY at Buffalo, 1981.

[CJS91]   J. Case, S. Jain, and A. Sharma. Complexity issues for vacillatory function identification. In *Proceedings, Foundations of Software Technology and Theoretical Computer Science, Eleventh Conference, New Delhi, India. Lecture Notes in Computer Science 560*, pages 121–140. Springer-Verlag, December 1991.

[CNM79]   J. Case and S. Ngo Manguelle. Refinements of inductive inference by Popperian machines. Technical Report 152, SUNY/Buffalo, 1979.

[CS83]   J. Case and C. Smith. Comparison of identification criteria for machine inductive inference. *Theoretical Computer Science*, 25:193–220, 1983.

[Fel72]   J. Feldman. Some decidability results on grammatical inference and complexity. *Information and Control*, 20:244–262, 1972.

[Ful85]   M. Fulk. *A Study of Inductive Inference machines*. PhD thesis, SUNY at Buffalo, 1985.

[Gol67]   E. M. Gold. Language identification in the limit. *Information and Control*, 10:447–474, 1967.

[HU79]   J. Hopcroft and J. Ullman. *Introduction to Automata Theory Languages and Computation*. Addison-Wesley Publishing Company, 1979.

[Kop61]   Zdenek Kopal. *Numerical Analysis*. Chapman and Hall Ltd., London, 1961.

[KW80]   R. Klette and R. Wiehagen. Research in the theory of inductive inference by GDR mathematicians – A survey. *Information Sciences*, 22:149–169, 1980.

[Mar89]   Y. Marcoux. Composition is almost as good as s-1-1. In *Proceedings, Structure in Complexity Theory–Fourth Annual Conference*. IEEE Computer Society Press, 1989.

[MY78]   M. Machtey and P. Young. *An Introduction to the General Theory of Algorithms*. North Holland, New York, 1978.

[OSW86]   D. Osherson, M. Stob, and S. Weinstein. *Systems that Learn, An Introduction to Learning Theory for Cognitive and Computer Scientists*. MIT Press, Cambridge, Mass., 1986.

[Pop68]   K. Popper. *The Logic of Scientific Discovery*. Harper Torch Books, New York, second edition, 1968.

[Ric80]   G. Riccardi. *The Independence of Control Structures in Abstract Programming Systems*. PhD thesis, SUNY/ Buffalo, 1980.

[Ric81]   G. Riccardi. The independence of control structures in abstract programming systems. *Journal of Computer and System Sciences*, 22:107–143, 1981.

[Rog58]   H. Rogers. Gödel numberings of partial recursive functions. *Journal of Symbolic Logic*, 23:331–341, 1958.

[Rog67]   H. Rogers. *Theory of Recursive Functions and Effective Computability*. McGraw Hill, New York, 1967. Reprinted. MIT Press. 1987.

[Roy87]   J. Royer. *A Connotational Theory of Program Structure*. Lecture Notes in Computer Science 273. Springer Verlag, 1987.

[Wie78]   R. Wiehagen. *Zur Therie der Algrithmischen Erkennung*. PhD thesis, Humboldt-Universitat, Berlin, 1978.

Desiderata for
Generalization-to-N Algorithms

William W. Cohen

AI Principles Research Department, AT&T Bell Laboratories
600 Mountain Avenue Murray Hill, NJ 07974 USA
wcohen@research.att.com

Abstract. Systems that perform "generalization-to-N" in explanation-based learning generalize a proof tree by generalizing the *shape* of the tree, rather than simply changing constants to variables. This paper introduces a formal framework which can be used either to characterize or to specify the outputs of an algorithm for generalizing number. The framework consists of two desiderata, or desired properties, for generalization-to-N algorithms. In the paper, we first motivate and define these desiderata, then review one of several alternative frameworks for generalizing number: an automata-based approach first described in [Cohen, 1988]. Finally, we describe a generalization-to-N technique that provably meets these desiderata. As an illustration of the operation of the new algorithm, an implementation of it is applied to a number of examples from the literature on generalization-to-N.

1 Introduction

Generalizing number (also called generalization-to-N) in explanation-based learning is useful because standard EBL techniques often perform poorly on recursive domain theories. The reason for this is that usually the *size of a problem* is reflected in the *depth of recursion* of a proof, and hence in the shape of the proof tree that is generalized. Since explanation-based generalization (EBG) generalizes a proof tree by changing constants to variables, rather than generalizing the shape of the tree, for such problems EBG will produce a rule that is specific to a particular problem size. An example of the need for generalization-to-N, discussed in [Shavlik and DeJong, 1987], arises when EBL techniques are applied to a blocks world planner and the training example of building a 2-block tower. Standard EBG techniques cannot generalize from this example to the case of building an N-block tower.

Recently, several new techniques for generalizing number have been developed [Boström, 1990; Cohen, 1988; Letovsky, 1990; Shavlik, 1990; Subramanian and Feldman, 1990]. Given such a diversity of approaches, how can one choose among them? To date there have been relatively few comparisons of alternative techniques for generalizing number. We conjecture that *the lack of comparisons is due to the absence of formal tools for meaningfully characterizing the behavior of techniques for generalizing number*. Without such tools, analytic comparisons are impossible; and without at least a qualitative understanding of the behavior of two systems, empirical comparisons are extremely difficult to extrapolate to new domains or new problem distributions.

This paper attempts to alleviate this problem by introducing a *formal framework* which can be used to characterize (or alternatively, to specify) the outputs of an algorithm for generalizing number. The framework consists of two desiderata, or desired properties, for generalization-to-N algorithms. In the paper, we will first motivate and define these desiderata. We will then review one of several alternative frameworks for generalizing number, and describe a generalization-to-N technique that provably meets these desiderata.

2 Desiderata for Generalizing Number

Recall that *explanation based generalization (EBG)* takes as input an example x, a domain theory T_0, and an operationality criterion $\mathcal{O}$, and returns some rule R that generalizes x. More precisely, R is some *representation* of a set of objects, which we will denote $ext(R)$, such that $x \in ext(R)$, but $ext(R)$ is a subset of the deductive closure of the theory. In standard *EBG* algorithms (for example, Prolog_EBG [Kedar-Cabelli and McCarty, 1987]) the output R is a Horn clause rule such as the following:

$$EBG(T_0, \mathcal{O}, x) = \text{``cup(X)} \leftarrow \text{stable(X)} \wedge \text{liftable(X)} \wedge \text{holds\_fluid(X)''}$$

and $ext(R)$ denotes the sets of all objects that can be shown to be cups using the rule R. For the purposes of this paper, the first two inputs of *EBG* can considered to be fixed; thus we will normally drop the first two arguments and write simply $EBG(x)$.

In this paper, we will assume that a generalization-to-N (henceforth G-to-N) algorithm takes the same inputs, and also outputs some structure R that is a representation of a generalization of the training example x. For the moment, we will make no assumptions about the nature[1] of R; however we will continue to use $ext(R)$ to denote the set that R represents.

As motivation for our two desiderata, consider the following two "strawman" G-to-N algorithms. *Strawman-1* returns as output R the entire original domain theory T_0; in this case, $ext(R)$ denotes the deductive closure of the theory R. *Strawman-2* returns the rule output by Prolog_EBG; in this case $ext(R)$ has its usual meaning. We hope the reader will agree that both Strawman-1 and Strawman-2 are rather unsatisfying G-to-N algorithms. It is useful, however, to try and formalize the reasons that this is so.

What's wrong with Strawman-1? Simply put, Strawman-1's behavior is unsatisfying because its outputs are too general. In most EBL contexts, there is a penalty for overgeneralizing an example. If the learned rules are used to speed up problem solving, as in [Minton, 1988], then they will be overgeneral and (in most cases) needlessly inefficient; if the learned rules are used to construct a new theory that better models the data, as in [Cohen, 1990b], then they will be inaccurate.

How can one state formally that Strawman-1 generalizes too aggressively? Let us borrow a page from the literature on inductive learning and assume that the goal of EBL is to acquire a set of rules that handle some specific subset T_s of the queries that can be answered by the original domain theory; for example, T_s might be the

---

[1] One possible choice for R is a recursive theory, as in [Shavlik, 1990].

set of all queries that require building an N-block tower for $N \geq 1$. A desirable property for a G-to-N algorithm $EBGn$ to have is to never overgeneralize x with respect to that target subset, that is for

$$\forall x \in T_s, ext(EBGn(x)) \subseteq T_s$$

Since the target subset T_s is not normally known in advance, we must insist that this holds for some set $\mathcal{H}_1$ of possible target subsets T_s. Thus we arrive at the following definition: a G-to-N algorithm $EBGn$ is *conservative* for a set $\mathcal{H}_1 = \{T_{s,1}, T_{s,2}, \ldots\}$ of possible specializations of the initial domain theory T_0 iff

$$\forall T_s \in \mathcal{H}_1, \ \forall x \in T_s, ext(EBGn(x)) \subseteq T_s$$

Strawman-1 is conservative for only a trivial set $\mathcal{H}_1$: the set $\{T_{max}, \emptyset\}$, where T_{max} denotes the deductive closure of T_0 and $\emptyset$ is the empty set.

What's wrong with Strawman-2? Strawman-2 has the opposite problem: its outputs are, in many cases, too *specific*. There are two obvious penalties for undergeneralizing an example. First, more examples will be needed to learn the same information. Second, there is a often a cost associated with having several versions of a rule for different size problems; in other words, it is often true that a single rule which has been generalized-to-N is more efficient to use than a set of rules, one for each possible value of N.

One way to bound both the number of extra examples needed and the number of extra rules produced is to impose a bound on the number of different *possible outputs* for a G-to-N algorithm $EBGn$ given inputs from T_s. That is, one could require that the cardinality of the set

$$\{R : x \in T_s \text{ and } R = EBGn(x)\} \tag{1}$$

be bounded. For somewhat technical reasons, this does not quite work as a restriction; it is possible to devise algorithms that meet this restriction but do not actually generalize to N.[2] To strengthen this restriction, we will assume some *size measure* or complexity measure on representations,[3] denoted $size(R)$, and insist that the total size of the possible outputs of $EBGn$ is bounded by a constant times the size of T_s.

In particular, let $\mathcal{H}_2 = \{T_{s,1}, T_{s,2}, \ldots\}$ be a set of possible specializations of the initial domain theory T_0, and let PO be the set of possible outputs of $EBGn$ given T_s, as defined in Equation 1. A G-to-N algorithm $EBGn$ is defined to be *c-concise for $\mathcal{H}_2$* iff

$$\forall T_s \in \mathcal{H}_2, \left(\sum_{R_i \in PO} size(R_i) \right) \leq c \times size(T_s)$$

---

[2] The loophole is that there is nothing to prevent one from defining a algorithm that, given a problem x of size i (e.g, building an i-block tower), first constructs a large set of problems similar to x but of different sizes (e.g. building 1-block, 2-block, ..., 1000i-block towers), and then returns the union of the rules produced by standard EBG on these problems.

[3] One reasonable size measure is the number of bits needed to write encode the representation in some fixed encoding scheme. Notice that the size measure must also apply to a target subset T_s.

It can be shown that Strawman-2 fails this test for any $\mathcal{H}_2$ that contains "interesting" T_s's; in particular, if T_s requires G-to-N, then $\sum_{R_i \in PO} size(R_i)$ cannot be bounded. (For example, the sum of the sizes of the rules produced by Strawman-2 on block-towering problems cannot be bounded, since there are an infinite number of such rules.)

Discussion: From these remarks, we obtain the following desiderata for a G-to-N algorithm *EBGn*.

1. *EBGn* should be *conservative* for a nontrivial set $\mathcal{H}_1$.
2. *EBGn* should be *c-concise* for a nontrivial set $\mathcal{H}_2$: that is, a set $\mathcal{H}_2$ containing some T_s that (intuitively) requires generalization-to-N.

These desiderata can be used to further *specify* the problem of G-to-N, by choosing specific values for $\mathcal{H}_1$ and $\mathcal{H}_2$. For example, if we know some constraint that the target problem class T_s satisfies, we can define $\mathcal{H}_1$ to be the set of $T_{s,i}$'s that satisfies that constraint, and specify that the G-to-N algorithm be conservative for $\mathcal{H}_1$. Less obviously, these desiderata also comprise a framework for *analyzing* a G-to-N algorithm: determining sets $\mathcal{H}_1$ and $\mathcal{H}_2$ for which a G-to-N algorithm is conservative and c-concise would constitute a fairly complete characterization of its behavior.

A secondary motivation for these criteria stems from results in computational learning theory. In many contexts, the goal of explanation-based learning is to perform "knowledge-level learning"; that is, the goal is to produce to a set of rules that cover a particular subset of the domain (for an example of such a context see [Cohen, 1990b].) This problem is a type of inductive learning, where the possible hypotheses of the learner are specializations T_s of the domain theory. In [Cohen, 1990c] it is shown that, given a G-to-N algorithm which is *both* conservative and c-concise for some set of specializations $\mathcal{H}$, one can mechanically construct an algorithm which will learn (in Valiant's sense) any concept in $\mathcal{H}$.

3 Meeting the Desiderata

The desiderata above are only a partial specification of the problem of generalizing number: to complete the specification, it is necessary to choose values for the parameters $\mathcal{H}_1$ and $\mathcal{H}_2$. In the remainder of this paper, we will first argue for one particular version of $\mathcal{H}_1$. This $\mathcal{H}_1$ captures a fairly "weak" constraint: that is, a constraint which can be easily argued for, but which does not require the G-to-N algorithm to generalize very much. Next, we will treat this $\mathcal{H}_1$ as a specification, and produce an algorithm that is conservative for $\mathcal{H}_1$. Finally, we will give a result stating sufficient conditions for that same algorithm to be c-concise; that is, we will analyze the algorithm and find a set $\mathcal{H}_2$ such that the algorithm is c-concise for at least all T_s in $\mathcal{H}_2$.

For the convenience of the reader, however, we will first review the framework used for representing and generalizing explanations. This is an *automata-based* framework, a variant of that introduced in [Cohen, 1988].

Fig. 1. Code to generate a name tree and convert it to an explanation

name_tree(+G,-Tree) ← Tree is a name tree for some proof of the goal G

convert(+Tree,-Clause) ← convert a name tree into a Prolog clause

name_tree(G,nil) ←
    operational(G),!,call(G).
name_tree((G,H),(Tg,Th)) ← !,
    name_tree(G,Tg),name_tree(H,Th).
name_tree(G,(Name←Th)) ← !,
    clause(G,H,Name),name_tree(H,Th).

clause(A,B,Name) ← (A← B) is a clause in the domain theory with name Name

convert(Tree,(A←B)) ←
    goal_formula(A),convert(A,Tree,B).

convert(G,nil,G) ← !.
convert((G,H),(Tg,Th),(B1,B2)) ← !,
    convert(G,Tg,B1), convert(H,Th,B2).
convert(G,(Name←Th),Body) ← !,
    clause(G,H,Name), convert(H,Th,Body).

3.1 Representing and Generalizing Explanations

In EBL, explanations are usually represented as variablized proofs. However, the information in a proof variablized by *EBG* can also be represented by a record of the clauses of T_0 that were used in constructing the proof. In [Cohen, 1988] this information was expressed as a linear sequence of clause names; a more natural representation for this, however, is as a tree isomorphic to the proof tree, but with nodes that are labeled with the names[4] of the clauses used in the corresponding points of proof. To make this idea concrete, we give in Figure 1 Prolog meta-interpreters for first, generating such a data structure (which we call a *name tree*) and second, for converting it to a conventional EBL rule.

    The advantage of this representation for explanations is that it is easier to represent generalizations of the shape of this relatively simple data structure. One approach to representing generalizations of shape is to use a *tree automaton*, an extension of the familiar finite automaton that has been extensively studied in theoretical computer science [Thatcher, 1973]. Intuitively, a tree automaton can be thought of as a finite automaton that reads in, not a string, but a tree. The particular type of tree automata I will use is called a *deterministic root-to-frontier tree automaton* [Thatcher, 1973], which I will abbreviate as DTA. Such an automaton deterministically reads in a tree, starting from the root node and either accepts or rejects it. Just as DFAs can be represented by a directed graph with labeled edges, DTAs can be represented as a directed hypergraph[5] with labeled hyperarcs.

    As an example of a DTA, consider Figure 2, which shows an example DTA (henceforth A_0), an example of a tree (henceforce τ_0) that is accepted by the DTA,

---

[4] A *name* is simply some symbol that uniquely identifies a clause of the domain theory.

[5] Hypergraphs, as used here, are identical to AND-OR graphs as defined in [Nilsson, 1987]; each hyperarc corresponds to a "k-connector" in Nilsson's terminology. I will use Nilsson's graph notation for displaying hypergraphs, except that final states will be denoted with a double circle. The set of trees accepted by a DTA is the set of hyperpaths from the start state through the hypergraph that end only in final states.

Fig. 2. A DTA, the set of trees it accepts, and a sample tree

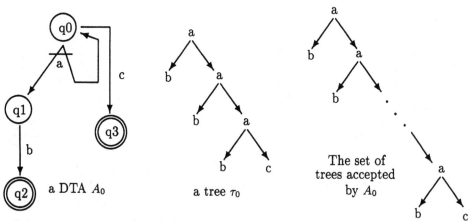

a DTA A_0 a tree τ_0 The set of trees accepted by A_0

and an informal description of the set of trees that the DTA accepts. In processing τ_0, A_0 begins from its start state q_0 and looks for a hyperedge with the same label as the root of τ_0 (this is precisely analogous to the operation of a DFA, which looks for an edge from the current state that has the same label as the first letter in the string that it is processing.) In this case, the hyperedge of A_0 that is labeled with a branches off to the two states q_1 and q_0. To process the remainder of the tree, A_0 will be recursively invoked on the first subtree of of τ_0 (the single leaf labeled b) starting in state q_1, and also will be recursively invoked in the second subtree of τ_0 (the root of which is also labeled with a) starting in the state q_0. The tree τ_0 will be accepted if both of these subtrees are accepted.

It can be easily verified that A_0 will indeed accept τ_0, and also all other trees of the form indicated in the figure. The point of all this is that *the appropriate generalization of the shape of τ_0 can be expressed as a DTA*. DTAs are thus one reasonable approach to representing generalizations-to-N. An alternative representation is a recursive logical theory [Shavlik, 1990]. An algorithm for translating a DTA into a recursive logical theory exists[6]; for a description, see [Cohen, 1990a] (a similar algorithm is also described in [Subramanian and Feldman, 1990].)

3.2 Specifying and Analyzing a G-to-N Algorithm

In this section, we will further specify the problem of G-to-N by arguing that a G-to-N algorithm should be conservative for *at least* a particular class of target problems,

---

[6] The basic idea of the algorithm is to gensym a new predicate name for each state of the DTA; each hyperedge of the DTA (from q_i to $\langle q_{j,1}, q_{j,2}, \ldots, q_{j,n} \rangle$) can be represented as a clause reducing a goal of the predicate associated with q_i to a conjunction of goals of the predicates associated with the q_j's. In the current implementation, states that have only a single exiting hyperarc are eliminated by a partial evaluation technique; the effect of this is that the result of generalizing number for proofs in which no iteration takes place is the same as the output of Prolog_EBG [Kedar-Cabelli and McCarty, 1987].

Fig. 3. Two types of trees that should be generalized

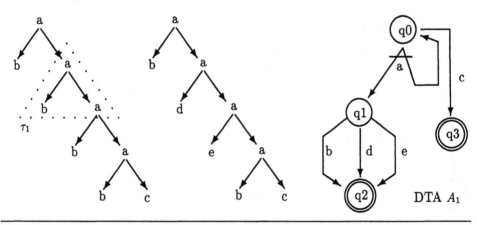

called the class of *t-threshold DTAs*.

The enterprise of generalizing number is based on the idea that, given a proof tree in which some subtree is repeated a number of times, one should generalize the number of repetitions of the subtree; for example, in the first name tree of Figure 3, any reasonable G-to-N algorithm should generalize the number of repetitions of the subtree τ_1. Does this principle include all of the situations in which a proof tree should be generalized? The second name tree of Figure 3 suggests another class of proof trees which arguably should be generalized. Even though there are no subtrees that repeat, there is clearly a repeating pattern along the rightmost path of the tree; hence this name tree can be generalized to the DTA A_1.

The second example suggests that a G-to-N algorithm should determine when to generalize a tree based on the repetition of *paths* through tree, rather than subtrees. Notice that a path through a tree can be represented by a sequence of natural numbers where each number i in the sequence denotes moving from a node to its i-th son; thus a *labeled path* (a path together with the labels of the nodes on that path) can be represented as a sequence of pairs $\langle a, i \rangle$ where a is the name of a clause in T_0 and i is a natural number. We argue that a reasonable choice to make (as to when to generalize a tree) is to assume that repetition exists if some subpath repeats more than t times for some threshold t. This corresponds to the assumption that the set P of labeled paths through the DTA defining the target class T_s has the property[7] that for all possible labeled paths w, x and y,

$$(wx^{t+1}y \in P \Rightarrow \forall j \geq 0, wx^{t+j}y \in P) \text{ and } (wx^{t+1}y \notin P \Rightarrow \forall j \geq 0, wx^{t+j}y \notin P)$$

A DTA that has this property is called a *t-threshold DTA*. A reasonable choice for

---

[7] This constraint is not entirely novel; it has close connections to the notion of a *noncounting language*, as defined in [McNaughton and Papert, 1971]. Specifically, it can be shown that a regular language is noncounting iff it is a *t*-threshold language for some *t*. In the context of learnability, it has been noted that many learnable classes of context-free languages are noncounting [Crespi-Reghizzi *et al.*, 1978].

the threshold is $t = 1$: in this case, a path is assumed to repeat arbitrarily many times if it repeats twice.

Fig. 4. Algorithm for inferring loops

Algorithm $XLI_t(\tau)$:

begin
    $A \leftarrow canonical\text{-}DTA(\tau)$
    for each pair of states p, q in A **do**
        if $similar_t(p, q)$ **then** mark p, q
    for each marked p, q **do**
        merge p and q
    call *determinize*
    return A
end

Algorithm *determinize*:

while A contains a state p with two
    exiting hyperarcs with identical labels
do
    let $\langle q_1, \ldots, q_r \rangle$ be the destinations
    of the first hyperarc
    let $\langle q_1', \ldots, q_r' \rangle$ be the destinations
    of the second hyperarc
    for $i = 1$ to r **do** merge q_i and q_i'
endwhile

The XLI_t algorithm shown in Figure 4 can be shown to be conservative for the class $\mathcal{H}_t = \{ext(A) : A$ is a t-threshold DTA$\}$; a companion paper [Cohen, 1990c] contains this analysis. The algorithm constructs the *canonical DTA* for a tree (that is, the most specific DTA accepting the tree) using a modification of the techniques used in [Cohen, 1988] to construct an initial tree automaton, and then generalizes the canonical DTA by first merging "similar" states and then invoking a special routine to make the resulting DTA deterministic.[8] The algorithm differs from the REDUCE* algorithm of [Cohen, 1988] in three respects. First, a slightly different type of tree automaton is being used; second, the top-level control structure is a little different; third and most importantly, a different criterion of "similarity" is used to decide which states to merge. Two states p and q are considered *similar* by XLI_t if they are the t-th and $(t + 1)$-th states in a series of states all connected by identical labeled paths. For $t = 1$, this means that p and q occur at corresponding positions in the a loop that is executed at least twice.

The companion paper [Cohen, 1990c] also defines a family $\mathcal{H}_2$ of DTAs for which XLI_t is c-concise. Languages in the family must be "strongly linearly recursive", and the recursive portion of the minimal automaton for every language in the family must (a) accept a t-threshold language and (b) have a simple iterative structure: specifically, a bounded number of non-nested loops. A *strongly linearly recursive DTA* is one which corresponds to a logical theory that is linearly recursive, and which also has the property that every goal not solved via recursion has only one proof. Notice that these are only sufficient conditions for XLI_t to be c-concise, however, not necessary ones: as the experiments described below show, XLI_t sometimes produces concise generalizations when these conditions do not hold.

As an further illustration of the operation of the algorithm, an implementation of it has been applied, using a threshold of $t = 1$, to a number of examples: specifically

---

[8] The *merge* procedure is also a slight modification of the procedure used in [Cohen, 1988].

all of the examples in [Cohen, 1988],[Shavlik, 1987], and [Shavlik, 1989]). The experimental results are summarized in Table 1. In each case, the intended generalization of each example is clear, and the generalization obtained by XLI_t is reasonable; however, the generalizations obtained by XLI_t are not always identical to those obtained by the earlier systems. For discussion of the differences, the reader is referred to [Cohen, 1990a, Chapter 6].

4   Conclusions

In this paper, we have described a formal framework which can be used to either characterize or to specify the behavior of a system for generalizing number. The framework consists of two desiderata, or desired properties, for generalization-to-N systems: any algorithm that generalizes number must be conservative and c-concise for some sets $\mathcal{H}_1$ and $\mathcal{H}_2$. These constraints constitute a partial specification of the problem of generalizing number; a G-to-N algorithm can also be analyzed by determining sets $\mathcal{H}_1$ and $\mathcal{H}_2$ for which the algorithm is conservative and c-concise. The paper also describe a G-to-N technique that provably meets these desiderata, analyzes it using this framework, and gives experimental results that illustrate its performance.

Acknowledgments

The author is grateful to Haym Hirsh for many stimulating discussions. The initial stages of this research were conducted while the author was supported by an AT&T Bell Laboratories Fellowship.

Table 1. Experimental results for generalizing number

Example	Source	Training Data/Generalization	Note
AND-NOR-1	Co88	implement [and,[not,f],[not,g]] by [nor,f,g]	
		implement [and,[not,f_1],...,[not,f_n]] by [nor,f_1,...,f_n]	
AND-NOR-2	Co88	implement [and,[or,a,b],[or,c,d]] by [nor,[nor,a,b],[nor,c,d]]	
		implement any and-or circuit by two levels of nor gates	
NOR-AND-1	Sh87	imp. not(or(or(not,not(b)),not(c))) by and(and(a,b),c))	
		imp. not(or(or(...or(not(f_1),not(f_2)),...),f_n)) by and(and(...and(f_1,f_2),...),f_n)	
NOR-AND-2	Sh89	imp. not(or(or(or(not(g6),not(g9)), or(not(g16),or(not(g32),not(g26))))), or(or(not(g37),not(g40)),not(g43)))) by and(and(and(g6,g9), and(g16,and(g32,g26))), and(and(g37,g40),g43)))	
		imp. not(or(or(...or(not(f_1),not(f_2)),...),f_n)) by and(and(...and(f_1,f_2),...),f_n)	
ADDER	Co88	implement 4-bit adder with ripple-carry	
		implement N-bit adder with ripple-carry	
MUX	Co88	implement 16:1 MUX as tree of 2:1 MUXs	
		implement 2^n:1 MUX as tree of 2:1 MUXs	
TABLE	Sh87	plan for setting 2 places at a table	
		plan for setting N places at a table	
TOWER-1	Sh87	plan for building a 3-block tower	(a)
		plan for building an N-block tower	
TOWER-2	Sh87	plan for building a 4-block tower	(a)
		plan for building an N-block tower	
CLEAR-1	Sh87	plan for clearing the last block in a 3-block tower	
		plan for clearing the last block in an N-block tower	
CLEAR-2	Sh87	plan for clearing 2 blocks off a supporting block	
		plan for clearing N blocks off a supporting block	
CLEAR-3	Sh87	plan for clearing 2 towers off a supporting block	(b)
		plan for clearing N towers off a supporting block	

Notes:

(a) The concepts learned by Shavlik's algorithm from TOWER-1 and TOWER-2 are different; the concepts learned by XLI_t are the same.

(b) This was an example of a problem too complex for the algorithm of [Shavlik, 1987] and illustrates a case where nested G-to-N is needed.

References

(Boström, 1990) Henrik Boström. Generalizing the order of goals as an approach to generalizing number. In *Proceedings of the Seventh International Conference on Machine Learning*, Austin, Texas, 1990. Morgan Kaufmann.

(Cohen, 1988) William W. Cohen. Generalizing number and learning from multiple examples in explanation-based learning. In *Proceedings of the Fifth International Conference on Machine Learning*, Ann Arbor, Michigan, 1988. Morgan Kaufmann.

(Cohen, 1990a) William W. Cohen. Concept learning using explanation based generalization as an abstraction mechanism. Technical Report DCS-TR-271, Rutgers University, 1990. (PhD thesis).

(Cohen, 1990b) William W. Cohen. Learning from textbook knowledge: A case study. In *Proceedings of the Eighth National Conference on Artificial Intelligence*, Boston, Massachusetts, 1990. MIT Press.

(Cohen, 1990c) William W. Cohen. Learning restricted classes of regular languages using loop induction. Bell Labs Technical Memoradum (Available from the author on request.), 1990.

(Crespi-Reghizzi *et al.*, 1978) S. Crespi-Reghizzi, G. Guida, and D. Mandrioli. Noncounting context-free languages. *Journal of the Association for Computing Machinery*, 25(4), October 1978.

(Kedar-Cabelli and McCarty, 1987) Smadar Kedar-Cabelli and L. Thorne McCarty. Explanation-based generalization as resolution theorem proving. In *Proceedings of the Fourth International Workshop on Machine Learning*, Irvine, California, 1987. Morgan Kaufmann.

(Letovsky, 1990) Stanley Letovsky. Operationality criteria for recursive predicates. In *Proceedings of the Eighth National Conference on Artificial Intelligence*, Boston, Massachusetts, 1990. MIT Press.

(McNaughton and Papert, 1971) R. McNaughton and S. Papert. *Counter-free automata*. MIT Press, 1971.

(Minton, 1988) Steven Minton. Learning effective search control knowledge: An explanation-based approach. Technical report, Carnegie-Mellon University Department of Computer Science, 1988.

(Nilsson, 1987) Nils Nilsson. *Principles of Artificial Intelligence*. Morgan Kaufmann, 1987.

(Shavlik and DeJong, 1987) J. Shavlik and G. DeJong. BAGGER: An EBL system that extends and generalizes explanations. In *Proceedings of the Sixth National Conference on Artificial Intelligence*, Seattle, Washington, 1987. Morgan Kaufmann.

(Shavlik, 1987) Jude Shavlik. Generalizing number in explanation based learning. Technical Report UILO-ENG-87-2276, Univ. of Illinois/Champaign, 1987. (PhD thesis).

(Shavlik, 1989) Jude Shavlik. Acquiring recursive concepts with explanation based learning. In *Proceedings of the Eleventh International Joint Conference on Artificial Intelligence*, Detroit, Michigan, 1989. Morgan Kaufmann.

(Shavlik, 1990) Jude Shavlik. Acquiring recursive and iterative concepts with explanation-based learning. *Machine Learning*, 5(1), 1990.

(Subramanian and Feldman, 1990) Devika Subramanian and Ronen Feldman. The utility of EBL in recursive domain theories. In *Proceedings of the Eighth National Conference on Artificial Intelligence*, Boston, Massachusetts, 1990. MIT Press.

(Thatcher, 1973) James Thatcher. Tree automata: An informal survey. In Alfred Aho, editor, *Currents in the Theory of Computing*. Prentice-Hall, 1973.

The Power of Probabilism in Popperian FINite Learning

(extended abstract)

Robert Daley   Bala Kalyanasundaram
Department of Computer Science
University of Pittsburgh
Pittsburgh, PA 15260

Mahe Velauthapillai
Department of Computer Science
George Town University
Washington, D.C. 20057.

Abstract

We consider the capabilities of probabilistic *FIN*-type learners who must always produce programs (i.e., hypotheses) that halt on every input. We show that the structure of the learning capability of probabilistic and team learning with success ratio above $\frac{1}{2}$ in *PFIN*-type learning is analogous to the structure observed in *FIN*-type learning. On the contrary, the structure of probabilistic and team learning with success ratio at or below $\frac{1}{2}$ is more sparse for *PFIN*-type learning than *FIN*-type learning. For $n \geq 2$, we show that the probabilistic hierarchy below $\frac{1}{2}$ for *PFIN*-type learning is defined by the sequence $\frac{4n}{9n-2}$, which has an accumulation point at $\frac{4}{9}$. We also show that the power of redundancy at the accumulation point $\frac{4}{9}$ is different from the one observed at $\frac{1}{2}$. More interestingly, for the first time, we show the power of redundancy even at points that are not accumulation points.

1   Introduction

A fundamental issue in multi-agent learning system is how various agents/learners cooperate in the learning process. We consider the learning process where the agents learn from examples. More precisely, given the graph of a function f from a class of total recursive functions $\mathcal{F}$, we want the learner to produce a program computing f.

Given a team of s learners we say that they can learn a class of functions $\mathcal{F}$ with plurality "*r out of s*" (denoted r/s) if given any function f from $\mathcal{F}$ at least r of the s members can correctly learn f. It is then natural to ask how the learning capability of a team of learners with plurality r/s compares to that of another team of learners with plurality x/y. Is it reasonable to expect that a single probabilistic learner which can successfully learn any function from the class $\mathcal{F}$ with probability $\frac{r}{s}$ can be simulated by a team of learners with plurality r/s ? While in many situations the capabilities of these two types of learners coincide, there are other situations where they are quite different and this gives rise to the phenomenon called *redundancy*. It is also natural to compare the capabilities of teams with different pluralities, and similarly for probabilistic learners.

For practical applications, it is important to devise templates for strategies useful for successful cooperation. Keeping this in mind, the research described in this paper deals fundamentally with the question of how teams of learners can work cooperatively to learn classes of functions which individually they would be unable to learn. On the other hand, from a theoretical point of view, we are interested in understanding and explaining the role of redundancy. Finally, we are interesting in investigating these questions for a broad spectrum of type of learners so that we can possibly identify the true nature and complexity of cooperation needed in a multi-agent learning system.

Work on these kinds of questions was begun by Freivalds [5] who showed that the learning capabilities of probabilistic learners beginning with probability 1 and ending with probability $\frac{1}{2}$ form discrete intervals such that any two probabilities in an interval yield equivalent learning power. This was extended to teams of learners by Daley et. al in [4]. The phenomenon of redundancy was first observed for such learners by Velauthapillai [11] who showed that a team of 2 with plurality 1/2 was less capable than a team of 4 with plurality 2/4. This showed that for the ratio $\frac{1}{2}$ the capabilities of probabilistic and team learners are different.

Our work has continued the investigation of these questions (see [1, 2, 3]) for a variety of different types of learners and has resulted in what appear to be general properties associated with the learning capabilities of teams of learners as well as probabilistic learners. Perhaps, the most interesting and important thing revealed by these investigations is the intimate nature of the mutual information which team members must possess about one another and the extremely complex nature of their interaction required in order for them to fully exploit their learning capability.

The work presented in this paper could be considered as a major stepping stone for other results [1, 3] in finite learning. The type of learners we consider in this paper must produce only total programs if they participate in the learning process. This helps us identifying the true combinatorial nature of cooperation. We could then expand the technique to devise learning strategies in other models (see [1]).

2   Previous Results

Consider a learning strategy L that receives values $(0, f(0)), (1, f(1)), (2, f(2)), \ldots$ of some (total recursive) function f from a class $\mathcal{F}$. In general, while observing this sequence of functional values, L will issue a sequence of hypotheses (i.e., programs) $h_1, h_2, h_3, \ldots$ not necessarily one for each new functional value L sees. Without loss of generality we may assume that $h_i \neq h_{i+1}$, so that each new conjecture represents a mind change from the previous hypothesis. We say that the algorithm L correctly learns the function f with respect to $\mathbf{FIN}\langle \mathbf{M} : m \rangle$-type learning (denoted

$f \in \mathbf{FIN}\langle\mathbf{M}\colon m\rangle[L])$ if after a finite amount of computation (and after seeing a finite number of values of f), L produces a final hypothesis for f after at most m mind changes and this final hypothesis is a correct program for f. We say that a class $\mathcal{F}$ of functions is $\mathbf{FIN}\langle\mathbf{M}\colon m\rangle$-learnable (denoted by $\mathcal{F} \in \mathbf{FIN}\langle\mathbf{M}\colon m\rangle$) if there is a strategy L that can correctly identify every function f in $\mathcal{F}$ with respect to $\mathbf{FIN}\langle\mathbf{M}\colon m\rangle$-type learning. We abbreviate $\mathbf{FIN}\langle\mathbf{M}\colon 0\rangle$ as $\mathbf{FIN}$(often denoted as EX_0 in the literature), and say that a class of functions $\mathcal{F} \in \mathbf{FIN}$ is *finitely* learnable. In this paper we are interested only in the case where there are no mind-changes. We will shortly define *PFIN*-type learners.

Gold [6] in his seminal paper, introduced the model of learning in the limit, where the learning algorithm is permitted an unbounded (but finite) number of mind changes. We denote by LIM (or EX in the literature) the family of classes $\mathcal{F}$ of functions such that there is a learning strategy L that correctly identifies every function in $\mathcal{F}$ in the limit.

Two different models of computation which we will be considering are probabilistic learning and pluralistic (or team) learning. First we will define the models.

As with any probabilistic algorithm, a probabilistic learning strategy L consults the outcome of a sequence of flips of a fair coin during the course of its computation. We say that the strategy L learns (with respect to *FIN*-type learning) a function f with probability p, if the probability, taken over all possible coin flips of L, that the strategy outputs a final correct program for f is at least p. We denote the fact that L so learns f by $f \in \mathbf{FIN}\langle\mathbf{P}\colon p\rangle[L]$, and we denote by $\mathbf{FIN}\langle\mathbf{P}\colon p\rangle$ the family of all classes of functions that are *FIN* learnable by some probabilistic strategy with probability at least p. Observe that one can extend these definitions to LIM-type learning.

Analogous to pluralistic scientific societies, one can consider learning by a team of strategies. Here, the strategies in the team can cooperate to learn functions. Let $L = \{L_1, L_2, \ldots, L_s\}$ be the team that cooperates to learn a class $\mathcal{F}$ of functions. Each member of the team receives the values of a function f in $\mathcal{F}$, and the team L correctly learns f (with respect to *FIN*-type learning) with plurality r/s, if at least r out of s members output a final program which is correct for f. Notice that the remaining $s - r$ learners need not even produce programs. The team L learns the class $\mathcal{F}$ (with respect to *FIN*-type learning) (with plurality r/s) of functions if the team L learns every f in $\mathcal{F}$ with respect to *FIN*-type learning. We denote the fact that the team L so learns f by $f \in \mathbf{FIN}\langle\mathbf{T}\colon r/s\rangle[L]$, and we denote by $\mathbf{FIN}\langle\mathbf{T}\colon r/s\rangle$ the collection of such classes of functions that are *FIN* learnable by some team of s learners with plurality at least r out of s. As before, one can analogously extend the definition to LIM-type learning. We are now ready to define *PFIN*-type learning.

Our objective is to devise learning strategy for learning some total recursive function f from a class $\mathcal{F}$. For deterministic *FIN*-type learning (no mind change) the learner will produce one and only one program that computes f. On the other hand, for probabilistic or team *FIN*-type learning (no mind change) potentially many programs are produced out of which some of them (depending on the success ratio) compute f correctly. In this case, those programs that do not compute f correctly, need not always compute a total function. Further, some learners (in team learning) may not even participate in the learning process by producing programs. In this paper we impose the condition that the programs produced by any participating learner must compute total functions. We call a learner who, if at all participate, always produce total programs a *PFIN*-type learner. One can then analogously define **PFIN**$\langle$**T**$:r/s\rangle$ and **PFIN**$\langle$**P**$:p\rangle$.

We will examine the capabilities of probabilistic and pluralistic *PFIN*-type learning. Throughout this paper we distinguish between the expressions $\frac{r}{s}$ and r/s: the former indicates the fraction and the latter indicates "r out of s".

The complete relationship between pluralistic and probabilistic learning for LIM-type learning was revealed in the work of Smith [10], Pitt [8], and Pitt and Smith [9]. In essence, in the case of learning in the limit, probability and plurality are the same, with the ratio r *out of* s corresponding to the probability $\frac{r}{s}$. On the other hand, for FIN-type learning, until recently only a part of the structure of the probabilistic hierarchy was known.

The learning power of probabilistic learners was first investigated by Freivalds [5] for *FIN*-type learners where it was shown

Theorem 1 *(Freivalds)*
a) *For integers $n \geq 1$, if $\frac{n+1}{2n+1} < p \leq \frac{n}{2n-1}$ then* **FIN**$\langle$**P**$:p\rangle =$ **FIN**$\langle$**P**$: \frac{n}{2n-1}\rangle$.
b) *For integers $n \geq 1$,* **FIN**$\langle$**P**$: \frac{n}{2n-1}\rangle \subset$ **FIN**$\langle$**P**$: \frac{n+1}{2n+1}\rangle$.

In the above (and subsequent) theorem we use $\subset$ to denote *proper* subset. Velauthapillai [11] extended Freivalds' result to pluralistic learning.

Theorem 2 *(Velauthapillai) For integers $n \geq 1$,* **FIN**$\langle$**T**$:(n)/(2n-1)\rangle \subset$ **FIN**$\langle$**T**$:(n+1)/(2n+1)\rangle$.

Daley and Velauthapillai [4] showed that Freivalds' simulation construction above also yields

Theorem 3 *(Daley and Velauthapillai) For integers $n \geq 1$, if $\frac{n+1}{2n+1} < p \leq \frac{n}{2n-1}$ then* **FIN**$\langle$**P**$:p\rangle =$ **FIN**$\langle$**T**$:(n)/(2n-1)\rangle$.

Thus for *FIN*-type learning probabilistic and pluralistic learners are equivalent with respect to their learning capabilities for ratios $> \frac{1}{2}$.

Corollary 1 *For natural numbers r and s such that $\frac{r}{s} > \frac{1}{2}$,* **FIN**$\langle$**P**$: \frac{r}{s}\rangle =$ **FIN**$\langle$**T**$:r/s\rangle$.

First evidence that the structure of the probabilistic hierarchy in FIN-type learning is different from LIM-type learning is shown by Velauthapillai [11].

Theorem 4 *(Velauthapillai)* **FIN**$\langle$**T**$:1/2\rangle \subset$ **FIN**$\langle$**T**$:2/4\rangle$.

This important result demonstrated several things. First, it showed for the ratio $\frac{1}{2}$ that redundancy pays, i.e., doubling the team size while keeping the same ratio of success can result in strictly more powerful teams of learners. Corollary 1 shows that redundancy does not pay for ratios $> \frac{1}{2}$. Secondly, probabilistic and pluralistic *FIN*-type learning are different (e.g., **FIN**$\langle$**T**$:1/2\rangle \neq$ **FIN**$\langle$**P**$: \frac{1}{2}\rangle$). Later, Jain and Sharma [7] showed that

Theorem 5 *(Jain and Sharma)*
a) For integers $n > 0$, $\mathbf{FIN}\langle\mathbf{T}:2n/4n\rangle \subseteq \mathbf{FIN}\langle\mathbf{T}:2/4\rangle$, *and*
b) For integers $n > 1$, $\mathbf{FIN}\langle\mathbf{T}:(2n-1)/(4n-2)\rangle \subseteq \mathbf{FIN}\langle\mathbf{T}:1/2\rangle$.

This result shows that there are *exactly* two pluralistic capability classes for the ratio $\frac{1}{2}$. It was also shown in [4], however, that at $\frac{1}{3}$ there is an unlimited increase in learning power possible by (continually) doubling the team size and retaining the success ratio of $\frac{1}{3}$, i.e., there is infinitely much redundancy possible at $\frac{1}{3}$.

Recently in [3] we revealed much more about the relationship between probabilistic and pluralistic strategies and about the power of redundancy.

Theorem 6 *(Daley, Kalyanasundaram and Veluathapillai)*
For $\frac{24}{49} < p \leq \frac{1}{2}$, $\mathbf{FIN}\langle\mathbf{P}:p\rangle = \mathbf{FIN}\langle\mathbf{T}:2/4\rangle$.

Observe that this theorem shows that $\mathbf{FIN}\langle\mathbf{P}:\frac{1}{2}\rangle = \mathbf{FIN}\langle\mathbf{T}:2/4\rangle$, thus completely characterizing the learning capability at probability $\frac{1}{2}$.

The following theorem shows that the simulation result of Theorem 6 is tight.

Theorem 7 *(Daley, Kalyanasundaram and Veluathapillai)*
$\mathbf{FIN}\langle\mathbf{T}:2/4\rangle \subset \mathbf{FIN}\langle\mathbf{T}:24/49\rangle$.

Theorem 5 showed that the amount of redundancy possible for the ratio $\frac{1}{2}$ is finite, i.e., there are exactly two capabilities consisting in $\mathbf{FIN}\langle\mathbf{T}:1/2\rangle$ and $\mathbf{FIN}\langle\mathbf{T}:2/4\rangle$. Finally, even more light was shed on the nature of this phenomenon, by the following theorem which shows that redundancy does not pay in the interval $(\frac{24}{49}, \frac{1}{2})$. Thus, the power of redundancy which exists at $\frac{1}{2}$ is an isolated case.

Theorem 8 *(Daley, Kalyanasundaram and Veluathapillai) For natural numbers r and s such that $\frac{24}{49} < \frac{r}{s} < \frac{1}{2}$,* $\mathbf{FIN}\langle\mathbf{T}:2/4\rangle \subseteq \mathbf{FIN}\langle\mathbf{T}:r/s\rangle$.

In this paper we investigate the learning capability structure (both probabilistic and pluralistic) for *PFIN*-type learning. We show that there are many parallels between the structure given above for *FIN*-type learning and for *PFIN*-type learning. In particular, the notion of redundancy also plays an important part in the structure of *PFIN*-type learning.

3   Results

We first show that the structure of probabilistic capability classes for *PFIN*-type learning coincides with that of *FIN*-type learning at success ratio $\frac{1}{2}$ and above. Simulation results are not so surprising since we deal with programs that compute total functions. On the other hand, diagonalization argument has be modified considerably to account for totality of the function computed by the programs used in the construction.

Theorem 9 *For integers $n \geq 1$,*
a) $\mathbf{PFIN}\langle\mathbf{T}:n/(2n-1)\rangle \subset \mathbf{PFIN}\langle\mathbf{P}:\frac{n+1}{2n+1}\rangle$.
b) if $\frac{n+1}{2n+1} < p \leq \frac{n}{2n-1}$, then $\mathbf{PFIN}\langle\mathbf{P}:p\rangle \subseteq \mathbf{PFIN}\langle\mathbf{T}:n/(2n-1)\rangle$.

Analogous to *FIN*-type learning, for ratios above $\frac{1}{2}$, probabilistic and pluralistic learning coincide, and there can be no redundancy.

Corollary 2 *For natural numbers* r *and* s *such that* $\frac{r}{s} > \frac{1}{2}$, **PFIN**$\langle$P:$\frac{r}{s}\rangle$ = **PFIN**$\langle$T:$r/s\rangle$.

Just as redundancy was discovered at the first accumulation point for the **FIN** probabilistic sequence, so too we can show that redundancy also occurs at the first accumulation point for the sequence of probabilistic **PFIN** capabilities.

Theorem 10
a) **PFIN**$\langle$T:$1/2\rangle \subset$ **PFIN**$\langle$T:$2/4\rangle$.
b) For integers $n \geq 0$, **PFIN**$\langle$T:$(2n+1)/(4n+2)\rangle =$ **PFIN**$\langle$T:$1/2\rangle$.
c) For integers $n \geq 1$, **PFIN**$\langle$T:$2n/4n\rangle =$ **PFIN**$\langle$T:$2/4\rangle$.

Likewise, we can show that this redundancy is isolated.

Theorem 11
For natural numbers r *and* s *such that* $\frac{r}{s} < \frac{1}{2}$, **PFIN**$\langle$T:$2/4\rangle \subseteq$ **PFIN**$\langle$T:$r/s\rangle$.

We now turn our attention to probabilistic hierarchy at or below $\frac{1}{2}$.

Theorem 12 *For integers* $n \geq 2$,
a) **PFIN**$\langle$P:$\frac{4n}{9n-2}\rangle \subset$ **PFIN**$\langle$P:$\frac{4(n+1)}{9(n+1)-2}\rangle$.
b) if $\frac{4(n+1)}{9(n+1)-2} < p \leq \frac{4n}{9n-2}$, *then* **PFIN**$\langle$P:$p\rangle \subseteq$ **PFIN**$\langle$P:$\frac{4n}{9n-2}\rangle$.

Notice that Theorem 10 (resp. Theorem 4) shows that it pays to increase the size of the team in *PFIN*-type (resp. *FIN*-type) learning, eventhough the success ratio is the same. We call this the power of *redundancy*. One way to explain this phenomenon is to observe the hierarchy of the learning capabilities defined by the success ratio. Notice that the sequence $\frac{n}{2n-1}$ converges to $\frac{1}{2}$ and the difference $I(n) = \frac{n}{2n-1} - \frac{n+1}{2(n+1)-1}$ converges to 0. Therefore, one can expect the efficacy of redundancy to appear at such accumulation points (e.g., ratio $\frac{1}{2}$ for the sequence $\frac{n}{2n-1}$). The following theorem shows some of the power of redundancy at the second accumulation point $\frac{4}{9}$ for the *PFIN*-type learning.

Theorem 13
a) **PFIN**$\langle$T:$4/9\rangle =$ **PFIN**$\langle$T:$8/18\rangle \subset$ **PFIN**$\langle$T:$16/36\rangle \subset$ **PFIN**$\langle$T:$12/27\rangle$.
b) For all integers $n \geq 1$, **PFIN**$\langle$T:$4n/9n\rangle \subseteq$ **PFIN**$\langle$T:$12/27\rangle$.
c) For all integers $m \geq 1$ *with* $m \neq 0 \bmod 3$ **PFIN**$\langle$T:$4m/9m\rangle \subseteq$ **PFIN**$\langle$T:$16/36\rangle$.

As a logical next step, it is interesting to see if the power of redundancy is observed only at accumulation points. We have the following interesting results that show that the phenomenon of *redundancy* is more complex and need not appear only at accumulation points. It is important to observe that $\frac{4(8k+2)}{9(8k+2)-2} = \frac{8k+2}{18k+4} = \frac{4k+1}{9k+2}$ and $\frac{4(4k+2)}{9(4k+2)-2} = \frac{4k+2}{9k+4}$.

Theorem 14 *For integers $k \geq 0$,*
a) $\mathbf{PFIN}\langle\mathbf{T}\colon (8k+2)/(18k+4)\rangle - \mathbf{PFIN}\langle\mathbf{T}\colon (4k+1)/(9k+2)\rangle \neq \emptyset.$
b) $\mathbf{PFIN}\langle\mathbf{T}\colon (4k+2)/(9k+4)\rangle - \mathbf{PFIN}\langle\mathbf{T}\colon (4k+1)/(9k+2)\rangle \neq \emptyset.$

Finally, we point out one additional fact regarding *PFIN* team capabilities for ratios below $\frac{1}{2}$, viz., for the values of $n = 30$ and $n = 31$ in the sequence $\frac{4n}{9n-2}$ we obtain incomparable capabilities.

Theorem 15
a) $\mathbf{PFIN}\langle\mathbf{T}\colon 120/268\rangle - \mathbf{PFIN}\langle\mathbf{T}\colon 124/277\rangle \neq \emptyset.$
b) $\mathbf{PFIN}\langle\mathbf{T}\colon 124/277\rangle - \mathbf{PFIN}\langle\mathbf{T}\colon 120/268\rangle \neq \emptyset.$

4   Diagonalization Proofs

The constructions in this section are all rather similar in nature, so we will give an illustrative example. The other diagonalization proofs can be obtained by consulting the relevant figures given at the end of this paper. We give here a sketch of the proof for Theorem 12a for the case where $n = 2$, i.e., we show $\mathbf{PFIN}\langle\mathbf{T}\colon 12/25\rangle$ is more capable than $\mathbf{PFIN}\langle\mathbf{T}\colon 8/16\rangle$ (which is an instance of probability $p = \frac{8}{16}$). The general case for Theorem 12a in terms of the probability p is depicted in Figure 6.

We begin by describing the class of functions $\mathcal{F}_3^2$ which can be learned by some $\mathbf{PFIN}\langle\mathbf{T}\colon 12/25\rangle$ learner $L = \{L_1, \ldots, L_{25}\}$ but not by any $\mathbf{PFIN}\langle\mathbf{T}\colon 8/16\rangle$ learner. It is best to think of $\mathcal{F}_3^2$ as the set of all (groups of) functions which have a certain shape. The reader should consult Figure 1. The set $\mathcal{F}_3^2$ consists of all functions f satisfying

$$f(x) = \begin{cases} 0, & \text{if } 1 \leq x \leq a \\ c_1, & \text{if } a < x \leq b^{c_1} \\ c_2, & \text{if } x > b^{c_1} \end{cases}$$

where a and b^{c_1} are integers, and $c_1 \in \{1, 2\}$, $c_2 \in \{3, 4\}$ if $c_1 = 1$ and $c_2 \in \{5, 6, 7\}$ if $c_1 = 2$. The value $e = f(0)$ is decoded as a set of learners $M_1, \ldots, M_s$ and a number r such that $r \leq s$ (e.g., $r = 8$ and $s = 16$). To simplify notation we will denote finite initial segments of functions by finite length sequences of their values. For example, $e0^m$ denotes the function which has value e for input 0 and value 0 for inputs $1, \ldots, m$. We introduce the predicate $P(\sigma, k, t, m, y)$ which means that m is the point at which M_k produces its first (and only) hypothesis when fed the initial segments of the function σt^*, where σ is some finite initial segment, and y is an upper bound on the time it takes to do this:

$$P(\sigma, k, t, m, y) \equiv \forall j \leq m \; \Phi_{M_k}(\sigma t^j) \leq y \text{ and } \forall j < m \; \phi_{M_k}(\sigma t^j) = 0 \text{ and } \phi_{M_k}(\sigma t^m) > 0$$

We use Φ_j to denote the computational complexity of the program with number j. In the definition P we have also adopted the convention that on each initial segment of a function a *PFIN* learner M will always produce *some* output, using the value 0 to indicate that it "doesn't know".

The values a and b^t (for $t = 1, 2$) are defined as follows:

$$a = \min y \; \exists \text{ distinct } i_1, \ldots, i_r \; \forall k \leq r \; \exists m \leq y \; P(e, i_k, 0, m, y)$$

$$b^t = \quad \min y \, \exists \text{ distinct } i_1, \ldots, i_r \, \forall k \leq r \text{ either } [\, \exists m \leq a \, P(e, i_k, 0, m, a)$$
$$\text{and } \Phi_{\phi M_{i_k}(e0^m)}(a+1) \leq y \text{ and } \phi_{\phi M_{i_k}(e0^m)}(a+1) = t\,]$$
$$\text{or } \exists m \leq y \, P(e0^a, i_k, t, m, y)$$

The expression $\phi_{\phi M_{i_k}(e0^m)}(a+1) = t$ indicates that the program produced by M_{i_k} (before a) is following the t-valued branch. It is possible for b^{c_1} to be undefined. In that case the function f will have value c_1 for all $x > a$. (see f^1 and f^2 in Figure 1). Similarly, it is possible for both b^{c_1} and a to be undefined and in that case f will have value 0 for all $x > 0$. (see f^0 in Figure 1). However, if these values exist, then they can be computed (in real time) from the information encoded in the value e.

We now describe how the 12/25 team can learn all the functions in the set $\mathcal{F}_3^2$. After seeing $e = f(0)$, L_1, ..., L_{12} produce programs S_1, ..., S_{12}. These programs follow f^0, i.e., they produce output 0 for all inputs $1 \leq x \leq a$. If a is undefined, then these programs will forever follow f^0. If a is defined, then at a they split into two groups. The group S_1, ..., S_5 follows f^1, i.e., they produce output 1 for all inputs $a < x \leq b^1$. If b^1 is undefined, then these programs will forever follow f^1. If b^1 exists, then at b^1 this group splits again into two subgroups. The subgroup S_1, S_2, S_3 follows f_1^1, i.e. they produce output 3 for all inputs $x > b^1$, and the subgroup S_4, S_5 follows f_2^1, i.e., they produce output 4 for all inputs $x > b^1$.

The group S_6, ..., S_{12} follows f^2, i.e., they produce output 2 for all inputs $a < x \leq b^2$. If b^2 is undefined, then these programs will forever follow f^2. If b^2 exists, then at b^2 this group splits again into three subgroups. The subgroup S_6, S_7, S_8 follows f_1^2, i.e., they produce output 5 for all inputs $x > b^2$, the subgroup S_9, S_{10} follows f_2^2, i.e., they produce output 6 for all inputs $x > b^2$, and the subgroup S_{11}, S_{12} follows f_3^2, i.e., they produce output 7 for all inputs $x > b^2$.

After seeing $f(a+1)$, the team of learners produce additional programs as follows: If $f(a+1) = 1$, then L_{13}, ..., L_{19} produce programs S_{13}, ..., S_{19}. These programs follow f^1. Again if b^1 is undefined, then these programs will forever follow f^1, and if b^1 exists, then at b^1 this group splits again into two subgroups. The subgroup S_{13}, S_{14}, S_{15} follows f_1^1, and the subgroup S_{16}, ..., S_{19} follows f_2^1. If $f(a+1) = 2$, then L_{13}, ..., L_{17} produce programs S_{13}, ..., S_{17}. These programs follow f^2. Again if b^2 is undefined, then these programs will forever follow f^2, and if b^2 exists, then at b^2 this group splits again into three subgroups. The subgroup S_{13} follows f_1^2, the subgroup S_{14}, S_{15} follows f_2^2, and the subgroup S_{16}, S_{17} follows f_3^2.

After seeing $f(b^t+1)$, the team of learners produce additional programs as follows: If $t = 1$ and $f(b^t + 1) = 3$ then L_{20}, ..., L_{25} produce programs S_{20}, ..., S_{25}, each of which follows f_1^1. If $t = 1$ and $f(b^t + 1) = 4$ then L_{20}, ..., L_{25} produce programs S_{20}, ..., S_{25}, each of which follows f_2^1. If $t = 2$ and $f(b^t + 1) = 5$ then L_{18}, ..., L_{25} produce programs S_{18}, ..., S_{25}, each of which follows f_1^2. If $t = 2$ and $f(b^t + 1) = 6$ then L_{18}, ..., L_{25} produce programs S_{18}, ..., S_{25}, each of which follows f_2^2. If $t = 2$ and $f(b^t + 1) = 7$ then L_{18}, ..., L_{25} produce programs S_{18}, ..., S_{25}, each of which follows f_3^2. The reader should consult Figure 2, where the distribution of the programs is illustrated and where [n],m denotes that n currently active programs (i.e., which already exist and have split) follow that branch and m new programs (created after the split) follow that branch. It is easy to see that no matter which function (f^0, f^1, f^2, f_1^1, f_2^1, f_1^2, f_2^2, or f_3^2) is given as the target function, there are always 12 programs produced by the team $L_1, \ldots, L_{25}$, which correctly compute it.

We now show that the set $\mathcal{F}_3^2$ cannot be learned by any team of 8 out of 16 learners. Let $M = \{M_1, \ldots, M_{16}\}$ be such a team. We consider function f from $\mathcal{F}_3^2$ where $M_1, \ldots, M_{16}$ and $r = 8$ are encoded as $f(0)$. The reader should consult Figure 3. We work from the top of the function tree to the bottom as follows. At the b^1 split, only 4 of the currently active programs can follow each branch, so 4 new programs are required on each branch (f_1^1 and f_2^1). Thus, the maximum remaining new programs which could be produced on the f^1 branch after the a split is 4, so 4 of the original 8 programs must follow the f^1 branch. This means that at most 4 of the original programs are available to follow the f^2 branch, and 4 new programs must be produced on the f^2 branch after the a split. At the b^2 split, at most 3 of the currently active programs can follow each branch, so at least 5 new programs are required on each branch (f_1^2, f_2^2, f_3^2). However, this is not possible since already 12 programs have been produced up to this point on the f^2 branch (8 original + 4 after the a split).

All other diagonalization arguments used in this paper are similar, and the function trees used along with the accompanying successful team distributions are given in the figures to be found at the end of this paper. ♠

5 Simulation Proofs

We omit the proofs of Theorems 9, 10 and 11 since they are analogous to proofs found in [5, 11, 7].

The constructions in this section share a number of basic ideas, which we outline here. Suppose M is a $\mathbf{PFIN}\langle \mathbf{P}{:}p \rangle$-type learner, and let L be a $\mathbf{PFIN}\langle \mathbf{P}{:}\frac{r}{s} \rangle$ that successfully simulates M and learns all that M can learn. Even though L is intended to be a probabilistic learner (with success ratio $\frac{r}{s}$), we will actually implement it as a team of learners (with plurality kr/ks, for an appropriate choice of k). Let $f \in \mathbf{PFIN}\langle \mathbf{P}{:}p \rangle[M]$ be an arbitrary function learnable by M. We will refer to M as the target learner and f as the target function, and we will refer to L as the pursuing team of learners. Observing the input graph of f, whenever M produces programs with a certain weight, L will also produce programs with a certain (but probably different) weight.

At the heart of the construction is Freivalds' idea of *following the functions*. The quantity $b \equiv 1 - p$ is the maximum weight of *bad* programs which can be produced by M on f. The construction involves a number of types of *events* which will cause the pursuing team to take different sorts of actions. Events are identified by observing that a certain number q (called a *quantum*) of programs produced by M concur in their output at least up to that point in time. Depending upon the quantity q, the events are classified as *initial, consensus* or *breakaway*. A key technique which is introduced here in order to simplify the construction is a reduction argument, which makes use of previously established relationships between probabilistic and team *PFIN*-type learners (especially Theorem 9).

Proof Sketch of Theorem 12b : For a sufficiently large integer $k \geq 1$, we will show that a learner L with plurality $k(4n)/k(9n - 2)$ can successfully simulate the learning by M of any target function f.

Initially, the simulator L will wait until M produces programs with weight at least p. We call this event the *initial event*, and the programs produced by M as part of this event the *initial programs*. At this point $4kn$ members output programs $\{S_1, \ldots S_{4kn}\}$.

For each input, the S_i's will classify the initial programs produced by M according to the finite function which they have thus-far computed. Since all of the programs produced by M must be total, this classification can be effectively completely carried out. This classification partitions the programs of M into groups. We say that a *consensus* event is witnessed if there is a group whose cumulative weight exceeds $T_1 \equiv 1 - \frac{3p}{2}$. When this happens, the S_i's follow the function computed by that group. If this ever results in an error of commission, then L knows that the weight of the bad programs produced by M exceeds T_1. Now, the rest of L's team will observe these bad programs (since M *always* produces programs which are defined on every input), and so they will wait until more than T_1 programs are produced by M to replace the bad ones. At that time, the remaining $5kn - 2k \geq 4kn$ (for $n \geq 2$) take a majority vote of the remaining p (or more) programs of M that seem to compute f thus far. Observe that the simulation will succeed since the cumulative weight of remaining bad programs for M is less than $\frac{1}{2}$.

If there is no group whose cumulative weight is at least $Q_1 \equiv \frac{5p}{2} - 1$, then L knows that the weight of the bad programs produced by M exceeds T_1. Analogous to our previous argument, there are at least $4kn$ of the S_i's left and they produce programs that compute f correctly. We say that a *breakaway* event takes place when a group with weight q ($Q_1 \leq q \leq T_1$) follows a path on which new programs with cumulative weight ν are produced by M, where $q + \nu = p$. In such a situation the breakaway path might be the path of the target function (where the weight ν of new programs produced by M replaces those initial programs of M which did not follow the breakaway path). Exactly what the team L must do when a breakaway event takes place depends on the value q, and we distinguish five cases (A through E below), defined by the following subintervals of $[Q_1, T_1]$: $[Q_1, \frac{8p}{3} - 1)$, $[\frac{8p}{3} - 1, \frac{11p}{4} - 1)$, $[\frac{11p}{4} - 1, \frac{14p}{5} - 1)$, $[\frac{14p}{5} - 1, \frac{17p}{6} - 1)$, and $[\frac{17p}{6} - 1, T_1]$. In each of the cases below we will assume that the breakaway path is the path of the target function f.

Case A. $Q_1 \leq q < \frac{8p}{3} - 1$: This case is possible only when $\frac{5p}{2} - 1 \leq 1 - \frac{3p}{2} \equiv p \leq \frac{1}{2}$, i.e., when $n \geq 2$. In this case, $k(n+2)$ programs of L will follow the path. Right after the breakaway event, L will produce $k(3n - 2)$ new programs along the breakaway path. Therefore, at this moment there are $k(4n)$ programs of L following the path. The number of programs lost by L (i.e., which did not follow the breakaway path) is $k(3n - 2)$ so that along the breakaway path L is reduced to a team with plurality $k(4n)/k((9n-2)-(3n-2)) = k(4n)/k(6n)$. Note that since redundancy doesn't pay for *PFIN*-type learning for ratios above $\frac{1}{2}$, we have that L actually reduces to a team with plurality 2/3. We call this plurality the *reduced follower plurality*. Similarly, M has lost $> p - (\frac{8p}{3} - 1) = 1 - \frac{5p}{3}$ programs which did not follow the breakaway path, so along the breakaway path M is reduced to a learner with success probability $> \frac{p}{1-(1-\frac{5p}{3})} = \frac{3}{5}$. We call this probability the *reduced target probability*. By Theorem 9b (for $n = 2$) it is clear that along the breakaway path (which is the path of the target function f) L can (by applying the corresponding strategy of Theorem 9b) simulate the learning of f done by M.

Case B. $\frac{8p}{3} - 1 \le q < \frac{11p}{4} - 1$: This case is possible only when $\frac{8p}{3} - 1 \le 1 - \frac{3p}{2} \equiv p \le \frac{12}{25}$, i.e., when $n \ge 3$. In this case, $k(\frac{5n}{3} + 2)$ programs of L will follow the path, and L will produce $k(\frac{7n}{3} - 2)$ new programs along the breakaway path. The reduced follower plurality in this case is $\frac{3}{5}$, and the reduced target probability is $> \frac{4}{7}$. By Theorem 9b (for $n = 3$) along the breakaway path L can simulate the learning of f done by M.

Case C. $\frac{11p}{4} - 1 \le q < \frac{14p}{5} - 1$: This case is possible only when $\frac{11p}{4} - 1 \le 1 - \frac{3p}{2} \equiv p \le \frac{8}{17}$, i.e., when $n \ge 4$. In this case, $k(2n + 2)$ programs of L will follow the path, and L will produce $k(2n - 2)$ new programs along the breakaway path. The reduced follower plurality in this case is $\frac{4}{7}$, and the reduced target probability is $> \frac{5}{9}$. By Theorem 9b (for $n = 4$) along the breakaway path L can simulate the learning of f done by M.

Case D. $\frac{14p}{5} - 1 \le q < \frac{17p}{6} - 1$: This case is possible only when $\frac{14p}{5} - 1 \le 1 - \frac{3p}{2} \equiv p \le \frac{20}{43}$, i.e., when $n \ge 5$. In this case, $k(\frac{11n}{5} + 2)$ programs of L will follow the path, and L will produce $k(\frac{9n}{5} - 2)$ new programs along the breakaway path. The reduced follower plurality in this case is $\frac{5}{9}$, and the reduced target probability is $> \frac{6}{11}$. By Theorem 9b (for $n = 5$) along the breakaway path L can simulate the learning of f done by M.

Case E. $\frac{17p}{6} - 1 \le q \le T_1$: This case is possible only when $\frac{17p}{6} - 1 \le 1 - \frac{3p}{2} \equiv p \le \frac{6}{13}$, i.e., when $n \ge 6$. In this case, $k(3n - 2)$ programs of L will follow the path, and L will produce $k(n + 2)$ new programs along the breakaway path. The reduced follower plurality in this case is $\frac{4n}{8n-4} = \frac{n}{2n-1}$. The reduced target probability is $\ge \frac{2p}{4-5p}$. Thus, L will be able to simulate the learning of f by M along the breakaway path when $\frac{2p}{4-5p} > \frac{n+1}{2n+1}$, which is precisely when $p > \frac{4(n+1)}{9(n+1)-2}$.

It is possible for multiple breakaways to occur, and so we must demonstrate that L has sufficient resources (i.e., programs) to handle all possibilities. For example, 2 Case A breakaways (denoted **2A**) are possible, when $2Q_1 \le p \equiv p \le \frac{1}{2}$ or $n \ge 2$. Fortunately if $n \ge 2$, then (precisely) $2k(n + 2) \le k(4n)$, so that L will have enough initial programs to send along both breakaways. Similarly, 3 Case A breakaways are possible when $p \le \frac{6}{13}$ (i.e., when $n \ge 6$), and for precisely $n \ge 6$, L will have sufficient programs to cover all 3 events. However, L will never have suffcient resources to cover 4 Case A breakaways, since that would require $\ge k(4n + 4) > k(4n)$ initial programs. Fortunately once more, 4 breakaways are possible only when $p \le \frac{4}{9}$ (i.e., $n \ge \infty$). Table 1 summarizes all the possibilities for multiple events, where **A+B** means a Case A breakaway and Case B breakaway. The table is ordered according to decreasing probability p (increasing n) in the Case Possible column. We have also listed the minimal impossible cases from which all other cases follow (e.g., the impossibility of **3B** follows from that for **A+2B**, since a **B** breakaway has a higher weight threshold than a **A** breakaway.).

♠

5.0.1 Proof sketch of Theorem 13

First we will prove that $\mathbf{PFIN}\langle \mathbf{T}: 4/9 \rangle = \mathbf{PFIN}\langle \mathbf{T}: 8/18 \rangle$. We will show that there is a team of plurality 4/9 who can successfully simulate a given team of plurality

Table 1: Multiple Events

Combination	Case Possible	L OK
2A	$n \geq 2$	$n \geq 2$
A+B	$n \geq 3$	$n \geq 3$
A+C	$n \geq 4$	$n \geq 4$
A+D	$n \geq 5$	$n \geq 5$
A+E	$n \geq 6$	$n \geq 6$
3A	$n \geq 6$	$n \geq 6$
2B	$n \geq 6$	$n \geq 6$
B+C	$n \geq 12$	$n \geq 12$
2A+B	$n \geq 18$	$n \geq 18$
B+D	$n \geq 30$	$n \geq 30$
4A	$n \geq \infty$	NO
2C	$n \geq \infty$	NO
2A+C	$n \geq \infty$	NO
B+E	$n \geq \infty$	NO
A+2B	$n > \infty$	NO

8/18. Assume that f is the target function that the teams are trying to learn.

At the beginning, the simulating team will wait until 8 members of the target team produce their hypothesis/program. The first 4 members of the simulating team will produce their programs (say S_i's) and they try to mimic the behavior of the 8 programs produced by the target team in the following way. As before S_i's will classify the events as either a consensus event ($T_1 = 6$), or as a quantum event ($2 \leq Q_1 \leq 6$).

First, observe that the programs of the target team must compute some total function. Therefore, the S_i's, can classify the programs of the target team according to consensus or quantum events. See Table 2 below. Suppose that the S_i's witness a consensus event and the path of the true function f will never witness it, then it must be the case that at least 7 initial programs produced by the target team are wrong. We call this *case A*. Therefore, the target team can produce at most 3 more bad programs. Therefore, the rest of the simulating team (at least 4) will see at least 8 target programs of which majority will compute f. Therefore, the simulating team produces programs that take majority vote of those 8 target programs.

We now consider the case where a quantum event $Q_1 \leq q \leq T_1$ took place. Observe that this rules out the possibility of a consensus event. The number of simulating programs following the quantum event depends upon the number q of the original programs of the target team participated in the quantum event.

Suppose that $Q_1 \leq q \leq 3$. We call this *case B*. In this case, only one of the four original programs of the simulating team follows this path. The simulation for this path enters the next level. If this were the path of f, then the target team will produce $8 - p$ additional programs to compensate for those $8 - q$ bad initial programs. Upon seeing this, the simulating team produces 3 more programs to join with the one original program to follow this path on the second level and apply *Strategy*$_3^2$ (the strategy used by a team with plurality 2/3 simulating another team

Table 2: 4/9 simulating 8/18

Case	Target Team	Target Ratio	Simulating Team	Simulating Ratio	Strategy
A	$0 \leq q \leq 1$	$\geq (8/11)$	0	$(4/5)$	$1/1$
B	$2 \leq q \leq 3$	$\geq (8/13)$	1	$(12/18)$	$2/3$
C	$q = 4$	$\geq (8/14)$	2	$(4/7)$	$4/7$
D	$5 \leq q \leq 6$	$\geq (8/16)$	3	$(4/8)$	$2/4$
E	$7 \leq q \leq 8$		4		

Table 3: Impossible Cases for 8/18 by 4/9

Combinations	Reason
E+B	$7 + 2 > 8$
D+C	$5 + 4 > 8$
5B	$10 > 8$

with plurality r/s where $r/s > 3/5$ (see Theorem 9)). Observe that the reduced plurality for the simulating team is $4/6 = 2/3$. On the other hand, the target team is also reduced to only $10 + q$ members out of which at least 8 must succeed, i.e., its reduced plurality is $8/(10 + q)$. By Theorem 9, the simulating team (4 out of 6) has a strategy $Strategy_3^2$ to simulate the target team (8 out of $10 + q$) if $\frac{8}{10+q} > \frac{3}{5}$. Therefore, the simulation succeeds if $3q < 10$ or $q \leq 3$.

For the case (say *case C*) where $q = 4$ and f follows the path of this quantum event, the number of original followers of the simulating team is 2. At the second level of the simulation, the S_i's will apply $Strategy_7^4$. Observe that the reduced plurality for the simulating team is $4/7$ and that for the target team is $8/14 = 4/7$.

Finally, for the case (say *case D*) where q is either 5 or 6, the number of original followers of the simulating team is 3. At the second level of the simulation, the S_i's will apply $RStrategy_8^4$ (the strategy used by a team with plurality $2/4$ to simulate teams with plurality $2n/4n$). Observe that the reduced plurality for the simulator is $4/8$ and that for the target team is $\geq 8/16$. Therefore, $RStrategy_8^4$ succeeds.

On the other hand, it could be the case that f did not witness either a consensus or a quantum event. In this case, none of the original programs of the simulating team will be correct. Observe that this is equivalent to *case A*. Therefore, at the second level, the remaining five S_i's apply $Strategy_1^1$. Fortunately, the reduced plurality for the target team is $8/11 > 2/3$. Therefore, $Strategy_1^1$ succeeds. We summarize various cases of the strategy in Table 2.

One should observe that some of these cases may co-exist. For example, it is possible for the simulator to witness two Case A type quantum events and a Case B quantum event simultaneously. A simple calculation shows that the simulator has enough of original programs to distribute according the strategy explained above. Table 3 illustrates the impossible combinations of various cases. Notice that not all bad combinations are illustrated.

We now prove that a team with plurality 12/27 can simulate any team with

Table 4: 12/27 simulating $4n/9n$, where $n \geq 1$

Case	Target Team	Target Ratio	Simulating Team	Simulating Ratio	Strategy
A	$0 \leq q < n$	$> (4n/6n)$	0	$(12/15)$	1/1
B	$n \leq q < \frac{5n}{3}$	$> (12n/20n)$	3	$(12/18)$	2/3
C	$\frac{5n}{3} \leq q < 2n$	$> (4n/7n)$	5	$(12/20)$	3/5
D	$2n \leq q < \frac{11n}{5}$	$> (20n/36n)$	6	$(12/21)$	4/7
E	$\frac{11n}{5} \leq q < \frac{17n}{7}$	$> (28n/52n)$	7	$(12/22)$	6/11
F	$\frac{17n}{7} \leq q \leq 3n$	$\geq (4n/8n)$	9	$(12/24)$	2/4
G	$3n < q \leq 4n$		12		

Table 5: Impossible Cases for $4n/9n$ by 12/27

Combinations	Reason
G+B	$q + n > 4n$ when $n \geq 1$ and $q > 3n$
F+C	$\frac{17n}{7} + \frac{5n}{3} > 4n$ when $n \geq 1$
E+2B	$\frac{11n}{5} + 2n > 4n$ when $n \geq 1$
D+C+B	$2n + \frac{5n}{3} + n > 4n$ when $n \geq 1$
C+3B	$\frac{5n}{3} + 3n > 4n$ when $n \geq 1$
5B	$5n > 4n$ when $n \geq 1$

plurality $4n/9n$ for $n \geq 1$. We summarize the strategy in Table 4, where the quantity $T_1 = 3n$ and $Q_1 = n$.

As before, Table 5 illustrates the success of the simulation by showing that bad combinations are impossible.

We now prove that a team with plurality 16/36 can simulate any team with plurality $4m/9m$ for $m \geq 1$ and $m \not\equiv 0 \mod 3$. We summarize the strategy in Table 6, where the quantity $T_1 = 3m$ and $Q_1 = m$.

As before, Table 7 illustrates the success of the simulation by showing that bad combinations are impossible. One should observe that the condition $m \not\equiv 0 \mod 3$

Table 6: 16/36 simulating $4m/9m$, where $m \geq 1$ and $m \not\equiv 0 \bmod 3$

Case	Target Team	Target Ratio	Simulating Team	Simulating Ratio	Strategy
A	$0 \leq q < m$	$> (4m/6m)$	0	$(16/20)$	1/1
B	$m \leq q < \frac{5m}{3}$	$> (12m/20m)$	4	$(16/24)$	2/3
C	$\frac{5m}{3} \leq q < 2m$	$> (4m/7m)$	7	$(16/27)$	3/5
D	$2m \leq q < \frac{11m}{5}$	$> (20m/36m)$	8	$(16/28)$	4/7
E	$\frac{11m}{5} \leq q < \frac{7m}{3}$	$> (12m/22m)$	9	$(16/29)$	5/9
F	$\frac{7m}{3} \leq q \leq 3m$	$\geq (4m/8m)$	12	$(16/32)$	2/4
G	$3m < q \leq 4m$		16		

Table 7: Impossible Cases for $4m/9m$ by $16/36$

Combinations	Reason
G+B	$q + m > 4m$ when $m \geq 1$ and $q > 3m$
F+C	$\lceil \frac{7m}{3} \rceil + \lceil \frac{5m}{3} \rceil > 4m$ when $m \geq 1$ and $m \neq 0 \bmod 3$
E+2B	$\frac{11m}{5} + 2m > 4m$ when $m \geq 1$
D+C+B	$2m + \frac{5m}{3} + m > 4m$ when $m \geq 1$
C+3B	$\frac{5m}{3} + 3m > 4m$ when $m \geq 1$
5B	$5m > 4m$ when $m \geq 1$

arise because the combination **F+C** will foil the simulation.

♠

6 Acknowledgements

The first author was supported in part by NSF Grant CCR-8901795, and the second author in part by NSF Grant CCR-9009318.

References

[1] R. Daley, and B. Kalyanasundaram, Capabilities of Probabilistic Learners with Bounded Mind Changes, Submitted for Publication.

[2] R. Daley, and B. Kalyanasundaram, Probabilistic and Pluralistic Learners with Mind Changes, In *Proceedings of Mathematical Foundations of Computer Science*, 1992.

[3] R. Daley, B. Kalyanasundaram, and M. Velauthapillai, Breaking the probability $\frac{1}{2}$ barrier in FIN-type learning, In *Proceedings of the 1992 Workshop on Computational Learning Theory*, 1992.

[4] R. Daley, L. Pitt, M. Velauthapillai, and T. Will, Relations between probabilistic and team one-shot learners, In *Proceedings of the 1991 Workshop on Computational Learning Theory*, pages 228-239, 1991.

[5] R.V. Freivalds, Finite Identification of General Recursive Functions by Probabilistic Strategies, Akademie Verlag, Berlin, 1979.

[6] E. M. Gold, Language identification in the limit, *Information and Control*, 10:447-474, 1967.

[7] S. Jain, and A. Sharma, Finite learning by a team, In *Proceedings of the 1990 Workshop on Computational Learning Theory*, pages 163-177, 1990.

[8] L. Pitt, Probabilistic inductive inference, *J. ACM*, 36(2):383-433, 1989.

[9] L. Pitt, and C. Smith, Probability and plurality for aggregations of learning machines, *Information and Computation*, 77(1):77-92, 1988.

[10] C. H. Smith, The power of pluralism for automatic program synthesis, *J. ACM*, 29:1144-1165, 1982.

[11] M. Velauthapillai, Inductive inference with a bounded number of mind changes, In *Proceedings of the 1989 Workshop on Computational Learning Theory*, pages 200-213, 1989.

[12] R. Wiehagen, R. Freivalds, and E. Kinber, On the power of probabilistic strategies in inductive inference, *Theoretical Computer Science*, 111-113, 1984.

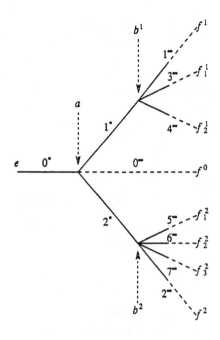

Figure 1
Function Tree

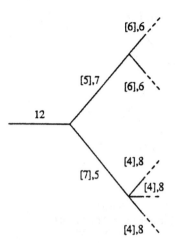

Figure 2
Stronger team Distribution (12/25)

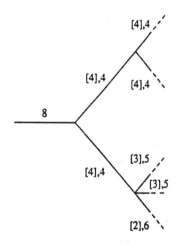

Figure 3
Weaker Team Distribution (8/16)

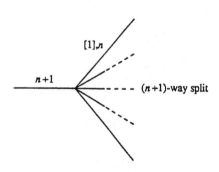

Figure 4
Stronger Team Distribution $((n+1)/(2n+1))$
(Theorem 9a)

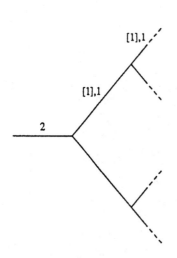

Figure 5
Stronger Team Distribution (2/4)
(Theorem 10a)

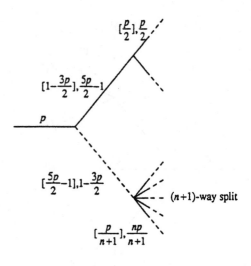

Figure 6
Stronger Team Distribution $(p \geq \dfrac{4(n+1)}{9(n+1)-2})$
(Theorem 12a)

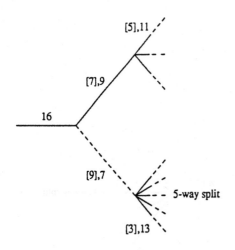

Figure 7
Stronger Team Distribution (16/36)
(Theorem 13a)

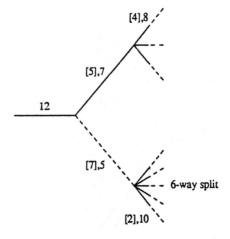

Figure 8
Stronger Team Distribution (12/27)
(Theorem 13a & 13c)

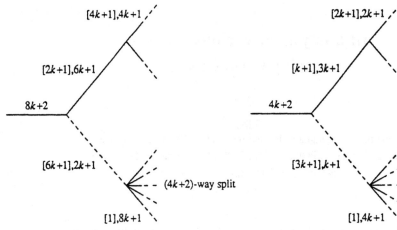

Figure 9
Stronger Team Distribution $((8k+2)/(18k+4))$
(Theorem 14a)

Figure 10
Stronger Team Distribution $((4k+2)/(9k+4))$
(Theorem 14b)

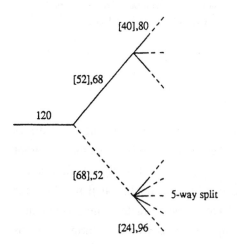

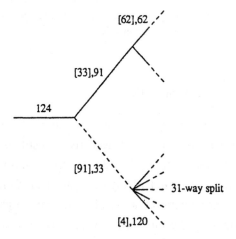

Figure 11
Stronger Team Distribution (120/268)
(Theorem 15a)

Figure 12
Stronger Team Distribution (124/277)
(Theorem 15b)

An analysis of various forms of
'jumping to conclusions'

Peter A. Flach

ITK

Institute for Language Technology and Artificial Intelligence
Tilburg University, PObox 90153, 5000 LE Tilburg, the Netherlands
☎ +31 13 663119, fax +31 13 663069
flach@kub.nl

Abstract. In this paper, we discuss and relate characterisations of different forms of 'jumping to conclusions': Kraus, Lehmann & Magidor's analysis of plausible reasoning, the present author's characterisation of inductive reasoning, Zadrozny's account of abductive reasoning, and Gärdenfors' theory of belief revision. Our main claims are that (*i*) inductive reasoning can be characterised in a way similar to plausible reasoning; (*ii*) inductive and abductive reasoning are special cases of explanatory reasoning; and (*iii*) there are strong relations between belief revision and explanatory reasoning. The ultimate goal of this research is a general account of jumping to conclusions.

1.   Introduction

A reasoning agent can be said to be 'jumping to conclusions' whenever it draws conclusions that are not deductively justified by the premises. In other words, the proof procedure ⊢ employed by the reasoner is unsound: $\alpha \vdash \beta$ does not imply $\alpha \models \beta$, where $\models$ denotes the standard logical semantics. Consequently, the conclusion β to which the reasoner jumps at a certain moment, might have to be retracted later, when new information becomes available: the conclusion jumped to is *defeasible*. In formal domains like mathematics, jumping to conlusions is inexcusable. However, humans typically employ many forms of defeasible reasoning, which justifies the study of these forms from the point of view of Artificial Intelligence.

Plausible reasoning provides a typical form of jumping to conlusions, allowing us to draw conclusions from incomplete information. For instance, we might have a general rule which normally holds, with a number of known exceptions, such as[1]

```
flies(X):-bird(X),¬abnormal(X). % normal birds fly
bird(X):-sparrow(X).             % sparrows are birds
```

---

[1] We use a Prolog-like notation for clausal logic; we are not restricted to Horn logic, but in this case we use negated literals in the body of a clause to make our point clear.

```
    :-abnormal(X),sparrow(X).        % which are not abnormal
    bird(X):-penguin(X).             % penguins are birds
    abnormal(X):-penguin(X).         % which are abnormal
```
Furthermore, we know three specific birds:
```
    bird(opus).
    sparrow(sparky).
    penguin(tweety).
```
In all Herbrand models of this set of clauses, bird(sparky) is true and abnormal(sparky) is false, so the conclusion that Sparky flies is deductively justified. Furthermore, in all models both bird(tweety) and abnormal(tweety) are true, but flies(tweety) is true in some models and false in others. We can only conclude that Tweety doesn't fly if the implication in the first clause is interpreted as an equivalence (Predicate Completion). Finally, we don't even know whether Opus is abnormal or not; we can only conclude that Opus is not abnormal by treating the unprovability of her abnormality as sufficient evidence (Closed World Assumption).

The two latter conclusions are defeasible: we can add the facts flies(tweety), flies(opus) and abnormal(opus) without making the theory inconsistent, while invalidating the conclusions. In general, plausible reasoning lacks the property of *monotonicity* of classical logic, which states that strengthening the premises of an argument never invalidates any conclusion: for any formulas α, β and γ, $\alpha \vdash \beta$ implies $\alpha, \gamma \vdash \beta$. For this reason, plausible reasoning is often called non-monotonic reasoning. However, none of the other forms of jumping to conclusions studied in this paper have the property of monotonicity. Therefore, a stronger characterisation of plausible reasoning is needed, as will be discussed in section 2.

Inductive reasoning derives general rules from particular cases. For instance, if we know that the following facts are true:
```
    bird(sparky).                    flies(sparky).
    bird(opus).                      flies(opus).
    :-bird(clyde).                   :-flies(clyde).
```
we might inductively conclude flies(X):-bird(X), since this rule deductively entails that Sparky and Opus fly, given that they are birds, while it does not entail that Clyde flies. We could say that the general rule provides an *explanation* for the fact that some objects fly while others don't.

In this case, explanations are identified with deductive proofs; however, that is not necessarily so. Consider the following facts from a deductive database, which list employees together with their managers:
```
    emp_mngr(smith,johnson).
```

```
emp_mngr(jones,johnson).
emp_mngr(clark,middler).
emp_mngr(kent,middler).
```

We might want to conclude that employees have at most one manager, which is expressed by the constraint

```
M1=M2:-emp_mngr(E,M1),emp_mngr(E,M2).
```

This general rule does not entail the above facts; still, it can be said to provide some sort of explanation for the fact that `emp_mngr(smith,middler)` is false. In section 3, we will provide a general framework for inductive reasoning, which unifies both types of inductive reasoning. The framework is built around an abstract notion of explanation, which can be structurally characterised by several properties.

Abductive reasoning is also concerned with finding explanations for observed facts. For instance, given the general rule `flies(X):-bird(X)` and the fact `flies(opus)`, we might want to conclude that `bird(opus)` is true, since it explains why Opus flies, given the general rule. The problem becomes interesting only when there are several general rules (such as `flies(X):-aeroplane(X)`). Here again explanation is identified with a deductive proof.

However, in some forms of *diagnostic reasoning*, which is closely related to abductive reasoning, different notions of explanation are employed. For instance, we might have the following model of the normal operation of two batteries in series (adapted from (Poole, 1989)):

```
plus(v(B1),v(B2),V):-voltage(series(B1,B2),V).
normal_range(v(B),1.2,1.6):-¬abnormal(B).
```

The term `v(B)` denotes the voltage of battery `B`. If we observe `voltage(series(b1,b2),1.456)`, we can prove from this observation and the above rules `abnormal(b1);abnormal(b2)`[2]. There are thus two minimal diagnoses, one stating the abnormality of `b1`, the other stating the abnormality of `b2`; however, neither of these explain the observation in terms of a deductive proof.

In section 4, it will will be shown that abductive reasoning can be abstractly characterised around a central notion of explanation, in a way very similar to inductive reasoning. In fact, we will argue that inductive and abductive reasoning are very similar with regard to the logical relations between premises and conclusion. Their main difference lies on the syntactical level: inductive reasoning derives general rules as explanations with specific facts as premises, while abductive reasoning derives specific facts as explanations with both general rules and other specific facts as premises.

---

[2]; denotes disjunction.

Belief revision is concerned with updating a set of beliefs (a deductively closed theory) with new information. This new information can consist of a new belief, or a previously held belief that is falsified. For instance, if our current beliefs include `flies(X):-bird(X),bird(tweety)` and `flies(tweety)`, and we find out that the latter fact is not true, we have to retract this fact from our belief set, as well as one of the other beliefs. This case of belief revision is handled by the contraction operator. Other cases are expansion, which incorporates non-conflicting information in the theory, and revision, which takes care of new information which contradicts the current theory. In (Gärdenfors, 1988) these operators are abstractly defined by structural properties called rationality postulates. This will be briefly discussed in section 5.

It will be clear by now that these various forms of jumping to conclusions have much in common. For instance, default rules in plausible reasoning can be invoked by a predicate `normal`; the statement `normal(tweety)` can then be seen as an abductive explanation for the observation `flies(tweety)` (Kakas et. al, 1992). Furthermore, if a belief set is revised, we would like to retain all plausible consequences of the new information as beliefs (Gärdenfors, 1990). In section 6, we will investigate various relations between the different forms of reasoning. One application of such relations is to rewrite structural properties of one form of reasoning to properties of another, which would enable us to capture them all in a single framework.

2. Plausible reasoning

(Kraus, Lehmann & Magidor, 1990) provides an extensive discussion of the structural properties a consequence relation $\vdash$ for plausible reasoning might have, based on the work of Gabbay (1985). These properties are expressed in a meta-language, as axiom schemes and Gentzen-style inference rules. We will present their work in some detail, since it formed the motivation for our own work on the structural characterisation of inductive reasoning. We assume a propositional language, and $\models$ denotes logical consequence in standard propositional logic.

Their weakest system is called C and models socalled *cumulative* consequence relations. This system is defined by the following axiom schema and inference rules:

- **Reflexivity:** $\qquad\qquad\qquad\qquad\qquad \alpha \vdash \alpha$

- **Left Logical Equivalence:** $\qquad\qquad \dfrac{\models \alpha \leftrightarrow \beta\,,\, \alpha \vdash \gamma}{\beta \vdash \gamma}$

- **Right Weakening:** $\qquad\qquad\qquad \dfrac{\models \alpha \rightarrow \beta\,,\, \gamma \vdash \alpha}{\gamma \vdash \beta}$

- **Cut:** $\qquad\qquad\qquad\qquad\qquad \dfrac{\alpha \wedge \beta \vdash \gamma\,,\, \alpha \vdash \beta}{\alpha \vdash \gamma}$

- **Cautious Monotonicity:** $$\dfrac{\alpha \vdash \beta , \alpha \vdash \gamma}{\alpha \wedge \beta \vdash \gamma}$$

Reflexivity states that any formula is a consequence of itself. *Left Logical Equivalence* expresses that logically equivalent formulas have the same consequences. *Right Weakening* states that consequences may be weakened. *Cut* states that if some part of the premises is a consequence of the rest, it may be cut away from the premises. Finally, *Cautious Monotonicity* is the reversal of Cut: premises may be extended with any of their logical consequences.

Cautious Monotonicity, as well as Left Logical Equivalence, are special cases of

- **Monotonicity:** $$\dfrac{\models \alpha \rightarrow \beta , \beta \vdash \gamma}{\alpha \vdash \gamma}$$

Adding Monotonicity to **C** results in the system **CM**, which stands for *cumulative monotonic reasoning*. The still stronger system **M** (monotonic reasoning) is obtained by adding the following rule to **CM**:

- **Contraposition:** $$\dfrac{\alpha \vdash \beta}{\neg \beta \vdash \neg \alpha}$$

M (which in fact has all the properties of classical logic) is strictly stronger than **CM**, which is in turn strictly stronger than **C**.

A system which is, like **CM**, strictly weaker than **M** and strictly stronger than **C** is the system **P**, which stands for *preferential reasoning*; it is however incomparable to **CM**. It is obtained from **C** by adding the following rule:

- **Or:** $$\dfrac{\alpha \vdash \gamma , \beta \vdash \gamma}{\alpha \vee \beta \vdash \gamma}$$

The authors suggest that anything which could possibly be called a consequence relation should obey the rules of **C**. Furthermore, they suggest that "a good reasoning system should validate all the rules of **P**".

Kraus *et al.* also give a semantic account of each of the above forms of reasoning, and prove the corresponding representation theorems (soundness and completeness). Intuitively, a model for a consequence relation consists of a set of states (possible states of affairs), and a binary relation on those states, which represents the preferences of the reasoner for certain states above others. Every state is labeled with the *set* of worlds the reasoner thinks are possible in that state[3]. In cumulative models, the preference relation satisfies a certain smoothness condition. In preferential models, all sets of worlds which label states are singletons. Models for cumulative monotonic reasoning are cumulative

---

[3]Considering a preference relation between states labeled by sets of worlds rather than between worlds is the main difference with Shoham's account of preferential reasoning (1987); this is essential for cumulative reasoning, but it also corrects some errors in Shoham's account.

models with an empty preference relation. Models for monotonic reasoning are preferential models with an empty preference relation.

3. Inductive reasoning

In this section, we give an account of inductive reasoning which is very similar to the discussion in the previous section. Thus, we consider an *inductive consequence relation* $\alpha \mathrel{\vdash_T} \beta$, which is a ternary relation between a *background theory* T, a conjunction of *examples* α, and an *inductive hypothesis* β, all of which are propositional formulas. Whenever this relation holds, we say that β is an *inductive consequence* of α, given T. Alternatively, we say that β (inductively) *explains* α, given T. We will limit attention to a fixed background theory, which reduces $\mathrel{\vdash_T}$ to a collection of binary relations between examples and inductive hypotheses, parametrised by T.

In (Flach, 1992), we argued that any inductive consequence relation should satisfy three rules, which jointly constitute the system **I**. Roughly, the argument is that these rules are necessary and sufficient for a kind of induction called *identification in the limit* (Gold, 1967), in which an infinite sequence of inductive hypotheses converges in the limit to a correct hypothesis. These three rules are the following:

- **Convergence:**

$$\frac{T \models \alpha \to \beta \ , \ \alpha \mathrel{\vdash_T} \gamma}{\beta \mathrel{\vdash_T} \gamma}$$

- **Conditional Reflexivity:**

$$\frac{\not\models \neg\alpha}{\alpha \mathrel{\vdash_T} \alpha}$$

- **Right Logical Equivalence:**

$$\frac{T \models \beta \leftrightarrow \gamma \ , \ \alpha \mathrel{\vdash_T} \beta}{\alpha \mathrel{\vdash_T} \gamma}$$

Convergence formalises the following intuition: suppose we have an inductive explanation for some set of examples α, then making this set of examples smaller (β) should not invalidate the explanation. Put differently: the addition of a new example should give us possibly more information about the correct explanation, but certainly not less. *Conditional Reflexivity* states that consistent examples explain themselves. *Right Logical Equivalence* expresses that logically equivalent inductive hypotheses explain the same examples. Together, these three rules constitute the system **I**. This system contains each of the systems that follow, and we consider it to be the weakest system for inductive reasoning still meaningful.

In the next system we consider, Conditional Reflexivity is strengthened to

- **Reflexivity:** $\qquad\qquad\qquad\qquad \alpha \mathrel{\vdash_T} \alpha$

i.e. any set of examples (consistent or not) inductively explain themselves. Together, Reflexivity and Convergence imply $T \models \alpha \to \beta \Rightarrow \beta \mathrel{\vdash_T} \alpha$, i.e. a hypothesis explains all its logical consequences given T. Adding Reflexivity to $\mathbf{I}$ amounts to accepting deductive proofs as inductive explanations. As already remarked in the introduction, we will later on consider alternative inductive explanations, which do not conform to the rule of Reflexivity.

The following two rules are similar to Cut and Cautious Monotonicity, discussed in the previous section.

- **Right Cut:**
$$\frac{\alpha \vdash_T \beta \wedge \gamma, \; \beta \vdash_T \gamma}{\alpha \vdash_T \gamma}$$

- **Right Extension:**
$$\frac{\alpha \vdash_T \gamma, \; \beta \vdash_T \gamma}{\alpha \vdash_T \beta \wedge \gamma}$$

Right Cut states that a part of an inductive hypothesis which is explained by the rest, may be cut away; *Right Extension* is the converse of Cut. Adding Reflexivity, Right Cut, and Right Extension to $\mathbf{I}$ results in the system $\mathbf{SC}$[4]. In this system, the following rule can be derived:

- **Compositionality:**
$$\frac{\alpha \vdash_T \gamma, \; \beta \vdash_T \gamma}{\alpha \wedge \beta \vdash_T \gamma}$$

This rule states that if an inductive hypothesis explains two examples separately, it also explains them jointly. It is a required property if we don't want to store the examples. In particular, if we can guarantee that a new hypothesis explains all the examples explained by the previous hypothesis, then we only need to test it against the last example which refuted the previous hypothesis.

The system **SP** is obtained from **SC** by adding the following rule:

- **Right Or:**
$$\frac{\alpha \vdash_T \beta, \; \alpha \vdash_T \gamma}{\alpha \vdash_T \beta \vee \gamma}$$

This rule states that the set of inductive explanations for a particular set of examples is closed under disjunction. The additional power gained by this rule is illustrated by the following rule, which states that part of the inductive hypothesis may be added as a condition to the example (the rule's name abbreviates Examples as Implications):

- **EI:**
$$\frac{\alpha \vdash_T \beta \wedge \gamma}{\beta \rightarrow \alpha \vdash_T \gamma}$$

The intuition behind this rule is the following. Suppose γ is a rule defining some concept, β is the description of some object, and α expresses whether this object belongs to the concept. Rule EI then states that if the rule plus the description of the object explains its classification, then the rule itself explains 'if object satisfies the description, then it has that classification'. We can thus use the second representation of hypotheses and examples

---

[4]The significance of the names we use will become clear later on.

as an alternative to the first.

Note that the two representations are only equivalent if the converse of EI holds. Since this converse is not a derived rule in **SC**, we obtain a strictly stronger system **SM** by adding it:

- **IE:**

$$\frac{\beta \to \alpha \mathrel{\vdash_T} \gamma}{\alpha \mathrel{\vdash_T} \beta \wedge \gamma}$$

Together, EI and IE establish a sort of reversed Deduction Theorem for inductive consequence relations: $\beta \to \alpha \mathrel{\vdash_T} \gamma \Leftrightarrow \alpha \mathrel{\vdash_T} \beta \wedge \gamma$. Consequently, in **SM** inductive explanations are identified with deductive proofs. As this is the case usually considered in the field of Machine Learning, it enables us to derive some classical results. In particular, the following two rules are derived rules in **SM**:

- **Explanation Strengthening:**

$$\frac{T \models \gamma \to \beta \,,\, \alpha \mathrel{\vdash_T} \beta}{\alpha \mathrel{\vdash_T} \gamma}$$

- **Explanation Updating:**

$$\frac{T \models \gamma' \to \gamma \,,\, \alpha \mathrel{\vdash_T} \gamma \,,\, \beta \mathrel{\vdash_T} \gamma'}{\alpha \wedge \beta \mathrel{\vdash_T} \gamma'}$$

Explanation Strengthening expresses that any γ logically implying some inductive explanation β of a set of examples α is also an explanation of α. We can therefore use the quasi-ordering of logical implication to structure the search space of possible inductive hypotheses. If $T \models \gamma \to \beta$, we say that γ is *at least as general as* β, relative to T. *Explanation Updating* states that if γ is a hypothesis explaining the examples seen so far α but not the next example β, it can be replaced by some γ' which logically implies γ and explains β. This is, in essence, the Version Space method of (Mitchell, 1982).

Inductive consequence relations satisfying the rules of **SC**, **SP** or **SM** will be called *strong* inductive consequence relations. We will now introduce an alternative family of systems for *weak* inductive reasoning, in which not every deductive proof is considered an explanation. Consequently, we need an alternative for Reflexivity. Consider the following 'weak' form of Reflexivity:

- **Weak Reflexivity:** $\qquad\qquad \neg\alpha \mathrel{\not\vdash_T} \alpha$

Together, Weak Reflexivity and Convergence imply $\alpha \mathrel{\vdash_T} \beta \Rightarrow T \wedge \beta \not\models \neg\alpha$, i.e. an inductive hypothesis does not imply the negation of an example. Thus, an inconsistent formula is not considered a valid inductive explanation under Weak Reflexivity (but it is under Reflexivity). We introduce some further weak versions of rules in **SC**:

- **Weak Right Cut:**

$$\frac{\alpha \mathrel{\vdash_T} \beta \wedge \gamma \,,\, \neg\beta \mathrel{\vdash_T} \gamma}{\alpha \mathrel{\vdash_T} \gamma}$$

- **Weak Right Extension:**

$$\frac{\alpha \mathrel{\vdash_T} \gamma \,,\, \neg\beta \mathrel{\not\vdash_T} \gamma}{\alpha \mathrel{\vdash_T} \beta \wedge \gamma}$$

The system **WC** consists of the rules of **I**, plus Weak Reflexivity, Weak Right Cut, and Weak Right Extension. It is the weak analogue of the strong system **SC**. It allows for the derivation of the following rule:

- **Weak Compositionality:**
$$\frac{\alpha \mathrel{\vdash_T} \gamma, \neg\beta \mathrel{\not\vdash_T} \gamma}{\alpha\wedge\beta \mathrel{\vdash_T} \gamma}$$

Weak Compositionality is much less powerful than its strong counterpart Compositionality. In general, we don't have Compositionality in weak inductive reasoning, since the implication $\neg\beta \mathrel{\vdash_T} \gamma \Rightarrow \beta \mathrel{\vdash_T} \gamma$ does not hold. Consequently, we must always store all previously seen examples, and check them each time we switch to a new inductive hypothesis.

The next system, which is called **WP**, is obtained by adding the following rule to **WC**:

- **Right Or Elimination:**
$$\frac{\alpha \mathrel{\vdash_T} \beta\vee\gamma, \alpha \mathrel{\not\vdash} \beta}{\alpha \mathrel{\vdash_T} \gamma}$$

This rule states that if α has a disjunctive inductive explanation, at least one of the disjuncts must explain α. It is a special case of Explanation Strengthening (which would require every disjunct to explain α). Right Or Elimination is therefore a valid rule in **SM**. Among the derived rules of **WP** is:

- **LR:**
$$\frac{\alpha\wedge\beta \mathrel{\vdash_T} \gamma}{\alpha \mathrel{\vdash_T} \beta\wedge\gamma}$$

LR states that if the left side is weakened by removing a conjunct, it can be used to strengthen the rigth side. Obviously, this rule follows from Convergence and Explanation Strengthening, and is therefore also a derived rule in **SM**.

The final system **WM** consists of the rules of **WP** plus the converse of LR:

- **RL:**
$$\frac{\alpha \mathrel{\vdash_T} \beta\wedge\gamma}{\beta\wedge\alpha \mathrel{\vdash_T} \gamma}$$

This rule requires some justification, since it seems counter-intuitive at first sight. How can we at the same time weaken the explanation, and strengthen the explained? The point is that in **WM** we have the equivalence $\alpha \mathrel{\vdash_T} \beta \Leftrightarrow T\wedge\beta \mathrel{\not\models} \neg\alpha$. Thus, the inductive explanations are exactly those formulas that are consistent with the examples and the background theory. This also means that the relation $\vdash_T$ becomes symmetric: $\alpha \mathrel{\vdash_T} \beta \Leftrightarrow \beta \mathrel{\vdash_T} \alpha$. But does it make sense for an inductive consequence relation to be symmetric? It seems that inductive reasoning is inherently irreversible, since it involves reasoning from the particular to the universal. We claim that this irreversibility is not a fundamental property of the inductive consequence relation, but rather a result of additional syntactical conditions regarding the logical form of examples and hypotheses. Such conditions are quite common in inductive reasoning. For instance, for inductive consequence relations satisfying Reflexivity the conjunction of examples is always a valid explanation. Since this constitutes a trivial inductive argument, it will frequently be avoided by making non-minimal generalisations. Although Reflexivity is a significant property of a class of inductive consequence relations, it is generally not meant to be exploited in the inductive reasoning process. The same holds for Symmetry in the case of inductive reasoning according to **WM**.

In one respect, **WM** is comparable in power to **SM**: the generality ordering can again be used to structure the search space of possible inductive hypotheses. However, search will proceed in the opposite direction of less general explanations, since the following rule replaces Explanation Strengthening:

- **Explanation Weakening:**
$$\frac{T \models \gamma \to \beta \, , \, \alpha \mathrel{\kappa_T} \gamma}{\alpha \mathrel{\kappa_T} \beta}$$

This reversal of the search direction can be intuitively understood, if we consider the case of inductive concept learning. Strong inductive reasoning finds *sufficient* conditions, which yield a positive classification of some instances. In contrast, weak inductive reasoning finds *necessary* conditions, which yield a negative classification of some other instances. In clausal logic, Horn theories constitute sufficient conditions, while their completion yields necessary condition. It is obvious that a more general Horn theory yields a less general completion.

Just as necessary conditions can be derived from sufficient conditions, weak inductive consequence relations can be derived from strong ones and *vice versa*. Let κ_T denote a given inductive consequence relation, and define $\alpha \mathrel{\kappa_T} \beta$ iff $\neg\alpha \mathrel{\not\kappa_T} \beta$. Then κ_T satisfies the rules of **SM** (**SP, SC**) iff κ_T satisfies the rules of **WM** (**WP, WC**). One may in fact define a system which is stronger than both **SM** and **WM**, but we will refer to (Flach, 1991) for details.

4. Abductive reasoning

Abduction is commonly studied in the context of Logic Programming (see (Kakas *et. al*, 1992) for an excellent survey). A first attempt to structurally characterise abductive reasoning can be found in (Zadrozny, 1991). In this section, we will briefly consider his approach. Zadrozny considers a relation of *explanation e—* on $P \times F$, where P is a set of possible explanations partially ordered by $\geq$, and F is a collection of well-formed formulas/terms in some formal language, which the system will try to explain. Instead of $<l,t> \in e—$, we write $l \mathrel{e—} t$ and say that l *explains* t. The partial ordering expresses that some explanations are better than others; e.g., explanations might be *minimal* sets of ground facts such that the observations are provable.

Explanation theories describe properties of explanation relations in a meta-language of axiom schemes and Gentzen-style inference rules. The following axiom scheme is assumed to hold:

- **Best Explanation:** $\forall l \ [l \ e\!-\!t \rightarrow \exists l_s \ [l_s \ e\!-\!t \ \& \ l_s {\geq} l \ \& \ \neg \exists l_s' \ [l_s' {>} l_s \ \& \ l_s' \ e\!-\!t]]]$

This axiom scheme states that for any explanation l, there is an explanation l_s which is at least as good, such that there is no explanation l_s' which is better than l_s. In other words, there are no infinite ascending chains in the ordering $\geq$. A rule proposed by Zadrozny is the following:

- **Downward Closure:** $$\frac{l \ e\!-\!t \ , \ l' {\leq} l}{l' \ e\!-\!t}$$

This rule expresses that if l explains t, any l' less good than l also does.

As an example, consider abductive diagnosis in Horn logic. Let T be a theory describing the behaviour of a system with components c_i. An explanation is a set of components considered faulty, partially ordered by reverse set inclusion (thus, smaller sets are better explanations). The following axioms are assumed: $\varnothing \ e\!-\!\psi$ for all ψ such that $T \models \psi$ (i.e. anything which can be deduced from T needs no explanation), and $\{c_i\} \ e\!-\!ab(c_i)$ (i.e. the diagnosis $\{c_i\}$ explains the abnormal operation of c_i). Then, rules are needed for the combination of explanations, such as

- **Horn Cut:** $$\frac{l \ e\!-\!X{\leftarrow}Y \ , \ l' \ e\!-\!Y{\leftarrow}Z}{l \cup l' \ e\!-\!X{\leftarrow}Z}$$

For instance, if T entails $o{\leftarrow}ab(c_0)$ and o is an observation to be explained, we combine $\varnothing \ e\!-\!o{\leftarrow}ab(c_0)$ and $\{c_0\} \ e\!-\!ab(c_0)$ to get $\{c_0\} \ e\!-\!o$.

Zadrozny also considers models of explanation theories. An important point is that alternative explanations of one observation may be incompatible (e.g., logically inconsistent). Therefore, a condition of *Cohesion* is imposed on models: for any model M of an explanation theory, if $M \models l \ e\!-\!t$ and $M \models l' \ e\!-\!t$, then there must be an l'' such that $l'' {\geq} l$, $l'' {\geq} l'$, and $M \models l'' \ e\!-\!t$. In other words, every model contains a single best explanation.

5. Belief revision

Our discussion of belief revision follows (Gärdenfors, 1988) to a large extent. We assume a propositional language, and $\models$ denotes standard logical consequence. A *belief set* is a set of formulas which is deductively closed[5]. That is, if K is a belief set, then $K \models B \Rightarrow B \in K$.

---

[5]This condition is actually a bit of a weakness, since in general we are not interested in revising an entire

The *expansion* of K by A is denoted K_A^+; it models the incorporation of new information in the belief set K. This operation is abstractly defined by the following postulates:

(K$^+$1) K_A^+ is a belief set;

(K$^+$2) $A \in K_A^+$;

(K$^+$3) $K \subseteq K_A^+$;

(K$^+$4) if $A \in K$, then $K_A^+ = K$;

(K$^+$5) if $K \subseteq H$, then $K_A^+ \subseteq H_A^+$.

By means of these postulates, it is for instance possible to show that $(K_A^+)_B^+ = K_{A \wedge B}^+ = (K_B^+)_A^+$, that is, the order of the new pieces of information is irrelevant. Furthermore, if $Cn(F)$ denotes the set of logical consequences of the set of formulas F, then these postulates imply that $Cn(K \cup \{A\}) \subseteq K_A^+$. Since we don't want to add anything to K which is not strictly necessary, we add the following postulate:

(K$^+$6) K_A^+ is the smallest set satisfying (K$^+$1)—(K$^+$5).

It can now be shown that $Cn(K \cup \{A\}) = K_A^+$, i.e. $K_A^+ = \{B \mid K \wedge A \models B\}$. Thus, the above postulates fully characterise the operation of expansion.

If $K \models \neg A$, then K_A^+ will be inconsistent. The *revision* of K with A, K_A^*, extends expansion by demanding that the resulting belief set be consistent. Thus, the reasons for believing $\neg A$ in K must be retracted before A can be added. The following postulates are listed for revision:

(K*1) K_A^* is a belief set;

(K*2) $A \in K_A^*$;

(K*3) $K_A^* \subseteq K_A^+$;

(K*4) if $\neg A \notin K$, then $K_A^+ \subseteq K_A^*$;

(K*5) K_A^* is inconsistent if and only if $\models \neg A$;

(K*6) if $\models A \leftrightarrow B$, then $K_A^* = K_B^*$;

(K*7) $K_{A \wedge B}^* \subseteq (K_A^*)_B^+$;

(K*8) if $B \notin K_A^*$, then $(K_A^*)_B^+ \subseteq K_{A \wedge B}^*$.

Contrary to the expansion postulates, these postulates do not uniquely characterise an expansion operator. According to Gärdenfors, this can only be achieved by considering extra-logical factors, such as a preference ordering. Below, we will show how this can be done for the *contraction* operator K_A^- which removes all reasons for believing A from K. The corresponding revision operator is then defined as $K_A^* = (K_{\neg A}^-)_A^+$.

Gärdenfors gives the following postulates for contraction:

(K$^-$1) K_A^- is a belief set;

(K$^-$2) $K_A^- \subseteq K$;

theory, but only a set of axioms of which the theory is the deductive closure (Nebel, 1989).

(K⁻3)   if $A \notin K$, then $K_A^- = K$;

(K⁻4)   if $\not\models A$, then $A \notin K_A^-$;

(K⁻5)   if $A \in K$, then $K \subseteq (K_A^-)_A^+$;

(K⁻6)   if $\models A \leftrightarrow B$, then $K_A^- = K_B^-$;

(K⁻7) $K_A^- \cap K_B^- \subseteq K_{A \wedge B}^-$;

(K⁻8)   if $A \notin K_{A \wedge B}^-$, then $K_{A \wedge B}^- \subseteq K_A^-$.

In order to fully characterise a contraction operator, Gärdenfors proposes the ordering of *epistemic entrenchment*. This is a relation ≤ between logical formulas, satisfying the following postulates:

(EE1)   if $A \leq B$ and $B \leq C$, then $A \leq C$;

(EE2)   if $A \models B$, then $A \leq B$;

(EE3) $A \leq A \wedge B$ or $B \leq A \wedge B$;

(EE4)   if K is consistent, $A \notin K$ iff $A \leq B$ for all B;

(EE5)   if $B \leq A$ for all B, then $\models A$.

These postulates express that beliefs which are lower in the ordering are preferred to give up. For instance, (EE2) expresses that if B follows from A, it is preferred to give up A only, since if we chose to give up B, we still would have to give up A also. (EE4) is added to define the ordering also for formulas that are not believed at all; they are minimal elements. Similarly, tautologies are the maximal elements (EE5).

The connection between epistemic entrenchment and contraction is as follows. Suppose we have to give up the belief $A \wedge B$, i.e. at least one of A and B has to be given up. If we choose to give up B (that is, $B \notin K_{A \wedge B}^-$), this should be because A is at least as entrenched as B: $B \leq A$. In fact, it is the case that if we define $B \leq A$ iff $B \notin K_{A \wedge B}^-$, then ≤ satisfies (EE1)—(EE5) iff the contraction operator satisfies (K⁻1)—(K⁻8). In other words, epistemic entrenchment provides exactly the extra-logical factors needed for the definition of a contraction operator.

6.   Relations between different forms of reasoning

In the preceding four sections, we showed how different forms of jumping to conclusions can be abstractly described by structural properties. In this section, we will give a preliminary analysis of the relations between these different forms of reasoning.

Plausible reasoning and inductive reasoning. A plausible consequence relation ⊢ can serve as the underlying logic for inductive reasoning in two different ways. For strong inductive consequence relations, we define $T \wedge \beta \vdash \alpha$ iff $\alpha \hspace{2pt} \kappa_T \hspace{2pt} \beta$. It is then easily verified that the system **SC** for κ_T corresponds to the system **C** for ⊢. Similarly, **SP** corresponds to **P**, and **SM** corresponds to **M**. This relationship shows that strong inductive reasoning aims at finding a hypothesis which can replace the examples, since they can be (plausibly) derived from it.

For weak inductive consequence relations, we define $T \wedge \beta \not\vdash \neg\alpha$ iff $\alpha \mathrel{\vdash_T} \beta$. In this case, **WC** corresponds to **C**, **WP** corresponds to **P**, and **WM** corresponds to **M**. In these systems, inductive hypotheses delimit the intended model from the outside: they describe what is false in the intended model. Instead of replacing the examples, weak inductive hypotheses describe regularities contained in the examples. Applications of this type of inductive reasoning are described in (Flach, 1989; 1990).

Inductive reasoning and abductive reasoning. A minor notational difference between Zadrozny's framework and ours is, that Zadrozny writes $l \, e\!\!-\!\! t$ for l (abductively) explains t, while we write $\alpha \mathrel{\vdash_T} \beta$ for β (inductively) explains α. Our notation is motivated by the view of inductive reasoning as deriving inductive hypotheses from examples by means of an inductive consequence relation. A link between the two frameworks is readily established: if we define $l \, e\!\!-\!\! t \Leftrightarrow t \mathrel{\vdash_T} l$ and $l \geq l' \Leftrightarrow T \models l' \rightarrow l$, then Zadrozny's rule Downward Closure is equivalent to our Explanation Strengthening[6]. Best Explanation is not satisfied in the case of full first-order logic, but it is satisfied in propositional logic. We conclude that our system **SM** can be encoded in Zadrozny's framework, by associating 'best explanations' with 'most specific inductive hypotheses'. It can then be shown that the rule Horn Cut presented above can be derived by means of Explanation Strengthening, Compositionality, and Convergence. Similarly, it can be shown that **WM** can also be encoded as an explanation theory: simply use the reverse ordering (thus preferring more general inductive hypotheses). This is particularly interesting, since it seems to provide us with a link between provability-based and consistency-based approaches to diagnosis (Poole, 1989).

On the basis of this analysis, we claim that on the *logical* level (i.e., the consequence relation involved) there is no fundamental difference between inductive and abductive reasoning. The main difference manifests itself on the *syntactical* level (i.e. the type of formulas used for premises and conclusions). Inductive reasoning derives general rules as explanations with specific facts as premises, while abductive reasoning derives specific facts as explanations with both general rules and other specific facts as premises.

On the other hand, the remaining systems for inductive reasoning do not correspond to explanation theories as defined by Zadrozny, since they don't require the existence of any ordering on explanations. Thus, while it seems that both inductive and abductive reasoning are instances of what could be called *explanatory reasoning*, Zadrozny's

---

[6]This ordering is only a quasi-ordering, but it can be transformed into a partial ordering by means of the equivalence relation of logical equivalence, as stated by Right Logical Equivalence.

framework is too restrictive for some of the forms of inductive reasoning we considered. This being said, we conclude that these two independently developed frameworks are similar enough to be combined into one framework for explanatory reasoning.

Belief revision and plausible reasoning. Gärdenfors (1990) suggests a relation between belief revision and plausible inference, as follows. If we define $A \vdash_K B$ iff $B \in K_A^*$, then postulates (K^*1)—(K^*8) for revision can be translated to rules for plausible inference, and *vice versa*. While on one hand it seems obvious to include the plausible consequences of A given K in the revision of K with A, we think this approach will not fully work. Consider the belief set K: either it includes $\neg A$, or it doesn't. If it doesn't, then by (K^*3)—(K^*4), $K_A^* = K_A^+$. In order not to require monotonicity of $\vdash\sim$, we should then drop the minimality condition (K^+6). A problem arises if K includes $\neg A$, since this means that A is inconsistent with K, so it will plausibly entail anything, given K. On the other hand, according to (K^*5), K_A^* is inconsistent only if $\neg A$ is a tautology. It seems, therefore, that plausible reasoning is more closely related to non-minimal expansion, rather than revision.

Belief revision and inductive reasoning. Recall that in the system SM, $\alpha \vdash_T \beta \Leftrightarrow T \wedge \beta \models \alpha$; therefore, $K_A^+ = \{B \mid B \vdash_K A\}$. That is, the expansion of a belief set K with A is equal to the set of examples inductively explained by A, given K as background knowledge, if the inductive consequence relation satisfies the rules of SM. The rules of SM and the above postulates are thus closely related. For instance, (K^+2) corresponds to Reflexivity, and (K^+3) translates to $B \vdash_K \text{true} \Rightarrow B \vdash_K A$, which is a special case of Explanation Strengthening. If we again drop the minimality condition (K^+6), we may find similar relations between expansion and the other systems for strong inductive reasoning.

Belief revision operators can also be used to describe the dynamic properties of inductive reasoning. For instance, expansion is invoked if the current theory does not explain a new example α. The result is a generalisation of the sufficient conditions. In general, the expansion operator used will be non-minimal, otherwise we would simply collect the examples. If the theory includes necessary conditions, it might even explain $\neg \alpha$. In that case, we need to apply a revision operator in order to both generalise the sufficient conditions, and to specialise the necessary conditions. As shown above, this can be done by first contracting the theory with $\neg \alpha$, and expanding the result with α. If the reasoning process includes negative examples, that are not to be explained, we also have to apply contraction.

This concludes our preliminary analysis of the various connections between different kinds of defeasible reasoning. We think that it will be useful to investigate these connections in more detail. Our confidence in the outcome of such investigations is further increased by the observation, that all four frameworks presented here use, at some point, an ordering which is somehow connected to logical implication. In belief revision, this is the ordering of epistemic entrenchment. In inductive reasoning, we encountered the generality ordering, which in fact equals logical implication. In abductive reasoning, we used a preference ordering between explanations; this could be minimality, which is also easily formulated in terms of logical implication. In plausible reasoning, one has the preference ordering on sets of worlds. We hope to have convinced the reader that the connections between belief revision and various types of reasoning, be they plausible, inductive, or abductive, are worth studying.

7. Concluding remarks

In this paper, we have presented characterisations of different forms of 'jumping to conclusions': Kraus, Lehmann & Magidor's analysis of plausible reasoning, the present author's characterisation of inductive reasoning, Zadrozny's account of abductive reasoning, and Gärdenfors' theory of belief revision. We have stressed the similarities between these frameworks, and identified several ways in which they can be related. Our main claim is that it is worthwhile to develop a general theory of jumping to conclusions. More specifically, we made the following claims:

- inductive reasoning can be characterised in a way similar to plausible reasoning;
- inductive and abductive reasoning are special cases of explanatory reasoning;
- there are strong relations between belief revision and explanatory reasoning.

Future work will include a further elaboration of these relations, as well as a model-theoretic characterisation of inductive reasoning. We hope to report on this work on a future occasion.

References

P.A. Flach (1989), 'Second-order inductive learning'. In Analogical and Inductive Inference AII'89, K.P. Jantke (ed.), Lecture Notes in Computer Science 397, Springer Verlag, Berlin, pp. 202-216. Full version appeared as ITK Research Report no. 10.

P.A. FLACH (1990), 'Inductive characterisation of database relations'. In *Proc. International Symposium on Methodologies for Intelligent Systems*, Z.W. Ras, M. Zemankowa & M.L. Emrich (eds.), pp. 371-378, North-Holland, Amsterdam. Full version appeared as ITK Research Report no. 23.

P.A. FLACH (1991), *The role of explanations in inductive learning*, ITK Research Report no. 30, Institute for Language Technology & Artificial Intelligence, Tilburg University, the Netherlands.

P.A. FLACH (1992), *On the validity of inductive reasoning*, manuscript.

D.M. GABBAY (1985), 'Theoretical foundations for non-monotonic reasoning in expert systems'. In *Logics and Models of Concurrent Systems*, K.R. Apt (ed.), pp. 439-457, Springer Verlag, Berlin.

P. GÄRDENFORS (1988), *Knowledge in flux*, MIT Press, Cambridge, Massachusetts.

P. GÄRDENFORS (1990), 'Belief revision and nonmonotonic logic: two sides of the same coin?' In *Proc. Ninth European Conference on Artificial Intelligence*, pp. 768-773, Pitman, London.

E.M. GOLD (1967), 'Language identification in the limit', *Information and Control* **10**, pp. 447-474.

A.C. KAKAS, R.A. KOWALSKI & F. TONI (1992), *Abductive Logic Programming*. Imperial College, London, January 1992.

S. KRAUS, D. LEHMANN & M. MAGIDOR (1990), 'Nonmonotonic reasoning, preferential models and cumulative logics', *Artificial Intelligence* **44**, pp. 167-207.

T.M. MITCHELL (1982), 'Generalization as search', *Artificial Intelligence* **18**:2, pp. 203-226.

B. NEBEL (1989), 'A knowledge level analysis of belief revision'. In *Proc. First International Conference on Principles of Knowledge Representation*, Morgan Kaufmann, Los Altos, CA.

D. POOLE (1989), 'Normality and faults in logic-based diagnosis'. In *Proc. Logics in Computer Science*, pp. 275-279, Ithaca, NY.

Y. SHOHAM (1987), 'A semantic approach to nonmonotonic logics'. In *Proc. Eleventh International Joint Conference on Artificial Intelligence*, pp. 1304-1310, Morgan Kaufmann, Los Altos, CA.

W. ZADROZNY (1991), *On rules of abduction*. IBM Research Report, August 1991.

An inductive inference approach to classification

Rusins Freivalds

The University of Latvia

Inst. of Mathematics & Comp. Science

Raina boulevard 29

Riga 226250, Latvia

E-mail: rusins@lumii.su

Achim G. Hoffmann

Technische Universität Berlin

Department of Computer Science

FR 5-11, Franklinstr. 28/29

D-1000 Berlin 10

E-mail: achim@cs.tu-berlin.de

Abstract

In this paper, we introduce a formal framework for investigating the relationship of inductive inference and the task of classification. We give the first results on the relationship between functions that can be identified in the limit and functions that can be acquired from unclassified objects only. Moreover, we present results on the complexity of classification functions and the preconditions necessary in order to allow the computation of such functions.

1 Introduction

In the literature on neural networks, one finds a number of papers on so-called *self-organizing* networks (e.g. [3, 6]). The basic idea is, to have a system (preferrably in the style of a neural network) which learns to behave useful in a certain sense by just getting some *unclassified* objects of the respective domain. Here, the system gets *no* feedback whether its learning approach is correct or not. This contrasts most of the approaches in inductive inference, where for example the system is confronted with preclassified objects or feedback whether its predictions have been correct.

As a consequence, the only source of information for the system is the fact, that not all possible objects will be presented, but only a certain 'meaningful' subset. This subset is hoped to show some 'natural' clusters which should be recognized by the self-organizing system. See Figure 1. A possible application may be to extract compound features for a (high level) symbolic learning approach.

In the following, we are interested in the general computational abilities of such systems. We consider on the one hand the computational abilities of systems to infer certain classification functions from a given set of functions. On the other hand, we will consider the kind of information that is necessary to extract certain meaningful information from a given sample of 'representative' objects. Here the amount of information that has to be provided to self-organizing systems in advance is of particular interest.

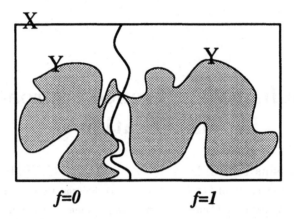

Figure 1: The subset Y of the basic set X and a separation function f.

The paper is organized as follows. The formal framework for our considerations is presented in section 2. In the following section the general abilities of systems for computing separation functions are investigated. In section 4 the complexity of separation functions that can be acquired from unclassified samples is investigated. Section 5 contains concluding remarks.

2   Preliminaries

In the following, we will consider two kinds of total recursive functions: On the one hand, we consider classification *functions*, usually denoted by f or f', which are supposed to determine the class of particular objects.
On the other hand, we consider inference *strategies* (resp. classification strategies), usually denoted by Φ, which are supposed to choose a certain classification function f.

2.1   Notation

The value of a total recursive function Φ given the first n values $f(0), f(1), \ldots, f(n-1)$ of the function f as input is denoted by $\Phi[f(0), \ldots, f(n-1)]$ or shorter by $\Phi[f^n]$. In the following, we interpret the value of a total recursive function Φ as the index of another total recursive function f in a certain fixed numbering τ. However, often the numbering τ will not be mentioned explicitly. By $\Phi[f^n](i)$ we denote the value for the argument i of the function with the index $\Phi[f^n]$ in the numbering τ. So, we write (somewhat sloppy) also $\Phi[f^n]$ for the *function* with the index $\Phi[f^n]$.
Hence, $\Phi[f^n](i)$ denotes the value which will be computed for i by the classification function which has been determined by the strategy Φ after reading the first n values of the function f.

2.2 The classification task

Formally, we consider an infinite basic set X of objects. For that we simply use the set of all positive integers. The subset containing only the first n objects is denoted by X_n, i.e., $X_n = \{0, \ldots, n-1\}$.

The goal of a *self-organizing system* S is to define classes of objects in some set X_n. More precisely, the goal is that finally, S will for each possible object $x_i \in X_n$ respond with a positive integer, indicating the class to which x_i belongs. The response $f(x_i)$ will be computed by some recursive function f that has been determined by S while reading the presented sequence of objects.

The only source of information for S is the following: Only examples which belong to a certain fixed subset $Y \subset X$ are presented to S. Moreover, Y_n denotes the set $X_n \cap Y$.

In the activities of our self-organizing system S we distinguish two different stages:

1. The learning phase: A sequence of unclassified objects is presented to the system. Additionally, the system is supplied with a range of the possible number of classes together with a specification of a certain metric g for determining the different classes. This is also called the *cluster criterion* and is defined in the following. In this paper, we only consider the case of *two* classes.

2. The classification phase: The system responds with the index of the class assigned to the presented object. I.e. the system determines the index of a function $f : \mathbf{N} \rightarrow \{0, \ldots, (\#classes - 1)\}$ in a fixed numbering τ of total recursive functions. In our case of only two classes, the domain of the function f is $\{0, 1\}$.

Definition 1 *The **metric** g which represents the 'a priori knowledge' of a system S is encoded in some total recursive function g. The function g has as its arguments two classifications of the same sequence of objects $s = o_1, \ldots, o_n$ with $o_i \in X_n$ for $1 \leq i \leq n$.*

$$g : (c_1(s), c_2(s)) \rightarrow \{-1, 1, 0\}$$

where g indicates whether classification c_1 is to be preferred over c_2 or vice versa or that both are equivalent. $c_1(s)$ and $c_2(s)$ are given as a sequence of pairs. Each pair consists of an object and an associated class. The sequence can be of arbitrary but finite length. If the sequence of objects s is given by

$$s = o_1, \ldots, o_n$$

then $c_i(s)$ is given by

$$c_i(s) = \langle o_1, class_{c_i}(o_1)\rangle, \ldots \langle o_n, class_{c_i}(o_n)\rangle$$

for $i \in \{1, 2\}$.

Furthermore, we identify a **self-organizing system** S with a classification strategy Φ which gets as input a metric g and some or all elements of a fixed subset Y_n of X_n.

2.3 Probabilistic setting

For the following probabilistic setting we assume some probability distribution P_n on X_n for all n. Since objects are only allowed to be chosen from Y_n, $P_n(X_n \setminus Y_n) = 0$. Moreover,

$$(\forall y \in Y_n))\ P_n(y) > 0 \wedge \sum_{y \in Y_n} P_n(y) = 1.$$

In other words, Y_n represents the set of 'naturally' appearing objects. Thus, Y_n represents the kind of information that is potentially provided to the system.

For a growing number of objects randomly drawn according to P_n the probability for getting the complete set Y_n approaches 1 arbitrarily closely, since Y_n is always a finite set.

Moreover, we are **not** interested in the values of an inferred classification function on the elements of $(X \setminus Y)$. I.e. the values for elements in $(X \setminus Y)$ has to be defined but are allowed to be arbitrary. See section 4 for more details.

2.4 Classification vs. inductive inference

Our setting for *classification* contrasts the usual setting for *inductive inference* as follows:

The setting for identification in **inductive inference** looks usually as follows:
Given is a set of functions F. Given is a set of initial values of an unknown function $f \in F$ which has to be **identified**:

$$f(0), f(1), f(2), f(3), \ldots, f(n)$$

There is an identification algorithm Φ which identifies the set of functions F in the limit, if

$$(\forall f \in F)\ (\exists i)\ \Phi[f(0), f(1), \ldots, f(i)] = f$$

Definition 2 *A function f can be **identified in the limit**, if there is a numbering of functions τ and*

$$(\exists \Phi)\ (\exists i)\ \Phi[f(0), f(1), \ldots, f(i)] = f$$

Our setting for **classification** contrast this as follows:
Given is a sequence of values of the function y, which describes the particular subset $Y_n \subseteq X_n$. I.e.

$$(\forall i < n)\ y(i) = \begin{cases} 1 & \text{if } i \in Y_n \\ 0 & otherwise \end{cases}$$

To each particular function y and for each particular n the classification strategy Φ will **infer** a particular function f_n classifying the set X_n. As mentioned in 2.2, only the values of f_n for the set Y_n are important. However, in the following we will consider classification in two disjoint classes. This special case is also called *separation*.

3   Computable separations

In this section we prove theorems on the possibility of inferring a separation function on X_n depending on a given subset $Y_n \subseteq X_n$. I.e. we assume that the complete set Y_n is presented to the learning algorithm Φ.
Thus, the learning algorithm Φ is provided with all y-values $y(0), \ldots, y(n-1)$.

Definition 3 *A separation function f is* **inferrable from unclassified examples only,** *if there is an inference strategy Φ such that $\forall n\ \Phi[y(0), y(1), \ldots, y(n-1)] = f_n$ and $(\forall i < n)\ f(i) = f_n(i)$.*
Note: *No specific assumptions are made on the class F of functions from which f is chosen.*

Theorem 1 *There exists a separation function which is inferrable from unclassified examples, but cannot be identified in the limit.*

Proof: We assign increasing numbers to the elements of Y according to their integer values starting with the smallest integer in Y. I.e., we define a function $n : \mathbf{N} \to \mathbf{N}$, where $n(i) = |\{x \,|\, x \le i \wedge x \in Y\}|$.

Example:

$j =$	0	1	2	3	4	5	6	7	8	9	10	11	12	$\cdots$
$j \in Y$	no	yes	yes	no	yes	no	no	no	no	yes	yes	yes	no	$\cdots$
$n(j) =$	0	1	2	2	3	3	3	3	3	4	5	6	6	$\cdots$

Then, let f be a function which classifies exactly each odd numbered element of Y positively and each even numbered element of Y negatively. Obviously, f can be inferred from unclassified examples only. However, f cannot be identified in the limit from any set of functions F. This can be seen by contradiction: We assume f can be identified in the limit. That means, there is some classification strategy Φ and some i_0 such that

$$(\forall i > i_0)\ \Phi[f(0), \ldots, f(i-1)] = \Phi[f(0), \ldots, f(i_0 - 1)] = f.$$

Let f' denote the function determined by Φ after reading the first i_0 values of f, i.e. $f' = \Phi[f^{i_0}]$. We consider the values $f'(i_0)$, $f'(i_0 + 1)$ and the classification $f'(k)$ of the next element k in Y_n. I.e. it holds $n(k) = n(i_0 + 1) + 1$. In table 1 all eight possible combinations are shown.
However, the set Y, i.e. the membership of i_0 and $(i_0 + 1)$ in Y can always be chosen in order to contradict the values of $f(i_0)$ and $f(i_0 + 1)$. In table 1 for any possibly inferred function f a contradicting construction of Y for i_0 and $i_0 + 1$ is provided. Hence, f cannot be identified in the limit of i_0. This proves the theorem.

$\square$

At next, we are interested, how often a classification function has to be revised (how many mindchanges have to be performed), in order to infer a function of a certain complexity. The complexity is expressed as the index of the function in a given numbering.

$f'(i_0)$	$f'(i_0+1)$	$f'(k)$, where $n(k) = n(i_0+1)+1$	$i_0 \in Y$	$(i_0+1) \in Y$	value on which $f'(.) \neq f(.)$
0	0	0	yes	yes	i_0 or (i_0+1)
0	1	0	yes	no	i_0 or k
1	0	0	any value	yes	(i_0+1) or k
1	1	0	yes	yes	i_0 or (i_0+1)
0	0	1	yes	yes	i_0 or (i_0+1)
0	1	1	any value	yes	(i_0+1) or k
1	0	1	yes	no	i_0 or k
1	1	1	yes	yes	i_0 or (i_0+1)

Table 1: For any possibly inferred function $f' = \Phi[f^{i_0}]$ there exists a set Y such that f' differs from f. The membership of the two objects in an appropriately contradicting Y is given in the fourth and fifth colomn.

Given a set of total recursive functions U and a numbering τ of these functions, $\Phi^{MC}(\tau_i)$ denotes the number of mindchanges Φ will do, when Φ finally determines the function indexed by τ_i.
Moreover, we define

$$\Phi^{MC}_{U,\tau}(n) := \max_{i \in \{0,\ldots,n\}} \Phi^{MC}(\tau_i).$$

I.e., among the first $n+1$ functions in the numbering τ there is at least one function, which requires $\Phi^{MC}_{U,\tau}(n)$ mindchanges in order to become determined by Φ.

The following theorem gives lower bounds on the number of mindchanges for inferring functions of a given complexity from unclassified examples only.

Theorem 2 *There is an enumerated class of functions (U,τ) such that for an arbitrary classification strategy Φ and arbitrary positive integer k:*

1. $\forall n \ \Phi^{MC}_{U,\tau}(n) > \log_2 n - 3$

2. $\exists^\infty n \ \Phi^{MC}_{U,\tau}(n) > \log_2 n + \log_2 \log_2 n + \ldots + \underbrace{\log_2 \log_2 \ldots \log_2 n}_{k}$

Proof: Analogously to the proof in [1].

4　The complexity of separation functions

In this section we will investigate the *complexity* of separation functions, that can be inferred from unclassified examples only. For that purpose, we use Kolmogorov's notion of the complexity of finite objects as introduced in [4]. According to this idea, the complexity of a function f in a fixed numbering of functions is the binary logarithm of its minimum index and is called its Kolmogorov complexity of f and is denoted by $K(f)$. This notion has also been used for investigations of learning complex functions within connectionist models of computation in [2]. In the following, we are interested in the separation of the subset Y resp. the subsets Y_n. For the purpose of measuring the complexity of a separation of Y, we consider for each possible separation function f the class F_{f,Y_n} of separation functions which are equivalent on their values of Y_n. I.e., $F_{f,Y_n} = \{h|(\forall i \in Y_n)\ f(i) = h(i)\}$.

Moreover, we denote by $K_{Y_n}(f)$ the minimal Kolmogorov complexity among all separation functions in F_{f,Y_n}.

$$K_{Y_n}(f) = \min_{f' \in F_{f,Y_n}} K(f').$$

I.e. $K_{Y_n}(f)$ is the Kolmogorov complexity of the least complex description of the separation of the subset Y_n according to f.

We use Kolmogorov complexity for our considerations, since it is often claimed that neural networks or *self-organizing systems* are capable of acquiring complex functions.

For such subsymbolic approaches to learning and classification various more or less complicated and, as a consequence, more or less incomprehensible models of computation have been proposed. Hence, we use Kolmogorov complexity in order to distinguish between seemingly complicated functions - distributed over the entire network - and really complex functions[1] that have been acquired.

The provided upper bounds hold for arbitrary classification strategies - i.e. they hold for arbitrary kinds of *self-organizing systems* or *networks* as well.

The first theorem in this section gives a rather trivial but very general upperbound on the complexity of inferrable separation functions.

Theorem 3 *For all separation functions f on X_n, all $Y_n \subseteq X_n$, any classification strategy Φ and any metric g holds the following: The minimal Kolmogorov complexity of a separation function f' equivalent on Y_n to f which can be inferred by Φ is upperbounded as follows:*

$$K_{Y_n}(f) \le K(g) + K(Y_n) + const$$

Proof: By a subprogram of length $K(Y_n)$ the input to Φ can be generated by the subprogram. Thus, the complexity of any function computable by Φ in combination with the metric g and the input of the set Y_n is limited by the term given in the theorem.

□

The general upperbound in theorem 3 shows that the complexity of inferrable functions is basically limited by the complexity of the system itself (i.e. the function g) and by the complexity of the provided sample $K(Y_n)$. In theorem 1, we have already seen that the possible amount of information provided by a sample is unbounded. However, we are particularly interested in how far the complexity of the provided sample can contribute to the complexity of a 'meaningful' and inferrable separation function.

---

[1] We mean complex in terms of their description, i.e. in terms of possible encoding length.

For that purpose, we consider initially the case of monotonic classification strategies. The next theorem presents a tighter bound on the complexity of inferrable separation functions, if *no* mindchanges are allowed.

Definition 4 *A* **monotonic classification strategy** Φ *is a classification strategy which classifies incrementally the presented objects and never changes the classification of previously classified objects. I.e., the classification strategy Φ is* **monotonic**, *if*

$$(\forall k)(\forall j < k) \ \Phi[y_1, \ldots, y_k](y_j) = \Phi[y_1, \ldots, y_k, y_{k+1}](y_j).$$

Theorem 4 *Assume an arbitrary but fixed $Y_n \subseteq X_n$ and a fixed probability distribution P_n on Y_n for arbitrary n. Then, for any monotonic classification strategy Φ nd any metric g holds the following: If for any sequence of objects randomly drawn according to P_n, Φ finally acquires the same target separation function f, then the Kolmogorov complexity of f is upper bounded as follows:*

$$K_{Y_n}(f) \leq K(g) + 2 \log_2 n + const.$$

Proof: We prove the theorem by contradiction. Assume Φ determines a separation function f with $K_{Y_n}(f) > K(g) + 2 \log_2 n + const$. ($\log_2 n$ is due to the information of limiting the set X_n to n elements and $\log_2 n$ is the amount of information necessary for describing one object of X_n.) Then, there must be an object $y_1 \in Y_n$ as follows. Provide y_1 as the first element of a 'randomly' drawn sequence to Φ. Then, there must be another object $y_2 \in Y_n$, which cannot be classified according to f. This is since the amount of information provided so far $(K(g) + 2 \log_2 n)$ does not suffice for determining the function f. Since $K_{Y_n}(f)$ is by definition the smallest amount of information in order to compute all values of f on Y_n, there must be an $y_2 \in Y_n$ for which $f(y_2)$ differs from $\Phi[y_1](y_2)$ for at least one appropriate y_1.

$\square$

The restriction of being a monotonic classification strategy in theorem 4 is very strong. In other words, theorem 4 provides rather a lower bound, while theorem 3 gives an upperbound on what can be expected from self-organizing systems.

However in the following, we consider limits for approximations of a complex target separation function.

Definition 5 *Assume for some n a fixed $Y_n \subseteq X_n$ and a fixed probability distribution P_n on Y_n. Then, we say a function f ε-approximates a target function f_t, if*

$$\sum_{x \in \{x | x \in Y_n \wedge (f(x) \neq f_t(x))\}} P_n(x) \leq \varepsilon$$

The following theorem strongly upperbounds the complexity of separation functions, which can be ε-approximated with a reasonable probability of success.

Theorem 5 *For all $0 < \varepsilon < \frac{1}{2}$ and $0 < \delta < 1$, an arbitrary but fixed sample size s an arbitrary probability distribution P_n on X_n and a target separation function f_t with a complexity*

$$K_{Y_n}(f_t) > K(g) + 3\log_2 n + const,$$

the following holds:
There is no metric g and no inference strategy Φ which infers a function f from a sample of size s randomly drawn according to P_n, which ε-approximates f_t with probability at least $1 - \delta$.

Proof: We will construct a suitable probability distribution P_n on Y_n for which the theorem holds. First of all, note that $|Y_n| > 2$. Moreover, the following proposition holds:

Proposition 1 For all classification strategies Φ and all metrics g, there must be three objects $y_1, y_2, y_3 \in Y_n$ with the following property:

$$\Phi[y_1, y_2](y_1) \neq \Phi[y_1, y_2, y_3](y_1)$$

Proof: Assume, the proposition is false. Then, there exists a function f'_t which is equivalent to f_t on the set Y_n with $K_{Y_n}(f_t) \leq K(g) + 3\log_2 n + const$. Hence, a contradiction.

$\square$

I.e. there is an element $y_1 \in Y_n$, whose classification changes, when Φ gets the third object as input. This fact is due to the complexity of f_t. I.e. $\log_2 n$ is required for limiting the set X_n to n elements and $2\log_2 n$ is the amount of information for describing y_1 and y_2.

Let P_n be given by $P_n(y_1) = P_n(y_2) = \frac{1-\gamma}{2}$ and $P_n(y_3) = \gamma$ for some $0 < \gamma < 1$. we may choose γ arbitrarily close to 0. Hence, for all δ there is an appropriate γ as follows:
The probability that y_3 occurs in a sample of size s randomly drawn according to P_n is less than $1 - \delta$.
I.e., y_1 will be misclassified with probability greater than $1 - \delta$, since it will be classified according to $\Phi[y_1, y_2]$.

$\square$

Theorem 5 indicates that the complexity of 'meaningful' classification functions, which can be inferred from unclassified examples only is rather limited.
However, the probabilistic setting certainly does not properly cover real applications of self-organizing systems. On the other hand, it is not obvious that different circumstances in real applications will enhance the abilities of self-organizing systems.

5 Conclusion and further work

We have shown, that the complexity of classification functions acquired under reasonable preconditions is seriously limited. Moreover, in a probabilistic setting - related to Valiant's PAC-learning model [5] - the complexity of a function that can be acquired does not exceed significantly the complexity of the used inference strategy. Our probabilistic setting requires to determine a separation function that misclassifies a randomly drawn object with probability of at most ε. The difference to Valiant's model of concept learning is basically the fact that in our setting the system is provided with *unclassified* objects only. I.e., the source of information of the learning system is quite different from the PAC-model.

Further work will be concerned with investigating the relationship between classification functions inferred through a number of mindchanges and the number of mindchanges necessary in a corresponding inductive inference setting. Moreover, the probabilistic setting of classification presented in this paper will be investigated in more depth.

Acknowledgement: The authors thank an anonymous referee for helpful comments on this paper.

References

[1] R. Freivalds, J. Barzdin, and K. Podnieks. Inductive inference of recursive functuions: complexity bounds. In *Lecture Notes in Computer Science*, volume 502, pages 111–151. Springer-Verlag, 1991.

[2] A. G. Hoffmann. Connectionist functionality and the emergent network behavior. *Neurocomputing - An International Journal*, 2(2):161–172, 1991.

[3] T. Kohonen. *Self-Organization and Associative Memory*. Springer-Verlag, Heidelberg, West-Germany, 1984.

[4] A. N. Kolmogorov. Three approaches to the quantitative definition of information. *International Journal for Computer Mathematics*, 2:157–168, 1968. (originally published in Russian: Problemi peredachi informacii, vol. 1, No. 1, 1965, p. 3–11.).

[5] L. Valiant. A theory of the learnable. *Communications of the ACM*, 27:1134–1142, 1984.

[6] C. von der Malsburg. Network self-organization. In S. F. Zornetzer, J. L. Davis, and C. Lau, editors, *An Introduction to Neural and Electronic Networks*, pages 421–432. Academic Press, New York, 1990.

Asking Questions Versus Verifiability

William I. Gasarch[†]
Department of Computer Science and
Institute for Advanced Computer Studies
The University of Maryland
College Park, MD 20742
gasarch@cs.umd.edu

Mahendran Velauthapillai
Department of Computer Science
Georgetown University
Washington, D.C. 20057, USA
mahe@cs.georgetown.edu

ABSTRACT

Case and Smith studied learning machines whose conjectures are verifiable (i.e. the conjectures are total programs). They discovered that such machines are *weaker* than machines whose conjectures are not verifiable. Gasarch and Smith studied learning machines that ask questions. They discovered that such machines are *stronger* than passive machines. We raise the question *Can the weakness of verifiability be overcome by the strength of asking queries?*

We answer many interesting questions along the way. These include a full examination of PEX and the resolution of some open problems of Gasarch Smith.

The motivating question has two answers: if unbounded mind changes are allowed then queries *do not* increase learning power of verifiable machines, where in the bounded case they do.

[†] Supported by NSF grants CCR-880-3641 and CCR 9020079

I. Introduction

Inductive inference is the study of learning in the limit. The model is that the learner sees data $f(0), f(1), \ldots$, makes conjectures $e_1, e_2, \ldots$ (these are programs) eventually always outputs the same program, which is a program for f. This model was introduced by Gold [12] and extensively studied by several people (see [1]) including [3,4,17].

Case and Smith [4] studied learning machines whose conjectures are verifiable (i.e. the conjectures are total programs). They discovered that such machines are weaker then machines that are allowed to conjecture non-total programs (in symbols $PEX \subset EX$).

Gasarch and Smith [9] studied machines that learn functions by asking questions about the function (see [9,10,11] for subsequent work). They discovered that machines that can ask questions can usually learn more than machines that do not (in symbols $EX \subset Q_1 EX[*]$).

These two adjustments on the original model, and the results about them, lead to the following question: *Can the weakness of verifiability be overcome by the strength of asking questions?* While studying this question several other issues arise, including a more detailed study of verifiability and the resolution of an open question from [9].

II. Definitions

In this section we formalize our notions and state our results precisely. Our machines will learn recursive functions which are taken to encode an arbitrary phenomenon, see the discussion in [4]. We assume $\varphi_0, \varphi_1, \varphi_2, \cdots$ is an acceptable programming system. An (standard, passive) *inductive inference machine* (IIM) is a total algorithmic device that takes as input the graph of a recursive function (an ordered pair at a time) and outputs (from time to time) programs intended to compute the function whose graph serves as input [3,12]. An IIM M learns a recursive function f, if, when M is given the graph of f as input, the resultant sequence of outputs converges (after some point there are no more mind changes) to a program that computes f. This is denoted by $M(f) \downarrow$. Learning has occurred since we can use the program output by the IIM to predict the value of $f(x)$, for all x, after having seen only finitely many examples. In this case we write $f \in EX(M)$. EX stands for "explains" [4]. The class EX is the collection of all sets $EX(M)$ (or subsets thereof) of functions learned by an IIM. We say that $f \in PEX(M)$ if the IIM only outputs programs which computes total recursive functions, and eventually converges to a single program which computes f. This enables one to check whether the programs output by the IIM computes f. The collection of all the sets $PEX(M)$ is called PEX. The PEX stands for "popperian" [4]. If σ is an initial segment of some function f, then $M(\sigma)$ denotes the last conjecture about f made by M, after seeing all of σ as input, but prior to requesting . additional input.

Each time an IIM outputs a conjecture we say that another *learning trial* has been completed. Since it is never known if enough trials have been completed, it is sometimes desirable to fix an a priori bound on the number of trials that will be permitted. If convergence is achieved after only c changes of conjecture we write $f \in EX_c(M)$, ($f \in PEX_c(M)$) for $c \in N$, where N denotes the set of natural numbers. The class of sets of functions identifiable by IIMs restricted to c mind changes is denoted by EX_c (PEX_c). The number of mind changes needed by an IIM to make a successful inference is a crude measure of the complexity of performing the inference [5].

The requirement that M on input f must converge to to a program that must compute the function f is too stringent. So one possible relaxation of this to allow the the machine to converge to a program that computes f except at some finite number of points. So given an IIM M we say $f \in EX_b^a(M)$ if and only if M on some initial segment of f will converge a program e after atmost b mind calnges, and $|\{x|\varphi_e(x)i \neq f(x)\}| \leq a$. For $PEX_b^a(M)$ we require the errors to be errors of commnision. Smith defined team inference, for definitions of $[1,n]EX_b^a$ and the motivation see [17]. $[1,n]PEX_b^a$ can be defined similary.

A *query inference machine* (QIM), defined by Gasarch and Smith [9] is an algorithmic device that asks a teacher questions about some unknown function, and while doing so, outputs programs. In this way, the QIM learns about some phenomenon, encoded by a recursive function, by asking finitely many questions. We assume that the teacher always returns the correct answer to any question asked by a QIM. The questions are formulated in some query language L. A variety of different query languages are considered. The languages that we consider have different expressive power. The more expressive the query language, the more questions the QIM can ask. In a sense, giving a QIM a more expressive query language to use makes the QIM more articulate. Formally, a QIM is a total algorithmic device which, if the input is a string of bits $\vec{b}$, corresponding to the answers to previous queries, outputs an ordered pair consisting of a guess which is a (possibly null) program e, and a question ψ. For more details and technical results about QIM's see [9,10,11,15,].

Define two functions g (*guess*) and q (*query*) such that if $M(\vec{b}) = (e, \psi)$ then $g(M(\vec{b})) = e$ and $q(M(\vec{b})) = \psi$. By convention, all questions are assumed to be sentences in prenex normal form (quantifiers followed by a quantifier-free formula, called the matrix of the formula) and questions containing quantifiers are assumed to begin with an existential quantifier. This convention entails no loss of generality and serves to reduce the number of cases needed in several proofs. A QIM M learns a recursive function f if, when the teacher answers M's questions about f truthfully, the sequence of output programs (total programs) converges to a program that computes f. In this case, we write $f \in QEX[L](M)$ ($f \in PQEX[L](M)$). For a fixed language L, the class $QEX[L]$ ($QPEX[L]$) is the collection of all sets $QEX[L](M)$ ($QPEX[L](M)$) as M varies over all QIMs that use the query language L. Note in the case of $QPEX[L](M)$, even if the QIM M is given the wrong answers, it has to output total programs. $QEX_c[L]$ ($QPEX_c[L]$) is defined similarly.

All the query languages that we will consider allow the use of quantifiers. Restricting the applications of quantifiers is a technique that we will use to regulate the expressive power of a language. Of concern to us is the alternations between blocks of existential and universal quantifiers. Suppose that $f \in QEX[L](M)$ ($f \in QPEX[L](M)$) for some M and L. If M only asks quantifier-free questions, then we will say that $f \in Q_0EX[L](M)$

($f \in Q_0 PEX[L](M)$). If M only asks questions with existential quantifiers, then we will say that $f \in Q_1 EX[L](M)$ ($f \in Q_1 PEX[L](M)$). In general, if M's questions begin with an existential quantifier and involve $a > 0$ alternations between blocks of universal and existential quantifiers, then we say that $f \in Q_{a+1} EX[L](M)$ ($f \in Q_{a+1} PEX[L](M)$). The classes $Q_a EX[L]$, $Q_a PEX[L]$, $Q_a EX_c[L]$ and $Q_a PEX_c[L]$ are defined analogously. By convention, if a QIM restricted to c mind changes actually achieves that bound, then it will ask no further questions.

Now we introduce the query languages that will be used. Every language allows the use of $\wedge$, $\neg$, $=$, $\forall$, $\exists$, symbols for the natural numbers (members of N), variables that range over N, and a single unary function symbol $\mathcal{F}$ which will be used to represent the function being learned. Inclusion of these symbols in every language will be implicit. The *base* language contains only these symbols. If L has auxiliary symbols, then L is denoted just by these symbols. For example, the language that has auxiliary symbols for plus and less than is denoted by $[+, <]$ and is Presburger arithmetic with a function symbol. The language that has auxiliary symbols for plus and times is denoted by $[+, \times]$ and is Peano arithmetic with a function symbol. The language with extra symbols for successor and less than is denoted by $[S, <]$, where S indicates the symbol for the successor operation. The symbol "$\star$" will be used to denote an arbitrary language that includes all the symbols common to all the languages we consider and some (possibly empty) subset of operational symbols denoting computable operations. e.g. $+$, $<$, $\times$ and S. Such a language will be called *reasonable*.

III. Notations

Throughout this paper, φ_0, φ_1, φ_2, ... denotes an acceptable programming system [13], also known as a Gödel numbering of the partial recursive functions [16]. The function φ_e is said to be computed by the program e. Let $\mathcal{R}$ denote the class of all recursive functions. Throughout this section we assume that L is an arbitrary, but fixed, reasonable query language.

Recall that for our purposes the language L contains the usual logical operators, the symbol $\mathcal{F}$, relational symbols, and operational symbols. The relational and operational symbols are to be interpreted in the obvious way (e.g. "+" denotes plus and "<" denotes less than). It is assumed that any sentence without quantifiers or the symbol $\mathcal{F}$ can be effectively assigned a truth value (e.g., $2 + 2 < 5$ is TRUE).

IV. Technical Summary

Before comparing PEX to $QPEX$ it is necessary to examine PEX in more detail. In Section (V) we look at the four parameter problem for PEX, namely, 'for what values of a, b, c, an d does $PEX_b^a \subseteq PEX_c^d$?' It turns out that, unlike the case for EX, there are interesting tradeoffs. In Section VI we look at how PEX_* compares to $Q_*PEX_*[*]$. We show that $Q_*PEX[*] = PEX_*$, which answers the motivating question of this paper: The strength of asking questions *does not* make up for the weakness of outputting verifiable conjectures. If mind changes are bounded then the situation changes. We show that a there are classes that are in $Q_*PEX_0[*]$ but not in PEX_a for any fixed a.

Sections VII, VIII, and IX refine what is known by looking at the particular languages $[+, \times]$, $[+, <]$, and $[S, <]$. In section VII we show that there are classes in PEX_{a+1} that are not in $QEX_a[+, <]$ (and hence not in $QPEX_a[+, <]$. This proof uses k-good sets (as introduced in [11] in a novel way. The proof also shows that there is a proper mind change hierarchy for $QEX_a[+, <]$ and for $QEX_a[S, <]$, thus cracking two open problems from [9].

V. PEX Learning

The first two results presented here shows the mind change anomaly trade-offs for PEX machines. The next two results extends the previous results when multiple machines are involved. These results are interesting, and important since we will see how these compare with the results in the latter sections. The theorems proved in this section uses techniques that have been used before [4,8,17]. The following theorem gives necessary and sufficient conditons to patch up $a - c$ anomalies when b mind changes are allowed. This shows the important parameter here is the mind changes.

THEOREM 1. $(\forall a, b, c, d \in N)$ such that $(a \geq c)$ then $PEX_b^a \subseteq PEX_d^c$ if and only if $d \geq \left(b+1 \right) \left(\left\lfloor \frac{a}{c+1} \right\rfloor + 1 \right) - 1$

Proof: ($\Longleftarrow$) Let $(a, b, c, d \in N)$ such that $(a \geq c)$ be given. Let $S \in PEX_b^a$. Hence there exists an IIM M such that $S \subseteq PEX_b^a(M)$. We will construct an IIM M' such that if $d \geq \left(b+1 \right) \left(\left\lfloor \frac{a}{c+1} \right\rfloor + 1 \right) - 1$ then $S \subseteq PEX_d^c(M')$. Note that by proof of   for each program output by M, M' has to output a maximum of $\left\lfloor \frac{a}{c+1} \right\rfloor + 1$ programs to reduce the errors from a to c. Now M outputs a total of $b+1$ programs, hence M' has to output $\left(b+1 \right) \left(\left\lfloor \frac{a}{c+1} \right\rfloor + 1 \right)$ programs in total to reduce the errors from a to c. That is if $d \geq \left(b+1 \right) \left(\left\lfloor \frac{a}{c+1} \right\rfloor + 1 \right) - 1$ then $PEX_b^a \subseteq PEX_d^c$.

($\Longrightarrow$)

We will show that if $d < \left(b+1 \right) \left(\left\lfloor \frac{a}{c+1} \right\rfloor + 1 \right) - 1$ then $PEX_b^a - PEX_d^c \neq \emptyset$. To show this we will construct a set S of recursive functions. All the functions will be constant functions (almost constant), except possibly for the initial segments of the functions which will be described below:

1) The functions have at most $(b+1)$ steps with each step starting with at least $(a+1)$ constant values. That is initially the functions starts with at least $(a+1)$ zeros then if it steps up, it will start with $(a+1)$ ones and so on.

2) After the initial $(a+1)$ constants have at most a non constant values. That is in the initial segment after $(a+1)$ zeros have at most a non zero values, and if ever there is a jump, then after the $(a+1)$ values of ones, have at most a values not equal to one.

Consider an IIM M, when fed with input from any recursive function that executes the following steps in order:

Begin M

1) Look for $(a+1)$ consecutive constant values.

2) Output an index for a program which has an initial segment of all the values M has seen so far and the rest with the constant value seen in step (1).

3) Go to step (1).

End M

Clearly $S \in PEX_b^a(M)$. Now we will show that for any IIM M' $S \not\subseteq PEX_d^c(M')$. We will construct an $f \in S$ such that $f \notin PEX_d^c(M')$. The construction of f will proceed in stages. At stage s f^s will denote the initial segment of f that has been constructed so far. We will use the variables V_o, V_n to indicate the values by which the functions is extended. Set $V_n = 0$, $M'(\emptyset) = \emptyset$, $f^0 = \emptyset$

For $s = 0$ to b do begin

1) Set $V_o = V_n$. Extend f^s with at least $(a+1)$ values of V_o and more, until M' on (f^s) outputs a new guess.

2) Let the maximum value at which f^s is defined be denoted by x_m. The last guess output by M' on f^s be p_l. Set $f^s(x_m + i) = 1 \dot{-} \varphi_{p_l}(x_m + i)$ for $i = 1 \cdots (c+1)$. This can be done since p_l is total. Extend f^s with more and more values of V_o until another new guess appears.

3) Repeat step (2) $\left\lfloor \frac{a}{c+1} \right\rfloor$ times.

4) Set $V_n = MAX(\varphi_{p_l}(x_m + 1), \cdots, \varphi_{p_l}(x_m + c + 1)) + 1$.

End

Clearly if the above loop does not terminate f becomes total and $f \in S$. If the above loop terminates then set $f = f^b \cup \{V_0 \,|\, x > x_m\}$. Observe that f has at most $(b+1)$ jumps, and on each segment maximum of $(c+1)(\left\lfloor \frac{a}{c+1} \right\rfloor)$ i.e $\leq a$ non constant values. Hence $f \in S$. Now M' for each time through the loop outputs $(1 + \left\lfloor \frac{a}{c+1} \right\rfloor)$ programs. But the loop is repeated $(b+1)$ times hence the total number of programs output by M' is $\left(b+1\right)\left(\left\lfloor \frac{a}{c+1} \right\rfloor + 1\right)$. Hence if $d <$ allowed less than $\left(b+1\right)\left(\left\lfloor \frac{a}{c+1} \right\rfloor + 1\right) - 1$ then $f \notin PEX_d^c(M')$. ☒

COROLLARY 2. $(\forall a, b, c \in N)$ such that $(a \geq b)$, $PEX_0^a \subseteq PEX_c^b$ if and only if $c \geq \left\lfloor \frac{a}{b+1} \right\rfloor$

The next theorem shows how to trade mind changes for machines precisely.

THEOREM 3. $(\forall n \geq 1)\ (\forall a \in N)\ [1,n]PEX_0^a = PEX_{n-1}^a$

Proof: Let $n \geq 1$ be given. Clearly $PEX_{n-1}^a \subseteq [1,n]PEX_0^a$. Now to show that $[1,n]PEX_0^a \subseteq PEX_{n-1}^a$. Let $M_1,\ M_2,\cdots,M_n$ be any PEX_0^a IIMs. We will construct an IIM M' such that it can simulate $M_1,\ M_2,\cdots,M_n$ IIMs. M' executes the following algorithm in steps.

Begin M'

1) Output the lexicographically the least program output by the by the team (which has not been previously output by M').

2) Run the program output in step (1) and check for $(a+1)$ errors. If $(a+1)$ errors are found then go to step (1).

END M'

Clearly the maximum number of mind changes is $n-1$ and M' will lock on to the correct program output by the team. ☒

The following theorem gives a necessary and sufficient conditions for trade-offs between machines anomallies and mind changes.

THEOREM 4. $(\forall a,b,c,d \in N)$ such that $(a \leq c)\ (\forall n \geq 1)\ [1,n]PEX_b^a \subseteq PEX_d^c$ if and only if $d \geq n(b+1)(\left\lfloor \frac{a}{(c+1)} \right\rfloor + 1) - 1$

Proof: $(\Rightarrow)$ Let (a,b,c,d) such that $(a \leq c)$ and $(n \geq 1)$ be given. We will first prove that $[1,n]PEX_b^a = PEX_{n(b+1)-1}^a$. This proof is very similar to the proof of Theorem 3, therefore we will only provide the essential details of the proof. In the proof of Theorem 3 We constructed a machine which simulated $[1,n]PEX_0^a$ by guessing n programs (hence $n-1$ mind changes). Now since each machine in the $[1,n]PEX_b^a$ class can output $(b+1)$ programs a machine that simulates the class $[1,n]PEX_b^a$ must output $n(b+1)$ programs, therefore $[1,n]PEX_b^a = PEX_{n(b+1)-1}^a$. Now by Theorem 1 result follows.

VI. PEX Learning with Any Language

The next theorem shows that if you are only allowed to ask quatifier free questions then there is no power increase. This result is similar to the result $Q_0EX_a[\star] = EX_a$ proved in [9].

THEOREM 5. $(\forall a \in N) \; Q_0 PEX_a[\star] = PEX_a$

Proof: Let $a \in N$ be given and $S \in Q_0 PEX_a[\star]$ as witnessed by a QIM M. Note that M can only pose queries involving constants. An IIM can simulate the QIM M by waiting for enough input to answer the query. With sufficient data, the IIM can deduce the answers to such queries. Also the IIM outputs whatever program M outputs, since M is allowed only a mind changes, the IIM will also make a mind changes

On the other hand, suppose that $S \subset PEX_a(M)$, where M is an IIM. Let $f \in S$. A QIM can simulate M on input f by asking "is $f(0) = 0$?" "$f(0 = 1$?" until the value of $f(0)$ is found. Similarly it can find the values of $f(1)$, $f(2), \cdots$ and simulate M. ⊠

Note that in the proof of the above theorem the QIM found the values of f by asking questions only involving constants. We will use this technique extensively in the rest of the paper.

The next theorem shows that asking questions will not increase power when unbounded mind changes are allowed. The earliar results obtaind for EX [9] says otherwise. The reason for this is verifiability. That is we require the machines to output total programs.

THEOREM 6. $Q_\star PEX_\star[\star] = PEX_\star$.

Proof: Clearly $PEX_\star \subseteq Q_\star PEX_\star[\star]$. Now we will show that $Q_\star PEX_\star[\star] \subseteq PEX_\star$. Let $S \in Q_\star PEX_\star[\star]$. Then there exists a QIM M such that $S \subseteq Q_\star PEX_\star[\star](M)$. Now we will construct an IIM M' such that $S \in PEX_\star(M)$. The proof of the theorem is based on the fact that if QIM M infers any $f \in S$. Then there exists a sequence of answers (YES NO, which we represent by bits) to the queries posed by M which will eventually lead to the correct program. M' executes the following algorithm for any $f \in S$.

Begin M'

Let $BITSTRINGS = 0, 1^*$.

1) Let $\vec{b}$ be lexicographically the least string from $BITSTRINGS$.

2) Let $e = g(M(\vec{b}))$, output e. Note that c is a total program.

3) Check more and more values of f with φ_e, until an error is found (this may never happen).

4) If an error is found in step (3) delete $\vec{b}$ from $BITSTRINGS$ and go to step (1).

End M'

Let $\vec{b}$ be the answers (the sequence of bits) to the queries by M which will lead to the correct guess which will compute f. Suppose the algoritm does not converge to a single program, then step (1) thru (4) are being executed infinitely often. This implies that M' would have eliminated $\vec{b}$ (the correct sequence of ibits) from $BITSTRINGS$. This is a contradiction, hence result. ⊠

We have proved in Theorem 1 that you can trade off anomallies for mind changes for PEX classes. Next we show that you can do the same for $QPEX$ classes.

THEOREM 7. $(\forall a \in N)\ Q_*PEX_0^a[\star] \subseteq Q_*PEX_a^0[\star]$.

Proof: The proof of this theorem is similar to the proof of Theorem 3. Here the M' looks for errors one at a time and outputs a patched version of the program. Since there is at most a errors M' needs only a mind changes. ⊠

In Theorem 6 we proved that when unbounded mind changes are allowed the ability to ask questions does not increase power. However in the next theorem we will show that if the mind changes are bounded the ability to ask questions with just one quantifier will increase power.

THEOREM 8. $(\forall a \in N)\ Q_1PEX_0^0[\star] - PEX_a^* \neq \emptyset$.

Proof: Let S be set of recursive functions that step at most $a + 1$ times, and whenever it steps up, it does so by value one. Note that for every $f \in S$ the range of f is a subset of $\{0, 1, \cdots, a + 1\}$.

We will construct a QIM M such that $S \in Q_*PEX_0^0[\star](M)$.

Begin M

1) Ask $(\exists x) f(x) = a+1$. If the answer is NO. Try $(\exists x) f(x) = a$. Continue these questions for less and less values until the answer is YES for some constant c, $c \le a + 1$.

2) Find the value of $f(0)$ by asking questions of the form "is $f(0) = 0$?", $f(0) = 1$? and so on. Similarly find the values of $f(1), f(2), \cdots f(x-1)$.

3) Using the values found in step (1) and (2) output a index for a program which is almost constant c with the initial segment patched with the values $f(0), \cdots, f(x-1)$.

End M

Clearly $S \in Q_*PEX_0^0[*](M)$.

Now its easy to show that $S \notin PEX_a^*$. Let M be any IIM M and $a \in N$ be given. We will construct an $f \in S$ such $f \notin PEX_a^*(M)$. The construction of f will proceed in stages. f^s denotes the initial segment of f constructed at stage s. Set $f^0 = \emptyset$. Extend f^0 with more and more values of zero until M outputs a program on f^0.

For $s = 1$ **to** $a+1$ **do begin**

1) Let $\sigma_1 = f^{s-1}$ and $\sigma_2 = f^{s-1}$.

2) Extend σ_1, σ_2 with more and more values of $s-1$ and s respectively until $M(\sigma_1) \ne M(f^{s-1})$ or $M(\sigma_2) \ne M(f^{s-1})$. One of these must happen, since program output by the machine cannot be correct on both segments.

3) If $M(\sigma_1) \ne M(f^{s-1})$ then set $f^s = \sigma_1$ else set $f^s = \sigma_2$.

End

Clearly the loop must terminate. Let the maximum domain value at which f^{a+1} is defined be x_{a+1}. Now set $f = f^{a+1} \cup \{f^{a+1}(x_{a+1}) | x > x_{a+1}\}$ Clearly the IIM M will change its mind $a+1$ times on f. It is only allowed a mind changes $\boxtimes$

THEOREM 9. $(\forall a, b, c \in N \cup \{*\})$ $Q_*PEX_b^a[*] \subseteq PEX_c^0$ if and only if $c = *$.

Proof: ($\Rightarrow$) Let ($\forall a, b, c \in N \cup \{\star\}$). Suppose $c \neq \star$, then by Theorem 8 $Q_\star PEX_b^a[\star] - PEX_j^0 \emptyset$. Hence if $Q_\star PEX_b^a[\star] \subseteq PEX_c^0$ implies that $c = \star$.

($\Leftarrow$) Let $c = \star$, then by the result follows. ☒

VII. PEX Learning with $[+, \times]$

In this section we will show that the ability to ask question using $[+, \times]$ its a "all or nothing process".

The next theorem shows that a QIM with no queries no mind changes has the same power as an IIM with no mind changes.

THEOREM 10. $Q_0 PEX_0[+, \times] = PEX_0$.

Proof: By definitions.

The next theorem shows that a QIM with the ability to ask questions with one quatifier and zero mind chages has the same power as a an IIM with unbounded number of mind changes.

THEOREM 11. $Q_1 PEX_0[+, \times] = PEX_\star$.

Proof: First we will prove that $PEX_\star \subseteq Q_1 PEX_0[+, \times]$. Let $S \in PEX_\star$. Hence there exists an IIM M such that $S \subseteq PEX_\star(M)$. Now we will construct a QIM M' such that $S \subseteq Q_1 PEX_0[+, \times](M')$. Let $\langle ., . \rangle$ denote a pairing function from $N \times N \to N$ found in [16] and e be a index of any program such that φ_e is total. Consider the set $A_e = \{\langle x, y \rangle \mid \varphi_e(x) \neq y\}$. Clearly since e is total, A_e recursive. By work done in solving Hilberts 10th problem [6,7,14] (also theorem 8 in [9]) there is an effective list of polynomials $p_0, p_1, \cdots$ such that for all i,

$\langle x, y \rangle \in A_i \Leftrightarrow \exists \vec{z}[p_i(\vec{z}, \langle x, y \rangle) = 0]$. That is $\varphi_i(x) \downarrow \neq y \Leftrightarrow \exists \vec{z}[p_i(\vec{z}, \langle x, y \rangle) = 0]$.

Let $f \in S$. The QIM M' finds the values of $f(0)$, $f(1), f(2), \cdots$ and feeds them into M. Whenever M outputs a new guess c_1 it asks the following question.

$$\exists x \exists \vec{z}[\varphi_{e_1}(\vec{z}, \langle x, f(x) \rangle) = 0]$$

Note that the above question is equivalent to $\exists x[f(x) \neq \varphi_{e_1}(x)]$.

If the answer is NO, then M' outputs e and stops, else it waits for a new guess e_2 from M and asks the question

$$\exists x[f(x) \neq \varphi_{e_2}(x)].$$

until it gets the answer YES. Clearly $S \subseteq Q_1 PEX_0[+, \times](M')$. Hence $PEX_* \subseteq Q_1 PEX_0[+, \times]$.

Now by $Q_* PEX_*[*] = PEX_*$, hence $Q_1 PEX_0[+, \times] \subseteq PEX_*$. ☒

VIII. QEX/PEX Learning with $[+, <]$

THEOREM 12. $(\forall a \in N) \ Q_* PEX_a[+, <] \subset PEX_*$.

Proof: Let $a \in N$ be give. By $Q_* PEX_a[+, <] \subseteq PEX_*$. By Theorem 11 in [11] $PRIMREC \in PEX_* - Q_* PEX_a[+, <]$. ☒

The next few definitions and theorems will enable us to obtain a mind change hierarchy for $QEX[+, <]$. Also this we will prove that for all a, $QEX_a[+, <] \subset QEX_{a+1}[+, <]$, which resolves an open question from [9]. From the proof of this theorem we also obtain that $PEX_{a+1} - QEX_a[+, <] \neq \emptyset$.

We use the machinery of k-good sets introduced in [11].

In this section we study infering recursive sets. Questions now have one free set variable X instead of one free function f, $q(X)$ denote a query.

DEFINITION 13. For $k \geq 1$, a k-good set is an infinite set $\{s_0 < s_1 < \cdots\}$ such that (1) for all i, k divides s_i; (2) $k < s_0$; (3) for all i, $ks_i < s_{i+1}$. (The intuition is that the elements of a k-good set are very far apart and have nice divisibility properites.)

DEFINITION 14. For $k \geq 1$ and $\sigma \in \{0,1\}^*$, a (k, σ)-good set is a set $S \subseteq N$ such that (1) $\{x \mid x \geq |\sigma|\} \cap S$ is k-good; (2) for all $x \leq |\sigma$ $x \in S$ iff $\sigma(x) = 1$.

These sets are important because of the following lemma from [11].

LEMMA 15. Given $\sigma \in \{0,1\}^*$, $k \in N$, and a query $q(X)$ there exists σ', k', and $b \in \{T, F\}$ such that σ' extends σ, k divides k', and for all (k', σ')-good sets A $q(A)$ is b (True or False). The values of σ', k', and b can be found by a primitive recursive algorithm.

This Lemma can be used to prove the following

LEMMA 16. There exists a recursive set G such that (1) given any finite sequence $\vec{q}(X)$ of queries (in $[+, <]$) and answers $\vec{b}$ such that $\vec{q}(G)$ is answered by $\vec{b}$, there exists σ (an initial segment of G) and $k \in N$ such that for any (k, σ)-good set A, $\vec{q}(A)$ is answered by $\vec{b}$; (2) for every k there exists a σ such that G is (k, σ)-good; (3) if F is any finite set then $G - F$ has properties (1) and (2).

Convention: If M is a QIM and $A \subseteq N$ then the phrase 'simulate M with A' means to run machine M and supply the answers that are true for A. This is done nonconstructively.

THEOREM 17. $(\forall a \in N)$ $PEX_{a+1}[+, <] - QEX_a[+, <]$.

Proof: Let G be the set in the above lemma. Let

$$S = \{G - F \mid F \text{ has } \leq a + 1 \text{ elements}\}.$$

It is easy to see that $S \in PEX_{a+1} \subseteq QEX_{a+1}[+, <]$. We show that $S \notin QEX_a[+, <]$. Let M be a QIM using $[+, <]$ that makes at most a mind changes while inferring functions in S. We show that S is not inferred by M.

Simulate M with G until a conjecture e is made. If e is not an index for G then keep simulating with G. If e is an index for G then we do the following. Let $\vec{q}$ be the queries made and $\vec{b}$ be the answers supplied. Let (k, σ) be the parameters guaranteed to exist by the above lemma. Let n_1 be the least number such that $n_1 > |\sigma|$ and $n_1 \in G$. Continue the simulation with $G - \{n_1\}$. Since $G - \{n_1\}$ is (k, σ)-good (by the above lemma) the simulation up to this point is valid for $G - \{n_1\}$.

By repeating this process a times, we can defeat machine M. ╳

COROLLARY 18. $(\forall a \in N)$ $QEX_a \subset QEX_{a+1}[+, <]$. ╳

COROLLARY 19. $(\forall a \in N)\ Q_*PEX_a[+,<] \subset Q_*PEX_{a+1}[+,<]$.

Proof: Let $a \in N$ be given. By definition $QPEX_a[+,<] \subseteq QPEX_{a+1}[+,<]$. Now by definitions $PEX_{a+1} \subseteq QPEX_{a+1}[+,<]$ and $QPEX_a[+,<] \subseteq QEX_a[+,<]$ hence result ⊠

IX. QEX/PEX Learning with $[S,<]$

In this section we will obtain some results about QIM's when their query language is restricted to $[S,<]$. It is interesting to note that most of the results here parallels the results for QIM's with query language $[+,<]$.

COROLLARY 20. $(\forall a \in N)\ QEX_a[S,<] \subset QEX_{a+1}[S,<]$.

Proof: This result can be obtained as a corollary to Theorem 17.

It is of interest to note that this result could not be obtained using ω-automata; the machinery of k-good sets was needed, even though the language was $[S,<]$.

THEOREM 21. $(\forall a \in N)\ Q_*PEX_a[S,<] \subset PEX_*$.

Proof: By $Q_*PEX_*[S,<] = PEX_*$, hence $Q_*PEX_a[S,<] \subseteq PEX_*$. The proof of theorem 18 in [9] essentially gives the following result $PRIMREC \in PEX_* - Q_*PEX_a[S,<]$, hence result. ⊠

THEOREM 22. $(\forall a \in N)\ Q_*PEX_0^0[S,<] - PEX_a^* \neq \emptyset$.

Proof: Result follows from Theorem 8 ⊠

THEOREM 23. $(\forall a \in N)\ PEX_{a+1} - Q_*PEX_a[S,<] \neq \emptyset$.

Proof: This result follows from Theorem 17

⊠

X. Open Problems

Problem: Given $a,b,c,d \in N$ and $n,m > 0$ does there exists a predicate P such that $[1,n]PEX_b^a \subseteq [1,m]PEX_d^c$ if and only if $P(a,b,c,d,m,n)$.

Problem: Given $a,b,c,d \in N$ does there exists a predicate P such that $Q \star PEX_b^a[\star] \subseteq Q \star PEX_d^c[\star]$ if and only if $P(a,b,c,d)$.

References

1. ANGLUIN, D. AND SMITH, C. H. Inductive inference: theory and methods. *Computing Surveys 15* (1983), 237–269.

2. ANGLUIN, D. AND SMITH, C. H. Inductive inference. In *Encyclopedia of Artificial Intelligence*, S. Shapiro, Ed., John Wiley and Sons Inc., 1987.

3. BLUM, L. AND BLUM, M. Toward a mathematical theory of inductive inference. *Information and Control 28* (1975), 125–155.

4. CASE, J. AND SMITH, C. Comparison of identification criteria for machine inductive inference. *Theoretical Computer Science 25, 2* (1983), 193–220.

5. DALEY, R. P. AND SMITH, C. H. On the complexity of inductive inference. *Information and Control 69* (1986), 12–40.

6. DAVIS, M., , H. PUTNAM, AND ROBINSON, J. The decision problem for exponential diophantine equations. *Annals of Mathematics 74* (1961), 425–436.

7. DAVIS, M. Hilbert's 10th problem is unsolvable. *American Mathematical Monthly 80* (1973), 233–269.

8. FREIVALDS, R., SMITH, C., AND VELAUTHAPILLAI, M. Trade–offs amongst parameters effecting the inductive inferribility of classes of recursive functions. *Information and Computation 82, 3* (1989), 323–349.

9. GASARCH, W. AND SMITH, C. *Learning via Queries.* to appear in JACM.

10. GASARCH, W., KINBER, E., PLESZKOCH, M., SMITH, C., AND ZEUGMANN, T. *Learning via queries with teams and anomalies.* Manuscript.

11. GASARCH, W., PLESZKOCH, M., AND SOLOVAY, R. *Learning via queries with plus and less than.* to appear in JSL.

12. GOLD, E. M. Language identification in the limit. *Information and Control 10* (1967), 447–474.

13. MACHTEY, M. AND YOUNG, P. *An Introduction to the General Theory of Algorithms.* North-Holland, New York, New York, 1978.

14. MATIJASEVIC, Y. Enumerable sets are diophantine. *Doklady Academy Nauk. SSSR 191* (1970), 279–282. Translation in Sov. Math. Dokl. 11, 1970, pp. 354–357.

15. PLESZKOCH, M., GASARCH, W., JAIN, S., AND SOLOVAY, R. *Learning via queries to an oracle.* Manuscript.

16. ROGERS, H. JR. *Theory of Recursive Functions and Effective Computability.* McGraw Hill, New York, 1967.

17. SMITH, C. H. The power of pluralism for automatic program synthesis. *Journal of the ACM 29, 4* (1982), 1144–1165.

Predictive Analogy and Cognition

Bipin Indurkhya

Computer Science Department, Boston University
Boston, MA 02215, USA

Abstract. The most prevalent sense of 'analogy' in cognitive science and AI literature, which I refer to as *predictive analogy,* is the process of inferring further similarities between two given situations based on some existing similarities. Though attempts to validate predictive analogy on logical grounds have been singularly unsuccessful, it is claimed that all the empirical evidence points to the usefulness of predictive analogy in cognition. In this article I critically analyze this claim. I argue that the classroom experiments by cognitive psychologists to demonstrate predictive analogy as a problem-solving heuristic do not really do so. Moreover, the few studies of real-world problem-solving situations definitely point away from predictive analogy. I present some examples where predictive analogy prevents one from seeing things as they are, thereby hindering cognition. Having exposed its 'dark side', I argue for a balanced perspective where predictive analogy is best seen as a psychological process that is as likely to be a liability as an asset to cognition.

1 Introduction

There are two prevalent ways in which the term 'analogy' is used in the literature. One refers to the act of seeing (or describing) one object (or situation) as another object. For instance, in Stephen Spender's classic poem *Seascape,* the sunlight reflecting on the waves in the ocean is seen as if someone were strumming a harp. This process is not limited to poetry and art, but is also known to underlie creative problem solving including scientific discoveries. For example, it has been documented that Niels Bohr's theory of quantum mechanics was deeply influenced by the cubist style of painting that depicted perspectives on an object from several different angles at once [2, 20]. This can be characterized as Bohr's wanting to see the atom as a cubist painting. Another example is provided by Gruber [12]. On analyzing Sir Charles Darwin's notebooks in which he kept notes while working on his celebrated theory of evolution, Gruber noted that the image of an irregularly branching tree kept recurring in Darwin's thoughts, and may have served as the primal metaphor for his natural selection principle. I refer to this sense of analogy as *interpretive analogy* here. (It is also referred to as *analogy by rendition* in [15].)

The other sense of analogy concerns the process of inferring further similarities between two objects and situations based on some existing similarities. For instance, suppose a person has never steered a boat before. However, she has driven automobiles, and from what she knows about boats and automobiles, she sees many similarities between the two. From these similarities, she might conclude that pushing the rudder to the left in the boat—being analogous to turning the steering wheel to the left in the automobile—would cause the boat to turn left. I refer to this sense of analogy as *predictive analogy,* which is also variously known as 'analogical reasoning' and 'analogical inference'. It is in this sense that the term 'analogy' is mostly used in cognitive science and artificial intelligence research.

There are two important differences between these two senses of analogy that must be appreciated. One is that prior similarities do not play any significant role in interpretive analogy. On the contrary, it works by changing the representation of the object or situation being described (the target), and *creates* the similarities—or, as some may feel more comfortable in saying, *discovers* unsuspected similarities—between it and the object (or situation) being used to describe (the source.) For instance, Gruber's [12] account cites several excerpts from Darwin's notebooks to show that it was not some existing similarities between the tree image and whatever was known about the evolution at that time that kept Darwin searching for what other similarities might be found. On the contrary, it was an emotional drive that kept up his intellectual commitment to articulating an account of evolution that matched the tree image. It was not as if Darwin was searching for similarities, rather he was formulating them. This process was actually fraught with several problems that appeared to invalidate the analogy, but Darwin's intellectual commitment to the idea kept him from throwing away the analogy altogether. Instead, he improvised and sought different ways to render the analogy meaningful.

On the contrary, prior, or already known, similarities between the source and the target play a major role in predictive analogy, for it is they that justify the conclusion about the target. It is the fact that the boat is similar to the automobile that justifies the hypothesis that pushing the rudder to the left would cause the boat to turn left. If there were no existing similarities between the two, the conclusion would be considered unjustified, perhaps no better than a random guess.

The other major difference between the two senses of analogy is that interpretive analogy does not suggest any heuristic for choosing an appropriate source for a given target. In seeing the target as something else, a source might or might not provide a meaningful and interesting perspective on it, and might or might not be successful in solving whatever problem that one wishes to solve about the target object or situation. But the likelihood of success of a particular source is not correlated in any way to the prior similarities between the source and the target.

Predictive analogy does precisely that: it suggests that a source that is already known to be similar to the target is more likely to be successful than a source that is perceived as dissimilar. Given a number of potential sources for a given target, one's best bet, according to predictive analogy, is to choose the source that one see as most similar to the target. Thus, predictive analogy appears to provide a useful heuristic for problem solving. It is exactly for this reason that cognitive science and artificial intelligence research has focused on predictive analogy.

The spell of predictive analogy is so strong that many researchers take the term analogy to mean only predictive analogy. For instance, when I was presenting a paper on interpretive analogy and its role in learning [16] at a conference in Tokyo, one member of the audience asked me if I have some way of selecting a source. When I said "No!" the member of the audience declared that then I was not talking about analogy.

Of course, on the surface, this seems to be a quibble over the terminology. Certainly, there is nothing wrong in saying "By 'analogy' I mean predictive analogy and nothing else!" But then it remains to be shown that predictive analogy is indeed such a useful problem-solving heuristic as it is purported to be, for most examples of reasoning by analogy in real-world problem-solving situations (as opposed to problem solving in artificial classroom experiments—I will talk about it more later), including scientific discoveries, turn out to be instances of interpretive analogy. Darwin did not pick out the image of an irregularly branching tree as the source because he saw it as very similar to the phenomenon of natural selection. In fact, until he formulated his theory of evolution, one cannot even say that an irregularly branching tree had any similarities with the phenomenon of natural selection, for the phenomenon did not exist in anyone's mind before that. The same point can be made about Bohr's quantum theory and the cubist style of painting.

Not distinguishing between the two senses of analogy has been the root cause of making predictive analogy seem much bigger than it is, and most cognitive science and artificial intelligence researchers seem to have fallen into this trap. However, when we keep the distinction between interpretive analogy and predictive analogy in the foreground, the role of predictive analogy in cognition needs to be reevaluated. I made a brief attempt at this earlier [15], where I essentially pointed out that there is no logical basis for predictive analogy. (See also [17], Chap. 9, Sec. 3, pp. 322–329.) In this article, I analyze the role of predictive analogy in cognition from an empirical point of view.

The paper is organized as follows. In the next section, I consider the classroom experiments that have been done by psychologists to demonstrate the usefulness of predictive analogy as a problem-solving heuristic. In Section 3, I review the evidence from real-world problem-solving situations to see how far it lends support to predictive analogy.

As the proponents of predictive analogy always present only those examples where an inference from predictive analogy turns out to be useful, the 'dark side' of predictive analogy, containing examples where predictive analogy hinders cognition and becomes a liability rather than an asset, is never seen. To put predictive analogy and its role in cognition in proper perspective, I present several examples in Section 4 where predictive analogy becomes a stumbling block to cognition. Finally, in Section 5, I conclude by presenting what I believe to be a more balanced perspective on predictive analogy than what is currently seen in cognitive science and artificial intelligence literature.

2 Evidence from Classroom Experiments

A number of psychologists have tried to show that predictive analogy is a useful problem-solving heuristic by conducting classroom experiments in a somewhat artificial setting [3, 7, 9, 10]. For instance, in Gick and Holyoak's study [9], five different experiments were conducted to investigate how exactly people use analogy in problem solving. One of the problems that were used in their experimental set-up was that of coming up with some way to use electromagnetic radiation to destroy a tumor without destroying the surrounding healthy tissue.

In one of Gick and Holyoak's experiments, three groups of subjects were given an analog source (army maneuvers to capture an enemy fortress) and a way (different for each group) to solve the analogous problem in the source, while a fourth group was supplied with no such source. The results indicated that for the three groups who were given the analog source, the given solution to the source problem had a marked influence in their proposed solution to the target problem. Moreover, the fourth group did rather poorly: about half of the subject ended up suggesting that the patient be operated upon to clear a path for the electromagnetic rays. None of the subjects in this group suggested what was considered to be the most creative solution: that weak electromagnetic rays be sent from different directions so as to converge on the tumor. The experiment was conducted with the experimenter interacting with the subjects during problem solving, and with no interaction, which was found to have no significant effect on the results (except that more incomplete solutions were generated in the non-interactive version of the experiment). This, according to Gick and Holyoak, clearly demonstrated the power of predictive analogy in solving an unfamiliar problem.

In another experiment, it was found that even when the solution to the source problem was not explicitly given, and the subjects were allowed to develop their own solution of it, they were still able to use the solution of the source problem to solve the target problem. This is purported to show that even when the subject does not already know the solution of a similar problem in the source, making the analogy is still helpful because the subject can proceed by first solving the analogous source problem (which ought to be easier, as the subject is more familiar with it) and then transferring the solution to the target.

In yet another experiment, the subjects were divided into two groups. Both groups were presented with three stories, one of which was a potential source analog for the target problem. Then each group was given the target problem to solve. The subjects in one group were told that one of the stories presented earlier could provide a hint in solving the problem. The results of this experiment were that a large fraction (92%) of subjects in the group that was given the hint were able to find the right source and apply it successfully to solve the target problem, whereas only a small fraction (20%) of subjects in the 'no-hint' group were able to solve the problem at all. This showed that predictive analogy is not an automatic problem-solving strategy, but needs to be consciously applied.

Before analyzing to see if these experiments do indeed provide an empirical support for predictive analogy, let me review one more set of experiments that was published more recently [3]. In their experiments, Clement and Gentner made up a scenario about some hypothetical creatures called 'Tams' as the potential source (referred to as 'base' by Clement and Gentner). The scenario had two different causal structures in it that explained why Tams, which habitually grind and consume minerals through their underbellies, sometimes stop using their underbellies, and why they cannot work on a new terrain. One causal structure explained that when the mineral in one spot is exhausted, then Tams stop using their underbellies. The other causal structure explained that the underbelly of a Tam gets specialized to the texture of a particular rock through adaptation, and so it is unable to function on a rock with a different texture.

The subjects were given two different versions of a target scenario involving robots that gather data on planets using probes. In one version, the subjects were told that when robots exhaust data from one place, they must move to another place; and that the robots are designed with delicate probes that cannot survive flight to another planet. In the other version, the subjects were told that when the robots gather a lot of data, their internal computers overheat; and that the probes adapt and become specialized to one planet.

Then the subjects were asked to make predictions about the target scenario. Clement and Gentner argued that there are two potential predictions with respect to each version of the target. For instance, with respect to the first version, it might be predicted that the robots would stop using the probes at some point (when the data is exhausted) or that the robots cannot function on another planet (since they have delicate probes that cannot survive flight to another planet). Only one of these predictions (the first one) fits the systematicity model of Gentner [6], which was shown to be the most favored prediction in the experiment. Thus, Clement and Gentner not only claimed to have demonstrated that people use predictive analogy for making predictions, but also that the predictions derived from a 'systematic' mapping (which means a mapping that includes higher order relations and not the attributes) between the source and the target are more likely to occur.

Let us now see if any of these experiments do provide empirical support for predictive analogy as a useful problem-solving heuristic. First consider Gick and Holyoak's experiments. Interestingly, one condition that was true in all of their experiments, and not mentioned explicitly at all by them, was that *the analog source did lead to the solution of the target problem*. Even when two other seemingly irrelevant sources were included, those two sources were not analogous to the target problem. In other words, that predictive analogy would work in this example was satisfied a priori. What the experiment did confirm was that whenever that is the case (that it is known a priori that predictive analogy would work), then the subjects were capable of using predictive analogy to arrive at the solution (as long as it was explicitly hinted).

This point might seem rather subtle, but it can be emphasized by an analogy (and this is not predictive analogy!). The existing similarities between the source and the target might be thought of as a trail of bread crumbs, and the solution of the target problem can be thought of as arriving at home. Now the empirical problem of justification of predictive analogy is to show that by following the trail of crumbs you do indeed get home more often (demonstrated by actually following the trail of crumbs a few times and getting home). But what Gick and Holyoak's experiments show that *if the trail of crumbs leads home,* and if you follow the trail, then you get home.

To validate predictive analogy as a problem-solving heuristic, an issue must be addressed that Gick and Holyoak's experiments ignore altogether: how to select the source domain? To appreciate this, consider a real-world problem-solving situation. There is a problem that no one knows how to solve. Now if some source (similar to the target) provides a solution to the problem, then applying predictive analogy with that source would lead us to it (and we will know afterwards that the source is, in fact, the correct one). However, there are a large number of potential sources; how do we decide which one to use? There is no oracle here to point us to the correct source. Predictive analogy purports to fill this gap by suggesting that a source that is similar in certain respects (according to systematicity or some other such criterion) is more likely to be the correct one. But then it must be empirically demonstrated that this is the case, something that Gick and Holyoak's study fails to do.

Clement and Gentner's study is even weaker in providing an empirical justification for predictive analogy as a problem-solving heuristic. The target domain is quite artificial, and there is no way to tell whether a solution would or would not work. What it does manage to show is that people tend to favor certain kinds of predictions based on analogy over certain others. But there is no correlation between what people might predict and the solution of a real-world problem. If the subjects in Clement and Gentner's study were to solve a real-world problem, and there was no oracle to give them the 'right' source, then it is not clear whether the kind of predictions they made in the experiments would be useful at all.

3 Evidence from Real-World Problem-Solving Activities

I faulted Gick and Holyoak's study above in its inability to provide an empirical justification for predictive analogy on the grounds that the success in their classroom experiments does not translate into success with real-world problem solving. This suggests that if one were to look at real-world problem-solving situations, and if it could be shown that predictive analogy is responsible for leading to the solutions of even some of these situations, then predictive analogy would receive some empirical justification.

Problem solving in the real world has not been extensively studied; but the few studies that have been done [11, 18, 26] point away from predictive analogy by revealing that most creative insights are generated by using a source that, at least on a first glance, is very *dissimilar* to the target—so much that the juxtaposition of the source and the target seems bizarre initially—a process that Gordon very aptly named *making the familiar strange.*

It must be emphasized with respect to these studies that when a 'strange' source is used to get a new perspective on the target, the process ends up creating similarities between the source and the target. That is, there are always similarities between the source and the target *after the fact.* Many proponents of predictive analogy, not making any distinction between before-the-fact and after-the-fact states of affairs, cite these same studies as if they provide empirical justification for predictive analogy, when, in fact, they do not.

There are, nevertheless, a few examples of real-world problem-solving studies that do provide a small support to predictive analogy. For instance, Gentner and Jeziorski [8] note that in creating the theory of thermodynamics, Carnot used an analogy from the flow of fluids. Gentner and Jeziorski provide a long quotation from Carnot that lays out the analogy. From the existing similarities between the fluid flow and the heat flow, namely that fluid flows from a higher level to a lower level and heat flows from a higher-temperature body to a lower-temperature body, Carnot suggested the hypothesis: could it be that the rate of heat-flow is proportional to the temperature difference between the two bodies? (Just like the rate of fluid-flow is proportional to the difference in levels.)

Gordon's 'direct analogy' ([11], pp. 42–45) provides another set of examples that might be construed as instances of predictive analogy. For instance, in one of Gordon's examples, a group of product-development researchers was faced with the task of designing a dispenser for various products such as glue, nail polish, etc. The dispenser was to be in one piece (without a reclosable top), and therefore its mouth must open for dispensing and then close tightly after each use. The direct analogy that led to solving this problem came from that of a horse excreting. As a member of the group reminisced:

> "When I was a kid I grew up on a farm. I used to drive a hayrack behind a pair of draft horses. When a horse would take a crap, first his outer ... I guess you'd call it a kind of mouth, would open. Then the anal sphincter would dilate and a horse ball would come out. Afterwards, everything would close up again. The whole picture would be as clean as a whistle."
> ([11], p. 42).

The important thing, however, is that Gordon does not suggest that the most similar source is most likely to lead to the solution of a problem, or that the existing similarities between two situations have anything to do with being able to apply the known solution of a problem in one situation to solve a similar problem in the other situation. His examples of direct analogy do not suggest any such simple-minded solution to the creativity problem. His whole point is that sometimes recalling a similar image may suggest a new way to solve a problem.

In fact, most researchers who study creative problem solving are cautious and do not throw their weight behind predictive analogy for two reasons. One is that the insights obtained by predictive analogy are not always deep or insightful. For instance, Carnot's hypothesis "The rate of heat-flow is proportional to the temperature difference between two bodies," if it was derived as described by Gentner and Jeziorski [8], seems rather obvious. Contrast this with an example of interpretive analogy discussed in Schön ([26], pp. 74–76), where a product-development team used the 'paintbrush as a pump' analogy to improve the performance of the synthetic-fiber paintbrush. In this example, the paintbrush (the target) was not perceived as similar to a pump (the source) initially. But after the analogy was assimilated, a radical change took place in the way in which the process of painting, and the role of the paintbrush in it, was perceived. It was only from this changed perspective on painting that the problem of making the synthetic-fiber paintbrush perform as well as the natural-fiber paintbrush could be addressed. As another example, you could compare any theorem that is derived by predictive analogy (for example, a theorem about rings derived from a similar known theorem about groups) with Cantor's theorem that there are more real numbers than integers.

The second reason for most people who have had a first-hand experience with creative problem solving in the real world to not put their trust in predictive analogy is that they realize that truly creative insights require completely new and revolutionary perspectives. When a problem seems hard to solve, it is often because the familiar and conventional perspective on the problem is not sufficient to address it. In such situations, using a similar source is only going to reinforce the familiar perspective. Thus, if the problem were such that a radical change of perspective is needed—as in the paintbrush example mentioned above—then predictive analogy would become a severe handicap rather than an asset. This conclusion is also borne by the myriad of scientific, economic and social problems that exist in the world today, despite being attacked repeatedly by some very bright people. If predictive analogy were such a useful problem-solving heuristic as it is claimed to be, one would expect that many of these problems would be resolved by now.

To summarize this discussion, we see that the only empirical evidence for predictive analogy from problem solving in the real world is that occasionally using a source that is similar to the target can lead to a successful solution to the target problem. Moreover, the solution to the target problem suggested by predictive analogy in these cases is usually not a particularly deep or insightful one. Given that, for real-world problems, deep insights come from using 'strange' sources that do not initially seem similar to the target at all, a system that puts its faith in predictive analogy as a problem-solving strategy is sure to miss most such insights. Consequently, predictive analogy is not such a wonderful problem-solving heuristic as it is purported to be.

4 The 'Dark Side' of Predictive Analogy

Given that no one has been able to provide reasonable empirical support for predictive analogy, one wonders if there are any examples where predictive analogy is not an aid to cognition and problem solving. One even wonders if there are examples where predictive analogy hinders cognition and problem solving.

Perhaps not surprisingly, all the research on predictive analogy cites only what one might consider reasonable and useful examples of predictive analogy. Most of the predictive analogy examples used in the literature make correct predictions about their targets, and their sources are quite useful in understanding the unfamiliar targets. This only shows the careful attention these researchers give in selecting (or making up) their examples, so as to present predictive analogy in the best possible light. The 'dark side' of predictive analogy, which contains instances when an inference from predictive analogy is quite unreasonable (that is, *not justified* but not necessarily incorrect) and when predictive analogy becomes a hindrance rather than an aid to cognition, is never seen at all.

To fill this vacuum, I provide several examples below that provide a glimpse of the dark side of predictive analogy. For each example, I argue why the suggestion from predictive analogy is not justified, or why predictive analogy becomes an obstacle to cognition by blocking the information that might otherwise be received from the environment.

- In a study of the first-time users of computer text-editors, Allwood and Eliasson [1] found that many of their difficulties emanate from the fact that they use the typewriter analogy to understand text-editors. These subjects were familiar with using a typewriter, and they automatically formulated an analogy between it and the text-editor (there are many structural similarities between the two). They then proceeded to apply this analogy to understand the text-editor. Ironically, as documented by Allwood and Eliasson, this analogy became a stumbling block to their understanding. In particular, it led to a number of errors (keeping a key pressed too long so that multiple instances of a command were issued) and inefficiencies (moving the cursor characterwise when it would have been more efficient to move wordwise) in their use of the text-editor. (See also [13] for difficulties of using analogical models in explaining some computer-related concepts.)

  Here the role of predictive analogy in hindering cognition is clearly seen. If it were not for analogy, these subjects would be open-minded about learning the text-editor. As it was, they rushed into it thinking that they understand it through predictive analogy, and failed to realize the important differences and the vastly superior power of text-editors. I have had similar experiences in teaching Lisp to students whose earlier programming experience had been with Fortran or Basic.

- Gentner and Jeziorski [8] provide some examples of alchemists' use of analogies. For instance, they cite Stillman [28] who noted that the egg was used as a source of many analogies. In one such analogy, "[T]he shell, skin, white, and yolk of the egg were thought to be analogous to the four metals involved in transmutations—copper, tin, lead, and iron—although the pairings could vary between the components and the metal." ([8], p. 313.)

  Such analogies amount to no more than fanciful whims that are not 'justified' in any sense of the word. In fact, they often hinder the true objective of scientific inquiry by making irrational arguments that refuse to acknowledge facts when the facts do not fit these whimsical analogies. For instance, it has been reported that Francesco Sizzi used the following argument against Galileo's discovery of the satellites of Jupiter:

  > "There are seven windows in the head, two nostrils, two eyes, two ears, and a mouth; so in the heavens there are two favorable stars, two unpropitious, two luminaries, and Mercury alone undecided and indifferent. From which and many other similar phenomena of nature, such as the seven metals, etc., which it were tedious to enumerate, we gather that the number of planets is necessarily seven." (This is quoted on page 822 in [22].)

- In investigating the *Challenger* space shuttle disaster with the Presidential commission, famous physicist and Nobel laureate Richard Feynman noted the gross abuse of reasoning from predictive analogy as one of the factors contributing to the tragic mishap:

  "...[T]he phenomenon of accepting seals that had shown erosion and blowby in previous flights is very clear. The *Challenger* flight is an excellent example: there are several references to previous flights; the acceptance and success of these flights are taken as evidence of safety. But erosion and blowby are not what the design expected. They are warning that something is wrong. The equipment is not operating as expected, and therefore there is a danger that it can operate with even wider deviations in this unexpected and not thoroughly understood way. The fact that this danger did not lead to a catastrophe before is no guarantee that it will not the next time, unless it is completely understood. When playing Russian roulette, the fact that the first shot got off safely is of little comfort for the next." (See [4]. The quote here is from p. 223 of the reprint in *What do you care....*)

- On January 14, 1991, as the multinational force allied against Iraq and led by the United States stood poised to attack Iraq in a bid to liberate Kuwait, an article appeared in the *Wall Street Journal* [25] that made an analogy between the arguments used by the representatives of the U.S. Congress during the debate to authorize the President the use of force against Iraq, and the arguments used in the Congress during a similar debate in 1939, when Europe was standing on the brink of what was to become World War II. Besides a three-sentence introduction, the article contained nothing other than pairs of quotations; one quotation of every pair was taken from the 1939 debate and the other from the 1991 debate, with an appropriate heading for each pair. Both the arguments in each pair made essentially the same point. For instance, under the heading "To save democracy?" Senator Charles Tubey was quoted as arguing in 1939, "[This is] a war not to save democracy but to preserve territorial powers of certain European nations." And Representative William Gray was quoted as arguing in 1991, "Is [our policy] to defend democracy? Hardly! Kuwait is no democracy, neither is Saudi Arabia or Syria." Thus, there is a clear analogy between the debate of 1939 and the debate of 1991. (And since the arguments involved causal structure and higher order relations, there is an obvious 'systematicity' in the analogy.)

What is the point of analogy? Taken as it is (without the predictive power), it merely shows that Congress is cautious about rushing into war and committing billions of dollars and putting lives of hundreds of thousands of people in jeopardy when the security of the country is not directly threatened. But the author seems to be implying something more. In one of the three sentences preceding the quotations, the author claimed that "The similarity is more than superficial," but no further explanation was offered as to how. Of course, if one uses predictive analogy, a number of other hypotheses are at once suggested. For instance, one might conclude that if we did not go to war right away, a World War would ensue with significantly greater loss of life, or that the Iraqi war machinery was as formidable as Germany's was in 1939, or that all reservations put forward in the 1991 debate are meaningless because they turned out to be not valid in 1939. One can go on and on here. Perhaps the author, using predictive analogy as a psychological sleight of hand, meant people to draw all (or some) of these conclusions subconsciously. God forbid, if artificial intelligence systems that used the 'systematicity' principle or some other such form of predictive analogy to make predictions about the future had ever anything to do with political decision making, they would be easy prey to such sleight of hand. (See also [30].)

Analogies like these are quite common in political rhetoric. They essentially work by hiding what is significantly different about two situations, and by presenting a very distorted picture so that people may draw the conclusion that the politician wishes them to draw. Since the conclusion is not always stated explicitly (as in this example), it seems all the more convincing. (Everyone thinks that they arrived at it themselves!) By not questioning the basis of predictive analogy, we only make ourselves more vulnerable to such manipulation.

- Another example in the same vein is provided by Eleanor Clift's criticism of President George Bush's handling of the U.S. economy. She was quoted as saying, "The rhythm method is about as good in economic planning as it is in family planning."[1] (The comment was a response to President Bush's remark on waiting in the 'natural cycle' of the economy as a strategy to combat the recession.) This analogy makes a completely irrelevant comparison to support a conclusion. Of course, the conclusion (that waiting in the 'natural cycle' of the economy is not a successful strategy to combat recession) can be independently analyzed, and one can argue for or against it. But the analogy tries to give an aura of justification to the conclusion without bringing in a shred of evidence or considering a single fact about the economy.

- A third example of what I consider as the misuse of predictive analogy in politics is provided by Galbraith's article [5] that appeared in *The Boston Globe* in December 1991. The article drew a parallel between the current recession in the U.S. and the recession of 1930s. After noting some broad parallels, such as the fact that each recession followed a decade of wild speculation in the stock market, it went on to make a number of very specific analogies. For instance, the administration's reluctance to acknowledge the recession at first, and the flood of tax-reduction proposals from both the major parties to counter recession were noted in each case. Finally, the article ended by suggesting some possible ways in which the current recession might be dealt with. The suggestions, needless to say, were derived from predictive analogy using the recession of 1930 as the source. It was suggested, for instance, that tax reductions and lowering of interest rate would not work, and the administration would eventually resort to initiating large public works projects to boost employment. It was also suggested that such proposals will be severely condemned at first, as they were in the '30s.

---

[1]This appeared in "Quotes of Notes," (p. 27) in *The Boston Globe* on Saturday, November 30, 1991.

If one plays into the hand of predictive analogy, the article succeeds in putting all those proposals that suggest tinkering with the monetary policy (as in lowering of taxes and interest rates) to counter recession in an unfavorable light, and in taking some of the edge off the criticisms of those proposals that suggest more direct government involvement (as in initiating public works projects and in offering more extensive unemployment benefits). Here again, the conclusion from predictive analogy, namely that tinkering with monetary policy is not going to work and more direct government involvement is necessary, can be independently analyzed, and arguments based on economic theories can be made for or against it. However, the article, in using predictive analogy, introduces completely irrelevant factors in order to make the conclusion seem justified. For instance, what does the fact that in each situation the administration was reluctant to acknowledge the recession at first have to do with whatever effects tax reductions might have on the economy? And Galbraith ought to know better, for he is a professor emeritus of economics at Harvard University.

- Finally, a historical example where predictive analogy, justified or not, would have been a grave liability. During the French revolution, the political situation was in such a state of flux that what was 'politically correct' at one point in time would become the reason for sending someone to the guillotine a little later. How predictive analogy would have led to disaster in this period might be best appreciated from Shurkin's [27] description of a computer simulation of the French revolution designed by historian Michael Carter:

> "Students at Dartmouth can ... play a game that simulates the French revolution. The student assumes the role of a Jacobin who undergoes political interrogation. He or she must answer the questions according to the party line at a certain time during the revolution or be swept off to the guillotine. Given a second chance at the questions, they frequently find that what was right before is fatally wrong now; the rules have been changed and they are still doomed. A number of real Jacobins died that way." ([27], p. 317.)

Political revolutions provide an excellent source of examples where a cognitive agent reasoning from predictive analogy is doomed. Consider the recent failed coup in the Soviet Union. During the coup, the rules changed as to what was considered right. When the coup was overthrown, the rules changed again to the other extreme. In fact, even sitting on the fence in not opposing the coup was also punished in various ways. All this shows that predictive analogy is not such a great asset to cognition as it is purported to be, and an artificial system that uses it as a source of heuristics is not necessarily going to survive any revolutions.

I hope these examples give you at least a cause for concern about predictive analogy: that an inference from predictive analogy (whether 'systematic' or not) is not always justified, and is not always useful to cognition. On the contrary, predictive analogy can become a major stumbling block to one's ability to be objective and see things as they are, with possibly fatal consequences.

5 Conclusions: Towards a Balanced Perspective

Now that we have seen the dark side of predictive analogy, we can get a balanced perspective on it. Clearly, and this is what the psychological studies by Gentner and by Holyoak have effectively demonstrated, people find arguments from predictive analogy psychologically compelling. I have no problem understanding this point. Also, from this point of view, predictive analogy seems an important cognitive phenomenon that ought to be researched, so that we can understand it better, and become aware of the pitfalls it creates in cognition. But this has not been the spirit of the cognitive science and artificial intelligence research on predictive analogy, where the attitude towards predictive analogy has been nothing short of awe and reverence: "Predictive analogy is good. Predictive analogy works most of the time. Predictive analogy is the key to learning and problem solving. Predictive analogy is a key ingredient of intelligence. Predictive analogy must be incorporated in computational models of intelligence." And so on. Almost no effort has been spent to examine the negative effects of predictive analogy in cognition. The fact that an inference from predictive analogy appears psychologically convincing often prevents a person from seeing things as they are, some examples of which I presented above. In fact, my examples show only the tip of the iceberg. Once you become aware of the potential abuses of predictive analogy, you start to notice how much more often predictive analogy is abused than it is used. But the abuses are rarely, if at all, discussed in the literature about predictive analogy. This essentially negative contribution of predictive analogy to cognition raises some doubts as to whether it is always useful to incorporate predictive analogy in an artificial intelligence system.

Looking at predictive analogy as a cognitive process, successful some of the times but misleading at others, some observations can be made here. One is that there is no correlation between the existing similarities between the source and target situations, and the likelihood of finding some additional feature of the source situation in the target situation. Indeed, if this correlation were as it is assumed to be in predictive analogy, then most problems (whether they be proving a theorem, developing a new product, coming up with a new physical theory, or settling a political crisis) would be solved by merely finding a similar source. On the contrary, we find that in real-world situations, predictive analogy often leads to mundane and trite observations. The key to creativity lies in bringing in a fresh perspective, in perceiving unsuspected similarities where none were recognized before, and in noticing things that are hidden by the conventional ways of categorizing the world. All of this is accomplished by trying to see the target situation in terms of a *very dissimilar* source situation—that is, by interpretive analogy. However, there is no correlation here either between the dissimilarities between the source and target situations, and what fresh perspective, if any at all, would be provided by interpretive analogy. Given a problematic target, many dissimilar sources fail to create any insights at all, let alone the useful ones. Thus, the fact remains that some sources work—in terms of creating a useful perspective on the target that results in getting the problem solved—whereas many others do not, and this difference cannot be explained on the basis of the existing similarities between the source and target situations.

The second observation is that even though an inference from predictive analogy does not have an increased likelihood of success, one could still use the term 'justified' in a psychological sense to distinguish reasonable inferences based on predictive analogy (such as inferring the cost of an automobile from the cost of another automobile with the same make, model, year, and mileage) from unreasonable ones (such as the examples presented above). This is where Weitzenfeld's [29] approach is most illuminating, which presents predictive analogy as a deductive process that assumes the premise that the given similarities between the source and the target determine the inferred similarities.

In order to realize the full implications of Weitzenfeld's approach, it would be useful to contrast a theory-based inference with an inference from predictive analogy. A theory-based inference is logically deduced from a theory. For instance, from Newton's laws of motion, one might infer that when a force of 100 dynes is applied to a body of mass 20 grams that is moving in a certain direction at a constant velocity of 15 cms per second, and the force is applied in the direction that is opposite to the direction in which the body is traveling, then the body will come to rest in three seconds. Notice that even though such an inference is logically deduced from a theory, it does not automatically make it correct in the real world. Theories are essentially logico-deductive networks of concepts that are constructed by people in order to understand, explain and predict changes in the environment. However, the environment has its own autonomy, and is not bound by any of our theories. Even a cursory examination of the prehistory of any scientific theory or invention attests to this fact. (See, for instance, [14].) The autonomy of the environment is even more blatantly obvious when we consider theories in social sciences such as economics and psychology, which often make predictions that turn out to be incorrect.

In spite of the fact that a theory-based inference may turn out to be incorrect, it is quite meaningful to consider whether it is justified or not; in fact, such considerations are crucial in determining our course of actions such as the design and construction of an airplane or the economic policies of a government. A theory-based inference, however, inherits its justification from the theory itself. So the process essentially boils down to figuring out how much justification we attach to the theory. There is no simple way to determine it, but at least philosophers of science have suggested a number of criteria that can be taken into account [23, 24] such as the attempts that have been made to refute the theory, the number of confirming instances of the theory, and so on. This process is inevitably laborious; it may take many years to feel confident about a theory and it may involve many researchers.

Predictive analogy, on the other hand, shortcuts this laborious justification process of theory-based inferences. All you need is an example that is similar to the given target situation, and you are home! By claiming predictive analogy itself to be a justified process, any need to further justify an inference derived from it is easily dispensed with. (I must emphasize here that I am not talking about operationally verifying the inference in the environment, which is something to which a theory-based inference must eventually be subjected also, for it is not infallible. I am talking about the confidence one puts in the inference before operationally testing it in the environment.) Notice that syntactic criteria such as 'systematicity' [6] do not really provide anything even remotely close to justification, for justification is essentially a semantic notion. To appreciate this point, imagine how ridiculous the systematicity principle would look like in the context of theory-based inferences: it would basically be saying that if a theory makes use of relations, rather than attributes, and higher-order relations at that, then an inference derived from it is justified. Surely, any self-respecting scientist would not put her faith in such superficial properties of a theory, for semantic factors such as the results of the experimental attempts at verifying or refuting the theory far outweigh any syntactic consideration.

In Weitzenfeld's approach, an inference from predictive analogy is seen essentially as a theory-based inference. The idea here is that predictive analogy assumes a second-order generalization as a premise. The difference between a first-order generalization and a second-order generalization is that whereas a first-order generalization links first-order variables (as in "if an automobile is of the year 1990, is made by Ford, is model Taurus, and has 30,000 miles on it, then it will cost approximately $8,000"), which makes the source superfluous in making an inference about the target, a second-order generalization links second-order variables (as in "if two automobiles have the same make, the same model, were made in the same year, and were driven approximately the same distance, then they cost approximately the same"), which requires a source in order that the second-order variables of the generalization can be given a value. Moreover, in Weitzenfeld's account, the justification for an argument from predictive analogy comes from the assumed second-order generalization, which is a theory-based inference. That is, in determining whether an inference from predictive analogy is justified or not, one must determine whether there is a justified theory which supports the second-order generalization underlying the predictive analogy.

Weitzenfeld's account contains two key insights. One is that if an inference from predictive analogy is based *only on already-perceived similarities* between the source and target situations, then there is absolutely no justification for it; it is quite irrelevant whether or not the already-perceived similarities satisfy some syntactic criteria such as systematicity. However compelling such an inference may seem, the compellingness is really a result of implicitly assuming that an argument from predictive analogy is always justified, an assumption that is easily refuted by the examples presented above. It is this implicit but false assumption that makes an argument from predictive analogy cast a spell that is exploited in various abuses of analogy. Certain similarities are pointed out between the source and target situations as a justification for reaching an erroneous conclusion about the target situation—a technique all too often employed in propaganda and political rhetoric. It is this spell which undermines the educational and explanatory usage of analogy and its cousin, metaphor [21]. Once the spell is broken, we realize that an argument that is based only on some already-perceived similarities between the source and target situations, and nothing else, is utterly un-justified. We learn to exercise extreme caution in trusting an argument based solely on some already-perceived similarities. Every such argument is a potential snare. One must find some other piece of knowledge, some other theory, some other fact—besides the already-perceived similarities between the source and target situations—that jus-tifies the argument from predictive analogy. And if no such justification can be found, the so called argument from analogy ought to be discarded.

The second insight of Weitzenfeld is that the justification of an inference from predictive analogy lies in how far the second-order generalization that is assumed in the predictive analogy is justified from the background knowledge. This, however, introduces a semantic component to predictive analogy, because the justification to predictive analogy comes from the background 'knowledge', and not from some syntactic properties of the representations. For instance, in the example of inferring the cost of an automobile from the cost of a similar automobile, it is the background knowledge that automobiles of the same make and model cost approximately the same in any given year, and that they depreciate at roughly the same rate with years and mileage, that makes the inference justified.

I must emphasize that I am talking about justification in a psychological sense here. Given the autonomy of the external world, one's background knowledge is fallible, and, therefore, there is no guarantee, even in a probabilistic sense, that a justified inference will turn out to be correct. The psychological nature of this justification can be better appreciated by emphasizing its subjectivity. Different people have different conceptual systems, with different types of causal links and different ways of giving ontologies to the world by instantiating these concepts. Yet, all these conceptual systems can quite reasonably be considered background 'knowledge'. For instance, to a believer in astrology, there is a causal relationship between the positions of the stars and the planets in the sky and certain events taking place on Earth. This relationship might well be coherent with the actual experiences of such a person. To her, the generalization that two people, if they were born when the planet Mars was in the same position, would have certain character traits in common would be perfectly justified. Yet to a non-believer in astrology, this is about as justified as saying that two cars of the same make, model, and year are of the same color.

Taken in this sense, predictive analogy can be more fruitfully studied along with its justification. For instance, we might find out what it is that makes unjustified inferences psychologically compelling to people. Is it that they subconsciously, as in the phenomenon of apparent motion [19], fill in the requisite second-order generalization needed to make the inference from predictive analogy justified? Or is it that they have some background knowledge that is being made overt by the inference from predictive analogy? Focusing on issues such as these is bound to increase our understanding of predictive analogy, prepare us better to counter the negative role it plays in cognition, and heighten our awareness of its potential abuses so that we are less vulnerable to it.

Acknowledgments: The work described in this paper was supported in part by the National Science Foundation under grant No. IRI-9105806. I am grateful to Professor Doug Hofstadter for his painstakingly thorough reading of an earlier draft of this article, and to Scott O'Hara for his comments on the final draft.

References

1. Allwood C.M. and Eliasson M., 1987, "Analogy and Other Sources of Difficulty in Novices' Very First Text-Editing," *International Journal of Man-Machine Studies* *27*, pp. 1–22.

2. Andersen M., 1967, "An Impression," in S. Rozental (ed.) *Niels Bohr: His life and work as seen by his friends and colleagues,* North-Holland, Amsterdam, The Netherlands, pp. 321–324.

3. Clement C.A. and Gentner D., 1991, "Systematicity as a Selectional Constraint in Analogical Mapping," *Cognitive Science 15*, pp. 89–132.

4. Feynman R., 1986, "Personal Observations on the Reliability of the Shuttle" by Richard Feynman, Appendix F to the *Report to the President by the Presidential Commission on the Space Shuttle Challenger Accident*, Washington D.C. (1986); reprinted in *What do you care what other people think?* by Richard Feynman, W.W. Norton and Co. (1988), New York, pp. 220–237.

5. Galbraith J.K., 1991, "Recession: Parallels With the 30s," *The Boston Globe*, December 17, 1991, p. 23.

6. Gentner D., 1983, "Structure-Mapping: A Theoretical Framework for Analogy," *Cognitive Science 7*, pp. 155–170.

7. Gentner D., 1989, "The Mechanisms of Analogical Learning," in S. Vosniadou and A. Ortony (eds.) *Similarity and Analogical Reasoning*, Cambridge University Press, London, U.K., pp. 199–241.

8. Gentner D. and Jeziorski M., 1989, "Historical Shifts in the Use of Analogy in Science," in B. Gholson *et al.* (eds.) *The Psychology of Science: Contributions to Metascience*, Cambridge University Press, London, U.K,, pp. 296–325.

9. Gick M.L. and Holyoak K.J., 1980, "Analogical Problem Solving," *Cognitive Psychology 12*, pp. 306–355.

10. Gick M.L. and Holyoak K.J., 1983, "Schema Induction and Analogical Transfer," *Cognitive Psychology 15*, pp. 1–38.

11. Gordon W.J.J., 1961, *Synectics: The Development of Creative Capacity*, Harper and Row, New York, NY.

12. Gruber H.E., 1978, "Darwin's 'Tree of Nature' and Other Images of Wide Scope," in J. Wechsler (ed.) *On Aesthetics in Science*, MIT Press (1978), Cambridge, Mass., pp. 121–40.

13. Halasz F. and Moran T.P., 1982, "Analogies Considered Harmful," *ACM Proc. of Human Factors in Computer Systems*, pp. 383–386.

14. Hart C., 1985, *The Prehistory of Flight*, University of California Press, Berkeley, Calif.

15. Indurkhya B., 1989, "Modes of Analogy," in K. P. Jantke (ed.) *Analogical and Inductive Inference*, Lecture Notes in Artificial Intelligence 397, Springer-Verlag (1989), Berlin, GDR, pp. 217–230.

16. Indurkhya B., 1990, "On the Role of Interpretive Analogy in Learning," *Proceedings of the First International Workshop on Algorithmic Learning Theory*, Japanese Society for Artificial Intelligence, Tokyo, Japan, pp. 174–189; reprinted in *New Generation Computing 8*, (1991), pp. 385–402.

17. Indurkhya B., 1992, *Metaphor and Cognition: An Interactionist Approach*, Kluwer Academic Publishers, Dordrecht, The Netherlands.

18. Koestler A., 1964, *The Act of Creation*, Hutchinsons of London; 2nd Danube ed., 1976.

19. Kolers P.A., 1972, *Aspects of Motion Perception*, Pergamon Press, Oxford, U.K.

20. Miller A.I., 1978, "Visualization Lost and Regained: The Genesis of the Quantum Theory in the Period 1913–27," in J. Wechsler (ed.) *On Aesthetics in Science*, MIT Press (1978), Cambridge, Mass., pp. 73–102.

21. Miller R.M., 1976, "The Dubious Case for Metaphors in Educational Writing," *Educational Theory 26*, (Spring 1976), pp. 174–181.

22. Newman J.R., 1956, *The World of Mathematics*, Volume 2, Simon and Schuster, New York.

23. Popper K.R., 1959, *The Logic of Scientific Discovery*, Hutchinson, London.

24. Popper K.R., 1962, *Conjectures and Refutations: The Growth of Scientific Knowledge*, Basic Books, New York; 2nd ed. 1965; Harper and Row: 1968.

25. Robbins J., 1991, "Echoes of 1939 on Capitol Hill," *Wall Street Journal*, January 14, 1991, p. A12.

26. Schön D.A., 1963, *Displacement of Concepts*, Humanities Press, New York, NY.

27. Shurkin J., 1984, *Engines of the Mind: A History of the Computer*, W.W. Norton and Co., New York, NY.

28. Stillman J.M., 1924, *The Story of Early Chemistry*, D. Appleton and Company, New York, NY; republished as *The Story of Alchemy and Early Chemistry*, Dover Publications (1960), New York, NY.

29. Weitzenfeld J.S., 1984, "Valid Reasoning by Analogy," *Philosophy of Science 51*, pp. 137–149.

30. Weizenbaum J., 1976, *Computer Power and Human Reason: From Judgment to Calculation*, W.H. Freeman and Company, New York, NY.

Learning A Class of Regular Expressions via Restricted Subset Queries

Efim Kinber

Institute of Mathematics and Computer Science,
University of Latvia
Rainis blvd., 29, Riga, Latvia 226250
kinber@lumii.lat.su

Abstract

A wide class of regular expressions non-representable as unions of "smaller" expressions is shown to be polynomial-time learnable via restricted subset queries from arbitrary representative examples "reflecting" the loop structure and a way the input example is obtained from the unknown expression. The corresponding subclass of regular expressions of loop depth at most 1 is shown to be learnable from representative examples via membership queries. A wide class of expressions with loops A^+ of arbitrary loop depth is shown to be learnable via restricted subset queries from arbitrary examples.

1 Introduction

Trying to learn programs from examples of their behavior, one comes across an important problem of loop identification. If, learning programs, we concentrate primarily on the loop structure identification (the place of a loop in the program, the ordering of loops, etc.) then we deal actually with purely syntactical synthesis of programs from examples (semantics is not taken into account). Various models of syntactical program synthesis were developed in [1,2,3]. All these models rely on the presence of counters in loops; respectively, learning methods are based on the identification of counting (primarily, arithmetical progressions) in input examples. Counting arguments proved to be quite powerful for syntactical program synthesis. However, counting apparently can be treated as an element of the program semantics. So, whenever one is interested in purely syntactical learning of the loop structure from examples, the most appropriate simple model to represent combinations of loops in a program seems to be the class of regular expressions. Consequently, we come across the problem of (syntactical) polynomial-time learning regular languages using the regular expressions as the hypotheses space; the problem that is interesting itself.

Learning regular languages has attracted much attention in the recent years. However, unlike to regular expressions and NFAs (generating devices), DFAs are usually used as the hypotheses space for learning (see survey [4], covering basic developments in this area). True, some negative results follow from the corresponding results for DFAs. For example, no poly-time algorithm can be guaranteed to find a consistent regular expression of size opt^k, where opt^k is the size of a smallest regular expression consistent with the sample ([5]).

However, to our knowledge, until recently no positive results are obtained for learning regular expressions.

In this paper we use a model of deterministic learning in a dialogue with a "teacher" (formally, an oracle). This approach was formally developed and applied for learning regular languages by D.Angluin ([6,7,8]). For example, if DFAs are used as the hypotheses space then regular languages are learnable via equivalence and membership queries. We use so-called restricted subset queries to learn regular expressions. The oracle of this kind is queried whether the language defined by a current hypothesis is a subset of the language to be learned. Our goal is to learn a regular expression containing no unions ($\cup$) from one example (an arbitrary one, if possible). However, expressions of this kind are hardly learnable from arbitrary examples. For instance, the example a of the language representable by the expression b^*c^*a tells nothing about the loops b^* and c^*. It is quite clear that an input example ought to "reflect" somehow the full structure of the target expression. In particular, it obviously has to contain values ("unfoldments") of all loops occurring in the expression. Moreover, an example has to represent the ordering of loops in the target expression. For instance, the expression $(a^*b^*c^*d)^*$ hardly can be learned from the example $cdbdad$; on the other hand, $aabcd$ seems to contain enough information to learn $(a^*b^*c^*d)^*$(of course, using an oracle). However, no example of the latter kind exists for expressions like $(ab^*)^*b^*$: to "reflect" just the loop b^*, one should drop the loop $(ab^*)^*$. The expression $(ab^*)^*b^*$ is, in fact, the union of two distinct "proper subexpressions":

$$(ab^*)^*b^* \equiv (ab^*)^* \cup b^*.$$

Thus, we come to the class of indecomposable expressions: an expression is indecomposable if it is not contained in the union of its proper subexpressions. For example, the expressions $(a^*b^*c)^*, (ab^*)^*$ and b^*a^*a are indecomposable. Consequently, we require a sample to be representative for an expression R if it belongs to no proper subexpression of R; representative samples clearly exist for indecomposable expressions. For instance, each word $a^kb^mc^nd$ for arbitrary $k, m, n \geq 1$ is a representative example for the expression $(a^*b^*c^*d)^*$. On the other hand, the example $acbcd$ is not representative for this expression, as it belongs to the "proper subexpression" $((a^*d)^*(b^*c^*d)^*)^*$. Note that the examples $a^kb^mc^nd$ are representative for the expressions $a^*b^mc^nd, a^*ab^mc^nd, a^*b^*c^nd$ as well; to choose the correct one, one has to query the oracle.

However, the above requirement seems to be not enough to ensure the correct synthesis of the unknown expression. To get a deeper insight, let us consider the expression

$$R = (cbbcbbb)^*(cbb)^*c^*b(cbbcbbbcbbc)^*b^*(bbbbcbbcbbbcb)^*$$

and its example

$$cbbcbbbcbbcbcbbcbbbcbbcbbbbbcbbcbbbcb.$$

This example is contained in no proper subexpression of the given expression R. On the other hand, it belongs to the language

$$L(cbbcbbbcbbcb^* cbbcbbbcbbcbbbbbcbbcbbbcb),$$

which turns out to be a sublanguage of $L(R)$. There is no way to obtain the latter expression by a process of unfolding loops in R. Thus, if a learning algorithm synthesizes the "incorrect" loop b^* in

$$cbbcbbbcbbcb^* cbbcbbbcbbcbbbbbcbbcbbbcb,$$

it hardly will be able "to get rid" of this loop in order to find R or any its subexpression (in poly-time). This consideration forces us to require a representative example to "reflect" a way it could be obtained from the unknown expression. For instance, the example

$$cbbcbbbcbbcbcbbcbbbcbbccbbcbbbcbbcbbbbbcbbcbbbcb$$

of R (the loop $(cbbcbbbcbbc)^*$ is unfolded twice) gives a chance to avoid "incorrect" loops like b^* just after $cbbcbbbcbbc$, as

$$L(cbbcbbbcbbcb^* cbbcbbbcbbccbbcbbbcbbcbbbbbcbbcbbbcb)$$

is not a sublanguage of $L(R)$). Thus, we require a representative example to "reflect" (implicitly) an according derivation from the unknown expression. A similar idea is accomplished in [9] for learning context-free languages via so-called structural membership and equivalence queries; however, in [9] derivations are presented in input examples in a much more explicit way.

In [8] D.Angluin proposed a method of learning DFAs via membership queries based on a different approach to representativeness: automata are learned from *state representatives* that represent ways from each "live" state to the accepting state.

In this paper we give a polynomial-time algorithm learning indecomposable regular expressions of loop depth at most 2 from arbitrary representative examples via restricted subset queries. We also show the subclass of indecomposable expressions of loop depth 1 to be learnable from representative examples via membership queries.

An interesting problem is to find out reasonable classes of regular expressions learnable from arbitrary examples. In this paper we show a wide class of expressions containing loops A^+ (instead of A^*) to be learnable from arbitrary examples via restricted subset queries.

2 Notation and Definitions

Let F denote a finite alphabet, F^* denote the set of all words (strings) over F (including the empty word λ). For any $w \in F^* w^k$ denote the concatenation of k words w, $| w |$ stands for the length (the number of symbols) of the word w. Any language is a subset in F^* for some F. Later on we consider only regular languages. Consequently, we consider alphabets F containing no symbols $(,)$, * and $\cup$.

Let RE denote the class of all regular expressions without unions over some fixed alphabet F. For an arbitrary $R \in RE$, let $L(R)$ denote the corresponding regular language. Similarly, given a regular language, $R(L)$ denote a regular expression R such that $L = L(R)$. $Pr(R)$ stands for the word obtained from R dropping all brackets and symbols *.

Definition 2.1 $R \in RE$ is said to be a *proper subexpression* of $R \in RE$ if $L(R') \subset L(R)$ and, to obtain R,
(1) at least one loop C^* is replaced by λ,
or
(2) at least one loop C^* is replaced by $(C_1^* C_2^* \ldots C_r^*)^*$, where each C_i is obtained from C by dropping at least one loop.
For example, $(ab^*)^*, b^*, (ab)^*$ are proper subexpressions of $(ab^*)^* b^*$; $((a^* c)^* (b^* c)^*)^*$ is a proper subexpression of $(a^* b^* c)^*$ (the rule (2) is applied to obtain it from $(a^* b^* c)^*$).

Definition 2.2. If C^* is of loop depth 1 then any word in $L(C^*)$ is called a *partial unfoldment* of C^*.

Definition 2.3. If C^* is of loop depth 2 then any word $C_1 C_2 \ldots C_m$ is called a *partial unfoldment* of C^* if each C_i is obtained from C or C^* by replacement some subloops to their partial unfoldments.

For instance, $aab^*(a^*bbc)^*$ is a partial unfoldment of $(a^*b^*c)^*$.

Definition 2.4. Let $R \in RE$ be any expression of loop depth at most 2. Any R' obtained from R by replacement some loops in R to their partial unfoldments is called a *partial unfoldment* of R.

Definition 2.5. Let $v \in L(R)$ for $R \in RE$. The expression v' obtained by replacement any subword u in v to the loop u^* is called a *reduction* of R if $L(v')$ is a subset of $L(R)$ and v' is not a partial unfoldment of R.

The word
$$cbbcbbbcbbcb^*\, cbbcbbbcbbcbbbbbcbbcbbbbcb$$
is a reduction of
$$R = (cbbcbbb)^*(cbb)^*c^*b(cbbcbbbcbbc)^*b^*(bbbbcbbcbbbcb)^*,$$
as it defines a sublanguage of $L(R)$, but is not a partial unfoldment of R.

Definition 2.6. An expression $R \in RE$ is called *indecomposable* if it is not contained in the union of $L(R')$ for proper subexpressions and reductions R' of R.

For example, $(ab^*)^*b^*$ is decomposable, $((ab^*)^*b^* \equiv (ab^*) \cup b^*)$, whereas ab^* and b^* are indecomposable.

Definition 2.7. Let $R \in RE$. A word $v \in L(R)$ is called a *representative* example of R if $v \notin L(R')$ for every proper subexpression and reduction R' of R.

As it easily follows from the definition of indecomposable expressions, representative examples do exist for them. For instance, $aababbbcbbc$ is a representative example for $R = (ab^*)^*(b^*c)^*$. On the other hand, $abbc$ is not representative for R, since it can be represented by a proper subexpression $(ab^*)^*c^*$. Furthermore, $aabbc$ is representative for $(a^*b^*c)^*$, whereas $bcac$ is not representative, as $bcac \in L(R')$ for a proper subexpression $R' = ((b^*c)^*(a^*c)^*)^*$.

Let IREk denote the class of indecomposable expressions of loop depth at most k.

Definition 2.8. An expression $R \in \text{IRE2}$ is said to be *canonical* if no transformation $CC^* \Rightarrow C^*C$ is applicable to it.

Now, let CRE$^+$ (*convex regular expressions*) denote the class of regular expressions in RE containing loops A^+ instead of A^*. We call an expression $R \in \text{CRE}^+$ *simple* if it does not contain loops $(A^k)^+$ for $k > 1$. For example, the expression $(aaa)^+(aaaaa)^+$ is not simple, whereas $(ba)^+a^+a$ is simple. Let SCRE$^+$ denote the class of all simple expressions in CRE$^+$. Similarly, we can define simple regular expressions $R \in RE$.

Definition 2.9. An expression $R \in \text{CRE}^+$ is said to be *canonical* if no transformation $CC^+ \Rightarrow C^+C$ is applicable to it and no loop $(A)^+$ can be replaced by A without violating equivalence.

For example, expressions $(((a^+)^+a^+)^+a^+)^+$ and aaa^+ are not canonical. The both expressions have the equivalent canonical expression a^+aa.

Let INIT[A] denote the set of all initial subwords of a word A. FIN[A] stands, respectively, for the set of all tails of the word A.

3 Learning Algorithm for IRE2: Example Run

First we define the following auxiliary transformation over regular expressions. For any expression P of loop depth at most 2, if P is a concatenation of loops

$$(C_1^* C_2^* ... C_i^*)^* (C_{i+1}^* C_{i+2}^* ... C_m^*)^*$$

then $TR(P)$ is $C_{j_1}^* C_{j_2}^* ... C_{j_s}^*$ for all pairwise distinct loops $C_{j_r}^*$ in $\{C_1^*, C_2^*, ..., C_m^*\}$, and $TR(P) = P$, otherwise.

Given a representative example v, our learning algorithm synthesizes loops of increasing length from left to right. Coming across any word α in the current expression R, it computes $TR(\alpha)$. If $TR(\alpha)$ is of the current length, it replaces α in P by $(TR(\alpha))^*$ and queries the oracle. If the answer is positive, it replaces α in R by $(TR(\alpha))^*$ and cuts off all possible δ around $TR^{-1}(\alpha)$ obtained from subwords w in v belonging to $L((TR(\alpha))^*)$. To demonstrate the basic ideas of the learning algorithm, we consider its run on the representative example

$$v = bbbbbcaabc$$

of the expression $bb(a^*b^*c)^*$.

Let L_* denote the target language.

The learning algorithm first synthesizes all loops of the length 1. In accordance with the strategy, it makes the first replacement $\alpha \to \alpha^*$ for the first symbol in v, getting the intermediate expression

$$b^* bbbbcaabc.$$

Now, having recognized that the right neighbour bb of the given b in v is in $L(b^*)$ and it can be cut off from v together with the first b (the oracle replies YES to the query

$$L(b^* bbbbcaabc) \subseteq L_*?),$$

the loop b^* "eats" the subword bb. Now the algorithm tries to replace the leftmost c by the loop c^*:

$$L(b^* bbc^* aabc) \subseteq L_*?$$

As the replay is negative, it moves to the next a. Using this strategy, the algorithm synthesizes all loops of the length 1 and obtains the expression

$$b^* bbca^* b^* c.$$

Then it synthesizes the only loop $(b^*c)^*$ of the length 2, moving the loop b^* to the right as far as possible (using replacements $\alpha^*\alpha \Rightarrow \alpha\alpha^*$) in order to insert it into the loop to be synthesized:

$$bb(b^*c)^* a^* b^* c.$$

All further attempts to synthesize loops of the length 2 fail, and the algorithm begins to synthesize loops of the length 3. After some unsuccessful attempts it comes across the subword $TR(\alpha) = a^*b^*c$ of the length 3. As $L((a^*b^*c)^*) \subseteq L_*$, the algorithm replaces α by the loop $(a^*b^*c)^*$. Further, since the subword bbc the left neighbour $(b^*c)^*$ is obtained from is in $L(\alpha^*)$, the loop α^* "eats" $(b^*c)^*$. Finally, we come to the target expression $bb(a^*b^*c)^*$. Note that the example $bbacabc$ of the above expression is not representative, as it belongs to a reduction

$$bbac^* abc$$

of the given expression.

4 Learning Algorithm for IRE2: Formal Definition

Theorem 4.1. There exists an algorithm that, for each $R \in$ IRE2, given any representative example $v \in L(R)$, finds out $R'(L)$ in time $O(|v|^9)$(including $O(|v|^3)$ queries).

Without loss of generality, we can assume that the target expression is canonical.

Let we are given an arbitrary representative example $v = a_1 a_2 \ldots a_n$ of some expression in IRE2. The algorithm, transforming v into the target expression, defines also an auxiliary function ϕ with values in the set
$$\{w \mid w \text{ is a subword in } v\}$$
defined on all subwords $P \in RE$ in the current expression that are not contained in loops. This function points out the subword w in v the subword $\phi^{-1}(w)$ is obtained from.

First we define the auxiliary procedure $\text{SINT}(R, P, \phi)$ that tests whether the loop P^* can replace P in R, makes this replacement if the test is successful, and indicates the failure, otherwise. It itself contains the subprocedure TESTLOOP defined below. Given $T \in RE$, let $l(T)$ denote $|\text{Pr}(T)|$.

$SINT(P, R, \phi)$:
begin

Let $P = P_1 P P_2; SintI := 0$;
If $P_1 = S\beta^* \beta^m$ and $P = \beta P'$ then $P := \beta^* P'$ and $P_1 := S\beta^{m+1}$;
$\qquad\qquad\qquad\qquad\qquad\qquad\qquad\qquad\qquad$ (try loop $(\beta^* P')^*$)
If $l(TR(P)) = length$ then execute $\text{TESTLOOP}(P, R)$;
If $SintI = 0$ and $P = \beta^* P'$ and $P_1 = S\beta$ then
begin $\qquad\qquad\qquad\qquad\qquad\qquad\qquad\qquad\qquad$ (try loop $(\beta P')^*$)
$P_1 := S\beta^*; P := \beta P'$;
If $l(TR(P)) = length$ then execute $\text{TESTLOOP}(P, R)$;
end;
If $SintI = 0, P = P'\beta^*$ and $P_2 = \beta S$ then

$\qquad$ **begin** $\qquad\qquad\qquad\qquad\qquad\qquad\qquad\qquad$ (try loop $(P'\beta)^*$)
$\qquad P_2 := \beta^* S; P := P'\beta$;
$\qquad$ If $l(TR(P)) = length$ then execute $\text{TESTLOOP}(P, R)$
$\qquad$ **end**;
$\qquad$ If $SintI = 1$ then
$\qquad$ **begin**
$\qquad$ Let $P := TR(P)$;
$\qquad$ Find out the longest concatenation of
$\qquad$ loops $T \in RE$ such that $P_1 = ST$
$\qquad$ (applying, if necessary transformation
$\qquad$ $C^* C \Rightarrow CC^* a$ finite number of times),

$$\phi(T) \in L(P^*) \text{ and } L(SP^* P_2) \subseteq L_*.$$

Set $P_1 := S$ and $\phi(P^*) := \phi(TP^*)$; $\qquad$ (P^* ''eats'' its left
$\qquad\qquad\qquad\qquad\qquad\qquad\qquad\qquad\qquad\qquad$ neighbour generated by
$\qquad\qquad\qquad\qquad\qquad\qquad\qquad\qquad\qquad\qquad$ a subword in $L(P^*)$)
Find out the longest $T \in RE$ such that $P_2 = TS$,

$$\phi(T) \in L(P^*) \text{ and } L(P_1 P^* S) \subseteq L_*;$$

Set $P_2 := S$ and $\phi(P^*) := \phi(P^*T)$;   (P^* "eats" its right neighbour generated by a subword in $L(P^*)$)

Replace $\phi^{-1}(P^*)$ in R by P^*
end
end.

TESTLOOP(P, R):
begin
   Set $P := TR(P)$;

$$\text{If } L(P_1 P^* P_2) \subseteq L_* \text{ then SintI} := 1$$

end.

Now we define the main procedure.
   PROC(v):
begin
$R := v$; $length := 0$; $\phi(a) := a$ for each symbol a in v;
while $length \leq n$ do
begin
$length := length+1$; $i := 0$; while $i \leq l(R)$ do

   begin
   $i := i + 1$;   (the left border of possible loop)
   $r := 0$;
   while $i + r \leq l(R)$)do
      begin
      until (P is of loop depth at most 1 or P is a
      concatenation of two loops that are concatenations
      of loops, i=the number of the first symbol of $Pr(P)$
      for $P \in RE$ and $i + r$=the number of the last symbol of $Pr(P)$) do
      $r := r + 1$;
      $SINT(P, R, \phi)$;
      If SintI=1 then $r := l(R) + 1$ and $i :=$ the number
      of the last symbol of $Pr(P^*)$ for the loop P^* been synthesized
      else $r := r + 1$
      end;
   end
end
end.

The running time of testing $w \in L(P)$ for any $P \in RE$ and $w \in F^*$ is $O(|\ w\ |^3)$. To test the existence of any loop and to "eat" neighbours the algorithm uses a linear number of queries. The total number of loops to be synthesized is at most quadratic. Therefore, the total running time can be bounded by $O(|\ v\ |^9)$, including $O(|\ v\ |^3)$ queries.

In fact, any reasonable algorithm complying the principle "miss no loop" would suffice to learn expressions in the given class.

Quite simple arguments show that at least a linear number of queries is necessary to learn the class IRE2 from representative examples. The general problem of bounds for the number of queries for learning expressions in IRE2 from representative examples remains open.

5 Correctness

Let R be any expression in IRE2. Let us consider the following generating process for an arbitrary $v \in L(R)$: on each step some loop C^* is to be replaced by some its partial unfoldment; the final expression has to be v. Such a process is called an *unfolding process*, and each intermediate expression is called an *unfoldment* of R. The word v is called a *final unfoldment* of R. At least one unfolding process clearly exists for every word $v \in L(R)$.

Definition 5.1.
(1) any word C^k for $k > 0$ for a loop C^* of depth 1 is called
its *final full unfoldment*;
(2) for each loop C^* of depth 2,

(2a) if $C^* = (C_1^* C_2^* \ldots C_r^*)^*$ then any concatenation of words C_i^k for $k > 0$ containing at least one C_i^k for each $i \in \{1, 2, \ldots r\}$ is called a *final full unfoldment* of C^*;

(2b) else, a word obtained from C replacing each subloop B^* by some word B^k for $k > 0$ is called a *final full unfoldment* of C^*.

For example, $aabbc$ is a final full unfoldment of $C = (a^* b^* c)^*$, whereas $acbc$, being a final unfoldment of C, is not a final full unfoldment. The aim of the final full unfoldment is to represent fully the structure of the loop C.

Let C^* be an expression in IRE2, and $C_1, C_2, \ldots, C_r$ be all proper subexpressions of C.

Lemma 5.1. A word $v \in L$ is a final full unfoldment of C^* iff

$$v \notin L(C_1^* C_2^* \ldots C_r^*)^*.$$

Proof. The statement immediately follows from the definitions of proper subexpressions, final full unfoldments and from the indecomposability of C^*: dropping any loop yields a "smaller" language.

Now we prove the lemma the correctness proof is based on.

Let $R \in$ IRE2 and $v \in L(R)$. Having fixed a process Γ unfolding R into v, one can clearly define, for each loop C^* in R, the set $M(\Gamma, R)$ of all subwords in v that are unfoldments of C^*.

Lemma 5.2. Let v be a representative example of R. For every process Γ unfolding R into v and for every loop C in R the set $M(\Gamma, C)$ contains a final full unfoldment of C.

Proof. Suppose $M(\Gamma, C)$ contains no final full unfoldment of C for some C and Γ. Then all $w \in M(\Gamma, C)$ are in various $L(C_1^* C_2^* \ldots C_r^*)^*$, where $C_1, C_2, \ldots, C_r$ are proper subexpressions of C. Thus, v is not representative. Q.E.D.

Now we will define a specific unfolding process of an $R \in IRE2$ called *canonical*. Canonical unfoldments are, in fact, expressions the learning algorithm outputs on intermediate stages of the synthesis.

Definition 5.2. Let $C^* \in$ IRE2.

(1) If C^* is of loop depth 1 then any word C^k is called its *canonical unfoldment*;

(2) if C in C^* is a concatenation of loops then any expression

$$A_1 A_2 \ldots A_m B_1 B_2 A_{m+1} \ldots A_k$$

is called a *canonical unfoldment* of C^* if B_1 and B_2 are pairwise distinct proper subexpressions of C^*, $B_1 B_2$ contains all subloops of C^* and $A_1, A_2, ..., A_k$ are proper subexpressions of C^* such that each A_i is a proper subexpression of neither A_{i-1}, nor A_{i+1};

(3) if C in C^* of loop depth 2 is not a concatenation of loops then any expression

$$D = A_1 C A_2 C \ldots A_m C A_{m+1}$$

is called a *canonical unfoldment* of C^* if each $A_i, 1 \leq i \leq m$, is a concatenation $C_1^* C_2^* \ldots C_r^*$, where all C_j are proper subexpressions of C^*, and, for each i C_i is a proper subexpression of neither C_{i-1}, nor C_{i+1}.

For example, $(b^* c)^* (a^* cd^*)$ is a canonical unfoldment of $(a^* b^* cd^*)^*$. $(b^* c^*)^* (a^* c^*)^*$ is a canonical unfoldment of $(a^* b^* c^*)^*$.

Definition 5.3. An unfolding process Γ is called *canonical* if, on each step, just the rightmost loop of the maximal length is replaced by its canonical unfoldment , and then the expression is transformed to the equivalent canonical form.

Definition 5.4. Each intermediate expression D in a canonical unfolding process Γ of an expression R is called a *canonical unfoldment of R with respect to Γ*.

Not every example v of $P \in$ IRE2 can be obtained by a canonical unfolding process. For instance, no canonical unfolding process can be guaranteed for an example $abab$ of $(a^* c^* b)^* (a^* d^* b)^*$. However, as it follows from Lemma 5.2, canonical unfolding processes do exist for representative examples; we leave details to the reader.

It is worth to note that, in general, many different canonical unfolding processes may generate an example. For instance, the subword abc in the example

$$aabcabcabcc$$

of the expression $(a^* bc)^* (abc^*)^*$ can be a value either of $(a^* bc)^*$, or $(abc^*)^*$. Our learning algorithm replaces a in abc by a^* (the leftmost possible loop of the length 1), so choosing $(a^* bc)^*$ to generate abc.

One obviously can represent any canonical unfolding process Γ as the sequence

(5.1) $$R_0 \Rightarrow R_1 \Rightarrow R_2 \Rightarrow \ldots \Rightarrow v,$$

where each R_i is obtained from R_{i-1} unfolding the rightmost loop of the maximal length in R_{i-1}.

Lemma 5.3. If the learning algorithm has been synthesized an intermediate expression R_s in the representation (5.1) of some canonical process Γ unfolding the target expression R_0, and for each outer loop C^* in R_s

$$M(\Gamma, C^*) = \{\phi(C^*)\}$$

then it outputs an intermediate canonical expression R' via some canonical unfolding process Γ', and for each outer loop C^* in R'

$$M(\Gamma', C^*) = \{\phi(C^*)\}.$$

Sketch of proof. Let $R(= R_s$ for some canonical $\Gamma)$ be a current expression. We choose the canonical unfolding process Γ that, to obtain R, replaces the leftmost loop C^* of the given *length* by a canonical unfoldment B. Our goal is to prove that the algorithm transforms R replacing just B by the loop C^*.

If the algorithm comes across $TR^{-1}(C^*)$ then it successfully replaces the whole canonical unfoldment of C^* by the corresponding loop. Therefore, we have to prove that the algorithm will not synthesize an illegal loop unless it comes across $TR^{-1}(C^*)$. However, an illegal replacement could happen obviously only if the input example would belong to a reduction of the target expression, and, consequently, would not be representative. Q.E.D.

The correctness of the learning algorithm easily follows from the lemma.

6 Learning Expressions of Loop Depth 1

In this section we show that the membership oracle suffices to learn simple indecomposable regular expressions of loop depth 1 in poly-time.

Theorem 6.1. There exists an algorithm that, for each simple $R \in$IRE1, given a representative example $v \in L(R)$, finds out $R'(L)$ via membership oracle in poly-time (including $O(|v|^3)$queries).

Proof sketch. The corresponding learning algorithm is very similar to that via restricted subset queries. Instead of any replacement $C \Rightarrow C^*$ in a current expression (to query the restricted subset oracle), it queries the membership oracle for each replacement $C \Rightarrow C^k, k = 0, 1, ..:, 2|v| + 1(v$ is the input example). Consider the word obtained by replacement $C \Rightarrow C^k$ for $k = 2|v| + 1$. First, note that C^k cannot be generated by neighbouring loops $(AC^m)^*$ and $(C^r B)^*$, as both m and r are less than k. Thus, since the target expression is simple, C^k can be generated only by a loop C^*. Consequently, positive answers for all above queries justify the replacement $C \Rightarrow C^*$ in the current expression. As the given input example is contained in no reduction of the target expression, the new current expression is an unfoldment via some (canonical) unfolding process.

As the number of queries to synthesize any loop is linear, and the total number of stages is quadratic, the total number of queries is $O(|v|^3)$. An open problem is whether this number of queries can be reduced.

It is very likely that all expressions $R \in RE$ of loop depth at most 1 are indecomposable. However, it is an open problem.

7 Learning from Arbitrary Examples

In this section we show expressions in the class SCRE$^+$ to be learnable from arbitrary input examples.

Theorem 7.1. There is an algorithm via restricted subset queries that, given an arbitrary example v of an expression $R \in$SCRE$^+$, finds out R' equivalent to R in poly-time (including $O(|v|^3)$ queries).

Proof sketch. Without loss of generality, we assume the target expression to be canonical. Given an input example v, the algorithm first finds the shortest word w in the target language (using $O(|v|^2)$ queries). Then, on each stage it synthesizes the shortest leftmost loop, replacing the leftmost subword A of the given length in a current expression by A^+ and querying the oracle. Sometimes there may be need to shift some loops. For instance, given the example

$$abcabcabcabcabcabc$$

of the expression

$$abca(bcabcabc)^+(abc)^+abc,$$

and having synthesized the intermediate expression
$$(abc)^+abcabcabcabcabc,$$
the algorithm must check all three possibilities
$$(abc)^+a(bcabcabc)^+abcabc,$$
$$abca(bc(abc)^+abc)^+abcabc$$

and

$$abca(bcabcabc)^+(abc)^+abc$$

in order to choose the correct one. A different complication arises in cases like

$$(ba^+aa)^+(a^+bc)^+.$$

Having synthesized the intermediate expression

$$(baaa)^+(a^+bc)^+$$

(the loop $(baaa)^+$ is synthesized after the loop $(a^+bc)^+$, as it is longer), the algorithm has to check the occurrence of the leftmost right "neighbour" a^+ in $(baaa)^+$. Similarly, having synthesized an intermediate unfoldment

$$(ba(b^+a^+b^+)^+)^+(ba^+b^+cccc)^+$$

of the expression

$$(ba(b^+a^+b^+)^+)^+((b^+a^+b^+)^+cccc)^+,$$

the algorithm has to try consequently words $b^+a^+b^+$ and $(b^+a^+b^+)^+$ (as the test for $b^+a^+b^+$ succeeds) on the place of ba^+b^+ in $(ba^+b^+cccc)^+$; b^+ and $(b^+a^+b^+)^+$ are the rightmost neighbouring loops to the left from $(ba^+b^+cccc)^+$ in the intermediate unfoldment. In the general case, the learning algorithm, having synthesized a loop $(ABCD...E)^+$, adds (or not) consequently loops $(A^+BCD...E)^+,((A^+B)^+CD...E)^+,(((A^+B)^+C)^+D...E)^+,\ldots$; each loop P^+added in this way is obtained from some left neighbouring loop by shifting to the place of P (without violating equivalence) and omitting some $^+$. The similar procedure has to be performed for the tail of the loop $(ABCD...E)^+$. Thus, the synthesis of each loop requires a linear number of queries.

As the target expression is simple, we are able to avoid distributing loops $(A^k)^+$ for various k among neighbouring outer loops (like in the case

$$(b(aaa)^+(aaaaaaa)^+)^+((aaaa)^+(aaaaaa)^+)^+c)-$$

the problem that looks to be hardly tractable.

The total number of stages is evidently quadratic. Thus, the total number of queries is bounded by $O(|v|^3)$. It can be proved (by induction) that all loops will appear on the correct places, and no loop will be missed.

An open problem is whether the bound $O(|v|^3)$ for the number of queries is tight.

8 Conclusion

Representative examples in our approach do not belong to reductions of regular expressions. This restriction ensures poly-time learning indecomposable expressions from arbitrary examples of this kind by quite natural algorithms. However, in many practical cases slight modifications of these algorithms learn indecomposable expressions from representative examples not satisfying this restriction. For instance, the example $acabc$ of the expression $(a^*b^*c)^*$ suffices to learn the latter expression, being not representative in our setting (as it belongs to the reduction ac^*abc of $(a^*b^*c)^*$). Lifting the restriction, we get representative examples consistent with the only principle "representative examples reflect all loops and their ordering". Besides, this property of representativeness is clearly decidable (it is not clear in our setting). An open problem is to find out reasonable classes of indecomposable regular expressions learnable in poly-time from representative examples of this kind.

Perhaps, the most important point in our approach to representativeness is its method-independence. It would be interesting to apply this approach for learning various classes of languages representable by generating devices. For example, it would be worth to find an appropriate method-independent notion of representativeness for linear grammars.

ACKNOWLEDGEMENTS

The author is very grateful to A.Brazma for many discussions motivated this research. The author thanks also Prof. Starke for a fruitful discussion.

REFERENCES

[1] J.M.Barzdin. Some rules of inductive inference and their use for program synthesis. In: *Information Proc'83*, North-Holland, 1983, 333-338.

[2] A.N.Brazma. Inductive synthesis of dot expressions. *Lecture Notes in Comp. Sci.*, v.502, 1991, 156-212.

[3] E.B.Kinber. Some models of inductive syntactical synthesis from sample computations. *Lecture Notes in Comp. Sci.*, v.502, 1991, 213-252.

[4] L.Pitt. Inductive inference, DFAs, and computational complexity. *Proc. of International Workshop AII'89, Lecture Notes in Comp. Sci.*, v.397, 1989, 18-44.

[5] L.Pitt, M.K.Warmuth. The minimum consistent DFA problem cannot be approximated within any polynomial. *Report NO.UIUCDC−R−89−1499*, Urbana, Illinois, 1989.

[6] D.Angluin. Queries and concept learning. *Machine learning*, 2, 1987, 319-342.

[7] D.Angluin. Learning regular sets from queries and counterexamples. *Information and Computation*, v.75, 2, 1987, 87-106.

[8] D.Angluin. A note on the number of queries needed to identify regular languages. *Information and Computation*, v.51, 1981, 76-87.

[9] Y.Sakakibara. Learning context-free grammars from structural data in polynomial time. *Proc. of the 1988 Workshop on Comp.Learn.Theory*, D.Haussler, L.Pitt eds., Morgan Kaufmann, San Mateo, 1988, 330-344.

A Unifying Approach to Monotonic Language Learning on Informant

Steffen Lange*

TH Leipzig

FB Mathematik und Informatik

PF 66

O–7030 Leipzig

steffen@informatik.th-leipzig.de

Thomas Zeugmann

TH Darmstadt

Institut für Theoretische Informatik

Alexanderstr. 10

W–6100 Darmstadt

zeugmann@iti.informatik.th-darmstadt.de

Abstract

The present paper deals with strong-monotonic, monotonic and weak-monotonic language learning from positive and negative examples. The three notions of monotonicity reflect different formalizations of the requirement that the learner has to produce always better and better generalizations when fed more and more data on the concept to be learnt.

We characterize strong-monotonic, monotonic, weak-monotonic and finite language learning from positive and negative data in terms of recursively generable finite sets. Thereby, we elaborate a unifying approach to monotonic language learning by showing that there is exactly one learning algorithm which can perform any monotonic inference task.

1 Introduction

The process of hypothesizing a general rule from eventually incomplete data is called inductive inference. Many philosophers of science have focused their attention on problems in inductive inference. Since the seminal papers of Solomonoff (1964) and of Gold (1967), problems in inductive inference have additionally found a lot of attention from computer scientists. The theory they have developed within the last decades is usually referred to as *computational or algorithmic learning theory*. The today state of the art of this theory is excellently surveyed in Angluin and Smith (1983, 1987).

Within the present paper we deal with identification of formal languages. Formal language learning may be considered as inductive inference of partial recursive functions. Nevertheless, some of the results are surprisingly in that they remarkably differ from

---

*This research has been supported by the German Ministry for Research and Technology (BMFT) under grant no. 01 IW 101.

solutions for analogous problems in the setting of inductive inference of recursive functions (cf. e.g. Osherson, Stob and Weinstein (1986), Case (1988), Fulk (1990)).

The general situation investigated in language learning can be described as follows: Given more and more eventually incomplete information concerning the language to be learnt, the inference device has to produce, from time to time, a hypothesis about the phenomenon to be inferred. The information given may contain only *positive examples*, i.e., exactly all the strings contained in the language to be recognized, as well as both *positive and negative examples*, i.e., the learner is fed with arbitrary strings over the underlying alphabet which are classified with respect to their containment to the unknown language. The sequence of hypotheses has to converge to a hypothesis which correctly describes the language to be learnt. In the present paper, we mainly study language learning from positive and negative examples.

Monotonicity requirements have been introduced by Jantke (1991A, 1991B) and Wiehagen (1991) in the setting of inductive inference of recursive functions. Subsequently we have adopted their definitions to the inference of formal languages (cf. Lange and Zeugmann (1991, 1992A, 1992B)). The main underlying question can be posed as follows: Would it be possible to infer the unknown language in such a way that *only* better and better hypotheses are inferred?

The strongest interpretation of this requirement means that we are forced to produce an augmenting chain of languages, i.e., $L_i \subseteq L_j$ iff L_j is guessed later than L_i (cf. Definition 3 (A)).

Wiehagen (1991) proposed to interpret "better" with respect to the language L having to be identified, i.e., now we require $L_i \cap L \subseteq L_j \cap L$ iff L_j appears later in the sequence of guesses than L_i does (cf. Definition 3 (B)). That means, a new hypothesis is never allowed to destroy something what a previously generated guess already *correctly* reflects.

The third version of monotonicity, which we call weak–monotonicity, is derived from non–monotonic logics and adopts the concept of cumulativity. Hence, we only require $L_i \subseteq L_j$ as long as there are no data fed to the inference device after having produced L_i that contradict L_i (cf. Definition 3 (C)).

In all what follows, we restrict ourselves to deal exclusively with the learnability of indexed families of non–empty uniformly recursive languages (cf. Angluin(1980)). This case is of special interest with respect to potential applications. The first problem arising naturally is to relate all types of monotonic language learning one to the other as well as to previously studied modes of inference. This question has been completely answered in Lange and Zeugmann (1991, 1992A). In particular, weak–monotonically working learning devices are exactly as powerful as *conservatively* working ones. A learning algorithm is said to be *conservative* iff it only performs justified mind changes. That means, the learner may change its guess only in case if the former hypothesis "provably misclassifies" some word with respect to the data seen so far. Considering learning from positive and negative examples in the setting of indexed families it is not hard to prove that conservativeness does not restrict the inference capabilities. Surprisingly enough, in the setting of learning recursive functions the situation is totally different (cf. Freivalds, Kinber and Wiehagen (1992)). Another interesting problem consists in characterizing monotonic language learning. In general, characterizations play an important role in inductive inference (cf. e.g. Wiehagen (1977, 1991), Angluin (1980), Freivalds, Kinber and Wiehagen (1992)). On the one hand, they allow to state precisely what kind of requirements a class of target objects has to fulfil in order to be learnable from eventually incomplete data. On .the other hand, they lead to deeper insights into the problem how algorithms performing the desired learning task may be designed. Angluin (1980) proved a characterization theorem for language learning from positive data that turned out to be very useful in applications. In Lange and Zeugmann (1992B), we adopt the underlying idea for characterizing all types of monotonic language learning from positive data in terms of recursively generable finite sets.

Because of the strong relation between inductive inference of recursive functions and language learning on informant, one may conjecture that the characterizations for montonic learning of recursive functions (cf. Wiehagen (1991), Freivalds, Kinber and Wiehagen (1992)) do easily apply to monotonic language learning. However, monotonicity requirements in inductive inference of recursive functions are defined with respect to the graph of the hypothesized functions. This makes really a difference as the following example demonstrates. Let $L \subseteq \Sigma^*$ be any arbitrarily fixed *infinite* context-sensitive language. By $\mathcal{L}_{fin}$ we denote the set of all finite languages over Σ. Then we set $\mathcal{L}_{finvar} = \{L \cup L_{fin} \mid L_{fin} \in \mathcal{L}_{fin}\}$. In our setting, $\mathcal{L}_{finvar}$ is strong-monotonically learnable, even on text (cf. Lange and Zeugmann (1992A)). If one uses the same concept of strong-monotonicity as in Freivalds, Kinber and Wiehagen (1992), one immediately obtains from Jantke (1991A) that, even on informant, $\mathcal{L}_{finvar}$ cannot be learnt strong-monotonically. This is caused by the following facts. First, any IIM M that eventually identifies $\mathcal{L}_{finvar}$ strong–monotonically with respect to the graphs of their characteristic functions has to output sometime a program of a recursive function. Next, the first program of a recursive function has to be a correct one. Finally, it is not hard to prove that no IIM M can satisfy the latter requirement.

In order to develop a unifying approach to monotonic language learning, we present characterizations of monotonic language learning on informant in terms of recursively generable finite sets. In doing so, we will show that there is exactly one learning algorithm performing each of the desired inference tasks on informant. Moreover, it turns out that a conceptually very close algorithm may be also used for monotonic language learning from positive data (cf. Lange and Zeugmann (1992B)).

2 Preliminaries

By $N = \{1, 2, 3, ...\}$ we denote the set of all natural numbers. In the sequel we assume familarity with formal language theory (cf. e.g. Bucher and Maurer (1984)). By Σ we denote any fixed finite alphabet of symbols. Let Σ^* be the free monoid over Σ. The length of a string $w \in \Sigma^*$ is denoted by $|w|$. Any subset $L \subseteq \Sigma^*$ is called a language. By $co - L$ we denote the complement of L, i.e., $co - L = \Sigma^* \setminus L$. Let L be a language and $t = s_1, s_2, s_3, ...$ a sequence of strings from Σ^* such that $range(t) = \{s_k \mid k \in N\} = L$. Then t is said to be a *text* for L or, synonymously, a *positive presentation*. Furthermore, let $i = (s_1, b_1), (s_2, b_2), ...$ be a sequence of elements of $\Sigma^* \times \{+, -\}$ such that $range(i) = \{s_k \mid k \in N\} = \Sigma^*$, $i^+ = \{s_k \mid (s_k, b_k) = (s_k, +), k \in N\} = L$ and $i^- = \{s_k \mid (s_k, b_k) = (s_k, -), k \in N\} = co - L$. Then we refer to i as an *informant*. If

L is classified via an informant then we also say that L is represented by positive and negative data. Moreover, let t, i be a text and an informant, respectively, and let x be a number. Then t_x, i_x denote the initial segment of t and i of length x, respectively, e.g., $i_3 = (s_1, b_1), (s_2, b_2), (s_3, b_3)$. Let t be a text and let $x \in N$. We write t_x^+ as an abbreviation for $range^+(t_x) := \{s_k \mid k \leq x\}$. Furthermore, by i_x^+ and i_x^- we denote the sets $range^+(i_x) := \{s_k \mid (s_k, +) \in i, k \leq x\}$ and $range^-(i_x) := \{s_k \mid (s_k, -) \in i, k \leq x\}$, respectively. Finally, we write $i_x \sqsubseteq i_y$, if i_x is a prefix of i_y.

Following Angluin (1980) we restrict ourselves to deal exclusively with indexed families of recursive languages defined as follows:
A sequence $L_1, L_2, L_3, \ldots$ is said to be an *indexed family* $\mathcal{L}$ of recursive languages provided all L_j are non–empty and there is a recursive function f such that for all numbers j and all strings $w \in \Sigma^*$ we have

$$f(j, w) = \begin{cases} 1 & , \quad if \quad w \in L_j \\ 0 & , \quad otherwise. \end{cases}$$

As an example we consider the set $\mathcal{L}$ of all context–sensitive languages over Σ. Then $\mathcal{L}$ may be regarded as an indexed family of recursive languages (cf. Bucher and Maurer (1984)). In the sequel we often denote an indexed family and its range by the same symbol $\mathcal{L}$. What is meant will be clear from the context.

As in Gold (1967) we define an *inductive inference machine* (abbr. IIM) to be an algorithmic device which works as follows: The IIM takes as its input larger and larger initial segments of a text t (an informant i) and it either requires the next input string, or it first outputs a hypothesis, i.e., a number encoding a certain computer program, and then it requires the next input string (cf. e.g. Angluin (1980)).

At this point we have to clarify what space of hypotheses we should choose, thereby also specifying the goal of the learning process. Gold (1967) and Wiehagen (1977) pointed out that there is a difference in what can be inferred in dependence on whether we want to synthesize in the limit grammars (i.e., procedures generating languages) or decision procedures, i.e., programs of characteristic functions. Case and Lynes (1982) investigated this phenomenon in detail. As it turns out, IIMs synthesizing grammars can be more powerful than those ones which are requested to output decision procedures. However, in the context of identification of indexed families both concepts are of equal power. Nevertheless, we decided to require the IIMs to output grammars. This decision has been caused by the fact that there is a big difference between the possible monotonicity requirements. A straightforward adaptation of the approaches made in inductive inference of recursive functions directly yields analogous requirements with respect to the corresesponding characteristic functions of the languages to be inferred. On the other hand, it is only natural to interpret monotonicity with respect to the language to be learnt, i.e., to require containment of languages as described in the introduction. As it turned out, the latter approach increases considerably the power of monotonic language learning (cf. e.g. the example presented in the introduction). Furthermore, since we exclusively deal with indexed families $\mathcal{L} = (L_j)_{j \in N}$ of recursive languages we almost always take as space of hypotheses an enumerable family of grammars $G_1, G_2, G_3, \ldots$ over the terminal alphabet Σ satisfying $\mathcal{L} = \{L(G_j) \mid j \in N\}$. Moreover, we require that membership in $L(G_j)$ is uniformly decidable for all $j \in N$ and all strings $w \in \Sigma^*$. As it turns out, it is sometimes very important to choose the space of hypotheses appropriately in order to achieve the desired learning goal. Then the IIM outputs numbers j which we interpret as G_j.

A sequence $(j_x)_{x \in N}$ of numbers is said to be convergent in the limit if and only if there is a number j such that $j_x = j$ for almost all numbers x.

Definition 1, (Gold (1967)) *Let $\mathcal{L}$ be an indexed family of languages, $L \in \mathcal{L}$, and let $(G_j)_{j \in N}$ be a space of hypotheses. An IIM M LIM $-$ TXT $(LIM - INF)$–identifies L on a text t (an informant i) iff it almost always outputs a hypothesis and the sequence $(M(t_x))_{x \in N}$ $((M(i_x))_{x \in N})$ converges in the limit to a number j such that $L = L(G_j)$.*
Moreover, M LIM $-$ TXT $(LIM - INF)$–identifies L, iff M LIM $-$ TXT $(LIM - INF)$–identifies L on every text (informant) for L. We set:
$LIM - TXT(M) = \{L \in \mathcal{L} \mid M\ LIM - TXT - identifies\ L\}$ *and define* $LIM - INF(M)$ *analogously.*
Finally, let $LIM - TXT$ $(LIM - INF)$ denote the collection of all families $\mathcal{L}$ of indexed families of recursive languages for which there is an IIM M such that $\mathcal{L} \subseteq LIM - TXT(M)$ $(\mathcal{L} \subseteq LIM - INF(M))$.

Definition 1 could be easily generalized to arbitrary families of recursively enumerable languages (cf. Osherson et al. (1986)). Nevertheless, we exclusively consider the restricted case defined above, since our motivating examples are all indexed families of recursive languages. Note that, in general, it is not decidable whether or not M has already inferred L. Within the next definition, we consider the special case that it has to be decidable wether or not an IIM has succesfully finished the learning task.

Definition 2, (Trakhtenbrot and Barzdin (1970)) *Let $\mathcal{L}$ be an indexed family of languages, $L \in \mathcal{L}$, and let $(G_j)_{j \in N}$ be a space of hypotheses. An IIM M FIN $-$ TXT $(FIN - INF)$–identifies L on a text t (an informant i) iff it outputs only a single and correct hypothesis j, i.e., $L = L(G_j)$, and stops.*
Moreover, M FIN $-$ TXT $(FIN - INF)$–identifies L, iff M FIN $-$ TXT $(FIN - INF)$–identifies L on every text (informant) for L. We set:
$FIN - TXT(M) = \{L \in \mathcal{L} \mid M\ FIN - TXT - identifies\ L\}$ *and define* $FIN - INF(M)$ *analogously.*

The resulting identification type is denoted by $FIN - TXT$ $(FIN - INF)$. Next we formally define strong-monotonic, monotonic and weak-monotonic inference.

Definition 3, Jantke ((1991A), Wiehagen (1991)) *An IIM M is said to identify a language L from text (informant)*

(A) strong–monotonically

(B) monotonically

(C) weak–monotonically

iff

M LIM $-$ TXT $(LIM - INF)$–identifies L and for any text t (informant i) of L as well as for any two consecutive hypotheses j_x, j_{x+k} which M has produced when fed t_x and t_{x+k} (i_x and i_{x+k}), for some $k \geq 1, k \in N$, the following conditions are satisfied:

(A) $L(G_{j_x}) \subseteq L(G_{j_{x+k}})$

(B) $L(G_{j_x}) \cap L \subseteq L(G_{j_{x+k}}) \cap L$

(C) if $t_{x+k} \subseteq L(G_{j_x})$ then $L(G_{j_x}) \subseteq L(G_{j_{x+k}})$ (if $i^+_{x+k} \subseteq L(G_{j_x})$ and $i^-_{x+k} \subseteq co - L(G_{j_x})$, then $L(G_{j_x}) \subseteq L(G_{j_{x+k}})$).

We denote by $SMON - TXT$, $SMON - INF$, $MON - TXT$, $MON - INF$, $WMON - TXT$, $WMON - INF$ the family of all thoses sets $\mathcal{L}$ of indexed families of languages for which there is an IIM inferring it strong–monotonically, monotonically, and weak–monotonically from text t or informant i, respectively.

Note that even $SMON - TXT$ contains interesting "natural" families of formal languages (cf. Lange and Zeugmann (1991, 1992A)). Finally in this section we define *conservatively* working IIMs.

Definition 4, (Angluin (1980A))
An IIM M CONSERVATIVE-TXT (CONSERVATIVE-INF)–identifies L on text t (on informant i), iff for every text t (informant i) the following conditions are satisfied:

(1) $L \in LIM - TXT(M)$ $(L \in LIM - INF(M))$

(2) *If M on input t_x makes the guess j_x and then makes the guess $j_{x+k} \neq j_x$ at some subsequent step, then $L(G_{j_x})$ must fail to contain some string from t_{x+k} ($L(G_{j_x})$ must fail either to contain some string $w \in i^+_{x+k}$ or it generates some string $w \in i^-_{x+k}$).*

$CONSERVATIVE-TXT(M)$ and $CONSERVATIVE -INF(M)$ as well as the collections of sets $CONSERVATIVE-TXT$ and $CONSERVATIVE-INF$ are defined in an analogous manner as above.

Intuitively speaking, a conservatively working IIM performs *exclusively* justified mind changes. Note that $WMON - TXT = CONSERVATIVE-TXT$ as well as $WMON - INF = CONSERVATIVE-INF$. Finally, the figure below summarizes the known results concerning monotonic inference (cf. Lange and Zeugmann (1991, 1992A)).

$$FIN - TXT \subset SMON - TXT \subset MON - TXT \subset WMON - TXT \subset LIM - TXT$$

$$\cap \quad\not\equiv\quad \cap \quad\not\equiv\quad \cap \quad\not\equiv\quad \cap \qquad\qquad \cap$$

$$FIN - INF \subset SMON - INF \subset MON - INF \subset WMON - INF = LIM - INF$$

(* # denotes incomparability of sets. *)

3 Characterization Theorems

In this section we give characterizations of strong–monotonic, monotonic and weak–monotonic inference from positive and negative data as well as for $FIN - INF$. Characterizations play an important role in that they lead to a deeper insight into the problem how algorithms performing the inference process may work (cf. e.g. Blum and Blum

(1975), Wiehagen (1977, 1991), Angluin (1980), Zeugmann (1983), Jain and Sharma (1989)). Starting with the pioneering paper of Blum and Blum (1975), several theoretical framworks have been used for characterizing identification types. For example, characterizations in inductive inference of recursive functions have been formulated in terms of complexity theory (cf. Blum and Blum (1975), Wiehagen and Liepe (1976), Zeugmann (1983)) and in terms of computable numberings (cf. e.g. Wiehagen (1977), (1991) and the references therein). Surprisingly, some of the presented characterizations have been succesfully applied for solving highly nontrivial problems in complexity theory. Moreover, up to now it remains open how to solve the same problems without using these characterizations. It seems that characterizations may help to get a deeper understanding of the theoretical framework where the concepts for characterizing identification types are borrowed from. The characterization for $SMON - TXT$ (cf. Lange and Zeugmann (1992B)) can be considered as further example along this line. This characterization has the following consequence. If $\mathcal{L} \in SMON - TXT$, then set inclusion in $\mathcal{L}$ is decidable (if one chooses an appropriate description of $\mathcal{L}$). On the other hand, Jantke (1991B) proved that, if set inclusion of pattern languages is decidable, then the family of all pattern languages may be inferred strong-monotonically from positive data. However, it remained open whether the converse is also true. Using our result, we see it is, i.e.,if one can design an algorithm that learns the family of all pattern languages strong-monotonically from positive data, then set inclusion of pattern languages is decidable. This may show at least a promising way how to solve the open problem wether or not set inclusion of pattern languages is decidable.

Our first theorem characterizes $SMON - INF$ in terms of recursively generable finite positive and negative tell-tales. A family of finite sets $(P_j)_{j \in N}$ is said to be recursively generable, iff there is a total effective procedure g which, on every input j, generates all elements of P_j and stops. If the computation of $g(j)$ stops and there is no output, then P_j is considered to be empty. Finally, for notational convenience we use $L(\mathcal{G})$ to denote $\{L(G_j) \mid j \in N\}$ for any space $\mathcal{G} = (G_j)_{j \in N}$ of hypotheses.

Theorem 1. *Let $\mathcal{L}$ be an indexed family of recursive languages. Then: $\mathcal{L} \in SMON - INF$ if and only if there are a space of hypotheses $\hat{\mathcal{G}} = (\hat{G}_j)_{j \in N}$ and recursively generable families $(\hat{P}_j)_{j \in N}$ and $(\hat{N}_j)_{j \in N}$ of finite sets such that*

(1) $range(\mathcal{L}) = L(\hat{\mathcal{G}})$

(2) For all $j \in N$, $\emptyset \neq \hat{P}_j \subseteq L(\hat{G}_j)$ and $\hat{N}_j \subseteq co - L(\hat{G}_j)$.

(3) For all $k, j \in N$, if $\hat{P}_k \subset \hat{P}_j$ as well as $\hat{N}_k \subseteq co - L(\hat{G}_j)$, then $L(\hat{G}_k) \subseteq L(\hat{G}_j)$.

Proof. Necessity: Let $\mathcal{L} \in SMON - INF$. Then there are an IIM M and a space of hypotheses $(G_j)_{j \in N}$ such that M infers any $L \in \mathcal{L}$ strong-monotonically with respect to $(G_j)_{j \in N}$. We proceed in showing how to construct $(\hat{G}_j)_{j \in N}$. This will be done in two steps. In the first step, we define a space of hypotheses $(\tilde{G}_j)_{j \in N}$ as well as corresponding recursively generable families $(\tilde{P}_j)_{j \in N}$ and $(\tilde{N}_j)_{j \in N}$ of finite sets where $\tilde{P}_j$ may be empty for some $j \in N$. Afterwards, we define a procedure which enumerates a certain subset of $\tilde{\mathcal{G}}$.

First step: Let $c : N \times N \to N$ be Cantor's pairing function. For all k, $x \in N$ we set $\tilde{G}_{c(k,x)} = G_k$. Obviously, it holds $range(\mathcal{L}) = L(\tilde{\mathcal{G}})$. Let i^k be the lexicographically ordered informant for $L(G_k)$, and let $x \in N$.
We define:

$$\tilde{P}_{c(k,x)} = \begin{cases} range^+(i_y^k) & if \quad y = min\{z \mid z \le x,\ M(i_z^k) = k,\ range^+(i_z^k) \ne \emptyset\} \\ \emptyset & otherwise \end{cases}$$

If $\tilde{P}_{c(k,x)} = range^+(i_y^k) \ne \emptyset$, then we set $\tilde{N}_{c(k,x)} = range^-(i_y^k)$. Otherwise, we define $\tilde{N}_{c(k,x)} = \emptyset$.

Second step: The space of hypotheses $(\hat{G}_j)_{j \in N}$ will be defined by simply striking off all grammars $\tilde{G}_{c(k,x)}$ with $\tilde{P}_{c(k,x)} = \emptyset$. In order to save readability, we omit the corresponding bijective mapping yielding the enumeration $(\hat{G}_j)_{j \in N}$ from $(\tilde{G}_j)_{j \in N}$. If $\hat{G}_j$ is referring to $\tilde{G}_{c(k,x)}$, we set $\hat{P}_j = \tilde{P}_{c(k,x)}$ as well as $\hat{N}_j = \tilde{N}_{c(k,x)}$.

We have to show that $(\hat{G}_j)_{j \in N}$, $(\hat{N}_j)_{j \in N}$, and $(\hat{P}_j)_{j \in N}$ do fulfil the announced properties. Obviously, $(\hat{P}_j)_{j \in N}$ and $(\hat{N}_j)_{j \in N}$ are recursively generable families of finite sets. Furthermore, it is easy to see that $L(\hat{\mathcal{G}}) \subseteq range(\mathcal{L})$. In order to prove (1), it suffices to show that for every $L \in \mathcal{L}$ there is at least one $j \in N$ with $L = L(\hat{G}_j)$ and $P_j \ne \emptyset$. Let i^L be L's lexicographically ordered informant. Since M has to infer L on i^L, too, and $L \ne \emptyset$, there are k, $x \in N$ such that $M(i_x^L) = k$, $L = L(G_k)$, $range^+(i_x^L) \ne \emptyset$ as well as $M(i_y^L) \ne k$ for all $y < x$. From that we immediately conclude that $L = L(\hat{G}_j)$ and that $\tilde{P}_j \ne \emptyset$ for $j = c(k,x)$. Due to our construction, property (2) is obviously fulfilled. It remains to show (3). Suppose k, $j \in N$ such that $\hat{P}_k \subseteq L(\hat{G}_j)$ and $\hat{N}_k \subseteq co - L(\hat{G}_j)$. We have to show $L(\hat{G}_k) \subseteq L(\hat{G}_j)$. In accordance with our construction one can easily observe: There is a uniquely defined initial segment, say i_x^k, of the lexicographically ordered informant for $L(\hat{G}_k)$ such that $range(i_x^k) = \hat{P}_k \cup \hat{N}_k$. Furthermore, $M(i_x^k) = m$ with $L(\hat{G}_k) = L(G_m)$. Additionally, since $\hat{P}_j \subseteq L(\hat{G}_j)$ as well as $\hat{N}_k \subseteq co - L(\hat{G}_j)$, i_x^k is an initial segment of the lexicographically ordered informant i^j of $L(\hat{G}_j)$.

Since M infers $L(\hat{G}_j)$ on informant i^j, there exist r, $n \in N$ such that $M(i_{x+r}^j) = n$ and $L(\hat{G}_j) = L(G_n)$. Moreover, M works strong-monotonically. Thus, by the transitivity of $\subseteq$ we obtain $L(\hat{G}_k) \subseteq L(\hat{G}_j)$.

Sufficiency: It suffices to prove that there is an IIM M inferring any $L \in \mathcal{L}$ on any informant with respect to $\hat{\mathcal{G}}$. So let $L \in \mathcal{L}$, let i be any informant for L, and let $x \in N$.

$M(i_x) = $ "Generate $\hat{P}_j$ and $\hat{N}_j$ for $j = 1,...,x$ and test whether (a) $\hat{P}_j \subseteq i_x^+ \subseteq L(\hat{G}_j)$ and (b) $\hat{N}_j \subseteq i_x^- \subset co - L(\hat{G}_j)$. In case there is at least a j fulfilling the test, output the minimal one, and request the next input.

Otherwise output nothing and request the next input."

Since all of the $\hat{P}_k$ and $\hat{N}_k$ are uniformly recursively generable and finite, we see that M is an IIM. We have to show that it infers L. Let $k = \mu z[L = L(\hat{G}_z)]$. We claim that M converges to k. Consider $\hat{P}_1, ..., \hat{P}_k$ as well as $\hat{N}_1, ..., \hat{N}_k$. Then there must be an x

such that $\hat{P}_k \subseteq i_x^+ \subseteq L(\hat{G}_k)$ and $\hat{N}_k \subseteq i_x^- \subseteq co - L(\hat{G}_k)$. That means, at least after having fed i_x to M, the machine M outputs an hypothesis. Moreover, since $\hat{P}_k \subseteq i_{x+r}^+ \subseteq L(\hat{G}_k)$ and $\hat{N}_k \subseteq i_{x+r}^- \subseteq co - L(\hat{G}_k)$ for all $r \in N$, the IIM M never produces a guess $j > k$ on i_{x+r}. Suppose, M converges to $j < k$. Then we have $\hat{P}_j \subseteq i_{x+r}^+ \subseteq L(\hat{G}_j) \neq L(\hat{G}_k)$ and $\hat{N}_j \subseteq i_{x+r}^- \subseteq co - L(\hat{G}_j)$ for all $r \in N$.

Case 1: $L(\hat{G}_k) \setminus L(\hat{G}_j) \neq \emptyset$

Consequently, there is at least one string $s \in L(\hat{G}_k) \setminus L(\hat{G}_j)$ such that $(s, +)$ has to appear sometimes in i, say in i_{x+r} for some r. Thus, $i_{x+r}^+ \not\subseteq L(\hat{G}_j)$, a contradiction.

Case 2: $L(\hat{G}_j) \setminus L(\hat{G}_k) \neq \emptyset$

Then we may restrict ourselves to the case $L(\hat{G}_k) \subset L(\hat{G}_j)$, since otherwise we are again in case 1. Consequently, there is at least one string $s \in L(\hat{G}_j) \setminus L(\hat{G}_k)$ such that $(s, -)$ has to appear sometime in i, say in i_{x+r} for some r. Thus, $i_{x+r}^- \not\subseteq co - L(\hat{G}_j)$, a contradiction.

Therefore, M converges to k on informant i. In order to complete the proof we show that M works stong-monotonically. Suppose that M outputs k sometime and changes its mind to j in some subsequent step. Hence, $M(i_x) = k$ and $M(i_{x+r}) = j$, for some $x, r \in N$. Due to the construction of M, we obtain $\hat{P}_k \subseteq i_x^+ \subseteq i_{x+r}^+ \subseteq L(\hat{G}_j)$ and $\hat{N}_k \subseteq i_x^- \subseteq i_{x+r}^- \subseteq co - L(\hat{G}_j)$. This yields $\hat{P}_k \subseteq L(\hat{G}_j)$ as well as $\hat{N}_k \subseteq co - L(\hat{G}_j)$. Finally, (3) implies $L(\hat{G}_k) \subseteq L(\hat{G}_j)$. Hence, M works indeed strong-monotonically.

q.e.d.

Although, there are remarkable differences between formal language learning from positive data, on the one hand, and language learning from positive and negative data, on the other hand, the characterizations of $SMON - INF$ is formally quite similar to that one of $SMON - TXT$, (cf. Lange and Zeugmann (1992B)).

Theorem 2. Let $\mathcal{L}$ be an indexed family of recursive languages. Then: $\mathcal{L} \in SMON - TXT$ if and only if there are a space of hypotheses $\hat{\mathcal{G}} = (\hat{G}_j)_{j \in N}$ and a recursively generable family $(\hat{T}_j)_{j \in N}$ of finite and non-empty sets such that

(1) $range(\mathcal{L}) = L(\hat{\mathcal{G}})$.

(2) $\hat{T}_j \subseteq L(\hat{G}_j)$ for all $j \in N$.

(3) For all $j, z \in N$, if $\hat{T}_j \subseteq L(\hat{G}_z)$, then $L(\hat{G}_j) \subseteq L(\hat{G}_z)$.

Surprisingly enough, the characterizations of $MON - INF$ and $MON - TXT$ are quite different. This is caused by the following facts. For characterizing $MON - TXT$, one has to construct a recursively generable family of finite tell-tales that should contain both, information concerning the corresponding language as well as concerning possible intersections of this language L with languages L' which may be taken as candidate hypotheses. However, these intersections may yield languages outside the indexed family. Moreover, as long as the output of the IIM M performing the monotonic inference really depends on the *range*, the *order* and *length* of the textsegment fed to M one has to deal with a *non-recursive* component. The non-recursiveness directly results from the requirement that M has to infer each $L \in \mathcal{L}$ from any text, i.e., one has to find suitable approximations of the uncountable many non-recursive texts. In Lange and Zeugmann (1992B), a method is pointed out for overcoming these difficulties.

The problem explained above does not appear when characterizing $MON - INF$. For language learning on informant, one can make the following observation. Any IIM M performing a desired inference task can be always simulated by an *order-independent* IIM M' of the same inference power as M (cf. Blum and Blum (1975)). M' has simply to rearrange the incoming data in lexicographical order. Then, M' takes the longest initial segment of the rearranged informant which forms an initial segment of the lexicographically ordered informant of the language to be learnt as input and outputs the same hypothesis as M will do when proccesing this amount of data. This is quite different from what one can expect in language learning from positive data, since an IIM can never be sure to have already seen a complete initial segment of the lexicographically ordered text of a language to be learnt.

Next to, we present a characterization of $MON - INF$.

Theorem 3. *Let $\mathcal{L}$ be an indexed family of recursive languages. Then: $\mathcal{L} \in MON - INF$ if and only if there are a space of hypotheses $\hat{\mathcal{G}} = (\hat{G}_j)_{j \in N}$ and recursively generable families $(\hat{P}_j)_{j \in N}$ and $(\hat{N}_j)_{j \in N}$ of finite sets such that*

(1) $range(\mathcal{L}) = L(\hat{\mathcal{G}})$

(2) For all $j \in N$, $\emptyset \neq \hat{P}_j \subseteq L(\hat{G}_j)$ and $\hat{N}_j \subseteq co - L(\hat{G}_j)$

(3) For all $k, j \in N$, and for all $L \in \mathcal{L}$, if $\hat{P}_k \cup \hat{P}_j \subseteq L(\hat{G}_j) \cap L$ as well as $\hat{N}_k \cup \hat{N}_j \subseteq co - L(\hat{G}_j) \cap co - L$, then $L(\hat{G}_k) \cap L \subseteq L(\hat{G}_j) \cap L$.

Proof. Necessity: Let $\mathcal{L} \in MON - INF$. Then there are an IIM M and a space of hypotheses $(G_j)_{j \in N}$ such that M infers any $L \in \mathcal{L}$ monotonically on any informant with respect to $(G_j)_{j \in N}$. Without loss of generality, we can assume that M works conservatively, too, (cf. Lange and Zeugmann (1991, 1992)). The space of hypotheses $(\hat{G}_j)_{j \in N}$ as well as the corresponding recursively generable families $(\hat{P}_j)_{j \in N}$ and $(\hat{N}_j)_{j \in N}$ of finite sets are defined as in the proof of Theorem 1.

We proceed in showing that $(\hat{G}_j)_{j \in N}$, $(\hat{N}_j)_{j \in N}$, and $(\hat{P}_j)_{j \in N}$ do fulfil the announced properties. By applying the same arguments as in the proof of Theorem 1 one obtains (1) and (2). It remains to show (3). Suppose $L \in \mathcal{L}$ and $k, j \in N$ such that $\hat{P}_k \cup \hat{P}_j \subseteq L(\hat{G}_j) \cap L$ as well as $\hat{N}_k \cup \hat{N}_j \subseteq co - L(\hat{G}_j) \cap co - L$. We have to show $L(\hat{G}_k) \cap L \subseteq L(\hat{G}_j) \cap L$. Due to our construction, we can make the following observations. There is a uniquely defined initial segment of the lexicographically ordered informant i^k for $L(\hat{G}_k)$, say i_x^k, such that $range(i_x^k) = \hat{P}_k \cup \hat{N}_k$. Moreover, $M(i_x^k) = m$ with $L(\hat{G}_k) = L(G_m)$. By i_y^j we denote the uniquely defined initial segment of the lexicographically ordered informant i^j for $L(\hat{G}_j)$ with $range(i_y^j) = \hat{P}_j \cup \hat{N}_j$. Furthermore, $M(i_y^j) = n$ and $L(\hat{G}_j) = L(G_n)$. From $\hat{P}_k \subseteq L(\hat{G}_j)$ and $\hat{N}_k \subseteq co - L(\hat{G}_j)$, it follows $i_x^k \sqsubseteq i^j$. Since $\hat{P}_j \subseteq L$ and $\hat{N}_j \subseteq co - L$, we conclude that i_y^j is an initial segment of the lexicographically ordered informant i^L for L.

We have to distinguish the following three cases.

Case 1: $x = y$
Hence, $m = n$ and therefore $L(\hat{G}_k) = L(\hat{G}_j)$. This implies $L(\hat{G}_k) \cap L \subseteq L(\hat{G}_j) \cap L$.

Case 2: $x < y$

Now, we have $i_x^k \sqsubseteq i_y^j \sqsubseteq i^L$. Moreover, M monotonically infers L on informant i^L. By the transitivity of $\subseteq$ we immediately obtain $L(\hat{G}_k) \cap L \subseteq L(\hat{G}_j) \cap L$.

Case 3: $y < x$

Hence, $i_y^j \sqsubseteq i_x^k \sqsubseteq i^j$. Since M works conservatively, too, it follows $m = n$. Therefore, $L(\hat{G}_k) = L(\hat{G}_j)$. This implies $L(\hat{G}_k) \cap L \subseteq L(\hat{G}_j) \cap L$.

Hence, $(\hat{G}_j)_{j \in N}$, $(\hat{N}_j)_{j \in N}$ as well as $(\hat{P}_j)_{j \in N}$ have indeed the announced properties.

Sufficiency: It suffices to prove that there is an IIM M inferring any $L \in \mathcal{L}$ monotonically on any informant with respect to $\hat{\mathcal{G}}$. So let $L \in \mathcal{L}$, let i be any informant for L, and $x \in N$.

$M(t_x) = $ "Generate $\hat{P}_j$ and $\hat{N}_j$ for $j = 1, ..., x$ and test whether

    (A) $\hat{P}_j \subseteq i_x^+ \subseteq L(\hat{G}_j)$ and

    (B) $\hat{N}_j \subseteq i_x^- \subset co - L(\hat{G}_j)$.

    In case there is at least a j fulfilling the test, output the minimal one and request the next input.

    Otherwise, output nothing and request the next input."

Since all of the $\hat{P}_k$ and $\hat{N}_k$ are uniformly recursively generable and finite, we see that M is an IIM. We have to show that it infers L. Let $k = \mu z[L = L(\hat{G}_z)]$. We claim that M converges to k. Consider $\hat{P}_1, ..., \hat{P}_k$ as well as $\hat{N}_1, ..., \hat{N}_k$. Then there must be an x such that $\hat{P}_k \subseteq i_x^+ \subseteq L(\hat{G}_k)$ and $\hat{N}_k \subseteq i_x^- \subseteq co - L(\hat{G}_k)$. That means, at least after having fed i_x to M, the machine M outputs an hypothesis. Moreover, since $\hat{P}_k \subseteq i_{x+r}^+ \subseteq L(\hat{G}_k)$ as well as $\hat{N}_k \subseteq i_{x+r}^- \subseteq co - L(\hat{G}_k)$ for all $r \in N$, the IIM M never produces a guess $j > k$ on i_{x+r}.

Suppose, M converges to $j < k$. Then we have: $\hat{P}_j \subseteq i_{x+r}^+ \subseteq L(\hat{G}_j) \neq L(\hat{G}_k)$ and $\hat{N}_j \subseteq i_{x+r}^- \subseteq co - L(\hat{G}_j)$ for all $r \in N$.

Case 1: $L(\hat{G}_k) \setminus L(\hat{G}_j) \neq \emptyset$

Consequently, there is at least one string $s \in L(\hat{G}_k) \setminus L(\hat{G}_j)$ such that $(s, +)$ has to appear sometime in i, say in i_{x+r} for some r. Thus, we have $i_{x+r}^+ \not\subseteq L(\hat{G}_j)$, a contradiction.

Case 2: $L(\hat{G}_j) \setminus L(\hat{G}_k) \neq \emptyset$

Then we may restrict ourselves to the case $L(\hat{G}_k) \subset L(\hat{G}_j)$, since otherwise we are again in case 1. Consequently, there is at least one string $s \in L(\hat{G}_j) \setminus L(\hat{G}_k)$ such that $(s, -)$ has to appear sometime in i, say in i_{x+r} for some r. Thus, $i_{x+r}^- \not\subseteq co - L(\hat{G}_j)$, a contradiction.

Consequently, M converges to k on informant i. To complete the proof we show that M works monotonically. Suppose M outputs k and changes its mind to j in some subsequent step. Consequently, $M(i_x) = k$ and $M(i_{x+r}) = j$, for some $x, r \in N$.

Case 1: $L(\hat{G}_j) = L$

Hence, $L(\hat{G}_k) \cap L \subseteq L(\hat{G}_j) \cap L = L$ is obviously fulfilled.

Case 2: $L(\hat{G}_j) \neq L$

Due to the definition of M, it holds $\hat{P}_k \subseteq i_x^+ \subseteq i_{x+r}^+ \subseteq L(\hat{G}_j)$. Hence, $\hat{P}_k \subseteq L \cap L(\hat{G}_j)$. Furthermore, we have $\hat{N}_k \subseteq i_x^- \subseteq i_{x+r}^- \subseteq co-L(\hat{G}_j)$. This implies $\hat{N}_k \subseteq co-L(\hat{G}_j) \cap co-L$. Since $M(i_{x+r}) = j$, it holds that $\hat{P}_j \subseteq L$ and $\hat{N}_j \subseteq co-L$. This yields $\hat{P}_k \cup \hat{P}_j \subseteq L(\hat{G}_j) \cap L$ as well as $\hat{N}_k \cup \hat{N}_j \subseteq co-L(\hat{G}_j) \cap co-L$. From (3), we obtain $L(\hat{G}_k) \cap L \subseteq L(\hat{G}_j) \cap L$.

Hence, M $MON-INF$–identifies $\mathcal{L}$.

q.e.d.

From our characterization for $MON-INF$, it immediately follows that any family $\mathcal{L}$ which is inferrable on informant by a monotonically working IIM M can be learnt by a *rearrangment-independently* as well as monotonically working IIM M', too. Osherson, Stob and Weinstein (1986) defined *rearrangement-independent* IIMs as follows: An IIM M is rearrangement-independent iff its output depends only on the range and the length of its input. If we are dealt exclusively with monotonic inference from positive data by rearrangment independent IMMs, denoted by $MONR-TXT$, we obtain a quite similar characterization (cf. Lange and Zeugmann (1992B)).

Theorem 4. *Let $\mathcal{L}$ be an indexed family of recursive languages. Then: $\mathcal{L} \in MONR-TXT$ if and only if there are a space of hypotheses $\hat{\mathcal{G}} = (\hat{G}_j)_{j \in N}$ and a recursively generable family $(\hat{T}_j)_{j \in N}$ of finite sets such that*

(1) $range(\mathcal{L}) = L(\hat{\mathcal{G}})$

(2) For all $j \in N$, $\hat{T}_j \subseteq L(\hat{G}_j)$.

(3) For all $j, z \in N$, if $\hat{T}_j \subseteq L(\hat{G}_z)$, then $L(\hat{G}_z) \not\subset L(\hat{G}_j)$.

(4) For all $k, j \in N$, and for all $L \in \mathcal{L}$, if $L(\hat{G}_j) \neq L \neq L(\hat{G}_k)$ and $\hat{T}_k \subseteq L(\hat{G}_j) \cap L$ as well as $\hat{T}_j \subseteq L$, then $L(\hat{G}_k) \cap L \subseteq L(\hat{G}_j) \cap L$.

Because of $WMON-INF = LIM-INF$ as well as the following trivial proposition, there is no need at all for characterizing $WMON-INF$. It can be easily shown that an appropriate *identification by enumeration strategy* is able to infer every indexed family of recursive languages on informant.

Proposition *For any indexed family $\mathcal{L}$ of recursive languages: $\mathcal{L} \in LIM-INF$.*

Finally, we present a characterization of $FIN-INF$. Note that an analogous theorem has been obtained independently by Mukouchi (1991).

However, even the next theorem has some special features distinguishing it from the characterizations already given. As pointed out above, dealing with characterizations has been motivated by the aim to elaborate a unifying approach to monotonic inference. Concerning $MON-INF$ as well as $SMON-INF$ this goal has been completely met by showing that there is exactly one algorithm, i.e. that one described in Theorem 1 and Theorem 3, which can perform the desired inference task, if the space of hypotheses is appropriately chosen. Obviously, the same algorithms can be applied for weak-monotonic inference, if the corresponding recursively generable families of finite sets will be appropriately choosen. The next theorem yields even a stronger implication. Namely, it shows, if there is a space of hypotheses at all such that $\mathcal{L} \in FIN - INF$ with respect to this space, then one can always use $\mathcal{L}$ itself as space of hypotheses, thereby again applying essentially one and the same inference procedure.

Theorem 5. *Let $\mathcal{L}$ be an indexed family of recursive languages. Then: $\mathcal{L} \in FIN - INF$ if and only if there are recursively generable families $(P_j)_{j \in N}$ and $(N_j)_{j \in N}$ of finite sets such that*

(1) For all $j \in N$, $\emptyset \neq P_j \subseteq L_j$ and $N_j \subseteq co - L_j$.

(2) For all $k, j \in N$, if $P_k \subseteq L_j$ and $N_k \subseteq co - L_j$, then $L_k = L_j$.

Proof. Necessity: Let $\mathcal{L} \in FIN - INF$. Then there are a space $\mathcal{G} = (G_j)_{j \in N}$ of hypotheses and an IIM M such that M finitely infers $\mathcal{L}$ with respect to $\mathcal{G}$. We proceed in showing how to construct $(P_j)_{j \in N}$ and $(N_j)_{j \in N}$. This is done in two steps. First we construct $(\hat{P}_j)_{j \in N}$ and $(\hat{N}_j)_{j \in N}$ with respect to the space $\mathcal{G}$ of hypotheses. Then we describe a procedure yielding the wanted families $(P_j)_{j \in N}$ and $(N_j)_{j \in N}$ with respect to $\mathcal{L}$.

Let $k \in N$ be arbitrarily fixed. Furthermore, let i^k be the lexicographically ordered informant of $L(G_k)$. Since M infers $L(G_k)$ finitely on i^k, there exists a $x \in N$ such that $M(i_x^k) = m$ with $L(G_k) = L(G_m)$. We set $\hat{P}_k = range^+(i_x^k)$ and $\hat{N}_k = range^-(i_x^k)$. The desired families $(P_j)_{j \in N}$ and $(N_j)_{j \in N}$ are obtained as follows. Let $z \in N$. In order to get P_z and N_z search for the least $j \in N$ such that $\hat{P}_j \subseteq L_z$ and $\hat{N}_j \subseteq co - L_z$. Set $P_z = \hat{P}_j$ and $N_z = \hat{N}_j$. Note that at least one wanted j has to exist, since for any pair $(\hat{P}_k, \hat{N}_k)$ of sets there is an informant i of some language $L \in \mathcal{L}$ such that $\hat{P}_k \subseteq i^+$ and $\hat{N}_k \subseteq i^-$.

We have to show that $(P_j)_{j \in N}$ and $(N_j)_{j \in N}$ fulfil the announced properties. Due to our construction, property (1) holds obviously. It remains to show (2). Suppose $z, y \in N$ such that $P_z \subseteq L_y$ and $N_z \subseteq co - L_y$. In accordance with our construction there is an index k such that $P_z = \hat{P}_k$ and $N_z = \hat{N}_k$. Moreover, due to construction there is an initial segment of the lexicographically ordered informant i^k of $L(G_k)$, say i_x^k, such that $range(i_x^k) = \hat{P}_k \cup \hat{N}_k$. Furthermore, $M(i_x^k) = m$ with $L(G_k) = L(G_m)$. Since $\hat{P}_k \subseteq L_y$ and $\hat{N}_k \subseteq co - L_y$, i_x^k is an initial segment of some informant for L_y, too. Taking into account that M finitely infers L_y on any informant and that $M(i_x^k) = m$, we immediately obtain $L_y = L(G_m)$. Finally, due to the definition of P_z and N_z we additionally know that $\hat{P}_k \subseteq L_z$ and $\hat{N}_k \subseteq co - L_z$, hence the same argument again applies and yields $L_z = L(G_m)$. Consequently, $L_z = L_y$. This proves (2).

Sufficiency: It suffices to prove that there is an IIM M inferring any $L \in \mathcal{L}$ finitely on any informant with respect to $\mathcal{L}$. So let $L \in \mathcal{L}$, let i be any informant for L, and $x \in N$.

$M(t_x) =$ "Generate P_j and N_j for $j = 1, ..., x$ and test whether

(A) $P_j \subseteq i_x^+ \subseteq L_j$ and

(B) $N_j \subseteq i_x^- \subseteq co - L_j$.

    In case there is at least a j fulfilling the test, output the minimal one and request the next input.

    Otherwise, output nothing and request the next input."

Since all of the P_j and N_j are uniformly recursively generable and finite, we see that M is an IIM. We have to show that it infers L. Let $j = \mu n[L = L_n]$. Then there must be an $x \in N$ such that $P_j \subseteq i_x^+$ as well as $N_j \subseteq i_x^-$. That means, at least after having fed i_x to M, the machine M outputs an hypothesis and stops. Suppose M produces a hypotheses k with $k \neq j$ and stops. Hence, there has to be a z with $z < x$ such that $P_k \subseteq i_x^+$ and $N_k \subseteq i_x^-$. Since $z < x$, it follows $P_k \subseteq L_j$ and $N_K \subseteq co - L_j$. Hence, (2) implies $L_k = L_j$. Concequently, M outputs a correct hypotheses for L and stops afterwards.

q.e.d.

4 Conclusions

We have characterized strong-monotonic, monotonic, and weak-monotonic language learning from positive and negative data. All these characterization theorems lead to a deeper insight into the problem what actually may be inferred monotonically. It turns out that each of these inference tasks can be performed by applying exactly the same learning algorithm.

Next we point out another interesting aspect of Angluin's (1980) as well as of our characterizations. Freivalds, Kinber and Wiehagen (1989) introduced inference from good examples, i.e., instead of successively inputting the whole graph of a function now an IIM obtains only a finite set argument/value-pairs containing at least the good examples. Then it finitely infers a function iff it outputs a single correct hypothesis. Surprisingly, finite inference of recursive functions from good examples is *exactly* as powerful as identification in the limit. The same approach may be undertaken in language learning (cf. Lange and Wiehagen (1991)). Now it is not hard to prove that any indexed family $\mathcal{L}$ can be finitely inferred from good examples, where for each $L \in \mathcal{L}$ any superset of any of L's tell–tales may serve as good example.

Furthermore, as our results show, all types of monotonic languague learning have special features distinguishing them from monotonic inference of recusive functions. Therefore, it would be very interesting to study monotonic language learning in the general case, i.e., not restricted to indexed families of recursive languages.

Acknowledgement

The authors gratefully acknowledge many enlightening discussions with Rolf Wiehagen concerning the characterization of learning algorithms.

5 References

[1] Angluin, D., (1980), Inductive Inference of Formal Languagues from Positive Data, Information and Control 45, 117 - 135

[2] Angluin, D. and C.H. Smith, (1983), Inductive Inference: Theory and Methods, Computing Surveys 15, 3, 237 - 269

[3] Angluin, D. and C.H. Smith, (1987), Formal Inductive Inference, In Encyclopedia of Artificial Intelligence, St.C. Shapiro (Ed.), Vol. 1, pp. 409 - 418, Wiley-Interscience Publication, New York

[4] Blum, L. and M. Blum, (1975), Toward a Mathematical Theory of Inductive Inference, Information and Control 28, 122 - 155

[5] Bucher, W. and H. Maurer, (1984), Theoretische Grundlagen der Programmiersprachen, Automaten und Sprachen, Bibliographisches Institut AG, Wissenschaftsverlag, Zürich

[6] Case, J., (1988), The Power of Vacillation, In Proc. 1st Workshop on Computational Learning Theory, D. Haussler and L. Pitt (Eds.), pp. 196 -205, Morgan Kaufmann Publishers Inc.

[7] Case, J. and C. Lynes, (1982), Machine Inductive Inference and Language Identification, Proc. Automata, Languages and Programming, Ninth Colloquim, Aarhus, Denmark, M.Nielsen and E.M. Schmidt (Eds.), Lecture Notes in Computer Science 140, pp. 107 -115, Springer-Verlag

[8] Freivalds, R., Kinber, E. B. and R. Wiehagen, (1989), Inductive Inference from Good Examples, Proc. International Workshop on Analogical and Inductive Inference, October 1989, Reinhardsbrunn Castle, K.P. Jantke (Ed.), Lecture Notes in Artificial Intelligence 397, pp. 1 - 17, Springer-Verlag

[9] Freivalds, R., Kinber, E. B. and R. Wiehagen, (1992), Convergently versus Divergently Incorrect Hypotheses in Inductive Inference, GOSLER Report 02/92, January 1992, Fachbereich Mathematik und Informatik, TH Leipzig

[10] Fulk, M.,(1990), Prudence and other Restrictions in Formal Language Learning, Information and Computation 85, 1 - 11

[11] Gold, M.E., (1967), Language Identification in the Limit, Information and Control 10, 447 - 474

[12] Jain, S. and A. Sharma, (1989), Recursion Theoretic Characterizations of Language Learning, The University of Rochester, Dept. of Computer Science, TR 281

[13] Jantke, K.P., (1991A), Monotonic and Non–monotonic Inductive Inference, New Generation Computing 8, 349 - 360

[14] Jantke, K.P., (1991B), Monotonic and Non–monotonic Inductive Inference of Functions and Patterns, Proc. First International Workshop on Nonmonotonic and Inductive Logics, December 1990, Karlsruhe, J.Dix, K.P. Jantke and P.H. Schmitt (Eds.), Lecture Notes in Artificial Intelligence 543, pp. 161 - 177, Springer-Verlag

[15] Lange, S. and R. Wiehagen, (1991), Polynomial–Time Inference of Arbitrary Pattern Languages, New Generation Computing 8, 361 - 370

[16] Lange, S. and T. Zeugmann, (1991), Monotonic versus Non-monotonic Language Learning, in Proc. 2nd International Workshop on Nonmonotonic and Inductive Logic, December 1991, Reinhardsbrunn, to appear in Lecture Notes in Artificial Intelligence

[17] Lange, S. and T. Zeugmann, (1992A), On the Power of Monotonic Language Learning, GOSLER–Report 05/92, February 1992, Fachbereich Mathematik und Informatik, TH Leipzig

[18] Lange, S. and T. Zeugmann, (1992B), Types of Monotonic Language Learning and Their Characterizations, in Proc. 5th ACM Workshop on Computational Learning Theory, July 1992, Morgan Kaufmann Publishers Inc.

[19] Mukouchi, Y., (1991), Definite Inductive Inference as a Successful Identification Criterion, Research Institute of Fundamental Information Science, Kyushu University 33, Fukuoka, December 24, '91 RIFIS-TR-CS-52

[20] Osherson, D., Stob, M. and S. Weinstein, (1986), Systems that Learn, An Introduction to Learning Theory for Cognitive and Computer Scientists, MIT-Press, Cambridge, Massachusetts

[21] Solomonoff, R., (1964), A Formal Theory of Inductive Inference, Information and Control 7, 1 - 22, 234 - 254

[22] Trakhtenbrot, B.A. and Ya.M. Barzdin, (1970), Konetschnyje Awtomaty (Powedenie i Sintez), Nauka, Moskwa (in Russian)

[23] Wiehagen, R., (1976), Limes–Erkennung rekursiver Funktionen durch spezielle Strategien, J. Information Processing and Cybernetics (EIK) 12, 93 - 99

[24] Wiehagen, R., (1977), Identification of Formal Languages, Proc. Mathematical Foundations of Computer Science, Tatranska Lomnica, J. Gruska (Ed.), Lecture Notes in Computer Science 53, pp. 571 - 579, Springer-Verlag

[25] Wiehagen, R., (1991), A Thesis in Inductive Inference, in Proc. First International Workshop on Nonmonotonic and Inductive Logic, December 1990, Karlsruhe, J.Dix, K.P. Jantke and P.H. Schmitt (Eds.), Lecture Notes in Artificial Intelligence 543, pp. 184 - 207

[26] Wiehagen, R. and W. Liepe, (1976), Charakteristische Eigenschaften von erkennbaren Klassen rekursiver Funktionen, Journal of Information Processing and Cybernetics (EIK) 12, 421 - 438

[27] Zeugmann, T., (1983), A–posteriori Characterizations in Inductive Inference of Recursive Functions, Journal of Information Processing and Cybernetics (EIK) 19, 559 - 594

Characterization of Finite Identification

Yasuhito Mukouchi

Department of Information Systems,
Kyushu University 39, Kasuga 816, Japan

Abstract. A majority of studies on inductive inference of formal languages and models of logic programming have mainly used Gold's identification in the limit as a correct inference criterion. In this criterion, we can not decide in general whether the inference terminates or not, and the results of the inference necessarily involve some risks. In this paper, we deal with finite identification for a class of recursive languages. The inference machine produces a unique guess just once when it is convinced the termination of the inference, and the results do not involve any risks at all. We present necessary and sufficient conditions for a class of recursive languages to be finitely identifiable from positive or complete data. We also present some classes of recursive languages that are finitely identifiable from positive or complete data.

1 Introduction

Inductive inference is a process of hypothesizing a general rule from examples. As a correct inference criterion for inductive inference of formal languages and models of logic programming, we have mainly used Gold's identification in the limit[5]. An inference machine M is said to identify a language L in the limit if the sequence of guesses from M, which is successively fed a sequence of examples of L, converges to a correct expression τ of L, that is, all guesses from M become a unique τ within a certain finite time. Under this criterion, many productive results concerning inductive inference from positive data have been reported by Angluin[1], Wright[16], Shinohara[15] and Sato&Umayahara[13]. Also, many systems concerning inductive inference from complete data have been developed (cf. e.g. Shapiro[14] and Muggleton&Buntine[10]).

Considering ordinary learning process of human beings, the criterion of identification in the limit seems to be natural. However, we can not decide in general whether a sequence of guesses from an inference machine converges or not at a certain time, and the results of the inference necessarily involve some risks. Clearly, it is important to have a conclusive answer, when we want to use the result of machine learning. There are some classes of which concepts can be learned conclusively within a finite time.

In this paper, we deal with finite identification for a class of recursive languages. Originally, finite identification was introduced to inductive inference of recursive functions (cf. Freivald&Wiehagen[4], Klette&Wiehagen[7] and Jantke&Beick[6]). An inference machine M is said to finitely identify a language L if M, which is successively fed a sequence of examples of L, produces a unique guess at a certain time and the guess is a correct expression of L. That is, the inference machine does not produce a guess until it is convinced that the guess is correct.

In Section 2, we prepare some necessary concepts for our discussions. In Section 3 and 4, we discuss necessary and sufficient conditions for a class to be finitely identifiable from positive or complete data. Angluin[1] introduced the notion of a finite tell-tale of a language to discuss inferability of formal languages from positive data, and showed that a class is inferable from positive data if and only if there is a recursive procedure to enumerate all elements in the finite tell-tale of any language of the class. In this paper, we introduce a definite finite tell-tale and a pair of definite finite tell-tales of a language, and show that a class is finitely identifiable from positive or complete data if and only if they are uniformly computable for any language of the class. We also present some classes of recursive languages that are finitely identifiable from positive or complete data.

2 Preliminaries

Let U be a recursively enumerable set to which we refer as a *universal set*. Then we call $L \subseteq U$ a *language*. We do not consider the empty language in this paper.

Definition 1. A class of languages $C = L_1, L_2, \cdots$ is said to be an *indexed family of recursive languages* if there exists a computable function $f : N \times U \to \{0, 1\}$ such that
$$f(i, w) = \begin{cases} 1, & \text{if } w \in L_i, \\ 0, & \text{if } w \notin L_i. \end{cases}$$

From now on, we assume a class of languages is an indexed family of recursive languages without any notice.

Definition 2. A *positive presentation* of a language L is an infinite sequence $w_1, w_2, \cdots$ of elements of U such that $\{w_1, w_2, \cdots\} = L$.

A *complete presentation* of a language L is an infinite sequence $(w_1, t_1), (w_2, t_2), \cdots$ of elements of $U \times \{0, 1\}$ such that $\{w_i \mid t_i = 1, i \geq 1\} = L$ and $\{w_j \mid t_j = 0, j \geq 1\} = U - L$.

We denote by σ, δ positive or complete presentations and by $\sigma[n]$ (resp., $\sigma(n)$) the finite sequence (resp., the finite set) which consists of first $n \geq 0$ data in σ.

In this paper, we use a slightly different inference machine from that of identification in the limit. That is, the inference machine is an effective procedure that requests inputs from time to time and stops with a unique output. The unique output produced by the machine is called a *guess*.

Definition 3. A class C of languages is said to be *finitely identifiable from positive (resp., complete) data* if there exists an inference machine M which satisfies the following: For any language L_i of the class C and for any positive (resp., complete) presentation σ of L_i, M which is successively fed σ's data produces a unique guess, say j, after some finite time and $L_j = L_i$ holds.

In this criterion, an inference machine produces a unique guess when the inference process terminates.

3   Finite Identification from Positive Data

In this section, we discuss necessary and sufficient conditions for a class to be finitely identifiable from positive data.

From now on, let $C = L_1, L_2, \cdots$ be an indexed family of recursive languages.

In the criterion of identification in the limit, the following definition and theorem are well-known.

Definition 4 (Angluin[1]). A set S_i is said to be a *finite tell-tale* of L_i if
(1) S_i is a finite subset of L_i, and
(2) there is no index j such that $S_i \subseteq L_j \subsetneq L_i$.

Theorem 5 (Angluin[1]). *A class C is inferable in the limit from positive data if and only if there exists an effective procedure that enumerates all elements in a finite tell-tale of L_i for any index i.*

Now, we show our definition and theorem that form a remarkable contrast to the above definition and theorem.

Definition 6. A set S_i is said to be a *definite finite tell-tale* of L_i if
(1) S_i is a finite subset of L_i, and
(2') $S_i \subseteq L_j$ implies $L_i = L_j$ for any index j.

Clearly from the definition, the definite finite tell-tale has a more specific meaning than the finite tell-tale.

In this paper, a finite-set-valued function F is said to be *computable* if there exists an effective procedure that produces all elements in $F(x)$ and then halts uniformly for any argument x.

Theorem 7. *A class C is finitely identifiable from positive data if and only if a definite finite tell-tale of L_i is uniformly computable for any index i, that is, there exists an effective procedure that on input i produces all elements of a definite finite tell-tale of L_i and then halts.*

Proof. (i) The 'only if' part. Suppose the class C is finitely identifiable from positive data. Then there exists an inference machine M which satisfies Definition 3. A definite finite tell-tale of L_i is uniformly computable by the following procedure:

Procedure $Q(i)$;
begin
    let σ be a positive presentation of L_i;
    for $k := 1$ **to** ∞ **do begin**
        feed the next datum in σ to M;
        if M produces a guess **then** output $\sigma(k)$ and stop
    end
end.

Note that we can effectively take a positive presentation of L_i, because the universal set U is effectively enumerable and whether $w \in L_i$ or not is decidable for any $w \in U$.

Since M finitely identifies the class C, this procedure is guaranteed to terminate. Now, we show by contradiction that the output of this procedure, say S, is a definite finite tell-tale of L_i. Suppose S is not a definite finite tell-tale of L_i. Clearly, S is a finite subset of L_i. Therefore, there exists an index j such that $L_i \neq L_j$ and $S \subseteq L_j$. Since M infers L_i from $\sigma[\sharp S]$, it follows that M can not infer L_j from a positive presentation δ of L_j such that $\delta[\sharp S] = \sigma[\sharp S]$. This contradicts the assumption.

(ii) The 'if' part. Suppose a definite finite tell-tale of L_i is uniformly computable for any index i, and we denote by $S(i)$ the result of computation. The class C is finitely identifiable from positive data by the following procedure:

Procedure M;
begin
    $T := \phi$;
    for $j := 1$ **to** ∞ **do begin**
        read the next datum and add it to T;
        for $i := 1$ **to** j **do**
            if $S(i) \subseteq T$ **then** output i and stop
    end
end.

Note that whether $S(i) \subseteq T$ or not is decidable, because $S(i)$ and T are explicitly given finite sets. Suppose we are going to feed a positive presentation σ of L_h.

(1) When this procedure terminates, the output is a correct guess. In fact, let g be the output of this procedure. Since $S(g) \subseteq T \subseteq L_h$, it follows that $L_g = L_h$ by Definition 6.

(2) This procedure always terminates after some finite time. In fact, let

$$a = \min\{k \mid S(h) \subseteq \sigma(k)\} \qquad \text{and} \qquad b = \max\{a, h\}.$$

Note that $h \leq b$ holds. Suppose this procedure does not terminate. Then it reaches the case of $j = b$ and $i = h$. In this case, $S(i) \subseteq T(= \sigma(b))$ holds, which contradicts the assumption. $\qquad\qquad\square$

We can show that the above procedure M terminates with a guess c when it reaches the case $j = b$ and $i = c$, where

$$a_n = \min\{k \mid S(m_n) \subseteq \sigma(k)\}, \qquad\qquad (n \geq 1)$$
$$b = \min\{\max\{m_1, a_1\}, \max\{m_2, a_2\}, \cdots\},$$
$$c = \min\{m_k \mid \max\{m_k, a_k\} = b, \, k \geq 1\}$$

and $m_1, m_2, \cdots$ are all the m's with $L_m = L_h$. Note that $L_i = L_j$ does not imply $S(i) = S(j)$.

Lange&Zeugmann[9] has obtained similar results to the above theorem in the context of monotonic language learning from positive data, independently of ours.

The following corollary is obvious from Definition 6 and Theorem 7.

Corollary 8. *If a class C has two languages L_i, L_j with $L_i \subsetneq L_j$, then the class C is not finitely identifiable from positive data.*

Here, we present an example of a class of languages which is finitely identifiable from positive data.

Example 1. Let p_i be the i-th prime and put $L_i = \{n \mid n$ is a multiple of $p_i\}$ $(i \geq 1)$. Since p_i is a primitive recursive function of i, the class $C = L_1, L_2, \cdots$ is an indexed family of recursive languages. This class C is finitely identifiable from positive data. In fact, we can take the set $\{p_i\}$ as a definite finite tell-tale of L_i.

4 Finite Identification from Complete Data

In this section, we discuss necessary and sufficient conditions for a class to be finitely identifiable from complete data.

The following Definition 9 and Theorem 10 form a remarkable contrast to Definition 6 and Theorem 7 concerning positive data.

Definition 9. A language L is said to be *consistent* with a pair of sets $\langle T, F \rangle$ if $T \subseteq L$ and $F \subseteq U - L$. A pair of sets $\langle T_i, F_i \rangle$ is said to be *a pair of definite finite tell-tales of L_i* if
(1) T_i is a finite subset of L_i,
(2) F_i is a finite subset of $U - L_i$, and
(3) if L_j is consistent with the pair $\langle T_i, F_i \rangle$, then $L_i = L_j$.

Note that if S_i is a definite finite tell-tale of L_i, then the pair $\langle S_i, \phi \rangle$ is a pair of definite finite tell-tales of L_i.

Theorem 10. *A class C is finitely identifiable from complete data if and only if a pair of definite finite tell-tales of L_i is uniformly computable for any index i.*

Proof. (i) The 'only if' part. Suppose the class C is finitely identifiable from complete data. Then there exists an inference machine M which satisfies Definition 3. Then we consider the following procedure:

Procedure $P(i)$;
begin
    let σ be a complete presentation of L_i;
    for $k := 1$ **to** ∞ **do begin**
        feed the next datum in σ to M;
        if M produces a guess **then begin**
            $T := \{w_j \mid (w_j, 1) \in \sigma(k), j \geq 1\}$;
            $F := \{w_j \mid (w_j, 0) \in \sigma(k), j \geq 1\}$;
            output the pair $\langle T, F \rangle$ and stop
        end
    end
end.

The output of the above procedure $P(i)$ is shown to be a pair of definite finite tell-tales of L_i in a similar way to the proof of Theorem 7.

(ii) The 'if' part. Suppose a pair of definite finite tell-tales of L_i is uniformly computable for any index i, and we denote by $\langle T(i), F(i) \rangle$ the result of computation. Then we consider the following procedure:

Procedure M;
begin
    $T := \phi;$ $F := \phi;$
    for $j := 1$ **to** ∞ **do begin**
        read the next datum (w, v);
        if $v = 1$ **then** $T := T \cup \{w\}$ **else** $F := F \cup \{w\}$;
        for $i := 1$ **to** j **do**
            if $T(i) \subseteq T$ **and** $F(i) \subseteq F$ **then** output i and stop
    end
end.

We can show that the class C is finitely identifiable by the above procedure M in a similar way to the proof of Theorem 7. □

We present a sufficient condition for a class to be finitely identifiable from complete data. This condition has more specific meaning than the condition of "finite thickness", which Angluin[1] introduced as a sufficient condition for a class to be inferable in the limit from positive data.

Theorem 11. *A class C is finitely identifiable from complete data if*
(1) the set $\{i \mid w \in L_i\}$ is finite and uniformly computable for any $w \in U$, and
(2) whether $L_i = L_j$ or not is decidable for any indices i, j.

Proof. Suppose (1) and (2) hold. The definite finite tell-tale of L_i is uniformly computable by the following procedure, where the sequence $w_1, w_2, \cdots$ is an effective enumeration of the universal set U:

Procedure $P(i)$;
begin
    let k be the least number such that $w_k \in L_i$;
    $T := \{w_k\};$ $F := \phi;$
    compute the set $\{j \mid w_k \in L_j\}$ and set it to S;
    for each $j \in S$ **do**
        if $L_i \neq L_j$ **then begin**
            $m := 1;$
            while $(w_m \in L_i$ and $w_m \in L_j)$ or $(w_m \notin L_i$ and $w_m \notin L_j)$ **do** $m := m+1$;
            if $w_m \in L_i$ and $w_m \notin L_j$ **then** $T := T \cup \{w_m\}$ **else** $F := F \cup \{w_m\}$
        end;
    output the pair $\langle T, F \rangle$ and stop
end.

Since the while loop above is executed only when $L_i \neq L_j$, this while statement always terminates. Therefore, the procedure $P(i)$ always terminates. It is clear that the output of $P(i)$ is a pair of definite finite tell-tales of L_i. □

We present an example of a class of languages which is finitely identifiable from complete data.

Example 2. We consider the class of pattern languages. Here, we define a pattern and a pattern language briefly. (For more details, see Angluin[2] or Mukouchi[11].)

Fix a finite alphabet with at least two constant symbols. A pattern is a nonnull finite string of constant and variable symbols. The pattern language $L(\pi)$ generated by a pattern π is the set of all strings obtained by substituting nonnull strings of constant symbols for the variables of π. Since two patterns that are identical except for renaming of variables generate the same pattern language, we do not distinguish one from the other. We can enumerate all patterns recursively and whether $w \in L(\pi)$ or not for any w and π is effectively decidable. Therefore, we can consider the class of pattern languages as an indexed family of recursive languages, where the pattern itself is considered to be an index.

(i) The class of pattern languages satisfies the condition (1) of Theorem 11. In fact, fix an arbitrary constant string w. If $w \in L(\pi)$, then π is not longer than w. The set of all patterns shorter than a fixed length is finite and uniformly computable, and whether $w \in L(\pi)$ or not for any w and π is decidable. Therefore, the set $\{\pi \mid w \in L(\pi)\}$ is finite and uniformly computable.

(ii) Angluin[2] showed that $L(\pi) = L(\tau)$ if and only if $\pi = \tau$.

Therefore, we see that the class of pattern languages is finitely identifiable from complete data by Theorem 11.

By theorems in Angluin[2], we can also show that $\langle T, F \rangle$ is a pair of definite finite tell-tales of $L(\pi)$, where T is the set of all elements of $L(\pi)$ with the same length as π, and F is the set of all constant strings each of which is not longer than π and does not belong to T. Furthermore, we see that the class of pattern languages is not finitely identifiable from positive data by Corollary 8.

Note that Lange&Zeugmann[8] has obtained similar results concerning the class of pattern languages, independently of ours.

5 Concluding Remarks

In this paper, we have discussed conditions for a class of recursive languages to be finitely identifiable from positive or complete data. We also presented some classes that are finitely identifiable from positive or complete data.

Finitely identifiable classes are much smaller than those that are inferable in the limit, but the finite identification seems to be much more significant than it is thought of.

We conclude by pointing out some relations between the results on finite identification obtained in this paper and the results shown in Angluin[1]. As easily seen, the definite finite tell-tale has a more specific meaning than the finite tell-tale. Also, if a class C is finitely identifiable from positive data, then C is also inferable in the limit from positive data. It seems that whether finitely many "mind changes" are allowed or not makes the difference between recursive enumerability of a finite tell-tale and uniform computability of a definite finite tell-tale.

Acknowledgements

The author wishes to thank Setsuo Arikawa for many suggestions, that made me start this research, and productive discussions.

References

1. Angluin, D.: Inductive inference of formal languages from positive data, Information and Control **45** (1980), 117–135
2. Angluin, D.: Finding patterns common to a set of strings, Proc. 11th Annual Symposium on Theory of Computing (1979), 130–141
3. Angluin, D., Smith, C.H.: Inductive inference: theory and methods, ACM Computing Surveys **15** No. 3 (1983), 237–269
4. Freivald R.V., Wiehagen, R.: Inductive inference with additional information, Elektron. Informationsverarb. Kybern. (EIK) **15** (1979), 179–185
5. Gold, E.M.: Language identification in the limit, Information and Control, **10** (1967), 447–474
6. Jantke, K.P., Beick, H.-R.: Combining postulates of naturalness in inductive inference, Elektron. Informationsverarb. Kybern. (EIK) **17** (1981), 465–484
7. Klette, R., Wiehagen, R.: Research in the theory of inductive inference by GDR mathematicians – a survey, Information Sciences **22** (1980), 149–169
8. Lange, S., Zeugmann, T.: On the power of monotonic language learning, GOSLER-Report 05/92, Fachbereich Mathematik und Informatik, TH Leipzig (1992)
9. Lange, S., Zeugmann, T.: Types of monotonic language learning and their characterization, to appear in Proc. 5th Workshop on Comput. Learning Theory (1992)
10. Muggleton, S., Buntine, W.: Machine invention of first-order predicates by inverting resolution, Proc. 5th International Conference on Machine Learning (1988), 339–352
11. Mukouchi, Y.: Characterization of pattern languages, Proc. 2nd Workshop on Algorithmic Learning Theory (1991), 93–104
12. Mukouchi, Y.: Definite inductive inference as a successful identification criterion, RIFIS-TR-CS-52, Research Institute of Fundamental Information Science, Kyushu University, (1991)
13. Sato, M., Umayahara, K.: Inductive inferability for formal languages from positive data, Proc. 2nd Workshop on Algorithmic Learning Theory (1991), 84–92
14. Shapiro, E.Y.: Inductive inference of theories from facts, Technical Report 192, Department of Computer Science, Yale University, (1981)
15. Shinohara, T.: Inductive inference from positive data is powerful, Proc. 3rd Workshop on Comput. Learning Theory (1990), 97–110
16. Wright, K.: Identification of unions of languages drawn from an identifiable class, Proc. 2nd Workshop on Comput. Learning Theory (1989), 328–333

A Model of the 'Redescription' Process in the Context of Geometric Proportional Analogy Problems

Scott O'Hara

Computer Science Department, Boston University
Boston, MA. 02215, USA

Abstract

It has been recognized for some time that analogies can redescribe an object or situation sometimes resulting in a radically new point of view. While this creative aspect of analogy is often cited as a reason for its study, AI approaches to analogy have, for the most part, ignored this phenomenon and instead have focused on computing similarities between fixed descriptions. To study this 'redescription' process by which new points of view can be created, we seek a micro-world in which the redescription phenomenon occurs in its full subtlety but in which it can be isolated from extraneous and ill-understood factors. Proportional analogies (i.e., analogies of the form: A is to B as C is to D) in the abstract domain of geometric figures form just such a micro-world. In this paper, we describe an algebraic formulation of the redescription process in the context of geometric proportional analogies. We then discuss the design of a computer program called PAN which redescribes geometric figures while solving proportional analogy problems. Finally, we briefly discuss our plans for future work in this area.

1   Introduction: The Need for Redescription

The ability to respond creatively to a problem by looking at it from a different point of view is one of the hallmarks of intelligent behavior. A problem that is seemingly insoluble from one point of view often becomes trivial when looked at from a different perspective. How can this fundamental aspect of human intelligence be investigated? Hofstadter [10] argued that many of the crucial aspects of creative thought appear in the context of analogy problems and he has created a surprisingly rich micro-world involving strings of characters in which these processes can be investigated. Indurkhya [15] argued that the mechanism underlying such creative analogies is representational change, or in the terms used in this paper, redescription. Indurkhya suggested the domain of geometric figures as a domain for investigating creative analogies. Much more than the string domain, the geometric domain forces one to come to grips with the vast combinatorics of a very large space of possible descriptions. In this paper we will present our current work on the design of a computer program called PAN (for Proportional ANalogies) which models the process of redescription in the context of geometric proportional analogy problems. Our approach is based on the algebraic framework of Indurkhya [16, 17, Chaps. 5 and 6].

The discussion of our model will include the following terminology. A *description* is simply any representation of an object. An object or figure is said to be described if there exists some description which represents it. A figure is *redescribed* if by some process its original description is changed to some other description which nevertheless still represents it. If a description is never permitted to change during a process, it will be called a *fixed* description. *Proportional analogies,* the kind that commonly appear on intelligence tests, are analogies of the form A is to B as C is to D. These analogies are so called because of their close relationship to numerical proportions e.g., $\frac{1}{3} :: \frac{2}{6}$. While proportional analogies come in various forms, in this paper we will concentrate on proportional analogy problems of the following type: given the three items A, B and C, provide a fourth item D which forms a proportional analogy with the first three.

Proportional analogies are an excellent domain for studying the redescription process. The problem is clearly defined and permits a straight-forward way of evaluating a computational model by comparing its performance to that of an adult human. By concentrating at least initially on analogies in an abstract domain such as geometric figures, controversial issues surrounding descriptions and their meaning can be mininized. Most everyone agrees on what a triangle or polygon is. The focus then, can be on the redescription process.

Current work on analogy has focused on finding mappings between fixed descriptions. Much of the progress in this 'fixed description' approach to analogy may be viewed as discovering criteria by which components of one description are mapped to components of another description. For example, in Winston's [28] approach, the mappings were constrained to be from the most salient features of an initial, fixed description to the most prototypical features of another description. In later work, Winston [29] emphasized the mapping of "important" relations, such as causality relations, between descriptions. Gentner and her colleagues [4, 6] have stressed the mapping of higher-order relations between fixed descriptions. Holyoak and Thagard [14] also highlighted consistent structural correspondences between descriptions, but included other factors such as semantic similarity and the pragmatics of how the analogy is to be used. Greiner [7] addressed the problem of "what should be mapped" by requiring that the mappings support learning as well as the solution of a given problem. Mappings in Greiner's NLAG system were further constrained to be part of some pre-existing abstraction. Kedar-Cabelli [18] explicitly added a 'purpose' to the representation of an analogy in order to allow a system to choose an appropriate description. Kedar-Cabelli stays essentially within the fixed description approach since the given purpose determines which description is chosen. The ANALOGY program of Evans [3] solved proportional analogy problems in the geometric domain. ANALOGY is distinctive among analogy programs even today in that it built conceptual-level descriptions in terms of concepts such as closed-plane figures from lower-level descriptions in terms of lines and curves. However, its sharp division between a description-building phase and an analogy-making phase is a strong limitation (see [17, pp 378-84].) Evans also stays within the fixed description approach since no change in a description is possible once it is built. Other work on analogy described in a survey by Hall [8], while differing in many respects, all compute mappings between fixed descriptions.

The work of Douglas Hofstadter and Melanie Mitchell on the Copycat project [9, 10, 11, 12, 20] is a notable exception to the fixed description approaches to analogy. Copycat is a program that solves proportional analogy problems in the domain of character strings [10]. Unlike the programs described above, Copycat solves string analogy problems by building up descriptions of the terms of the analogy from minimal initial descriptions. While sharing the perspective that the ability to change descriptions flexibly is crucial to understanding creative analogies, PAN differs from Copycat in three important respects. First, in contrast to the non-deterministic architecture of Copycat, PAN uses a deterministic search in the space of possible descriptions based on the strategy depth-first iterative deepening [19]. Secondly, the respective representational schemes are significantly different: PAN uses an algebraic representation while Copycat uses a hybrid representation incorporating notions of both semantic networks and connectionist-style networks. Finally, while work on Copycat emphasizes the emergence of conceptual-level descriptions from minimal low-level descriptions, work on PAN aims to model the interaction of existing conceptual-level descriptions.

While the fixed-description research cited above has shed some light on the nature of analogical processes, Indurkhya [15] and Chalmers et al. [1] have pointed out that the fixed description approach has skirted some of the deeper issues presented by human analogical capabilities. In particular, present models of analogy fail to explain a certain class of analogies which require different descriptions of the same object or action as it appears in different analogies. There are many examples of such analogies. We draw your attention to three such examples in Figure 1 borrowed from Indurkhya [15] (with slight differences.) Notice that the third item in each proportional analogy is the Star of David figure. The Star of David can be described in many different ways. Let us now look more closely at these proportional analogies and show how the contexts of the other terms forces different descriptions on the Star of David.

In Figure 1(a), item A may be viewed as two overlapping rectangles in which the top rectangle is pulled up to produce item B. The Star of David figure is similarly transformed by viewing it as two overlapping triangles. In Figure 1(b), item A is a square with an osculating rectangle attached to each side. Item B is produced by removing these rectangles. The Star of David figure is analogously described as a hexagon surrounded by triangles. Finally, in Figure 1(c), item A is three intersecting line segments separated by sixty degree angles. item B is gotten by removing the vertical line segment. The Star of David figure is similarly transformed by viewing it as three parallelograms separated by sixty degree angles (this may be difficult to see at first). Notice that in Figure 1(a) the most appropriate description of the Star of David is of two overlapping triangles, while in Figure 1(b), the most appropriate description is of a central hexagon figure surrounded by osculating triangles, and in Figure 1(c) the appropriate description is of three overlapping parallelograms. All of these descriptions are needed to solve these analogies. If one of these descriptions were chosen as *the* way to describe the Star of David then only one of the analogies could be solved.

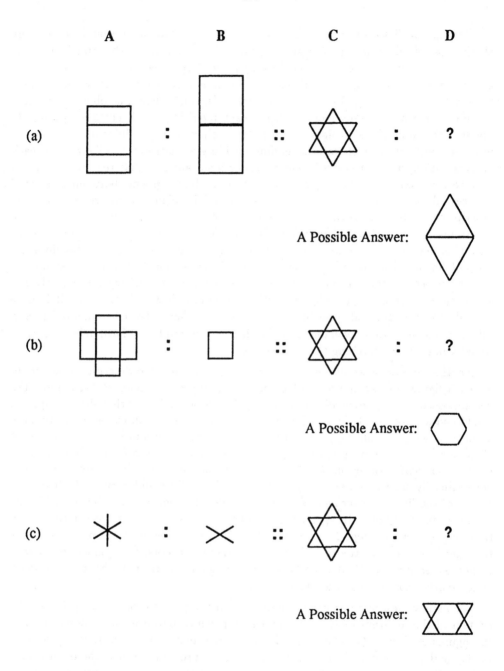

Figure 1: Three proportional analogies which require different descriptions of the Star of David (taken with modification from Indurkhya's "Modes of Analogy" [1989]).

One approach to automating the solution of these problems would be to store all the possible descriptions of a given figure. This is an approach implicit in many models of analogy-making. Many analogy programs have a recognition phase [8] where an appropriate description is retrieved from memory. However, while we have given three examples of analogies involving the Star of David, it should be obvious that it is possible to construct many more analogies each requiring a different description. By dividing the Star of David figure at arbitrary points, it is possible to decompose it in a very large number of ways depending on the granularity of the figure. For each decomposition, one can easily invent a proportional analogy that requires it. If one were to represent geometric figures as a list of the line segments between connected vertices, then for the Star of David, there would be eighteen line segments in its description. This would mean that there would be over a quarter million (2^{18}) ways of describing the Star of David as two subfigures. Further huge numbers of descriptions would be needed for decomposition into three or more subfigures and this does not account for descriptions involving overlapping figures or for descriptions that involve higher level conceptualizations such as squares, polygons, symmetry, etc. Clearly, the approach of storing all possible descriptions is impractical at best. Even if it were possible to enumerate all possible descriptions of a figure (which is doubtful) and sufficient memory were available to hold all these descriptions, formidable obstacles would still exist to searching this vast space.

Another approach would be to provide the richest possible description one could for each figure, say at the level of pixels. This approach would at least allow the decomposition of a figure in all possible ways. One problem here is that the descriptions would contain too much detail. Given two figures, there are an extraordinarily large number of ways of relating pixels in one figure to those in another figure and most of these relations are meaningless. Another more significant problem is that the pixel level is too sparse conceptually. When one looks at the figures in Figure 1, one does not ordinarily see the figures at the level of pixels (or lines and curves). Instead, one perceives the figures in terms of squares, triangles, hexagons i.e., in terms of higher-level concepts. Further, the perceived similarities between figures are *determined* by these higher-level concepts. In Figure 1(a), the rectangles in A are mapped to the triangles in C. Yet, at the pixel level, and without concepts, this connection cannot be noticed easily since there is no basis for picking out the triangle shapes as opposed to some other configuration of pixels.

Let us now describe our general approach to the problem of redescription in the context of the program PAN. PAN is initially given a conceptual-level description of the figures A, B and C. These initial descriptions may not be entirely appropriate to the analogy at hand but this will not be a fatal problem because the descriptions will be allowed to change and *interact* with one another. The descriptions will use each other as *contexts* as they interact and change to create a coherent picture of the proportional analogy. Our intuition is that people rarely approach a situation devoid of pre-existing notions. They usually have some pre-conceived idea of what a situation means, what is important, what is not, what are the components, and what are the relationships between the components. Our hypothesis is that these pre-conceived, initial descriptions bias the redescription process. In the context of proportional analogies, this would mean that different answers for D could be returned depending on the initial conceptualizations of items A, B and C.

This interactive redescription process, as we imagine it, is complex, and has proven difficult to model all in one step. We therefore have attempted to find simplifying restrictions that make the modeling problem easier. In the version of PAN described in this paper, we restrict the description of A to be fixed and in a normal form which we discuss in Section 5. We further require B and C to be described as structureless wholes (the meaning of this statement will become more clear as you read on.) Finally, we assume that processing can be broken up into a transformation phase and a mapping phase. We project a series of PAN versions each one more complex than the previous one as we relax the various restrictions placed on the previous versions. We discuss this further in Section 6.

2   Sensorimotor and Concept Networks: An Algebraic Approach

In a complex world where no two objects or experiences are ever really identical, a finite intelligence must seek a certain "cognitive economy" [25] in modeling the world, allowing the intelligence to respond to the world in an efficient and accurate fashion. Concepts serve this crucial representational role for any intelligent agent. Concepts allow an agent to make sense of the world by grouping together large amounts of data and experience and treating them as though they were the same. Concepts, by reducing the amount of information that an agent has to deal with, make possible learning, remembering, communication and reasoning [27]. In the absence of concepts, a cognitive agent would most likely be overwhelmed by the vast amount of information presented to it by the world.

Using an approach that is similar to the cognitive frameworks of Indurkhya [17] and Holland et al. [13], we capture the notion of a concept and its relation to sensory data by making a distinction between two levels of representation. The first level of representation, which we will call the *sensorimotor level*, models the rich complexity of data that a cognitive agent gets from its environment through its senses and motor capabilities. The information at the sensorimotor level is represented by a single *sensorimotor network*. The second level of representation, called the *conceptual level*, groups and simplifies the information represented at the sensorimotor level. A particular grouping at this level will be called a *concept network*. Since the sensorimotor data may be grouped in various ways, there may many different concept networks at the conceptual level.

We will model both the sensorimotor and concept networks as algebras. An *algebra* is a set of objects, possibly infinite, along with a set of operators defined over those objects. Each operator has a finite, fixed number of arguments and the operation of an operator is defined by a total function which maps a product of the set of objects to the set of objects itself. An algebra is closed over the set of objects in that every application of an operator to objects in the object set results in an object that is also in the object set. The operators of an algebra give structure to the set of objects by defining how the various objects are connected to one another.

How are the sensorimotor and concept network algebras related? Typically, a concept network is some algebra that is "simpler" in some sense than the sensorimotor network but which retains some of its structure. For our purposes here, a concept network is a *subalgebra* of the sensorimotor network where a subalgebra consists of a subset of the objects of the original algebra and a subset of the operators in the original algebra whose action is closed over the subset of objects. Indurkhya [17, Chap. 6] defines a concept network in terms of an algebra of classes, which is more general than we need here. Associated with each concept network is a *recognition procedure* which, given an object from the sensorimotor network, determines whether or not the object is in the object set of the concept network. We will discuss recognition procedures again when we talk about the mapping process in Section 5.

What is our motivation for using algebra as a representation language? We have two. First, Indurkhya [17, Chaps. 5 and 6] has created an algebraic framework in which questions concerning creative metaphor can be precisely formulated. The questions of most interest to Indurkhya have been those concerning metaphors in which a shift of viewpoint or change of represesentation takes place. Second, we are inspired by Piaget's use of an algebra-like formulation [23, pp. 164-236] to describe the mental structures found in children. In Piaget's view [22, 24], mental capacity develops as an interaction between the current capacities of a cognitive agent and the external world. An agent comes to know about the world by acting upon it and transforming it from one world state to another. According to Piaget, the physical actions of a cognitive agent become part of an agent's knowledge by being internalized and abstracted into mental actions or operations. These mental operations become part of a system of operations constituting an agent's knowledge about a world. Such networks of mental states and operations can be modelled in a natural way as algebras where the mental states are the algebraic objects and the mental operations are the operators which modify objects into other objects.

3 Sensorimotor and Concept Networks in the Domain of Geometric Figures

Let us now apply the notions of sensorimotor and concept networks discussed above to the domain of geometric figures. The algebra shown in Figure 2 will be our sensorimotor network for geometric figures.

Here, we can imagine some creature with eyes that are only able to see straight lines. It can track lines in straight or circular motions or detect that a line is reflected across some axis. It is also able to "chunk" lines together into arbitrary configurations. Our sensorimotor algebra is not intended to be an accurate psychological or phsysiological model. Instead, it is intended to capture in an abstract way the low-level sensory and motor information that a cognitive agent might have.

Each geometric figure is represented as a set of line segments. We will sometimes need to speak of a subfigure of a figure which is a subset of the line segments comprising the figure. Each line segment is represented as a pair of endpoints which are in turn represented as a pair of coordinates in the cartesian coordinate system. Points must

Objects

All geometric figures that can be constructed
within a 400 by 400 unit frame (represented by
the dotted rectangle) by combining straight line
segments.

Examples:

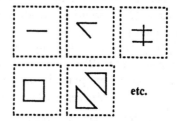

etc.

One-Argument Operators

TRANS[dx,dy]: A class of operators
that translates the argument figure dx
units along the x-axis and dy units along
the y-axis.(Note: dx and dy are parameters
that specify which TRANS operator is being
used. They are NOT arguments).

ROT[a,d]: A class of operators that
rotates the argument figure around axis
a by d degrees.

REFL[a]: A class of operators that
reflects the argument figure across axis
a. (a is specified by a slope and a
y-intercept.)

SCALE[c,k]: A class of operators
that changes the size and location of
its argument by multiplying the distance of each point in the figure from
some point p by the real constant k.

Two-Argument Operators

GLUE: Combine the two argument
figures together to produce a single
figure.

Figure 2: Objects and primitive operators for the geometric sensorimotor network.

fall within some range of values called the *frame*. The frame is currently set to be 400 by 400. A reflection axis is represented by a pair consisting of the axis' slope and its y-intercept. To avoid duplicate representations of the same geometric figure, two conditions are placed on the line segments. For any two line segments, (1) if they are parallel, they may not share any points. If they did, the two could be combined into a single line segment; (2) if they are not parallel, then the point of intersection, if there is one, must be an endpoint in both line segments. If this condition didn't hold, then one or both of the line segments could be split into two at the point of intersection.

The operators in our sensorimotor network are essentially those found in standard Euclidean geometry [2] plus the two-argument GLUE operator. The translation, rotation, and reflection operators together permit transformations between any arbitrarily positioned congruent figures, i.e. figures that don't change size or shape. With the addition of the scaling operators, figures may be increased or diminished in size. The GLUE operator permits the description of figures as being composed of subfigures which may be added or removed. Together, these operators allow us to represent a large class of geometric analogies such as those found in [3, 15, 16].

The algebra does not permit curved figures. We believe that this is not a significant problem since the notion of curvature could be added to our representation, say as a parameter in the line segment representation. The algebra also does not allow the deforming of figures such as stretching nor does it permit shading. Finally, the algebra does not permit the motion of an object relative to another object such as moving an object to the center of another. We are currently investigating how these capabilities might be added to our model.

Additional operators, which we will call *macro-operators*, may be formed by adding the identity and constant operators and then combining them with the primitive operators in Figure 2 by using composition [17, Chap 6, pp 204-5, p 216].

As we saw in the last section, even a figure of moderate complexity such as the Star of David has a huge number of decompositions. In order to prevent a cognitive agent from being overwhelmed by such complexity, concepts must be introduced. In our algebraic framework, a concept is modelled as a concept network, i.e. as a subalgebra of the sensorimotor network. This approach captures the simplifying aspect of concepts. An example of a concept in the geometric domain would be the concept of a square. The square concept network would be the set of all squares along with the set of all unary operators from the geometry sensorimotor network. The GLUE operator is not included since its application could result in a non-square.

In order to model the solution of geometric proportional analogies, we will need to define a number of more general geometric concepts some of which will be organized into hierarchies which we will call *concept network hierarchies*. Concept network hierarchies are modelled as trees where each node in the hierarchy is a concept network. Every node in a concept network hierarchy must be a subalgebra of its parent. Typically, though not necessarily, the root of a concept network hierarchy is the sensorimotor network.

The first concept network hierarchy that we will use is shown in Figure 3(a). The concept network hierarchy in Figure 3(a) has as its root the geometric sensorimotor network and divides it into connected and non-connected figures. It further divides

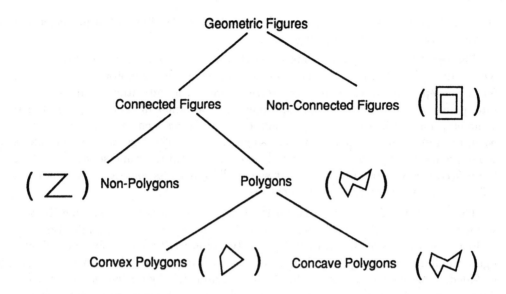

Figure 3(a): A concept network hierarchy containing connected figures, polygons and related concepts.

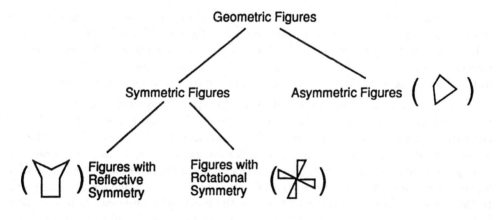

Figure 3(b): A concept network hierarchy containing symmetric and non-symmetric figures.

the connected figures into polygons and non-polygons and divides the polygons into convex polygons and concave polygons.

The second concept network hierarchy that we will use is shown in Figure 3(b) which, like Figure 3(a), has as its root the geometric sensorimotor network. This hierarchy represents finite, planar geometric figures with and without symmetry. Finite, planar geometric geometric figure may have two kinds of symmetry: rotational symmetry and reflective symmetry. A figure has *rotational symmetry* if it is invariant when rotated around its center by some angle less than 360 degrees. For example, a square, when rotated 90 degrees around its center is still the same square. A figure has *reflective* symmetry if it is invariant when reflected across some axis. A square has reflective symmetry across four different axes.

The operators in the concept networks of these hierarchies (not including the sensorimotor network, of course) include just the translation, rotation, reflection and scaling operators since the symmetry property, connectivity and "polygonicity" of a figure would not be changed by their application. However, the GLUE operator is not included, since its application could change a symmetric figure into an asymmetric figure, a connected figure into a non-connected figure, a polygon into a non-polygon, and conversely in all three cases.

We specify three other classes of concept network which are not organized into hierarchies. The *location* concept networks are a class of concept networks representing all geometric figures located at a single location. A figure's center is computed by averaging all the endpoints of all its line segments. This center is then considered the figure's location. The operators in a concept network in this class include only the rotation operators with a rotation axis at the figure's center and the reflection operators with reflection axes that pass through the figure's center.

The *size* concept networks represent geometric figures that are the same size. The size concept networks are currently only defined for figures with cyclic symmetry where it is possible to to find a center to the figure and a unique circle in which the figure is inscribed. The size of a figure is specified by the radius of this circle. The operators in this class of networks include all translation, rotation and reflection operators.

The *length and orientation* concept networks represent geometric figures that are the same length and oriented in the same direction. The length concept networks are currently only defined for figures with reflective symmetry. The orientation of a figure is determined by the slope of one of its reflective axes. A figure may be viewed as having different orientations if it has more than one axis of reflection. The length of a figure is determined by projecting perpendicular lines from each line segment endpoint to the reflective axis. The distance between the most extreme points of intersection is the length of the figure. Since figures may not be rotated, only the translation, reflection and scaling operators are included in this class of networks.

Further concept networks may be derived from existing concept networks by taking the intersection of two concept networks. For instance the intersection of the non-polygon concept network and the rotational symmetry concept network gives us the concept network of non-polygons with rotational symmetry. Given two algebras, the intersection of the respective object sets is closed under the set of operators formed by the intersection of the operator sets.

The concept networks in Figures 3(a) and 3(b) are all groupings of objects in the sensorimotor network. It is also possible to group the operators and macro-operators in the sensorimotor network. For example, we define the *copy rotations* as follows:

COPYROT[n,d,p]: A class of single argument macro-operators that returns n copies of its argument rotated in increments of d degrees around point p.

The Star of David may be viewed as a copy rotation of a single triangle with five copies at angle 60 degrees around the center of the figure. Since the macro-operators are not crucial to our development in this paper, we will leave it as an exercise to the reader to define the copy rotation macro-operators in terms of the operators in Figure 2.

We have included the macro-operators here in order to suggest how it might be possible to find an isomorphism between seemingly non-isomorphic figures as in the case of Figure 1(b). In that figure, the four osculating rectangles in figure A are mapped to the six osculating triangles in figure C. An isomorphism can be formed if one sees both the group of rectangles and the group of triangles as copy rotations. We are currently investigating how macro-operators might be fully integrated into our model.

4 Characterizing Proportional Analogy

Proportional analogies are analogies of the form A is to B as C is to D. In our characterization of proportional analogy, there are four different components. Let us take a look at each of these components.

The *items* in a proportional analogy are simply the objects A, B, C and D. Items may be any objects in the sensorimotor network. In the case of geometric figures, we will sometimes refer to items as figures.

A single *description* is associated with each item in a proportional analogy. A description is modelled as a tree where each *n*-ary internal node is labeled with an *n*-ary operator and each leaf node is labeled with an object. We will sometimes refer to a node labeled with an object or operator X as an 'X node.' The object that is described by a description may be discovered by a bottom-up evaluation of the tree. Given any description, a *subdescription* or *subtree* is a tree rooted at any node in the description. An *immediate subdescription* or *subtree* is a subdescription rooted at any child of the description's root. A *partial description* of a geometric figure is a description of any of its subfigures. The null partial description is symbolized by the $\perp$ symbol. Three different descriptions of the Star of David figure are shown in Figure 4. Notice that description 4(a) is the description needed in the proportional analogy in Figure 1(a), description 4(b) is the one needed in Figure 1(b) and description 4(c) is the one needed in Figure 1(c).

A *transformation* is any of a class of alterations that can be made to the description of an object, changing it into another description, usually of a different object. In this way, we can represent the change that is made to item A to get item B and to item C

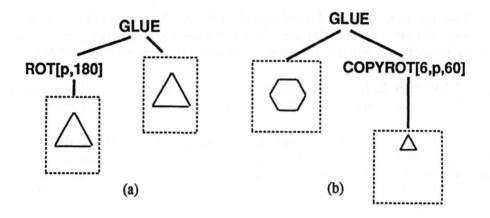

(a) (b)

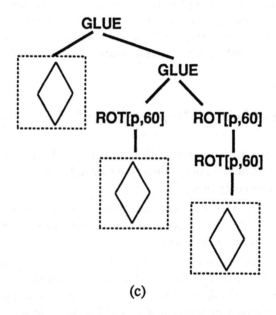

(c)

Figure 4:   Three descriptions of the Star of David.
The point p is the location <200,200>, i.e.
the center of the frame.

to get item D. In order to specify the transformations, we define an *insertion tree* to be a description where exactly one of its leaf nodes is labeled by a variable. There are two primitive transformations: insert an insertion tree into a description and delete an insertion tree from a description. An insertion tree is inserted into a description by replacing a subtree of the description with a new tree formed by instantiating the variable in the insertion tree with the subtree. The deletion of an insertion tree is done in an inverse fashion. A transformation then, is a sequence of primitive transformations which may be applied one after the other to a description.

The correspondence between the objects and operators in the descriptions of A and B to the object and operators in the descriptions of C and D will be called a *mapping*. In our characterization of proportional analogy, the mapping is restricted to be an *isomorphism*, i.e. a one-to-one, onto mapping. A consequence of the isomophism condition is that the descriptions of A and C have identical structures and there is a one-to-one correspondence between the object and operator labels in the description of A and the object and operator labels in the description of C. Identical conditions must hold between the descriptions of B and D.

The isomorphism requirement may seem excessively restrictive and perhaps requires a word of explanation. Our focus is on the process of redescription and NOT on the mapping process as is the case with most of the fixed description approaches to analogy. It thus makes sense to use as simple a mapping strategy as possible and try to make the redescription process do the work of forming analogies.

Now, let us put all the various components together to make a proportional analogy. To illustrate this, I call your attention to Figure 5 which shows how PAN would represent the geometric figures in the proportional analogy in Figure 1(c). Term A is described as three line segments where the sixty degree angle between the line segments is represented by the insertion of ROT[p,60] operators. The transformation of A into B is accomplished by deleting the insertion tree formed by the root GLUE node in A with the vertical line node as the left child and a variable as the right child. The objects and operators in the descriptions of A and B are mapped to the objects and operators of the descriptions of C and D by mapping the GLUE operator to the GLUE operator, the ROT[p,60] operator to the ROT[p,60] operator and the vertical line figure to the parallelogram figure. Notice that both the line figure and the parallelogram belong to a concept network formed by the intersection of five of the concept networks discussed in section 2. The concept network which contains the vertical line and the parallelogram, consists of all figures with rotational symmetry, reflective symmetry, a vertical orientation axis, the same length as the vertical line and located at point p.

5 How PAN Will Work

Let us now examine the current design of PAN. In this section, we sketch the overall organization and procedures of PAN as they are currently envisioned. The algorithms discussed here have not yet been implemented, so should be taken in a provisional spirit.

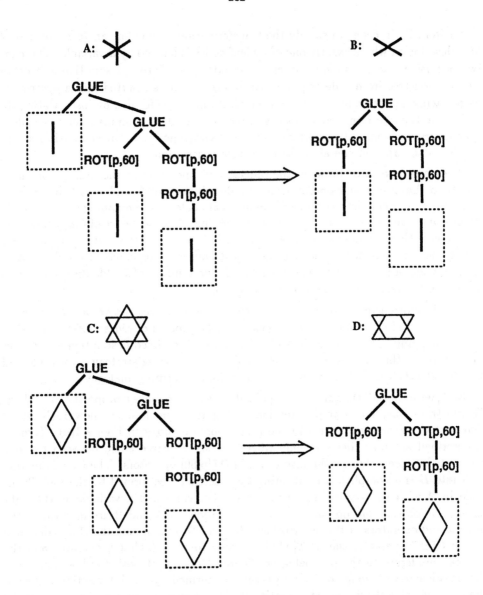

Figure 5: An algebraic representation of the proportional
analogy in Figure 1(c). The point 'p' is in the
center of the frame: <200,200>.

The top-level procedure of PAN is shown below. The input to PAN is a fixed description of item A in normal form (see below) and descriptions of items B and C consisting of single objects from the sensorimotor network. The output is a new description of B which is a transformation of A's description, a new description of C which is structurally identical to A's description, and an isomorphism M' between the objects and operators in the descriptions of A and B to the objects and operators in the descriptions of C and D.

PAN:

- *transform*:* Create a description of B which is a transformation of a given fixed description of A.

- *map*:* Create a description of C and an isomorphic mapping M which maps the objects and operators in the description of A to the objects and operators in the description of C.

- *apply-map:* Extend mapping M to M' maintaining the isomorphism condition by adding maps for all objects and operators in B's description but not in A's description. Apply M' to the description of B to get the description of D.

Note that this procedure and the ones to follow permit backtracking. Procedures which might return more than one set of outputs are marked with an asterick at the end of their name. For example, the *transform** procedure typically would find several ways to transform the description of A into a description of B. Sections of pseudocode that permit backtracking which are not labeled as procedures are also marked with an asterick. If a backtracking procedure or pseudocode section fails to complete execution, processing backs up to the last procedure or pseudocode section with an asterick. If the very first procedure or pseudocode section called within another procedure fails, then the calling procedure also fails. The reader may notice a similarity between our pseudocode and the computer language Prolog [26] in which we are planning to implement PAN. In presenting this pseudocode, we have decided not to show explicitly the arguments to the procedures so as not to overload the reader with too many symbols. However, for each procedure, the input and output arguments will be mentioned in the text.

In the remainder of this section, we discuss a global variable, called the Change Level, which helps control the search in the space of descriptions. We then define a normal form for the descriptions of A, and finally take a more detailed look at the transformation phase and the mapping phase.

5.1 The Change Level

Given any two descriptions, there may be many ways of transforming one into the other. Also, many different mappings are possible depending on the choice of descriptions. We would like to place an ordering on the possible transformations and mappings between two descriptions such that the "simplest" ones are attempted first, and more complicated ones are tried later. We model this in PAN by associating a weight with each transformation and each mapping as a measure of how much "mental effort" it takes to make that particular alteration to a description. The weight of a transformation is a function of the weights on its component insertions and deletions. Similarly, the weight of a mapping is a function of the weights on the individual maps. We define a global integer variable called the *Change Level* which defines the amount of overall change permitted to the descriptions. The sum of the weights of the transformation and the mapping must equal the Change Level. The Change Level acts as a kind of leash which is initially as tight as possible (zero) but is gradually loosened until some transformation and some mapping is found so that the proportional analogy problem can be solved.

Use of the Change Level gives rise to a search called depth-first iterative deepening [19]. In this search strategy, a depth-first search is made of the search space up to a bound on the depth of the search tree. In the case of PAN, the Change Level establishes this bound. If the thing being searched for is not found, then the bound is increased. The order of visitation of nodes in the search space is the same as a breadth-first search but has the advantage of linear space requirements as opposed to the exponential space requirements of breadth-first search.

In the procedures discussed below, in order to suppress some detail, the Change Level is not explicitly included. Instead it is implied that the Change Level is consulted whenever there is a choice between several different insertions, deletions or mappings. In a prototype version of PAN in the character string domain [21], an approach that seemed to work fairly well, uniform weight of one was assigned to every insertion and deletion.

5.2 A Normal Form for Descriptions

An examination of the descriptions that may be created from the objects and operators in the geometry algebra (sensorimotor network) reveals that classes of descriptions are essentially equivalent. This redundancy occurs because of the algebraic properties of the operators in the algebra. For instance, the GLUE operator is associative so, for all figures a, b and c, GLUE(GLUE(a,b),c) = GLUE(a,GLUE(b,c)). Thus a description containing two GLUE nodes in which one is the child of the other is equivalent to another description which was identical in all respects except that the GLUE nodes are "rotated" so the former child becomes the parent. Another property of interest is that the translation of any pair of figures that have been glued together is equivalent to gluing together two figures created by applying the same translation to each figure individually (in other words, for any figures a and b and any translation operator TRANS, TRANS(GLUE(a,b)) = GLUE(TRANS(a),TRANS(b))). The rotation, reflection and scaling operators also have this property with respect to GLUE.

To eliminate duplicate descriptions, we create a normal form for descriptions. Here, we sketch a normal form which eliminates some, but not all duplicate descriptions. We will also leave out the macro-operators pending a more detailed analysis of how the primitive operators (from Figure 1) and macro-operators interact with one another. To define our provisional normal form, we call any description which contains only translation, reflection, rotation and scaling operators a *TRRS-sequence*. Based on the above observations, we then say that a description is in *normal form* if it is either a TRRS-sequence or its root is a GLUE node where its left subtree is a TRRS-sequence and its right subtree is a description in normal form. Thus, a normal form description consists of a "superstructure" of n GLUE nodes in right-associative form below which there are $n + 1$ TRRS-sequences.

Could there possibly be any cognitive significance to the normal form for descriptions given its seemingly rigid mathematical structure? I would like to suggest that there might be. I speculate that the normal form represents a "compiling" (in the sense of a computer language compiler) of past experience with the operators of a concept network. After much experience with particular operations, a cognitive agent learns the properties of particular operators such as transitivity, commutativity etc. The agent thus settles on particular forms for descriptions eliminating any redundancy. I conjecture that this compiling process is related to the development of 'groupings' and algebraic group structure that Piaget has found in the thinking of children [23]. Of course, we are not attempting to model this development process, but simply assume that it has already taken place.

5.3 The Transformation Phase

The *transform** procedure, shown below:

---

transform*:

- *delete*:* delete insertion trees from the description of A creating a partial description of B.

- *insert:* insert further insertion trees creating a full description of B.

---

takes as input a description of A, an object B and, for each line segment in B, a boolean flag called a match flag. The *match flags* are used to monitor subfigure overlap. A line segment in B is *marked* if it is part of a subfigure that has been matched to a leaf node in A. Otherwise, a line segment in B is *unmarked*. *Transform** returns a description of B obtained by inserting and deleting insertion trees in A's description.

*Transform** proceeds by first deleting insertion trees from the description of A and matching what remains to the line segments in B and marking them. After this deletion and matching process, any unmarked line segments in B are assumed to have been inserted. The *insert* procedure then combines the remaining unmarked line segments into figures and appends them with GLUE operators to the partial description of B created by *delete**.

---

delete*:

- if (active subdescription (see explanation below) is a TRRS-sequence) then

    - *match-TRRS-sequence*:* Attempt to describe some subfigure of B as a TRRS-sequence which is a modification of the active subdescription.

- else

    - Call *delete** on all subtrees of active subdescription.
    - *adjust-root:* modify the active subdescription so that it reflects the structure of B.

The *delete** procedure, shown above, intertwines the deletion of insertion trees from the description of A with the matching of its leaf-nodes to subfigures in B. *Delete** is a recursive procedure which takes as input a subtree of the description of A which we will call the *active subdescription*, an object B from the sensorimotor network and a set of match flags. *Delete** returns a new, modified set of match flags as well as a partial description of B modified from the active subdescription. If no part of B can be described by modifying the active subdescription or if all line segments in B have been marked so the subdescription must be viewed as deleted, then instead of returning a partial description of B, the symbol ⊥ is returned.

The initial call of *delete** is made on an active subdescription consisting of the full description of A, a figure B, and a set of match flags indicating that B is completely unmarked. *Delete** executes a depth-first, postorder traversal of A's description with recursive calls being made on the immediate subtrees of the active subdescription. The basic idea is to try to first match the leaf-nodes of A's description to subfigures in B and then readjust A's description in a bottom-up fashion so that it reflects the structure of B.

Delete* consists of a base case and a recursive case. In the base case, *delete** tests if the active subdescription is a TRRS-sequence and, if it is, calls the *match-TRRS-sequence** procedure shown below. The input to the *match-TRRS-sequence** is a single TRRS-sequence, the figure B and the set of match flags for B. The output is either a new TRRS-sequence which describes a subfigure of B and which is formed from the original TRRS-sequence or the output is the ⊥ symbol. Also output is a new set of match flags marked appropriately.

Processing in *match-TRRS-sequence** is based on the fact that the result of applying a translation, reflection, rotation or scaling operator to a figure is a figure that is

---

match-TRRS-sequence*:

- Evaluate TRRS-sequence giving figure X.

- (*) Select line segment from X.

- (*) Select line segment from B.

- (*) Compute transformation that takes line segment in X to line segment in B.

- Apply transformation to all line segments in X.

- (*) if (every line segment in X matches a line segment in B, adjusting for line segment intersections and at least one of the matched line segments is unmarked) then

  - Mark all matched line segments in B

  - Insert the insertion tree corresponding to the transformation just discovered into the TRRS-sequence forming a new TRRS-sequence.

  - Return new TRRS-sequence.

- else

  - Return ⊥

---

similar to the original [2, Chap. 2] i.e., there exists some scaling factor that makes the figures congruent. Further, the effect of applying one of these operators to the whole figure is identical to applying the operator to each individual line segment in the figure. Procedure *match-TRRS-sequence** first evaluates the TRRS-sequence giving the figure it describes, X. It then selects one line segment from figure X and one from figure B and finds some transformation between them. Under the assumption that these two line segments are matching counterparts in two similar figures, all line segments in X are then transformed and matched against figure B. If a match is found, an insertion tree corresponding to the transformation is then inserted into the original TRRS-sequence giving a new TRRS-sequence. Note that all possible transformations can be reduced to one of the following: a single translation, a single reflection, a single rotation, a single translation followed by a single rotation across an axis parallel to the line of translation (called a *glide reflection*,) a rotation followed by a scaling, or a reflection followed by a scaling (see [2, Chap. 2].) It may be desirable to make further modifications to the TRRS-sequence by canceling inverse operators and by exploiting other interactions between operators. If no match is found, then backtracking occurs and a different pair of line segments is selected. We are investigating methods of ordering the choice of line segment pairs according to the amount of transformation required. The

GOSSAMER system desribed by Futrelle [5] looks like a promising approach for doing this efficiently. Processing continues until all possible pairs are exhausted or until the Change Level limit has been exceeded. The $\perp$ symbol is returned if the Change Level limit permits, (the $\perp$ symbol will force the delete of an insertion tree,) otherwise the procedure fails.

In the recursive case, *delete** is called on all immediate subtrees of the active subdescription. After this, the root of the active subdescription is "adjusted" by *adjust-root* in order to properly describe B. At present, the adjustment process is only applied to the GLUE operator since this is the only operator that would not be part of a TRRS-sequence, but we expect that it will become a much more complicated procedure when the capability of handling macro-operators is added. The *adjust-root* procedure, shown here:

---

adjust-root:

- if (root = GLUE) then

    - if (both partial descriptions are $\perp$) then return $\perp$
    - else if (left partial description is $\perp$) then return right-subtree
    - else if (right partial description is $\perp$) then return left-subtree
    - else return GLUE node composed with left and right partial descriptions.

- else handle other operators.

---

takes as input the partial descriptions of B returned by the recursive calls to *delete** and the root of the active subdescription. These are combined to output a new partial description of B.

5.4 The Mapping Phase

The *map** procedure is shown below. The input to *map** is a subtree of the description of A called as before, the *active subdescription*, a figure C from the sensorimotor network, a set of match flags for C, and a partial mapping from the objects and operators in the description of A to the objects and operators in the description of C. The output of *map** is a partial description of C, an updated set of match flags and a new mapping. The initial call to *map** is made with a full description of A, figure C, an unmarked set of match flags and an empty mapping. When the initial call to *map** terminates successfully, it returns a full description of C that has a structure that is identical to the structure of A's description, a fully marked set of match flags and an isomorphic mapping from the objects and operators of the description of A to the objects and operators of the description of C. Though this is not expressed explicitly in the *map** procedure, note that *map** may not terminate successfully unless all match flags have been marked. Otherwise, the description of C would only be partial.

---

map*:

- if (root of active subdescription (see explanation below) is an object node) then

    - *map-object*:* Find map from active subdescription to some subfigure in C which preserves isomorphism. Mark subfigure.

- else if (root of active subdescription is an operator node) then

    - Call *map** on immediate subtrees of the active subdescription. Result is a set of partial descriptions of C.

    - *map-operator*:* Find map from the root of the active subdescription to some operator that appropriately combines the partial descriptions of the previous step and preserves isomorphism.

Like *delete** from above, *map** is a recursive procedure that executes a postorder depth-first traversal of the description of A. Unlike the *delete** procedure, because of the isomorphism condition, no insertion trees are inserted or deleted. In the base case, where the active subdescription is an object, the procedure *map-object**, shown below, is called which tries to find a map from the active subdescription to some subfigure in C. The input to *map-object** is the active subdescription (renamed to X,) the object C, the set of match flags and the current isomorphic mapping. The output is a new set of match flags and an updated isomorphic mapping. *Map-object** starts by attempting to find a minimal concept network to which the active subdescription can belong. *Map-object** applies all of the recognition procedures for the concept networks (recall from Section 2 that a recognition procedure is a boolean function associated with a concept network which determines whether or not an object from the sensorimotor network is in the object set of the concept network.) The initial concept network for the active subdescription is then the intersection of every concept network for which its associated recognition procedure succeeded. *Map-object** then attempts to find a subfigure in C which is in the same concept network as the active subdescription. If this fails then the concept network of the active subdescription is generalized as described in the *map-object** box. The amount of effort expended on generalizing a concept network is constrained by the Change Level variable by associating a weight with each of the potential generalizations. If a subfigure in C is found, then *map-object** checks to see if the isomorphism condition is maintained and adds the new map to the mapping.

In the recursive case of *map**, recursive calls are made on the immediate subtrees

map-object*:

- Let X be the active subdescription.

- Apply all recognition procedures to object X.

- Let S be the set of all concept networks which were successfully recognized in the preceding step.

- Let CN_0 be the intersection of all the concept networks in S.

- (*) Specify concept network CN in which X is an object.

  - Initially, $CN = CN_0$.
  - On each successive backtracking call, form a new concept network CN for X by generalizing CN_0. Let S' be the result of removing one or more of the concept networks in S or by replacing one or more of the concept networks in S with an ancestor from one of the concept network hierarchies. Let CN be the intersection of all concept networks in S'.

- (*) Attempt to find a subfigure Y of C which is in CN.

- (*) if (the map X→Y satisfies the isomorphism condition with current partial mapping) then

  - Mark Y in C.
  - Add X→Y to mapping.

- else fail.

of the active subdescription. These calls create partial descriptions of C along with a partial isomorphic mapping. The procedure *map-operator** is then called. *Map-operator** combines the partial descriptions from the recursive calls to *map** into a new partial description of C with a root operator that is mapped to the root of the active subdescription. At present, only identity maps are allowed between operators so *map-operator** is currently a fairly simple procedure. However, we imagine that *map-operator** will develop into a procedure similar to *map-object** using concept networks defined over operators, like the copy rotations, instead of objects.

6   Future Work

Our immediate goal is to finish the PAN program as described here. We then will develop a series of PAN versions where each successive program relaxes one or more simplifying restrictions made in the previous program. Here are the successive versions of PAN as we currently envision them:

PAN(0): This is the version described in this paper. The restrictions made are (1) that the description of A is fixed; (2) the descriptions of B and C may change but start out as objects; and (3) the transformation phase and the mapping phase are separable.

PAN(1): Relax restriction 1 in PAN(0). We now have the following restrictions: (2') the descriptions of A, B and C may change but start out as objects; and (3) from PAN(0).

PAN(2): Drop restriction 2' from PAN(1) altogether. Allow any descriptions of A, B and C. Keep restriction 3 from PAN(1).

PAN(3): Drop assumption 3 from PAN(2). Allow the transformation phase to proceed concurrently with the mapping phase creating a completely free interaction of the descriptions.

Another aspect of our work is to find other domains in which to study the redescription problem. We are currently working on a version of PAN that solves proportional analogies in the domain of character strings described by Hofstadter [10]. A working prototype of PAN in the character string domain is discussed by O'Hara [21]. This 'proto-PAN' is similar in its overall approach to the PAN discussed in this paper. It is different in that it uses a a top-down preorder depth-first traversal of the descriptions compared to the bottom-up postorder traversal used here. The preorder traversal had the disadvantage of exploring descriptions of B and C which could not possibly have matching leaf-nodes in the description of A. A further difference is that the distinction between the sensorimotor network and the concept network is not made in 'proto-PAN'. Mappings between strings in 'proto-PAN' are instead based on a somewhat ad hoc similarity measure. The different set of operators used in the string domain helps bring out domain independent aspects of the redescription problem . For example, the concatenation operator which combines two strings into one string is not symmetric like the GLUE operator and so does not permit the transformation phase to be divided into a deletion phase and an insertion phase. We are also searching for other more real world domains such as verbal proportional analogies as well as other domains in which the redescription process is evident such as metaphor.

Acknowledgements. The work described in this paper was supported in part by National Science Foundation grant IRI-9105806. Much appreciation to Bipin Indurkhya for many discussions on the subject of this paper as well as comments on drafts of this paper. Thanks to Joyce Friedman for her comments after a very thorough reading of a draft of this paper. Also, thanks to Margo Guertin and Mary Atkins for comments on the introduction. Finally, thanks to Wayne Snyder for a discussion about normal forms and to Sivaramakrishnan Rajagopalan for a disussion about univeral algebra.

References

[1] Chalmers D., French R., Hofstadter D., 1991, "High-Level Perception, Representation and Analogy: A Critique of Artificial Intelligence Methodology", CRCC Technical Report 49 - March 1991, Center for Research on Concepts and Cognition, Indiana University, Bloomington, Indiana.

[2] Dodge, C., 1972, *Euclidean Geometry and Transformations*, Addison-Wesley Publishing Company, Inc., Reading, Massachusetts.

[3] Evans T.G., 1968, "A Program for the Solution of a Class of Geometric-Analogy Intelligence-Test Questions," in M. Minsky (ed.) *Semantic Information Processing*, MIT Press, Cambridge, Mass. (1968), Chap. 5, pp. 271–353.

[4] Falkenhainer B., Forbus K. and Gentner D., 1989, "The Structure-Mapping Engine: Algorithm and Examples," *Artificial Intelligence* **41**: 1-63.

[5] Futrelle R., 1990, "Strategies for Diagram Understanding: Generalized Equivalence, Spatial/Object Pyramids and Animate Vision," Proceedings of the 10th International Conference on Pattern Recognition, IEEE Computer Society Press.

[6] Gentner D., 1983, "Structure-Mapping: A Theoretical Framework for Analogy", *Cognitive Science 7*, pp. 155–170.

[7] Greiner R., 1988, "Learning by Understanding Analogies," pp 1-36, in *Analogica*, A. Prieditis (ed.), Morgan Kaufmann Publishers, Los Altos, California.

[8] Hall R. P., 1989, "Computational Approaches to Analogical Reasoning: A Comparative Analysis", *Artificial Intelligence 39*, pp. 39–120.

[9] Hofstadter D.R., 1984, "The Copycat Project: An Experiment in Nondeterminism and Creative Analogies," A.I. Memo 755, Artificial Intelligence Laboratory, MIT, Cambridge, Mass.

[10] Hofstadter D.R., 1985, "Analogies and Roles in Human and Machine Thinking", in *Metamagical Themas: Questing for the Essence of Mind and Pattern*, Basic Books, Inc., New York; Chap. 24 (pp. 547–603).

[11] Hofstadter D. and Mitchell M., 1988a, "Concepts, Analogies and Creativity", *Proceedings of the Canadian Society for Computational Studies of Intelligence*, Universtiy of Alberta, Edmonton, Alberta.

[12] Hofstadter D.R. and Mitchell M., 1988b, "Conceptual Slippage and Analogy-Making: A Report on the Copycat Project," *Proceedings of the Tenth Annual Conference of the Cognitive Science Society*, Lawrence Erlbaum Associates, Hillsdale, NJ.

[13] Holland J., Holyoak K., Nisbett R., Thagard P., 1989, *Induction: Processes of Inference, Learning, and Discovery*, MIT Press, Cambridge, Massachusetts.

[14] Holyoak K.J. and Thagard P., 1989, "Analogical Mapping by Constraint Satisfaction", Cognitive Science, Vol. 13, pp 295-355, 1989.

[15] Indurkhya B., 1989, "Modes of Analogy," in K. P. Jantke (ed.) *Analogical and Inductive Inference*, Lecture Notes in Artificial Intelligence 397, Springer-Verlag (1989), Berlin, GDR, pp. 217–230.

[16] Indurkhya B., 1991, "On the Role of Interpretive Analogy in Learning", *New Generation Computing*, Vol. 8, No. 4, pp. 385-402.

[17] Indurkhya B., 1992, *Metaphor and Cognition: An Interactionist Approach*, Kluwer Academic Publishers, Dordrecht, The Netherlands.

[18] Kedar-Cabelli S., 1988, "Toward a Computational Model of Purpose-Directed Analogy," pp 89-107, in *Analogica*, A. Prieditis (ed.), Morgan Kaufmann Publishers, Inc., Los Altos, California.

[19] Korf, R. E., 1985, "Depth-first iterative deepening: An optimal admissible tree search", *Artificial Intelligence*, $27(1)$:97-109.

[20] Mitchell M., and Hofstadter D., 1990, "The Emergence of Understanding in a Computer Model of Concepts and Analogy-Making," *Physica D*, 42:322-334.

[21] O'Hara S., 1992, "Modelling the 'Redescription' Process in the Context of Proportional Analogies," BU-CS Technical Report #92-002, Department of Computer Science, Boston University, Boston, Massachusetts.

[22] Piaget J., 1947, *The Psychology of Intelligence*, translated by M. Piercy and D. Berlyne, reprinted by Littlefield, Adams & Co., Totowa, New Jersey, 1981, by permission of Humanities Press Inc., New York, New York.

[23] Piaget J., 1953, *Logic and Psychology*, Manchester University Press, Manchester, UK.

[24] Piaget J., 1970, *Genetic Epistemology*, translated by E. Duckworth, W. W. Norton and Company, New York, New York.

[25] Rosch E., 1978, "Principles of Categorization," in *Cognition and Categorization*, E. Rosch and B. Lloyd (eds.), Laurence Erlbaum Associates, Hillsdale, New Jersey, pp. 27-77.

[26] Sterling L. and Shapiro E., 1986, *The Art of Prolog: Advanced Programming Techniques*, MIT Press, Cambridge, MA.

[27] Smith E., 1989, "Concepts and Induction," in *Foundations of Cognitive Science*, M. Posner (ed.), The MIT Press, Cambridge, Massachusetts.

[28] Winston P., 1978, "Learning by Creating and Justifying Transfer Frames," *Artificial Intelligence*, 10(2): 147-172.

[29] Winston P., 1980, "Learning and Reasoning by Analogy," *Communications of the ACM* 23(12): 689-703.

Inductive Strengthening: the effects of a simple heuristic for restricting hypothesis space search

Foster John Provost

Bruce G. Buchanan

Department of Computer Science
University of Pittsburgh
Pittsburgh, PA 15260 (USA)

Abstract

This paper examines the effects on a learning program of using a simple heuristic for restricting hypothesis space search and suggests the desirability of making the heuristic explicit so that it can be altered easily. The heuristic is: *only consider new hypotheses that cover at least one example not covered by the current concept description.* We study the use of the heuristic for three tasks: (i) restricting subsequent search after part of a concept description is learned, (ii) restricting search when partial concept descriptions are provided as initial knowledge, and (iii) restricting search when the heuristic is used as a constant bias to a higher level program that adjusts the bias of the learning program along different dimensions. We show that not only does this heuristic reduce the number of nodes searched, it also reduces the size of the resultant concept description and increases its predictive accuracy.

1. Introduction

Researchers in the machine learning community have been concentrating recently on *inductive biases*, defined by Mitchell as "any basis for choosing one generalization over another other than strict consistency with the observed training instances"[Mitchell, 1980]. The *strength* of a bias is the fraction of hypotheses considered by the learner within that bias relative to all possible hypotheses [Utgoff, 1984]. This paper studies the effects of a simple heuristic for restricting bias space search. This heuristic comes from a class of related heuristics that we call *inductive strengthening* heuristics. These heuristics restrict the search space dynamically, based on knowledge learned during search, as opposed to biases that statically restrict or order the hypothesis space (see [Rendell, 1986] for a discussion of different types of biases). "Strengthening" comes from the restriction of the hypothesis space--the overall bias of the system is made stronger; "inductive" is based on the non-deductive nature of the restriction--there is no guarantee that a better hypothesis might not be obscured by the restriction.

This type of heuristic is by no means new; in fact, most inductive learning programs use some form of inductive strengthening heuristic. The ever popular recursive splitting programs [Quinlan, 1986], [Breiman, Friedman, Olshen, & Stone, 1984] partition the data (*e.g.*, based on an information theoretic criterion), restricting their search from addressing hypotheses that require any other partition. In contrast to the recursive splitting algorithms, which attempt to specialize the most general concept description, the AQ algorithms take individual positive examples as seed hypotheses and attempt to find generalizations (see [Michalski, Mozetic, Hong, & Lavrac, 1986] for a brief description of AQ15 and more pointers). The AQ algorithms also use a form of inductive strengthening--when extending its current concept description, AQ takes a positive example that is not yet covered as its next seed. The CN2 algorithm [Clark, 1989] combines aspects of both the recursive splitting and AQ algorithms. It too uses a form of inductive strengthening: when the algorithm finds a good rule, it removes the examples the rule covers from the training set. In general, though, the contributions of this type of heuristic to the learning process are taken for granted in the literature.

This paper examines the effects of a simple heuristic for inductive strengthening in the context of the MC-RL learning program and suggests the desirability of making the heuristic explicit so that it can be altered easily. As described in Section 2, MC-RL performs a straightforward search of a space of conjunctive rules in an attempt to form a concept description in the form of a set of rules to be used in an evidence gathering inference engine. MC-RL's search is restricted by various heuristics. Section 3 examines the effects of the simple heuristic, *consider only rules that cover examples not covered by the current concept description*. We show that not only does this heuristic reduce the number of nodes searched, it also reduces the size of the resultant concept description and increases its predictive accuracy. We study the use of the heuristic for three tasks: (i) restricting subsequent search after part of a concept description is learned (the basic inductive strengthening task), (ii) restricting search when partial concept descriptions are provided as initial knowledge, and (iii) using learned knowledge across biases in a system that automatically adjusts MC-RL's inductive bias.

2. The MC-RL Learning Program

MC-RL is a multiclass version of the RL4 learning system [Clearwater & Provost, 1990], a descendent of Meta-DENDRAL [Buchanan & Mitchell, 1978]. RL4 searches for a disjunctive set of conjunctive rules that form the knowledge base for an evidence gathering performance system (a system which combines the evidence from several disjunctive rules to make a classification). RL4 structures its hypothesis space in a general to specific hierarchy rooted at the most general rule (every example is an element of the concept). Two types of specialization operators are used: (i) adding a conjunct, and (ii) specializing an existing conjunct. These operations are performed based on information provided in a partial domain model (PDM), which contains descriptions of the attributes, their types, possible values and value hierarchies for each attribute, along with other information used to determine when a rule is satisfactory, too general or too specific, and/or to restrict the hypothesis space.

RL4 Search Algorithm (Beam Search)

init-rule := (NIL ⇒ CONCEPT)
good-rules := ∅
too-general-rules := ∅
new-too-general-rules := { *init-rule* }
<u>repeat</u>
  too-general-rules := *beam width* best of *new-too-general-rules*
  new-too-general-rules := ∅
  <u>for</u> each *tg-rule* ∈ *too-general-rules* <u>do</u>
    specializations := feature-specializations(*tg-rule*)
        ∪ new-conj-specializations(*tg-rule*)
    <u>for</u> each *rule* ∈ *specializations* <u>do</u>
      compute positive and negative coverages of *rule*
      <u>if</u> *rule* is too specific <u>then</u> prune entire subtree rooted at *rule*
      <u>else if</u> *rule* is too general <u>then</u> add to *new-too-general-rules*
        (IS: if it covers an example not covered previously)
      <u>otherwise</u>
        save satisfactory *rule* in *good-rules*
          (IS: if it covers an example not covered previously)
        <u>if</u> learning maximally specific rules
        <u>then</u> add *rule* to *new-too-general-rules*
<u>until</u> *too-general-rules* = ∅ or stopping conditions met
retain maximally general/specific of *good-rules*

specialization functions (without automatic numeric marker selection)

feature-specializations(*rule*)
  specializations := { *r* | *r* is a rule created by replacing the last conjunct of *rule* with a
          more specific feature from the PDM which is not known to be
          too specific}
  <u>return</u> *specializations*

new-conj-specializations(*rule*)
  <u>if</u> adding a conjunct to *rule* would exceed the max conjunct limit
  <u>then</u> *specializations* := ∅
  <u>else</u> *specializations* := { *r* | *r* is a rule created by adding a feature *f* from the PDM
    that satisfies the following conditions:
      1) *f* is one of the most general features in its attribute's value hierarchy
      2) *f* is not known to be too specific
      3) *f*'s attribute follows that of all attributes mentioned in *rule* in the
        PDM's (heuristically) ordered list of attributes
        (eliminates redundancy in rule space) }
  <u>return</u> *specializations*

Fig. 1. RL4 Search Algorithm (Beam Search)

RL4's basic algorithm is given in Figure 1 (the two lines annotated with 'IS:' are the conditions used to implement the inductive strengthening heuristic). This learning procedure keeps statistics on the various tentative rules and compares these with the criteria specified in the PDM. If a rule is too general, it is specialized. If too specific, it is discarded along with the entire subtree rooted there. If satisfactory, it is saved. Several search methods are provided; the most commonly used is a beam search, which will be used throughout this paper. The evaluation function for the beam search is specified in the PDM, the default function rates node r_1 better than node r_2 if the ratio of true positives to false positives covered by r_1 is greater than that of r_2 (in a tie, the rule with the larger coverage wins). In summary, the search procedure is a beam search of the space of syntactically defined rules, in which sections of the rule space are pruned if they are guaranteed not to yield results that will prove satisfactory with respect to the criteria of the PDM.

It is straightforward to determine the worst-case time complexity of RL4's basic algorithm if the effects of the pruning heuristics are ignored. For the sake of this discussion, let us assume that there are a attributes, each having a maximum of v nominal values, n examples and a maximum of k conjuncts per rule. The search tree would have depth k and a maximum branching factor of av. At each node, RL4's search examines the n examples giving a time complexity of $O(kbav(n+\log bav))$, where b is the beam width. The log term comes from the need to sort the nodes after each level expansion in order to determine the b best to keep on the beam.

The simple inductive strengthening heuristic used for this paper is: *consider only rules that cover examples not covered by the current concept description*. This is implemented by **not** saving rules to the list *new-too-general-rules* if they do not cover a new example; before this point in the procedure, the coverages for the rules had not yet been computed.

MC-RL's learning procedure is identical to that of RL4, except that in MC-RL's search space, a node can represent rules for several different concepts (a node is essentially an antecedent with one or more possible consequents). *Too-general-nodes* take the place of *too-general-rules*, where a *too-general-node* is a node from which can be formed at least one "too-general" rule. Statistics are kept in a node for the different consequents; these consequents are eliminated one by one as the rules they form become too specific or are found to be satisfactory. The inductive strengthening heuristic in MC-RL is implemented by not saving a possible rule in a *too-general-node* unless it covers a positive example (for the corresponding concept) that was not covered by some other rule for the correct concept.

3. The Effects of the Simple Inductive Strengthening Heuristic

In this section, the effects of the simple IS heuristic are examined in three tasks. First, the heuristic is used to restrict subsequent search after part of a concept description is learned. Second, partial concept descriptions are provided to the learner as a starting bias of initial domain knowledge; the heuristic is then used to restrict search to complete the description. Finally, the heuristic is used as a constant bias in a program that adjusts the bias of the learning program along other dimensions.

Three domains are used for this study. Two were taken from the UCI repository: (i) a domain of mushrooms, where the task is to characterize a mushroom as being poisonous or edible (*cf.* [Schlimmer, 1987]), and (ii) a domain of automobiles (circa 1985), where the classification task was to place them into price categories (<$10K, $10K<price<$20K, >$20K). For the mushroom domain, unless otherwise indicated, 100 examples were used for training and 915 for testing; for the auto domain 100 examples were used for training and 99 for testing.

The third domain was an artificial domain with 22 attributes each with between 2 and 12 nominal values. Two learning tasks were created from this domain. The data for task 1 were generated from a set of 10 rules. Some of the rules are "heuristic" rules, in that they have non-null false positive coverage. Task 2 was to learn a set of 20 rules (or an equivalent set), similar to those in task 1. The size of the training sets used is 200, the size of the test sets is 2000.

In all three domains, an inference engine was used that collected all rules that covered an example and let them vote as to the correct classification. Each data point given in the tables and figures of this section is the result of averaging over 10 runs with randomly selected training and test sets; 95% confidence intervals are indicated (obtained using Student's t distribution).

3.1. Inductive Strengthening during Learning

Table 1 shows the results of running MC-RL on the four learning tasks with and without the inductive strengthening heuristic. The columns list the domain (and task), whether or not the heuristic was used (IS?), the number of nodes searched, the size of the resultant concept (number of rules), and the classification accuracy on the test data.

Domain	IS?	Nodes searched	# rules	Acc. on test data
Artificial - Task 1	no	953±45	125±7	96.6±0.4
Artificial - Task 1	yes	535±88	26±3	96.9±0.6
Artificial - Task 2	no	1939±157	370±21	95.3±0.1
Artificial - Task 2	yes	250±112	24±2	97.3±0.4
Automobiles	no	13219±972	4240±785	73.7±2.7
Automobiles	yes	8991±2004	72±16	82.3±2.6
Mushrooms	no	5245±436	901±178	94.2±1.5
Mushrooms	yes	2136±1477	26±6	94.3±1.8

Table 1. The effects of using IS heuristic during learning (averaged over 10 trials)

The results show that the heuristic is effective in reducing the number of nodes searched for each learning task. The amount of search reduction varied from a factor of eight for Task 2 to less than a factor of two in the automobile domain. Note that this search reduction was in addition to that achieved by MC-RL's other pruning methods. For example, the size of the syntactically defined hypothesis space searched for Task 1 is 2.7 E+5 rules.

The heuristic was also effective in reducing the size of the resultant concept definition. This is especially important if the rule set is intended to be viewed by humans; it is also important with respect to the efficiency of the performance system using the set of rules as a knowledge base. A similar reduction in the size of the concept description can be achieved by pruning the rule set to find a subset with maximal predictive accuracy (see [Quinlan, 1987]). This is a time consuming task, especially if the rule set is large. Even with a greedy procedure, for the tasks listed above pruning of the rule set takes longer than the learning itself.

The most surprising result is that in two of the four tasks, the classification accuracy on the test data is increased significantly with the use of the inductive strengthening heuristic. The reason is that the smaller rule sets contain good subsets of the satisfactory rules. This indicates that MC-RL's beam search evaluation function does a good job of ordering the rules so that the "better" rules are learned first. The inductive strengthening heuristic keeps the learner from acquiring rules that would lower the accuracy.

Table 2 shows the effect of the inductive strengthening heuristic in the mushroom and automobile domains when the heuristic pruning of the beam search has been reduced. More specifically, the beam width was increased from 100 to 1000, thereby excluding fewer nodes and their associated subtrees. In both domains although the total amount of search was increased, the effect of the simple inductive strengthening heuristic was also increased with respect to the number of nodes searched and the size of the rule set. The predictive accuracy of the searches that did not use the simple heuristic was increased by using the larger beam, but was still somewhat less than that achieved by using the inductive strengthening heuristic.

Domain	IS?	Nodes searched	# rules	Acc. on test data
Automobiles	no	99125±5176	33829±3224	80.8±2.0
Automobiles	yes	38966±30977	75±18	82.7±2.5
Mushrooms	no	29325±1938	3718±618	92.5±1.0
Mushrooms	yes	3108±3024	26±6	94.3±1.8

Table 2. The effects of using IS heuristic with the effects of beam search reduced (averaged over 10 trials)

These positive effects occur because the inductive strengthening heuristic focuses the hypothesis space search on rules that address incompleteness in the current concept description. The next section examines this effect further, showing that the heuristic scales the amount of search performed to the amount of concept description left to be learned.

3.2 Inductive Strengthening based on Prior Knowledge

This section investigates the use of the inductive strengthening heuristic to restrict search when a portion of the target concept description is provided as initial domain knowledge (the heuristic is also used during learning, as in Section 3.1). The artificial domain was used, since the "correct" concept could be known in advance.

Figures 2 & 3 show data generated by running MC-RL (on Task 1 and Task 2, respectively) starting with a randomly chosen subset of the "correct" rules, and using the simple IS heuristic to restrict subsequent search (95% confidence indicated). In Task 2, the difference was not very pronounced when 200 training examples were used. This was because MC-RL's beam search always searches a level completely; and the first level had 125 nodes (approximately one-half of the nodes needed for a complete search). With only 200 examples, the learner was unable to capture the subtle differences in the concept with 20 rules. Figure 3 shows the results of using 1000 training examples. On the average, with five times as many training examples, the accuracy was increased by about half a percent.

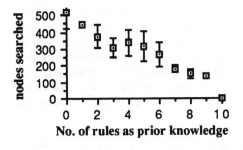 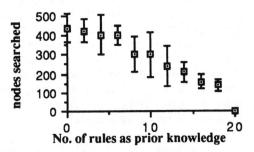

Fig 2. Linear decrease in the amount of search needed with the amount of prior knowledge available
(Task 1, averaged over 10 trials)

Fig 3. Linear decrease in the amount of search needed with the amount of prior knowledge available
(Task 2, averaged over 10 trials)

The figures show a linear relationship (in either case a line can be fit to the data with $R=0.97$) between the amount of the concept description still remaining to be learned (not given as prior knowledge) and the amount of search necessary to complete the concept description. The simple inductive strengthening heuristic is effective in directing MC-RL to those hypotheses that address incompleteness in the currently held concept description. Because it directs the search to incompleteness in the currently held concept description, the heuristic is useful in a system that constructs its concept description as it adjusts its inductive bias.

3.3. Inductive Strengthening in a Bias Adjustment System

Bias adjustment systems attempt to find a set of bias choices that is suitable for learning the concept at hand (see [Provost, 1991] for an overview of existing bias adjustment systems). For the results reported above, the strongest sufficient biases for the artificial domain's tasks were known *a priori*; suitable biases were determined empirically (by hand) for the automobile and mushroom domains. The ClimBS system [Provost, 1992], described below, performs a hill climbing search in MC–RL's bias space. Bias adjustment systems, however, must have biases of their own; otherwise, we would be trying to learn in the absence of any bias. In this section we examine the simple inductive strengthening heuristic as a static bias to ClimBS. Since the use of the inductive strengthening heuristic is represented explicitly in ClimBS as well as in MC-RL, an operator could be given to ClimBS which varied the bias along this dimension.

In bias adjustment, inductive strengthening heuristics can be used in the transfer of knowledge across biases. If a partial, but not satisfactory, concept description is learned with one bias, it can be used as prior knowledge after the bias is shifted. This is how the inductive strengthening heuristic is used in ClimBS.

ClimBS. The ClimBS system performs a hill climbing search in a multidimensional bias space, learning its concept description across biases. ClimBS' user specifies an initial bias in the form of a partial domain model (PDM), and bias transformation operators that operate on the PDM. ClimBS forms candidate biases by applying the transformation operators to the current bias; ClimBS then runs the learning system with each bias, collecting the concept descriptions learned with each. The biases are then compared based on the performance of the descriptions using a performance system and an evaluation function specified by the investigator. The current bias is set to be the best of these biases and the process iterates until the learned description satisfies some stopping criteria. The learning system used currently is MC-RL. The performance system used for these results is the voting inference engine. An in-depth treatment of ClimBS is provided in [Provost, 1992]. The search differs from strict hill climbing in that it will continue to search by random walk if no operator application makes an improvement; and the operators have preconditions, structuring the bias space.

The extended bias space that ClimBS navigates is delineated currently by four dimensions (initial value and transformed values given): (i) the positive performance threshold (0.9, 2/3*value), (ii) the negative performance threshold (0, +1%), (iii) the rule complexity (1, +1), and (iv) the beam width of the heuristic search (1, +2). The positive threshold specifies the percentage of positive examples a satisfactory rule must cover. The negative threshold specifies the maximum percentage of the negative examples that a satisfactory rule may cover. The rule sets are to be used in a system that can take advantage of imprecise rules when gathering evidence for a classification. The rule complexity specifies the number of conjuncts that may appear in the antecedent of a rule. A change in the beam width of the system indicates a change in the confidence in the heuristic hypothesis evaluation function. Additional dimensions can be addressed by adding the appropriate operators to ClimBS' operator set. In principle, an operator can change any aspect of the PDM.

Inductive Strengthening in ClimBS. The inductive strengthening heuristic is used as in section 3.2, considering the concept description learned in the previous biases to be the initial knowledge for the next run of the learner. Table 3 shows the results of running ClimBS on the four learning tasks with and without the inductive strengthening heuristic. The columns list the domain (and task), whether or not the heuristic was used (IS?), the number of nodes searched, the size of the resultant concept (number of rules), and the classification accuracy on the test data. Note that the subordinate learning system, MC-RL, used the inductive strengthening heuristic in all the runs. Thus, any effects observed are due to the presence of the heuristic in ClimBS.

Domain	IS?	Nodes searched	# rules	Acc. on test data
Artificial - Task 1	no	18185±3927	88±32	93.8±1.1
Artificial - Task 1	yes	11509±3342	29±8	95.5±1.5
Artificial - Task 2	no	14120±2517	77±25	96.0±0.9
Artificial - Task 2	yes	9633±2078	35±5	97.2±0.6
Automobiles	no	29133±8746	130±41	75.9±8.7
Automobiles	yes	16476±4468	48±10	80.4±4.5
Mushrooms	no	13365±7317	23±9	92.2±2.0
Mushrooms	yes	9801±4320	17±3	94.5±1.1

Table 3. The effects of using IS heuristic in ClimBS (averaged over 10 trials)

The results indicate that using the heuristic did reduce the amount of search, albeit not by the margins observed in Section 3.1. Similarly, the size of the concept learned was reduced; and the classification accuracy was increased. For these results, in addition to stopping when all the training examples were covered, ClimBS considered its search to have converged if no improvement was observed for 5000 nodes for the tasks from the artificial domain and 10000 nodes for the automobile and mushroom domains. If we compare the number of nodes searched to the size of the hypothesis space, as we did in Section 3.1, we see a much larger reduction for ClimBS. The syntactically defined search space for the artificial domain for ClimBS was 1.4 E+17 nodes. However, it is important to note that the convergence criteria used for these experiments were chosen based on the results observed with MC-RL. Different criteria may result if only the size of the search space was taken into consideration.

4. Conclusions

We have shown that this simple inductive strengthening heuristic is effective in reducing hypothesis space search, in reducing the size of the resultant concept descriptions, and in increasing the accuracy of the resultant concepts, even when used in a learning program with other effective hypothesis space restriction heuristics. Its utility in guiding the search to parts of the hypothesis space that address incompleteness in the currently held concept description can be seen in a scaling of the amount of search performed to the amount of concept description left to be learned. Finally, the heuristic can be used to transfer learned knowledge across biases in a bias adjustment system.

The heuristic examined was simple and the gains observed were modest. Future work includes studying the heuristic in more complicated domains, where there is a chance for a bigger win. Also, more complicated methods of inductive strengthening should be examined.

In none of the domains tested did using the heuristic increase the search time, the size of the rule set, or the predictive accuracy. However, there are cases when the heuristic does give a less desirable concept description. In the mushroom domain, for example, predictive accuracy is not the only criterion by which the value of a concept description should be measured. The cost of making predictions should also be taken into account. Results show that predictive accuracy can be traded for safety by altering the policy used for learning. Of the approximately 5 percent of the mushrooms misclassified by MC-RL's rule sets, half (on the average, about 2.6 percent) were "dangerous" predictions. One change in inductive policy, which included turning off the inductive strengthening heuristic and learning a large, redundant set of rules for the concept "poisonous," reduced the dangerous prediction rate to 0.04 percent [Provost & Buchanan, 1992]. We assert that such heuristics should be represented explicitly, to facilitate changes in inductive policy.

Acknowledgements

This work was supported by NLM grant 1-R01-LM05104 and an IBM Graduate Fellowship

References

Breiman, L., Friedman, J., Olshen, R., & Stone, C. (1984). *Classification and Regression Trees*. Belmont, CA: Wadsworth International Group.

Buchanan, B., & Mitchell, T. (1978). Model-directed Learning of Production Rules. In D.A.Waterman & F. Hayes-Roth (Ed.), *Pattern Directed Inference Systems* (pp. 297-312). New York: Academic Press.

Clearwater, S., & Provost, F. (1990). RL4: A Tool for Knowledge-Based Induction. In *Proceedings of the Second International IEEE Conference on Tools for Artificial Intelligence*, (pp. 24-30). IEEE C.S. Press.

Michalski, R., Mozetic, I., Hong, J., & Lavrac, N. (1986). The Multi-purpose Incremental Learning System AQ15 and its Testing Application to Three Medical Domains. In *Proceedings of the Fifth National Conference on Artificial Intelligence*, (pp. 1041-1045). AAAI-Press.

Mitchell, T. (1980). *The Need for Biases in Learning Generalizations* (Technical Report CBM-TR-117). Department of Computer Science, Rutgers University.

Provost, F. (1991). *ClimBS* (Technical Report ISL-91-1). Department of Computer Science, University of Pittsburgh.

Provost, F., & Buchanan, B. (1992). Inductive Policy. To appear in *Proceedings of the Tenth National Conference on Artificial Intelligence*. AAAI-Press.

Provost, F. J. (1992). ClimBS: Searching the Bias Space. Submitted to The Fourth International Conference on Tools for Artificial Intelligence.

Quinlan, J. (1986). Induction of Decision Trees. *Machine Learning*, 1, 81-106.

Quinlan, J. (1987). Generating Production Rules from Decision Trees. In *Proceedings of the Tenth International Joint Conference on Artificial Intelligence*.

Rendell, L. (1986). A General Framework for Induction and a Study of Selective Induction. *Machine Learning*, 1, 177-226.

Schlimmer, J. (1987). *Concept Acquisition Through Representational Adjustment*. Ph.D. Thesis, Department of Information and Computer Science, University of California at Irvine.

Utgoff, P. (1984). *Shift of Bias for Inductive Concept Learning*. Ph.D. Thesis, Rutgers University.

On Identifying DNA Splicing Systems from Examples

Yuji Takada

International Institute for Advanced Study of
Social Information Science *(IIAS-SIS)*
FUJITSU LABORATORIES LTD.
140, Miyamoto, Numazu, Shizuoka 410-03, Japan
email: yuji@iias.flab.fujitsu.co.jp

Rani Siromoney*

Madras Christian College
Tambaram, Madras 600 059, India

Abstract

DNA sequences are recombined with restriction enzymes and ligases. Splicing systems, generative devices introduced by Head [2], represent this DNA recombinant behaviors as operations on pairs of strings over a finite alphabet. Culik II and Harju [1] proved that a language generated by a splicing system is regular. We give a method to construct a splicing system from a deterministic finite state automaton. By combining a conventional inductive inference/learning method for deterministic finite state automata with our method, we have an effective inductive inference/learning method for splicing systems.

1 Introduction

DNA sequences are recombined with restriction enzymes and ligases; restriction enzymes cut sequences into several fragments and those fragments are pasted by ligases so that new sequences are constructed (cf. [5]). Using this kind of DNA recombinant behaviors, we can extract desirable parts from given sequences and create new sequences arranged in the desirable way.

Head [2] introduced new generative devices, called splicing systems, into formal language theory, which were defined to allow this DNA recombinant behaviors to be directly represented as operations on pairs of strings over a finite alphabet. Culik II and Harju [1] proved an important regularity of languages generated by splicing

---

*This work has been done during the author visit to FUJITSU LABORATORIES LTD.

systems through the use of their domino concept. Hence, we can use finite state automata to analyze a language generated by a splicing system.

In this paper, we consider the problem of finding a splicing system from examples. A solution of this problem provides us with an effective method to designate new DNA sequences; using this method, we can identify a splicing system from examples and from the identified splicing system, we can have ideas of restriction enzymes and initial sequences needed to create desirable sequences. Since a lot of inductive inference and learning methods for regular sets have been developed (cf. [4]) and as Culik II and Harju [1] have shown, the language generated by a splicing system is regular, we can have an inference method for the class of languages generated by splicing systems. However, that inference method does not give us an idea of splicing systems; we do not have any idea of restriction enzymes and initial sequences from representations for regular sets like finite automata.

Here we give a method to construct a splicing system, explicitly finding the initial sequences and the restriction enzymes, from a deterministic finite state automaton which accepts the language generated by the splicing system. By combining a conventional inductive inference/learning method for deterministic finite state automata with our method, we have an effective inductive inference/learning method for splicing systems.

2 Basic Definitions

Here we follow the formalization of Culik II and Harju [1] for splicing systems.

Let Σ be an alphabet, that is, a finite set of symbols. Then Σ^* denotes the free monoid generated by Σ with the identity element denoted by λ and Σ^+ denotes the set $\Sigma^* - \{\lambda\}$. The element λ is called the *null string* over Σ.

Let Δ be a subsemigroup of $\Sigma^* \times \Sigma^*$ generated by a finite subset of $\Sigma \times \Sigma$. (In [1], such a subsemigroup is called *alphabetic*.) Note that Δ need not have (λ, λ).

Since we are mainly interested in double stranded DNA sequences, throughout this paper, we may fix the alphabet $\Sigma = \{A, T, G, C\}$ and the semigroup Δ of $\Sigma^* \times \Sigma^*$ generated by the relation $\{(A, T), (T, A), (G, C), (C, G)\}$. Note that in this case $(\lambda, \lambda) \notin \Delta$, therefore, Δ is not a monoid.

A Δ-*domino* α is a triple $(l(\alpha), m(\alpha), r(\alpha))$, usually written as $\alpha = l(\alpha) \cdot m(\alpha) \cdot r(\alpha)$ where

$$l(\alpha), r(\alpha) \in (\Sigma^* \times \lambda) \cup (\lambda \times \Sigma^*), \quad m(\alpha) \in \Delta \cup \{(\lambda, \lambda)\},$$

and the products are in $\Sigma^* \times \Sigma^*$. The components of α are said to be its *left*, *middle*, and *right parts*. If $\alpha = m(\alpha)$, then α is called a *blunt domino*. For $i = 1, 2$, $f_i : \Sigma^* \times \Sigma^* \to \Sigma^*$ denotes the projection.

Two Δ-dominoes α and β can be *matched* together (in this order) to form a larger Δ-domino $\alpha \otimes \beta$ if $r(\alpha) \cdot l(\beta) \in \Delta$, that is, if the right part of α can be joined with the left part of β. The product $\alpha \otimes \beta$ is undefined if $r(\alpha) \cdot l(\beta) \notin \Delta$. In this case, we write $\alpha \otimes \beta = 0$, where 0 is a special element for this purpose. If we agree that 0 is a Δ-domino then the Δ-dominoes form a semigroup with a zero element. This semigroup is denoted by D_Δ. Also, $D_\Delta(I)$ denotes the subsemigroup of D_Δ generated by the subset I.

The set

$$BD_\Delta(I) = \{\alpha \in D_\Delta(I) \,|\, \alpha = m(\alpha)\}$$

is the *blunt language* generated by the subset I of D_Δ.

The set $\Delta_B = \Sigma \times \Sigma \cap \Delta$ is called the *base alphabet* of Δ. The sets $\Delta_l = \{(a, \lambda) \,|\, a \in \Sigma\}$ and $\Delta_r = \{(\lambda, b) \,|\, b \in \Sigma\}$ are called the *left-oriented alphabet* and the *right-oriented alphabet* of Δ, respectively. Then the set $\Delta_e = \Delta_B \cup \Delta_l \cup \Delta_r$ is called the *extended base alphabet* of Δ. If $\Sigma = \{A, T, G, C\}$ and Δ is a sub-semigroup of $\Sigma^* \times \Sigma^*$ generated by the relation $\{(A, T), (T, A), (G, C), (C, G)\}$ then $\Delta_B = \{(A, T), (T, A), (G, C), (C, G)\}$, $\Delta_l = \{(A, \lambda), (T, \lambda), (G, \lambda), (C, \lambda)\}$, and $\Delta_r = \{(\lambda, A), (\lambda, T), (\lambda, G), (\lambda, C)\}$. The graphical representations of Δ_B, Δ_l, and Δ_r are

$$\Delta_B = \left\{ \frac{A}{T}, \frac{T}{A}, \frac{G}{C}, \frac{C}{G} \right\},$$

$$\Delta_l = \left\{ \frac{A}{\cdot}, \frac{T}{\cdot}, \frac{G}{\cdot}, \frac{C}{\cdot} \right\}, \text{ and}$$

$$\Delta_r = \left\{ \frac{\cdot}{T}, \frac{\cdot}{A}, \frac{\cdot}{C}, \frac{\cdot}{G} \right\}.$$

Let P_l be a set of Δ-dominoes such that each $\sigma_l \in P_l$ is *left-oriented*:

$$l(\sigma_l) \in \Sigma^* \times \lambda \quad \text{implies} \quad r(\sigma_l) \in \lambda \times \Sigma^*$$

and P_r a set of Δ-dominoes such that each $\sigma_r \in P_r$ is *right-oriented*:

$$m(\sigma_r) \neq (\lambda, \lambda) \text{ and } l(\sigma_r) \in \lambda \times \Sigma^* \quad \text{implies} \quad r(\sigma_r) \in \Sigma^* \times \lambda.$$

Note that no P_l and P_r have a Δ-domino σ such that $l(\sigma) \in \lambda \times \Sigma^+$, $m(\sigma) = (\lambda, \lambda)$, and $r(\sigma) \in \Sigma^+ \times \lambda$.

Let $P = (P_l, P_r)$. We define the *splicing product* $\alpha \,|_P\, \beta$ of two Δ-dominoes α, β as $\alpha \otimes \beta$ if $\alpha \otimes \beta \neq 0$ and either

1. if $r(\alpha) \in \lambda \times \Sigma^*$ and $l(\beta) \in \Sigma^* \times \lambda$ then there exists $\sigma_l \in P_l$ such that

   (a) $m(\sigma_l) = r(\alpha) \cdot l(\beta)$,

   (b) $l(\sigma_l) = (x, \lambda)$ for some suffix x of $f_1(m(\alpha))$, and

   (c) $r(\sigma_l) = (\lambda, y)$ for some prefix y of $f_2(m(\beta))$,

   (then we say that σ_l *splices* $\alpha \otimes \beta$ *into* α, β) or

2. if $r(\alpha) \in \Sigma^+ \times \lambda$ and $l(\beta) \in \lambda \times \Sigma^+$ then there exists $\sigma_r \in P_r$ such that

   (a) $m(\sigma_r) = r(\alpha) \cdot l(\beta)$,

   (b) $l(\sigma_r) = (\lambda, x)$ for some suffix x of $f_2(m(\alpha))$, and

   (c) $r(\sigma_r) = (y, \lambda)$ for some prefix y of $f_1(m(\beta))$

   (then we say that σ_r *splices* $\alpha \otimes \beta$ *into* α, β).

Again we write $\alpha \mid_P \beta = 0$ if $\alpha \mid_P \beta$ is undefined above.

A subsemigroup T of D_Δ is called a *splicing semigroup* with respect to P if

$$\alpha \mid_P \beta \in T - \{0\} \quad \text{implies} \quad \alpha, \beta \in T.$$

Clearly, the splicing semigroups are closed under intersection (for fixed P) and each subset I of D_Δ generates a subsemigroup which is closed under splicing with respect to P. This smallest splicing semigroup of D_Δ containing I will be denoted by $D_\Delta^P(I)$.

A *splicing system* S for $D_\Delta^P(I)$ is a pair $S = (I, P)$ where I is the *initial set* and P is the set of *splicing dominoes* of S. In biological situation, splicing dominoes correspond to restriction enzymes and a splicing semigroup $D_\Delta^P(I)$ corresponds to the set of all DNA sequences constructed from sequences in I by recombination by restriction enzymes in P and ligations.

Note that the definition of the splicing product is slightly different from the one in [1]; we divide splicing dominoes into left-oriented dominoes and right-oriented ones so that blunt splicing dominoes can be distinguished. Also, the left part and right part of a splicing domino should be in middle parts of spliced dominoes in our definition, while this is not necessary in their definition.

The following remark immediately follows from the definition of the splicing product.

Remark 2.1 *Let $D_\Delta^P(I)$ be a splicing semigroup with $P = (P_l, P_r)$ and P' a pair (P_l', P_r') of sets of left-oriented and right-oriented Δ-dominoes such that $P_l \subseteq P_l'$ and $P_r \subseteq P_r'$. Then $D_\Delta^P(I) \subseteq D_\Delta^{P'}(I)$.*

Let $\alpha = l(\alpha) \cdot m(\alpha) \cdot r(\alpha)$ be a Δ-domino. A Δ-domino $\alpha' = l(\alpha') \cdot m(\alpha) \cdot r(\alpha')$ is said to be a *subdomino of α* if $l(\alpha')$ is a suffix of $l(\alpha)$ and $r(\alpha')$ is a prefix of $r(\alpha)$. Note that α is a subdomino of α itself.

For any sets D_1 and D_2 of Δ-dominoes we write $D_1 \prec D_2$ if for any $\alpha \in D_1$, D_2 has a subdomino α' of α.

The following lemma is obvious from the definitions of splicing semigroups and $\prec$ and Remark 2.1.

Lemma 2.2 *Let $D_\Delta^P(I)$ be a splicing semigroup with $P = (P_l, P_r)$ and P' a pair (P_l', P_r') of sets of left-oriented and right-oriented Δ-dominoes such that $P_l \prec P_l'$ and $P_r \prec P_r'$. Then $D_\Delta^P(I) \subseteq D_\Delta^{P'}(I)$.*

A *deterministic finite state automaton* (abbreviated DFA) over an alphabet Σ is a 5-tuple $\mathcal{M} = (K, \Sigma, \delta, q_0, F)$, where K is a nonempty finite set of *states*, q_0 in K is the *initial state*, F a subset of K is the set of *final states*, and δ a map from $K \times \Sigma$ to K is the *transition function* of $\mathcal{M}$. We extend δ in the usual way to a map from $K \times \Sigma^*$ to K such that $\delta(q, \lambda) = q$ for all $q \in K$, and $\delta(q, uv) = \delta(\delta(q, u), v)$ for all strings u and v in Σ^*. A string $w \in \Sigma^*$ is said to be *recognized* by $\mathcal{M}$ if $\delta(q_0, w) \in F$. The *language recognized* by $\mathcal{M}$ is the set of all strings recognized by $\mathcal{M}$ and is denoted by $L(\mathcal{M})$. For any state q of $\mathcal{M}$, $L(q, \mathcal{M})$ denotes the set $L(q, \mathcal{M}) = \{w \in \Sigma^* \mid \delta(q, w) \in F\}$. Clearly, $L(\mathcal{M}) = L(q_0, \mathcal{M})$.

A *regular set* over an alphabet Σ is a subset of Σ^* that is recognized by some DFA. If L is a regular set, then there is a DFA, unique up to isomorphism, with the smallest possible number of states of any *DFA* for L. This *DFA* is called the *minimum state DFA* for L.

Let $\mathcal{M} = (K, \Sigma, \delta, q_0, F)$ be a *DFA*. A state q is called *live* if there exist strings u and v such that $uv \in L(\mathcal{M})$ and $q = \delta(q_0, u)$. A state that is not live is called *dead*. It may be verified that the minimum state *DFA* has at most one dead state. Any pair (q, a) such that $q \in K$ and $a \in \Sigma$ is called a *transition* of $\mathcal{M}$. A string w is said to *exercise* (q, a) if there exist strings u and v such that $w = uav$ and $\delta(q_0, u) = q$. A transition is called *live* if there exists a string $w \in L(\mathcal{M})$ that exercises it.

Let T denote the set of all transitions of $\mathcal{M}$. Given a subset T' of T and a subset F' of F, we define the *DFA* $\mathcal{M}[T', F'] = (K', \Sigma, \delta', q_0, F')$ in the following way: The set K' of states is $K = F' \cup \{q \mid (q, a) \in T'\} \cup \{q_d\}$ where q_d is a dead state of $M(T', F')$ and not in K. For any $q \in K'$ and any $a \in \Sigma$, $\delta'(q, a) = q'$ if $\delta(q, a) = q'$ and $q' \in K'$, otherwise, $\delta'(q, a) = q_d$. Note that it is easy to verify that $L(\mathcal{M}[T', F']) \subseteq L(\mathcal{M})$.

The following theorem is due to Culik II and Harju [1].

Theorem 2.3 (Culik II and Harju [1]) *Let P be a pair of finite sets of left-oriented and right-oriented Δ-dominoes and I be a regular set over the base alphabet Δ_B. Then $D_\Delta^P(I)$ is a regular set over Δ_e.*

Culik II and Harju [1] have proved this theorem only for blunt languages. However, as they mentioned, this restriction is not essential. In their construction, for each splicing domino σ, we have only to add paths for $f_1(m(\sigma))$ and $f_2(m(\sigma))$; for each left-oriented splicing domino σ_l with $f_1(m(\sigma_l)) = a_1 \cdots a_n$ and $f_2(m(\sigma_l)) = b_1 \cdots b_n$, we add the path $(a_1, \lambda) \cdots (a_n, \lambda)$ from the initial state $(l, 1)$ to the state $(1, \tau, \sigma_l)$ and the path $(\lambda, b_1) \cdots (\lambda, b_n)$ from the state $(0, \rho, \sigma_l)$ to the final state $(r, 1)$. Similarly, we add paths for each right-oriented domino σ_r. Note that, since these added edges are never middle parts of Δ-dominoes in $D_\Delta^P(I)$, we do not have to consider these edges when we add paths for splicing. In the sequel, Theorem 2.3 follows from the proof of Culik II and Harju [1].

By Theorem 2.3, for each splicing language $D_\Delta^P(I)$ such that I is regular over Δ_B, we effectively have the minimum state *DFA* which recognizes $D_\Delta^P(I)$ and is unique up to isomorphism.

Since we are mainly interested in DNA recombinant behavior, in this paper we consider only the case where I is a finite set.

Example 2.4 Let I be the initial set:

$$A = \left\{ \begin{matrix} AT\,CG\,AT\,CG\,AT \\ TA\,GC\,TA\,GC\,TA \end{matrix}, \begin{matrix} GG\,CG\,CC\,GG\,CG\,CC \\ CC\,GC\,GG\,CC\,GC\,GG \end{matrix} \right\}.$$

Let P_l be the set of left-oriented dominoes:

$$P_l = \left\{ \begin{matrix} ATCG \cdot \cdot \\ \cdot \cdot GCTA \end{matrix} (ClaI), \begin{matrix} GGCG \cdot \cdot \\ \cdot \cdot GCGG \end{matrix} (NarI) \right\}$$

and P be the pair $(P_l, \emptyset)$, where ClaI and NarI are names of real restriction enzymes [5].

Then the splicing semigroup $D_\Delta^P(I)$ is recognized by $\mathcal{M}$ over Δ_e:

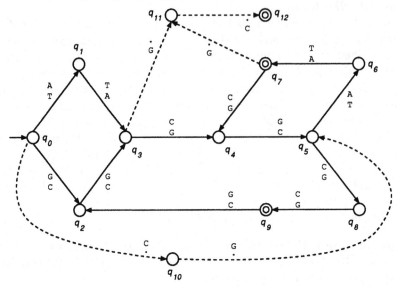

3 Finding Splicing Systems from Finite State Automata

In this section, we give an effective method to find a splicing system from a deterministic finite state automaton which accepts the language generated by the splicing system. By combining a conventional inductive inference/learning method for deterministic finite state automata with our method, we have an effective inductive inference/learning method for splicing systems.

3.1 Finding Splicing Dominoes

We first give a method to find a splicing dominoes.

Let $D_\Delta^P(I)$ be a splicing semigroup (regular set over Δ_e) such that I is finite, and $\mathcal{M} = (K, \Delta_e, \delta, q_0, F)$ be the minimum state DFA which recognizes $D_\Delta^P(I)$.

For any string $\omega \in \Delta_B^+$, $LE_l(\omega)$ is the set of all states of $\mathcal{M}$ such that for any q in $LE_l(\omega)$, (1) $\delta(q, \omega)$ is live and (2) $\delta(q, (\lambda, f_2(\omega))) \in F$.

Lemma 3.1 *For any two Δ-dominoes α and β with $r(\alpha) \in \Delta_r^+$, α and β are in $D_\Delta^P(I)$ and $\alpha \otimes \beta \neq 0$ if and only if $q = \delta(q_0, l(\alpha) \cdot m(\alpha))$ is in $LE_l(r(\alpha) \cdot l(\beta))$ and $\delta(q_0, \beta) \in F$.*

Proof.   Assume that α and β are in $D_\Delta^P(I)$ and $\alpha \otimes \beta \neq 0$. Then, since α is in $D_\Delta^P(I)$, $\delta(q_0, l(\alpha) \cdot m(\alpha) \cdot r(\alpha)) = \delta(q, r(\alpha))$ is in F. Since $\alpha \otimes \beta$ is in $D_\Delta^P(I)$, $\delta(q, r(\alpha) \cdot l(\beta))$ is live. Hence, q is in $LE_l(r(\alpha) \cdot l(\beta))$. Also, since β is in $D_\Delta^P(I)$, $\delta(q_0, \beta)$ is in F.

Conversely, if $q \in LE_l(r(\alpha) \cdot l(\beta))$, then $\delta(q_0, l(\alpha) \cdot m(\alpha) \cdot r(\alpha)) \in F$, therefore, $\alpha \in D_\Delta^P(I)$. Also, since $\delta(q_0, \beta)$ is in F, β is in $D_\Delta^P(I)$. Hence $\alpha \otimes \beta$ is defined and is in $D_\Delta^P(I)$. $\square$

Lemma 3.2 *For any Δ-domino $\gamma \in D_\Delta^P(I)$, if $\gamma = \alpha \mid_P \beta$ with $r(\alpha) \in \Delta_r^+$, then $q = \delta(q_0, l(\alpha) \cdot m(\alpha))$ is in $LE_l(r(\alpha) \cdot l(\beta))$ and $\delta(q_0, \beta) \in F$.*

Proof. Since γ is in $D_\Delta^P(I)$, $\gamma = \alpha \mid_P \beta$ implies that $\alpha, \beta \in D_\Delta^P(I)$ and $\alpha \otimes \beta \neq 0$. Hence, by Lemma 3.1, $q = \delta(q_0, l(\alpha) \cdot m(\alpha))$ is in $LE_l(r(\alpha) \cdot l(\beta))$ and $\delta(q_0, \beta) \in F$. $\square$

Note that the following example ensures that the converse of Lemma 3.2 is not always true.

Example 3.3 Let $\gamma_1 = (ATCGAT, TAGCTA)$, $\gamma_2 = (GGCGCC, CCGCGG)$, and $\gamma_3 = (AATCGCCA, TTAGCGGT)$. If $I = \{\gamma_1, \gamma_2, \gamma_3\}$ and $P = (\{(AT, \lambda) \cdot (CG, GC) \cdot (\lambda, TA), (GG, \lambda) \cdot (CG, GC) \cdot (\lambda, GG)\}, \emptyset)$, then

$$
\begin{aligned}
D_\Delta^P(I) \;=\; & I \cup \{(ATCGCC, TAGCGG), (GGCGAT, CCGCTA)\} \\
& \cup \{\alpha_1 = (AT, TA) \cdot (\lambda, GC), \alpha_2 = (GG, CC) \cdot (\lambda, GC)\} \\
& \cup \{\beta_1 = (CG, \lambda) \cdot (AT, TA), \beta_2 = (CG, \lambda) \cdot (CC, GG)\}.
\end{aligned}
$$

For the minimum state DFA $\mathcal{M}$ which recognizes $D_\Delta^P(I)$, $\delta(q_0, (AT, TA)) \in LE_l((CC, GG))$ but for $\alpha_1 \otimes \beta_2$, $\alpha_1 \mid_P \beta_2$ is undefined. Hence the converse of Lemma 3.2 is not always true.

A double string $\omega \in \Delta_B^+$ such that $LE_l(\omega)$ is not empty is said to be a *left-crossing* of $\mathcal{M}$.

Remark 3.4 *A left-crossing ω of $\mathcal{M}$ is effectively found.*

For any string $\omega' \in \Delta_B^+$, $NE_l(\omega')$ is the set of all states of $\mathcal{M}$ such that for any q in $NE_l(\omega')$, (1) $\delta(q, \omega')$ is a live state and (2) $\delta(q, (\lambda, f_2(\omega'))) \notin F$. From the definitions of $LE_l(\omega)$ and $NE_l(\omega')$, we have the following remark.

Remark 3.5 *For any $\omega \in \Delta_B^+$, $LE_l(\omega) \cap NE_l(\omega) = \emptyset$.*

Lemma 3.6 *Let $\gamma = \mu \cdot \omega \cdot \nu$ be a Δ-domino in $D_\Delta^P(I)$. If $\delta(q_0, \mu)$ is in $NE_l(\omega)$ or $\delta(q_0, (f_1(\omega), \lambda) \cdot \nu)$ is not in F then there is no left-oriented splicing domino of P which splices γ into two Δ-dominoes $\mu \cdot (\lambda, f_2(\omega))$ and $(f_1(\omega), \lambda) \cdot \nu$.*

Proof. By Remark 3.5, $\delta(q_0, \mu) \in NE_l(\omega)$ implies $\delta(q_0, \mu) \notin LE_l(\omega)$. Hence, this lemma follows from Lemma 3.2. $\square$

Let $\omega \in \Delta_B^+$ be a left-crossing of $\mathcal{M}$. Then $CP_l(\omega)$ denotes the set of all pairs of strings over Σ satisfying the following condition: a pair (u, v) is in $CP_l(\omega)$ if and only if

1. there exists $q \in LE_l(\omega)$ such that (1) there is a live state q_1 such that $\delta(q_1, \mu) = q$ for some $\mu \in \Delta_B^*$ with $f_1(\mu) = u$ and (2) $\delta(q_0, (f_1(\omega), \lambda) \cdot \nu)$ is live for some $\nu \in \Delta_B^*$ with $f_2(\nu) = v$,

2. for any $q \in LE_l(\omega)$ and any $\mu, \nu \in \Delta_B^*$ such that $f_1(\mu) = u$ and $f_2(\nu) = v$, if there is a live state q_1 with $\delta(q_1, \mu) = q$ and $\delta(q_0, (f_1(\omega), \lambda) \cdot \nu)$ is live, then $L(\delta(q, \omega \cdot \nu), \mathcal{M}) \subseteq L(\delta(q_0, (f_1(\omega), \lambda) \cdot \nu), \mathcal{M})$,

3. for any $q' \in NE_l(\omega)$, (1) for any $\mu' \in \Delta_B^*$ with $f_1(\mu') = u$ there is no live state q_2 such that $\delta(q_2, \mu') = q'$, or (2) for any $\nu' \in \Delta_B^*$ with $f_2(\nu') = v$, $\delta(q', \omega \cdot \nu)$ is not live,

4. there is no pair (u', v') in $CP_l(\omega)$ such that u is a suffix of u' and v is a prefix of v', and

5. for any μ and ν in Δ_B^* such that $f_1(\mu) = u$ and $f_2(\nu) = v$, μ and ν exercises each live transition of $\mathcal{M}$ at most one time.

Any element of $CP_l(\omega)$ is called a *context pair* of the left-crossing ω. For each $(u, v) \in CP_l(\omega)$, if μ and ν are double strings in Δ_B^* such that $f_1(\mu) = u$ and $f_2(\nu) = v$, then μ and ν exercises each live transition of $\mathcal{M}$ at most one time. Hence, $CP_l(\omega)$ is finite.

Remark 3.7 *Given a left-crossing ω of $\mathcal{M}$, $CP_l(\omega)$ is effectively found.*

For any left-crossing ω of $\mathcal{M}$, $P_l(\omega)$ denotes the set of left-oriented Δ-dominoes

$$P_l(\omega) = \{\sigma \mid (u, v) \in CP_l(\omega), \, l(\sigma) = (u, \lambda), \, m(\sigma) = \omega, \, r(\sigma) = (\lambda, v)\}.$$

Lemma 3.8 *Let ω be a left-crossing of $\mathcal{M}$ and $P_l(\omega)$ is the set of left-oriented Δ-dominoes constructed in the above way. For any $\gamma \in D_\Delta^P(I)$ and any $\sigma \in P_l(\omega)$, if σ splices γ into two Δ-dominoes α and β then $\alpha, \beta \in D_\Delta^P(I)$.*

Proof. Since σ splices γ into α and β, γ can be written as $\mu_1 \cdot \mu \cdot \omega \cdot \nu \cdot \nu_1$ where $l(\sigma) = (f_1(\mu), \lambda)$ and $r(\sigma) = (\lambda, f_2(\nu))$. Then $\alpha = \mu_1 \cdot \mu \cdot (\lambda, f_2(\omega))$ and $\beta = (f_1(\omega), \lambda) \cdot \nu \cdot \nu_1$. Let $q = \delta(q_0, \mu_1 \cdot \mu)$. Since γ is in $D_\Delta^P(I)$, $\delta(q_0, \mu_1)$ and $\delta(q, \omega \cdot \nu)$ are live, therefore, the construction of $P_l(\omega)$ ensures that q is in $LE_l(\omega)$. (If q were in $NE_l(\omega)$ then $\delta(q_0, \mu_1)$ should be dead or $\delta(q, \omega \cdot \nu)$ should be dead. Also, by Remark 3.5, if q is not in $NE_l(\omega)$ then $q \in LE_l(\omega)$.) Also, since $L(\delta(q, \omega \cdot \nu), \mathcal{M}) \subseteq L(\delta(q_0, (f_1(\omega), \lambda) \cdot \nu), \mathcal{M})$, $\delta(q_0, \beta)$ is in F. Hence, by Lemma 3.1, α and β are in $D_\Delta^P(I)$. $\square$

Similar to left-crossings, we define right-crossings and note that all the remarks and lemmas for left-crossings carry over similarly to right-crossings. For any string $\omega \in \Delta_B^+$, $LE_r(\omega)$ is the set of all states of $\mathcal{M}$ such that for any q in $LE_r(\omega)$, (1) $\delta(q, \omega)$ is live and (2) $\delta(q, (f_1(\omega), \lambda)) \in F$. A *right-crossing* ω of $\mathcal{M}$ is a string $\omega \in \Delta_B^+$ such that $LE_r(\omega)$ is not empty. For any string $\omega' \in \Delta_B^+$, $NE_r(\omega')$ is the set of all states of $\mathcal{M}$ such that for any q in $NE_r(\omega')$, (1) $\delta(q, \omega')$ is a live state and (2) $\delta(q, (f_1(\omega'), \lambda)) \notin F$. We also define $CP_r(\omega)$ and $P_r(\omega)$ for each right-crossing ω of $\mathcal{M}$ in the similar way to $CP_l(\omega)$ and $P_l(\omega)$.

The pair (λ, λ) is called a *null-crossing* of $\mathcal{M}$. Let $LE(\lambda)$ denote the set of all final states such that for any $q_f \in LE(\lambda)$ and any $\gamma \in \Delta_B^*$, $\delta(q_0, \gamma) \in F$ holds whenever $\delta(q_f, \gamma) \in F$. Then $CP(\lambda)$ denotes the set of all pairs of strings over Σ satisfying the following condition: (u, v) is in $CP(\lambda)$ if and only if

1. there exists $q_f \in LE(\lambda)$ such that (1) there is a live state q_1 such that $\delta(q_1, \mu) = q_f$ for some $\mu \in \Delta_B^*$ with $f_1(\mu) = u$ and (2) $\delta(q_f, \nu)$ is live for some $\nu \in \Delta_B^*$ with $f_2(\nu) = v$,

2. for any $q \in K - LE(\lambda)$, (1) for any $\mu' \in \Delta_B^*$ with $f_1(\mu') = u$ there is no live state q_2 such that $\delta(q_2, \mu') = q$, or (2) if $q \neq q_0$ then for any $\nu' \in \Delta_B^*$ with $f_2(\nu') = v$, $\delta(q, \nu')$ is not live,

3. there is no pair (u', v') in $CP(\lambda)$ such that u is a suffix of u' and v is a prefix of v',

4. for any μ and ν in Δ_B^* such that $f_1(\mu) = u$ and $f_2(\nu) = v$, μ and ν exercises each live transition of $\mathcal{M}$ at most one time, and

5. u or v is a non-null string.

Any element of $CP(\lambda)$ is called a *context pair* of the null-crossing. For each $(u, v) \in CP(\lambda)$, if μ and ν are double strings in Δ_B^+ such that $f_1(\mu) = u$ and $f_2(\nu) = v$, then μ and ν exercises each live transition of $\mathcal{M}$ at most one time. Hence, $CP(\lambda)$ is finite.

Remark 3.9 *Given $\mathcal{M}$, $CP(\lambda)$ is effectively found.*

$P(\lambda)$ denotes the set of left-oriented dominoes

$$P(\lambda) = \{\sigma \mid (u, v) \in CP(\lambda), l(\sigma) = (u, \lambda), m(\sigma) = (\lambda, \lambda), r(\sigma) = (\lambda, v)\}.$$

Lemma 3.10 *For any $\gamma \in D_\Delta^P(I)$ and any $\sigma \in P(\lambda)$, if σ splices γ into two dominoes α and β then $\alpha, \beta \in D_\Delta^P(I)$.*

Proof. Since σ splices γ into α and β, γ can be written as $\mu_1 \cdot \mu \cdot \nu \cdot \nu_1$ where $l(\sigma) = (f_1(\mu), \lambda)$ and $r(\sigma) = (\lambda, f_2(\nu))$. Then $\alpha = \mu_1 \cdot \mu$ and $\beta = \nu \cdot \nu_1$. Let $q = \delta(q_0, \mu_1 \cdot \mu)$. Since γ is in $D_\Delta^P(I)$, $\delta(q_0, \mu_1)$ and $\delta(q, \nu)$ are live, therefore, the construction of $P(\lambda)$ ensures that q is in $LE(\lambda)$. (If q were not in $LE(\lambda)$ then $\delta(q_0, \mu_1)$ should be dead or if $q \neq q_0$ then $\delta(q, \nu)$ should be dead.) Hence, by the definition, α and β are in $D_\Delta^P(I)$. $\square$

Let $O_l(\mathcal{M})$ be the set of all left-crossings of $\mathcal{M}$ and $O_r(\mathcal{M})$ be the set of all right-crossings of $\mathcal{M}$. Then $P(\mathcal{M})$ denotes the pair

$$P(\mathcal{M}) = (P(\lambda) \cup \bigcup_{w \in O_l(\mathcal{M})} P_l(w), \bigcup_{w' \in O_r(\mathcal{M})} P_r(w'))$$

of sets of all oriented Δ-dominoes constructed in the above way.

Lemma 3.11 *For every Δ-domino σ of P, $P(\mathcal{M})$ has a subdomino σ' of σ.*

Proof. Assume that σ is a left-oriented Δ-domino of P such that $m(\sigma) \neq (\lambda, \lambda)$. By Lemma 3.2, for any Δ-domino $\gamma \in D_\Delta^P(I)$, if σ splices γ into α and β then the state $q = \delta(q_0, l(\alpha) \cdot m(\alpha))$ is in $LE_l(m(\sigma))$. Then, since $\alpha, \beta \in D_\Delta^P(I)$, for any $\mu, \nu \in \Delta_B^*$ such that μ is a suffix of $m(\alpha)$ with $f_1(\mu) = f_1(l(\sigma))$ and ν is a prefix of $m(\beta)$ with $f_2(\nu) = f_2(r(\sigma))$, there exists a live state q_1 such that $\delta(q_1, \mu) = q$ and $\delta(q, m(\sigma) \cdot \nu)$ is live. Also, there should be a prefix ν' of $m(\beta)$ such that $f_2(\nu')$ is a prefix of $f_2(r(\sigma))$ and $L(\delta(q, m(\sigma) \cdot \nu'), \mathcal{M}) \subseteq L(\delta(q_0, (f_1(m(\sigma)), \lambda) \cdot \nu'), \mathcal{M})$. Clearly, there should be $u, v \in \Sigma^*$ such that u is a suffix of $f_1(l(\sigma))$, v is a prefix of $f_2(r(\sigma))$, and for any $q' \in NE_l(m(\sigma))$, for any $\mu' \in \Delta_B^*$ with $f_1(\mu') = u$ there is no live state q_2 such that $\delta(q_2, \mu') = q'$, or for any $\nu' \in \Delta_B^*$ with $f_2(\nu') = v$, $\delta(q', \omega \cdot \nu)$ is not live (otherwise, by Lemma 3.6, σ would splice Δ-domino in $D_\Delta^P(I)$ incorrectly).

Hence, the construction of $P_l(m(\sigma))$ ensures that $CP_l(m(\sigma))$ has a pair (u, v) such that u is a suffix of $f_1(l(\sigma))$ and v is a prefix of $f_2(r(\sigma))$. Hence $P_l(m(\sigma))$ has the subdomino $\sigma' = (u, \lambda) \cdot m(\sigma) \cdot (\lambda, v)$. We may similarly prove the cases where σ is a right-oriented Δ-domino and σ is a left-oriented Δ-domino with $m(\sigma) = (\lambda, \lambda)$. $\square$

Example 3.12 Consider the splicing semigroup $D_\Delta^P(I)$ in Example 2.4. For $\omega = \dfrac{CG}{GC}$, $LE_l(\omega) = \{q_3, q_7\}$ and therefore, ω is a left-crossing of $\mathcal{M}$. For any other ω', $LE_l(\omega')$ is empty. Then $NE_l(\omega) = \{q_8\}$, therefore,

$$CP_l(\omega) = \{(T, \lambda), (G, \lambda), (\lambda, T), (\lambda, G)\}.$$

Hence,

$$P_l(\omega) = \left\{ \dfrac{TCG}{\cdot GC}, \dfrac{GCG}{\cdot GC}, \dfrac{CG\cdot}{GCT}, \dfrac{CG\cdot}{GCG} \right\}.$$

Since for any string α if $\delta(q_9, \alpha)$ is a final state then $\delta(q_0, \alpha)$ is also a final state, the final state q_9 is a null-crossing state. Then,

$$CP(\lambda) = \{(CC, \lambda), (\lambda, CC)\}.$$

Hence,

$$P(\lambda) = \left\{ \dfrac{CC}{\cdot\cdot}, \dfrac{\cdot\cdot}{CC} \right\}.$$

Since there is no right-crossing of $\mathcal{M}$, the pair $P(\mathcal{M})$ is

$$P(\mathcal{M}) = (P(\lambda) \cup P_l(\omega), \emptyset).$$

Note that $P(\mathcal{M})$ has subdominoes of P.

Lemma 3.13 *Let ω be a left-crossing of $\mathcal{M}$ and q_1, q_2 states in $LE_l(\omega)$. Assume that for two splicing dominoes σ_1 and σ_2 in $P_l(\omega)$, there exist $\rho_1, \rho_2, \psi_1, \psi_2$*

1. *$\rho_1 \cdot \sigma_1 \cdot \psi_1$ and $\rho_2 \cdot \sigma_2 \cdot \psi_2$ are in Δ_B^*,*

2. *there exist live states q_1', q_2' such that $\delta(q_1', \rho_1 \cdot l(\sigma_1)) = q_1$ and $\delta(q_2', \rho_2 \cdot l(\sigma_2)) = q_2$,*

Then $\delta(q_1, \omega \cdot r(\sigma_1) \cdot \psi_1) = \delta(q_2, \omega \cdot r(\sigma_1) \cdot \psi_1)$ and $\delta(q_1, \omega \cdot r(\sigma_2) \cdot \psi_2) = \delta(q_1, \omega \cdot r(\sigma_2) \cdot \psi_2)$.

Proof. Let $\delta(q_1, \omega \cdot r(\sigma_1) \cdot \psi_1) = q_1^1$, $\delta(q_2, \omega \cdot r(\sigma_1) \cdot \psi_1) = q_2^1$, $\delta(q_1, \omega \cdot r(\sigma_2) \cdot \psi_2) = q_1^2$, and $\delta(q_1, \omega \cdot r(\sigma_2) \cdot \psi_2) = q_2^2$.

Let $\alpha_1, \alpha_2, \beta_1, \beta_2$ are Δ-dominoes in $D_\Delta^P(I)$ such that

1. $\alpha_1 = \mu_1 \cdot \rho_1 \cdot l(\sigma_1) \cdot (\lambda, f_2(\omega))$, $\beta_1 = (f_1(\omega), \lambda) \cdot r(\sigma_1) \cdot \psi_1 \cdot \nu_1$, $\alpha_2 = \mu_2 \cdot \rho_2 \cdot l(\sigma_2) \cdot (\lambda, f_2(\omega))$, $\beta_2 = (f_1(\omega), \lambda) \cdot r(\sigma_2) \cdot \psi_2 \cdot \nu_2$,

2. $\delta(q_0, \mu_1 \cdot \rho_1 \cdot l(\sigma_1)) = q_1$ and $\delta(q_0, \mu_2 \cdot \rho_2 \cdot l(\sigma_2)) = q_2$.

Then, since $\alpha_1 \otimes \beta_2$ and $\alpha_2 \otimes \beta_1$ are in $D_\Delta^P(I)$, $\delta(q_1^1, \nu_2)$ and $\delta(q_2^1, \nu_1)$ are in F. Since $\mathcal{M}$ is the minimum state DFA, $q_1^1 = q_2^1$. We can similarly prove $q_1^2 = q_2^2$. $\square$

We also have the similar result for right-crossings.

3.2 Finding Initial Sets

We next give a method to find an initial set.

Let $D_\Delta^P(I)$ be a splicing semigroup (regular set over Δ_e) such that I is finite, and $\mathcal{M} = (K, \Delta_e, \delta, q_0, F)$ be the minimum state DFA which recognizes $D_\Delta^P(I)$. Let $P(\mathcal{M})$ be the pair of sets of splicing dominoes for $\mathcal{M}$ constructed by the method in the previous section.

A live state q of $\mathcal{M}$ is said to be *pure* if for any $\mu \in \Delta_e^*$, if $\delta(q_0, \mu) = q$ then μ is in Δ_B^*. For any pure state q of $\mathcal{M}$ and $\pi \in \Delta_B$, the pair (q, π) is called a *pure transition* of $\mathcal{M}$ if there exists a double string $\gamma \in L(\mathcal{M}) \cap \Delta_B^*$ which exercises it. A pure final state q_f of $\mathcal{M}$ is said to be *pseudo* for $P(\mathcal{M})$ if for any μ and ν in Δ_B^* such that $\delta(q_0, \mu) = q_f$ and $\delta(q_f, \nu) \in F$, there exists a splicing domino $\sigma \in P(\lambda)$ such that $\rho \cdot l(\sigma) \in \Delta_B^*$ is a suffix of μ for some ρ and $r(\sigma) \cdot f \in \Delta_B^*$ is a prefix of ν for some ψ.

Let F_p be the set of all non-pseudo final states of $\mathcal{M}$ for $P(\mathcal{M})$ and T_0 be the set of all pure transitions of $\mathcal{M}$. Then let $\mathcal{M}_0 = \mathcal{M}[T_0, F_p]$ and $i = 0$. Note that $L(\mathcal{M}_0) \subseteq \Delta_B^*$. We first apply the following *Procedure 1* to $\mathcal{M}_i$:

Procedure 1:
Let ω be a left-crossing (or right-crossing) of $\mathcal{M}$. Let q_1, q_2 be two *distinct* states in $LE_l(\omega)$ (or $LE_r(\omega)$). If there are two *distinct* splicing dominoes σ_1 and σ_2 in $P_l(\omega)$ (or $P_r(\omega)$) such that for some $\rho_1, \rho_2, \psi_1, \psi_2$ with $\rho_1 \cdot \sigma_1 \cdot \psi_1, \rho_2 \cdot \sigma_2 \cdot \psi_2 \in \Delta_B^*$,

- there exist live states q_3, q_4 such that $\delta(q_3, \rho_1 \cdot l(\sigma_1)) = q_1$ and $\delta(q_4, \rho_2 \cdot l(\sigma_2)) = q_2$, and

- $\delta(q_1, \omega \cdot r(\sigma_1) \cdot \psi_1)$ and $\delta(q_2, \omega \cdot r(\sigma_2) \cdot \psi_2)$ are live,

where δ is the transition function of $\mathcal{M}_i$, then let $T_{i+1} = T_i - \{(q_1', \pi_2), (q_2', \pi_1)\}$ and $\mathcal{M}_{i+1} = \mathcal{M}[T_{i+1}, F_p]$ where (q_1', π_1) and (q_2', π_2) are two transitions of T_i such that $\delta(q_2, \mu_1) = q_2'$ for μ_1 with $\mu_1 \cdot \pi_1 = r(\sigma_1) \cdot \psi_1$ and $\delta(q_1, \mu_2) = q_1'$ for μ_2 with $\mu_2 \cdot \pi_2 = r(\sigma_2) \cdot \psi_2$.

Procedure 1 is applied for any left-crossing (and any right-crossing) ω of $\mathcal{M}$, any distinct two states q_1, q_2 in $LE_l(\omega)$ (and $LE_r(\omega)$), and any splicing dominoes $\sigma_1, \sigma_2 \in P_l(\omega)$ (and $P_r(\omega)$). After each application of *Procedure 1*, the counter i is incremented. Since the number of left-crossings and right-crossings of $\mathcal{M}$ is finite and for each left-crossing (or right-crossing) ω, the number of elements of $LE_l(\omega)$ (or $LE_r(\omega)$) and the number of splicing dominoes in $P_l(\omega)$ (or $P_r(\omega)$) are finite, we can apply *Procedure 1* to $\mathcal{M}$ finite times. Let $\mathcal{M}_n$ be a *DFA* after *Procedure 1* is finally applied. Since Lemma 3.13 ensures that by the construction of Culik II and Harju [1] for each i, σ_1 and σ_2 put transitions (q'_1, π_1) and (q'_2, π_2) into $\mathcal{M}_{i+1}$, we have the following:

Lemma 3.14 *For each i, $D_\Delta^P(I) = D_\Delta^{P(\mathcal{M})}(L(\mathcal{M}_i))$.*

In the sequel, $D_\Delta^P(I) = D_\Delta^{P(\mathcal{M})}(L(\mathcal{M}_n))$.

We next construct the finite subset $PCS(\mathcal{M}_n)$ of $L(\mathcal{M}_n)$ which satisfies the followings:

1. For every pure transition (q, π) of $\mathcal{M}_n$, there exists a double string γ in $PCS(\mathcal{M})$ which exercises (q, π).

2. For every pure state q of $\mathcal{M}_n$ and for any $\alpha_1 \cdot \beta_1$ in $RCS(\mathcal{M}_n)$ such that $\delta(q_0, \alpha_1) = q$, if there is $\alpha_2 \cdot \beta_2$ in $PCS(\mathcal{M}_n)$ such that $\delta(q_0, \alpha_2) = q$ and α_1 and α_2 are not prefix of each other, then $\alpha_1 \cdot \beta_2$ and $\alpha_2 \cdot \beta_1$ are in $PCS(\mathcal{M}_n)$.

To construct $PCS(\mathcal{M}_n)$, we have only to find all finite passes of the initial state to all final states of $\mathcal{M}_n$ until $PCS(\mathcal{M}_n)$ satisfies the condition 1.

Let $CS_0 = PCS(\mathcal{M}_n)$ and $i = 0$. Finally, we apply the following *Procedure 2* to CS_i repeatedly:

> *Procedure 2:*
> If there is $\gamma \in CS_i$ such that $\gamma = \alpha \otimes \beta$ but there is no splicing domino σ in $P(\mathcal{M})$ which splices γ into α and β then let $CS_{i+1} = CS_i - \{\gamma\}$ and apply this procedure to CS_{i+1}. Otherwise, output CS_i and halts.

Let $CS(\mathcal{M})$ be the output of *Procedure 2*. We call this constructed $CS(\mathcal{M})$ the *characteristic sample for $\mathcal{M}$ with respect to $P(\mathcal{M})$*.

The construction of $CS(\mathcal{M})$ and Lemma 3.14 ensure the following:

Lemma 3.15 $CS(\mathcal{M}) \subseteq L(\mathcal{M})$ *and $CS(\mathcal{M})$ is finite.*

A Δ-domino α in $D_\Delta^P(I)$ is said to be *atomic* if for any two Δ-dominoes β_1, β_2 in $D_\Delta^P(I)$, $\alpha \neq \beta_1 \otimes \beta_2$. Since Lemma 3.14 and the construction of $CS(\mathcal{M})$ ensure that for any atomic Δ-domino $\alpha \in D_\Delta^P(I)$, there is a Δ-domino $\mu \otimes \alpha \otimes \nu$ in $D_\Delta^{P(\mathcal{M})}(CS(\mathcal{M}))$, we have the following:

Lemma 3.16 *For any atomic domino $\alpha \in D_\Delta^P(I)$, there exists $\gamma \in D_\Delta^{P(\mathcal{M})}(CS(\mathcal{M}))$ such that $\gamma = \mu \mid_{P(\mathcal{M})} \alpha \mid_{P(\mathcal{M})} \nu$.*

Example 3.17 Consider the splicing semigroup $D_\Delta^P(I)$ in Example 2.4 and the pair $P(\mathcal{M})$ of sets of splicing dominoes in Example 3.12.

For $\mathcal{M}$ and $P(\mathcal{M})$, each state q_i $(1 \le i \le 9)$ is a pure state and only q_7 is a non-pseudo final state. Then, we have $\mathcal{M}_0 = \mathcal{M}[T_0, F_p]$:

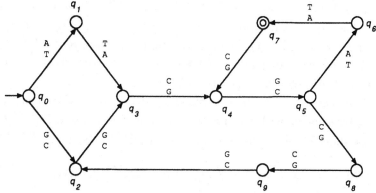

where $F_p = \{q_7\}$. *Procedure 1* does not change $\mathcal{M}_0$. For $\mathcal{M}_0$ we have

$$PCS(\mathcal{M}_0) \;=\; \left\{ \begin{array}{ll} \dfrac{AT\,CG\,AT}{TA\,GC\,TA}\,, & \dfrac{GG\,CG\,AT}{CC\,GC\,TA}\,, \\[2ex] \dfrac{AT\,CG\,AT\,CG\,AT}{TA\,GC\,TA\,GC\,TA}\,, & \dfrac{AT\,CG\,CC\,GG\,CG\,AT}{TA\,GC\,GG\,CC\,GC\,TA}\,, \\[2ex] \dfrac{GG\,CG\,AT\,CG\,AT}{CC\,GC\,TA\,GC\,TA}\,, & \dfrac{GG\,CG\,CC\,GG\,CG\,AT}{CC\,GC\,GG\,CC\,GC\,AT} \end{array} \right\} \,,$$

and *Procedure 2* does not remove any element in $PCS(\mathcal{M}_0)$ and therefore the characteristic sample $CS(\mathcal{M})$ for $\mathcal{M}$ with respect to $P(\mathcal{M})$ is $PCS(\mathcal{M}_0)$. It may be verified that $D_\Delta^P(I) = D_\Delta^{P(\mathcal{M})}(CS(\mathcal{M}))$.

As shown in Examples 2.4, 3.12, and 3.17, for any splicing semigroup $D_\Delta^P(I)$, if $\mathcal{M}$ is the minimum state DFA recognizing $D_\Delta^P(I)$, then any element in the pair $P(\mathcal{M})$ of sets of oriented Δ-domino may be a splicing domino and the characteristic sample $CS(\mathcal{M})$ for $\mathcal{M}$ with respect to $P(\mathcal{M})$ may be an initial set so that $D_\Delta^P(I) = D_\Delta^{P(\mathcal{M})}(CS(\mathcal{M}))$. The following theorem shows that this observation is always true.

Theorem 3.18 *Let $D_\Delta^P(I)$ be a splicing semigroup (regular set over Δ_e) such that I is finite and $\mathcal{M}$ be the minimum state DFA which recognizes $D_\Delta^P(I)$. Let $P(\mathcal{M})$ be the pair of sets of oriented Δ-dominoes constructed from $\mathcal{M}$ and $CS(\mathcal{M})$ be the characteristic sample for $\mathcal{M}$ with respect to $P(\mathcal{M})$. Then $D_\Delta^P(I) = D_\Delta^{P(\mathcal{M})}(CS(\mathcal{M}))$.*

We shall prove this theorem by a sequence of lemmas. Let $D_\Delta^P(I)$ be a splicing semigroup (regular set over Δ_e) with $P = (P_l, P_r)$ and $\mathcal{M} = (K, \Delta_e, \delta, q_0, F)$ be the minimum state DFA which recognizes $D_\Delta^P(I)$. Let $P(\mathcal{M})$ be the pair $(P_l(\mathcal{M}), P_r(\mathcal{M}))$ of sets of oriented Δ-dominoes constructed from $\mathcal{M}$ and $CS(\mathcal{M})$ be the characteristic sample for $\mathcal{M}$ with respect to $P(\mathcal{M})$.

Lemma 3.19 *Every element α in I is in $D_\Delta^{P(\mathcal{M})}(CS(\mathcal{M}))$.*

Proof. Let α be any element in I. Since α is in $D_\Delta^P(I)$, we shall write α as $\alpha_1 \otimes \cdots \otimes \alpha_n$ where for each i $(1 \leq i \leq n)$ $\alpha_i \in D_\Delta^P(I)$ is atomic.

For α_1, by Lemma 3.16, there exists $\beta_1 \in D_\Delta^{P(\mathcal{M})}(CS(\mathcal{M}))$ such that $\beta_1 = \alpha_1 \mid_{P(\mathcal{M})} \nu_1$ for some ν_1 with $l(\nu_1) = l(\alpha_2)$, therefore, α_1 is in $D_\Delta^{P(\mathcal{M})}(CS(\mathcal{M}))$.

For each α_i ($2 \leq i \leq n-1$), by Lemma 3.16, there exists $\beta_i \in D_\Delta^{P(\mathcal{M})}(CS(\mathcal{M}))$ such that $\beta_i = \mu_i \mid_{P(\mathcal{M})} \alpha_i \mid_{P(\mathcal{M})} \nu_i$ for some μ_i and ν_i with $r(\mu_i) = r(\alpha_{i-1})$ and $l(\nu_i) = l(\alpha_{i+1})$. Then α_i is in $D_\Delta^{P(\mathcal{M})}(CS(\mathcal{M}))$.

For α_n, by Lemma 3.16, there exists $\beta_n \in D_\Delta^{P(\mathcal{M})}(CS(\mathcal{M}))$ such that $\beta_n = \mu_n \mid_{P(\mathcal{M})} \alpha_n$ for some μ_n with $r(\mu_n) = r(\alpha_{n-1})$, therefore, α_n is in $D_\Delta^{P(\mathcal{M})}(CS(\mathcal{M}))$.

From the above observations, any $\alpha \in A$ is in $D_\Delta^{P(\mathcal{M})}(CS(\mathcal{M}))$. $\square$

Lemma 3.20 *Every Δ-domino α in $D_\Delta^P(I)$ is in $D_\Delta^{P(\mathcal{M})}(CS(\mathcal{M}))$.*

Proof. Since $P_l \prec P_l(\mathcal{M})$ and $P_r \prec P_r(\mathcal{M})$ by Lemma 3.11, $D_\Delta^P(I) \subseteq D_\Delta^{P(\mathcal{M})}(I)$ by Lemma 2.2. By Lemma 3.19, $I \subseteq D_\Delta^{P(\mathcal{M})}(CS(\mathcal{M}))$. Hence $D_\Delta^P(I) \subseteq D_\Delta^{P(\mathcal{M})}(I) \subseteq D_\Delta^{P(\mathcal{M})}(CS(\mathcal{M}))$. $\square$

Lemma 3.21 *Every Δ-domino α' in $D_\Delta^{P(\mathcal{M})}(CS(\mathcal{M}))$ is in $D_\Delta^P(I)$.*

Proof. Let α_1 and α_2 be any elements in $D_\Delta^{P(\mathcal{M})}CS(\mathcal{M})$. Assume that α_1 and α_2 are in $D_\Delta^P(I)$. For each i ($i = 1, 2$), if $P(\mathcal{M})$ has an oriented Δ-domino σ_i which splices α_i into μ_i and ν_i then, by Lemmas 3.8 and 3.10, $\mu_i, \nu_i \in D_\Delta^P(I)$. Hence, if μ_1 and ν_2, μ_2 and ν_1 can be matched together then by the definition of $D_\Delta^P(I)$, Δ-dominoes $\mu_1 \otimes \nu_2$ and $\mu_2 \otimes \nu_1$ are defined and in $D_\Delta^P(I)$.

By Lemma 3.15, $CS(\mathcal{M}) \subseteq D_\Delta^P(I)$. Any Δ-domino $\alpha' \in D_\Delta^{P(\mathcal{M})}(CS(\mathcal{M}))$ not in $CS(\mathcal{M})$ is constructed from elements in $CS(\mathcal{M})$ by repeatedly splicing and matching. Therefore, from the above argument, $\alpha' \in D_\Delta^P(I)$. $\square$

By combining Lemma 3.20 and Lemma 3.21, the proof of Theorem 3.18 is completed.

Theorem 3.22 *Let $D_\Delta^P(I)$ be a splicing semigroup (regular set over Δ_e) such that I is finite, and $\mathcal{M} = (K, \Delta_e, \delta, q_0, F)$ be the minimum state DFA which recognizes $D_\Delta^P(I)$. Given $\mathcal{M}$, the splicing system $\mathcal{S} = (CS(\mathcal{M}), P(\mathcal{M}))$ such that $D_\Delta^P(I) = D_\Delta^{P(\mathcal{M})}(CS(\mathcal{M}))$ is effectively found.*

Hence, given an inductive inference/learning method for deterministic finite state automata, we have an effective inductive inference/learning method for splicing systems.

4 Concluding Remarks

We did not show any computational complexity of our method. We expect that if we use the size of splicing systems and the size of examples as parameters then the running time of inference may be bounded by a polynomial. However, the running time is not bounded by any polynomial of the size of minimum state DFAs. Consider the initial set I consisting of all strings of length n over an alphabet consisting of k

symbols and the pair P of splicing dominoes whose both sets are empty. Then the minimum state DFA accepting $D^P_\Delta(I) = I$ has $n+1$ states but I has k^n number of strings. This implies that an inference algorithm may need an exponential number of examples.

We did not consider the case where initial sets are infinite regular sets. For this case, our method may construct splicing dominoes but does not work for initial sets. We also assume that it is possible to observe overhangs of spliced dominoes. Although our method still works well in biological situation, these restrictions may be removed in a future work.

References

[1] K. Culik II and T. Harju. Splicing semigroups of dominoes and DNA. *Discrete Applied Mathematics*, 31:261–277, 1991.

[2] T. Head. Formal language theory and DNA: An analysis of the generative capacity of specific recombinant behaviors. *Bulletin of Mathematical Biology*, 49(6):737–759, 1987.

[3] J. E. Hopcroft and J. D. Ullman. *Introduction to Automata Theory, Languages, and Computation*. Addison-Wesley, Reading, Massachusetts, 1979.

[4] L. Pitt. Inductive inference, dfas, and computational complexity. In K. P. Jantke, editor, *Proceedings of 2nd Workshop on Analogical and Inductive Inference, Lecture Notes in Artificial Intelligence, 397*, pages 18–44. Springer-Verlag, 1989.

[5] J. D. Watson, J. Tooze, and D. T. Kurtz. *Recombinant DNA: A Short Course*. Freeman, New York, 1983.

Lecture Notes in Computer Science

Lecture Notes in Artificial Intelligence (LNAI)